REMARKABLE RECOVERY

REMARKABLE RECOVERY

What Extraordinary Healings
Tell Us About
Getting Well
and Staying Well

CARYLE HIRSHBERG
&
MARC IAN BARASCH

RIVERHEAD BOOKS

New York   1995

RIVERHEAD BOOKS
a division of G. P. Putnam's Sons
Publishers Since 1838
200 Madison Avenue
New York, N.Y. 10016

Published simultaneously in Canada.

BOOK DESIGN BY
CAROL MALCOLM RUSSO/SIGNET M DESIGN, INC.

Library of Congress Cataloging-in-Publication Data

Hirshberg, Caryle, date.
Remarkable recovery : what extraordinary healings tell us
about getting well and staying well / Caryle Hirshberg and Marc Ian
Barasch.
p.   cm.
Includes index.
ISBN 1-57322-000-0 (acid-free paper)
1. Cancer regression, Spontaneous.   I. Barasch, Marc.   II. Title.
RC270.5.H57   1995
616.99′4—dc20   94-40641 CIP

Printed in the United States of America
1   3   5   7   9   10   8   6   4   2
This book is printed on acid-free paper. ∞

*To our parents
for their love, support,
and infinite tolerance*

ACKNOWLEDGMENTS

We would like to give heartfelt thanks to the many people who provided invaluable assistance in this remarkable endeavor:

Our editor, Amy Hertz, without whose vision, skills, and tenacity this work would not exist. Our agent, Ned Leavitt, whose acumen and polyrhythms were crucial catalysts.

Our project manager, Michele Paulet, whose undaunted belief in this work and organizational skills contributed immeasurably. Our research assistants, Elena Aquilar, Cousette Copeland, Helen Giffrow, Sarah Harman, Juliette Hollier, Nate Johnson, Matt Klein, Niki Lang, Anita Levy, Iris Paul, MD, Tanya Reeves, and Melinda Weinstein.

Our loyal friends, family, and companions: Leah Barasch, Pat Brown, Miriam and Alan Burdick, Joe Dryden, Rick Fields, Winston Franklin, Jan Hirshberg, David Kennard, Sam Matthews, Doug Murphey, Neva Newman, Claire Nuer, Lara Nuer, Stany Stuart, Libby Tanner, Ph. D., and Cybel Wolf.

The Institute of Noetic Sciences and the late Brendan O'Regan for their decade-long support of research in this field. Herbert Spiegel, MD, Marcia Greenleaf, Ph.D., Ian Wickramasekera, Ph.D., and Jeffrey Levin, Ph.D., for their encouragement, support, and participation in our research project.

Our colleagues who generously gave of their time and expertise: Jean Achterberg, Ph.D., Warren Berland, Ph.D., Bennett Braun, MD, Dee Brigham, Ph.D., Susan Buchbinder, MD, Rosy Daniel, MD, Marco DeVries, MD, Gerald Epstein, MD, Hans Eysenck, Ph.D., Steve Fahrion, Ph.D., Jimmie Holland, MD, Roxie Huebscher, Ph.D., Petrea King, Rudolf Moos, Ph.D., Pat Norris, Ph.D., Chris Northrup, MD, Paul O'Malley, Helen Coley Nauts, Karen Olness, MD, Rose Papac, MD, Candace Pert, Ph.D., Richard Rahe, MD, Rachel Naomi Remen, MD, Paul Roud, Ph.D., Beverly Rubik, Ph.D., Michael Ruff, Ph.D., Wallace Sampson, MD, Johannes Schilder, MD, Ph.D., Al Siebert, Ph.D., Stephanie Simonton, Ph.D., George Solomon, MD, David Spiegel, MD, Charles Spielberger, Ph.D., Leo Stolbach, MD, Auke Tellegen, Ph.D., and the many others who gave us their advice and constructive criticism.

And most of all, the remarkable people who spoke so revealingly of their struggles and triumphs, in hopes of helping others to find their own path through the wood.

Contents

CONTENTS

FOREWORD

A S A YOUNG DOCTOR I ONCE SAW A CASE OF UNTREATED metastatic lung cancer disappear. I sought out two of my professors and asked their opinion about what had happened. One simply responded, "We see this," and walked away. The other replied, "This is the natural course of the disease." In spite of the fact that these "explanations" explained nothing and I was as puzzled as ever, I felt somewhat consoled by them. Like my teachers, I felt threatened by this strange happening. I didn't want to have to confront what I could neither understand nor control. Cases of cancer that "just went away" were a reminder that doctors don't know everything. In the wake of this experience, I gradually drifted into the typical response of the medical profession toward this type of remarkable recovery. Ignore it.

Now, years later, I realize that my attitude and that of my profession are unbecoming to a scientist. Any wide-eyed, high-school science student would suspect that cases of spontaneous remission are a priceless treasure that might hold vital clues to a possible cure for this disease. But instead of studying spontaneous remissions scientifically, we've regarded these events as a virtual embarrassment. Like the placebo response, we've seen them as a nuisance, a monkey wrench in our theories, a reminder that our models are flawed and that our favored therapies are too often ineffective.

Our collective neglect of remarkable recoveries is astonishing and utterly irrational. What happened?

Einstein, perhaps the most famous scientist in history, once said, "Imagination is more important than knowledge." Imagination precedes knowledge. It tells scientists where to look for clues to stubborn questions and it sets the stage for experimentation. In ignoring remarkable recoveries, we have suffered a failure of the imagination. Nature seems to be shouting, "Here lies the treasure! Dig here!" But we have heard only noise, and have allowed narrowness and myopia to replace awe and wonder.

Because remarkable recoveries often occur unbidden and out-of-the-blue, they appear to be a blessing, a grace. We do not know the buttons to push to make them happen; we cannot compel them to do our bidding. This means we cannot control them. Control has become immensely important to generations of scientifically trained physicians. Could it be that we modern doctors, so desperate to control nature, have shunned these marvelous events because they are so uncontrollable? If so, our attitude toward remarkable recoveries may say as much about us as about the events themselves.

The fact is, a cancer mentality exists among physicians, just as it does among the public at large. Cancer is currently the illness onto which, more than any other, we project our fears of suffering and death. In many ways this is irrational. Statistics show, for instance, that coronary heart disease is far more prevalent and carries a much worse prognosis following diagnosis than cancer in general. But most of us ignore these facts; it is cancer, not heart disease, we fear most. We know cancer is a death sentence and that it will end in terrible wasting and dehumanizing agony. Doctors often act out these dismal beliefs about cancer in various ways—by grimly rehearsing "survival" statistics to someone newly diagnosed; by rushing to treatment before the sun goes down; by exuding pessimism and doom in their discussions with patients and their families. Yet, against the backdrop of the pervasive dread of cancer, there is a persistent tap-tap-tapping in the night—those cases in which cancer "just goes away." Cases of remarkable recovery are like proclamations nailed to doctors' doors declaring, "Cancer is not uniformly fatal; there is always hope; reevaluate your attitudes; dare to imagine."

One of the commonest ways doctors ignore this message is by saying, "These cases are rare. Discussing them causes 'false hope.' If patients believe a miraculous recovery might happen, they may refuse 'real' treatment—chemotherapy, surgery, irradiation—and do nothing except wait for the miracle. Or they may be seduced into quackish 'alternative treatments or mind cures' that don't work. For a patient's own good, it's best to emphasize the purely biological aspects of cancer."

These opinions, again, are not always rational. Physicians, like everyone else, have a variety of innate psychological characteristics that affect how they respond to disease and suffering and how they relate to patients. Many doctors seem always to see the glass half empty instead of half full. Some, including many cancer specialists, seem, for reasons entirely understandable, almost chronically depressed. This makes it less likely that they will even raise the possibility of remarkable recovery.

Should physicians "be negative" just to play it safe and avoid misleading patients? Many say yes. But what about the evidence that negative suggestions can result in fatal outcomes? All doctors know patients who die "on time" when provided the statistics about the course of their disease. Cases also abound in which patients die suddenly on receiving bad news, or when they interpret a casual, offhand comment of the physician in a negative way. Which is worse—false hope or excessive pessimism? If we physicians were more fully informed about the nature of remarkable recoveries, including the fact that these events are almost certainly more frequent than we've been taught, perhaps we could create a larger place for what authors Hirshberg and Barasch call "ethical hope." Ethical hope is different from false hope. It rests on real possibilities, not fantasy.

The psychology of each physician affects her or his attitude to remarkable recovery in another crucial way. Many physicians dismiss these events with disdain, saying that they are "just stories." They accord them no scientific value whatever and refer to them as "anecdotes." A physician with another perspective, however, may be favorably struck by a story of a remarkable recovery—in which case the story becomes not an anecdote but a "case history." Whether stories of remarkable recovery are regarded by physicians as worthless anecdotes or valuable case histories can depend on deep-seated psychological biases that physicians seldom acknowledge and that have little to do with science.

The stories that pepper *Remarkable Recovery* are immensely important. Almost all the great illnesses, from scurvy to appendicitis to tuberculosis, are the result of single-case observations—an inflated term meaning that a physician, at some point in history, was willing to sit patiently and listen attentively to a patient's story. Because the physicians of the past—such as Robert Graves, Thomas Addison, Richard Bright, James Parkinson, and Thomas Hodgkin—took stories seriously and correlated them with physical findings, we refer today to Graves', Addison's, Bright's, Parkinson's, and Hodgkin's diseases. The story is thus the foundation of medicine; without these gifted men, medicine as we know it would not exist.

Remarkable Recovery provides a host of stunning stories. These accounts give the reader the exquisite opportunity to step into the stream of medical history. Reading these case histories, one can feel medicine in motion—for out of the swirl of these accounts we can begin to perceive what some of the new concepts and theories of the origins and cure of cancer will eventually look like.

But *Remarkable Recovery* is far more than a collection of stories. For, unlike most writers who deal with unusual healings, authors Hirshberg and Barasch ask vital questions: Can we go beyond the stories? Can we apply science to the study of remarkable recoveries? Can we dare to imagine what the body's Healing System will eventually look like? The authors answer "yes" to these questions by weaving an enchanting tapestry from the twin threads of actual human experience and the research findings of contemporary science.

One of the greatest obstacles to understanding remarkable recoveries is the widespread assumption that the events that trigger them happen randomly, by chance. This attitude is conveyed by the term "spontaneous remission," which is widely used by physicians to refer to these happenings. "Spontaneous remission" has thus become a signpost saying, "Do Not Enter!" "Off Limits to Analysis!" Authors Hirshberg and Barasch explain why "remarkable recovery" is a more inclusive term. It runs the gamut from the traditional, unexplained cancer that "just went away" to exceptional survival after a terminal diagnosis, often remarkable in itself. If we unpack the term "spontaneous remission" as Hirshberg and Barasch have done, we can see that it is really an assortment of events. This is a valuable move. It helps clear the fog of mystery that less precise definitions have created. It gives the field a friendlier face.

Are remarkable recoveries "miracles"? Or are they natural events that are statistically uncommon and extremely complex, but which scientists shall eventually explain when science knows enough? We need seriously to set aside these carping, hairsplitting, pharasaical arguments. They are tiresome and they suffocate understanding. Because they obstruct progress in healing, they are inhumane. They are an echo of the long-standing enmity between science and religion, which should be allowed to fade away. Those who wish to use either scientific or spiritual interpretations of remarkable recoveries as a battering ram with which to demolish the opposition might do better to bear in mind another point of view, put forth by one of the greatest scientists in history, physicist Max Planck: "There can never be any real opposition between religion and science; for the one is the complement of the other . . . every advance in knowledge brings us face to face with the mystery of our own being."

Einstein said that the most important question anyone can ask is "Is the Universe friendly?" He gave a "yes" answer to this query because he saw evidence everywhere that Nature has a benevolent and compassionate side. If Einstein had had the opportunity to read *Remarkable Recovery,* I am certain it would have confirmed his opinion of the friendliness of the Universe. For this book makes clear that, although diseases such as cancer exist, Nature has provided along with them possibilities for cure.

Einstein said further, "Nature hides her secret because of her essential loftiness, but not by means of ruse." I suspect that Einstein would have found evidence of Nature's loftiness in the cases described in this book. The loftiness is expressed not just in terms of the awesome, physical complexity of the body's Healing System, but also in the way psychospiritual influences seem to figure so dramatically in healing after healing, case after case.

If Nature is indeed lofty and not merely complex, this suggests a different approach to the scientific investigation of remarkable recoveries. Perhaps our scientific experiments shall have to embody not just cleverness and ingenuity, but respect and veneration for the events and processes being investigated. Perhaps our experiments should be seen not as ways to force Nature to disclose her secrets, but as respectful invitations to Nature to reveal her essential sublimity—an attitude captured in the words of the paleontologist and Jesuit priest Teilhard de Chardin: "Research is the highest form of adoration." Could this be one of the reasons why a scientific understanding of remarkable recoveries has seemed so elusive? Is it that we have not embodied the requisite ways of being in our scientific endeavors, as opposed to our ways of doing? Planck again: "Indeed it was not by any accident that the greatest thinkers of all ages were also deeply religious souls. . . ."

According to an ancient teaching, if one really wants to hide a treasure, one should put it in plain sight, for then it will go unnoticed by everyone. As one account has it,

There was once an argument among the gods over where to hide the secret of life so men and women would not find it. One god said: Bury it under a mountain; they will never look there. No, the others said, one day they will find ways to dig up mountains and will uncover it. Another said: Sink it in the depths of the ocean; it will be safe there. No, the others objected, humans will one day find ways to plumb the ocean's depths and will find it easily. Finally another god said: Put it inside them; men and women will never think of looking for it there. All the gods agreed, and so that is how the secret of life came to be hidden within us.

Remarkable Recovery shows that one of life's great secrets—the healing of cancer—is hidden within us. May we have the courage—and the imagination—to notice.

—LARRY DOSSEY, MD

Larry Dossey, MD, is executive editor of *Alternative Therapies*. He is co-chair, Panel on Mind/Body Interventions, Office of Alternative Medicine, National Institutes of Health, and former Chief of Staff, Medical City Dallas Hospital. He is author of the best-seller *Healing Words, Meaning and Medicine, Recovering the Soul,* and *Space, Time and Medicine.*

REMARKABLE
RECOVERY

CHAPTER ONE

Who, What, Where, When, Why: In Quest of a Medical Mystery

THERE ARE NO MEDICAL JOURNALS DEVOTED TO THE STUDY OF remarkable recovery, those odd instances when a disease such as terminal cancer vanishes almost exorcismally from the body. There are no medical school courses explaining how, on certain irreproducible occasions, a malignant tumor disappears from a CT-scan like a glitch from a radar screen. Though there are institutions devoted to the study of most major diseases, and nationwide networks that trace epidemiology and treatment efficacies, there is no national remissions registry to track unexplained healings. It is not known how often they occur, in what diseases, and in what kinds of people, much less why.

Still they ply the circuit, these grateful, sometimes baffled beneficiaries of an unexpected grace: the woman on a talk show recounting how a tumor-the-size-of-an-orange that once straddled her left ovary just . . . dematerialized. If you retain a phosphor of native skepticism, you may well reserve judgment. But if you possess any curiosity, you cannot help but wonder, Can it be? Do such things really happen? It is only of late that you might hear some scientists reply, *They do.*

But such cases are only rarely investigated. Remarkable recovery is a phenomenon so spectacular, elusive, and almost scientifically disreputable that few researchers have bothered to look for it, let alone pursue its implications. When not dismissed as a mistaken diagnosis, it is considered almost a nuisance, its instances ruinous to the smooth, gracile arc of a statistical bell-shaped curve.

"There's an aura of spookiness about the subject," one doctor told an inquiring reporter at a 1976 conference, begging off a longer discussion. Such attitudes, surprisingly widespread in medicine, tend to obscure how truly consequential a phenomenon it is. The fascination of a handful of researchers with spontaneous remission may be seen as a secret engine of medical progress. The celebrated surgeon and medical researcher Dr. Steven Rosenberg of the National Cancer Institute, known for trail-blazing research into the body's natural cancer-killers, was set upon his career path by a man who had mysteriously recovered from stomach cancer.

Rosenberg's account briefly describes the patient, a fifty-one-year-old man with a "fist-sized" abdominal tumor and metastases to the liver—a fast-progressing, fatal condition. The man's stomach was operated on, but when his surgeons saw the spread of malignancy, they could do nothing more than close him up and send him home to die. However, twelve years later, the presumptively dead man showed up in the emergency room of a Boston-area veterans hospital and presented himself to Rosenberg.

Rosenberg was a bona fide prodigy: college at sixteen, an MD and PhD by his early twenties. This case, one of his very first as a junior surgical resident, looked routine enough, if a little depressing. The man, a grizzled old vet named Mr. DeAngelo, was now suffering from an infected gall bladder. Yet Mr. DeAngelo, with what Rosenberg would later remember as "an aura of secret triumph," regaled him with a story the young doctor was sure was a product of the befuddlements of old age and alcohol. Mr. DeAngelo insisted he had had terminal cancer and it just . . . went away. Digging out the original pathology report, Rosenberg discovered it was true—the feisty, self-congratulatory man before him was a species of medical freak.

Rosenberg performed the gall-bladder operation, taking time while in the abdominal cavity to probe the man's liver for the cancer he was sure would still be there. There was nothing. "I rushed out of the operating room," Rosenberg was later to write, "still dressed in green, still encrusted in drying blood. This didn't seem possible. There had been only four documented cases—not four a year in the United States, but four, ever, in the world—of spontaneous and complete remission of stomach cancer." Mr. DeAngelo, he immediately realized, "presented a mystery of ultimately enormous dimensions." From that moment on, Rosenberg dedicated himself to a quest to uncover the body's own cancer-fighting mechanisms, which he was now certain must exist.

But the question of what had made Mr. DeAngelo different from other patients was never answered, or even asked. Dr. Rosenberg's brief 1972 case report is almost maddeningly incurious. "No evidence of tumor or other masses could be found in the abdomen," he states simply. "No adenopathy could be palpated." To sieve through the medical annals of miracles is to be confronted with article after article dry to the point of dessication. If their subjects had personalities, relationships, or meaningful lives, the authors seem to be saying, these were of no more consequence than the oyster shell that accidentally incubates a rare, glimmering pearl.

During a discussion that turned on the story of Mr. DeAngelo—an alcoholic who polished off four quarts of bourbon a week—a doctor at a recent medical seminar interjected: "Did the guy quit drinking after they told him he had cancer?" Told no, he asked amid his colleagues' swelling laughter, "Well, then, what *kind* of whiskey did he drink?"

The lighthearted exchange belied its cut-to-the-chase significance: Medicine cannot explain why Mr. DeAngelo got better—if it could, it might have a cure for cancer. Sixty years ago, Dr.

Joseph DeCourcy wrote about spontaneous remission in the *Journal of Medicine:*

> There are no accidents in Nature. These apparent exceptions to the rule that every malignant tumor grows on ad infinitum are illustrations of the working of some natural law of which we are still ignorant. I believe it is of the very first importance to give close study to cases of this kind with a view to gaining an insight, if possible, into Nature's methods of healing, and to discover what can be done to make her work easier.

In a few words, Dr. DeCourcy summed up the promise of the study of spontaneous healing. But remission does not easily lend itself to rigorous research. For one thing, it is usually seen after the fact, presumably leaving no traces of how it occurred—if it did at all. A 1962 article on breast cancer sums up a still-prevalent attitude: "Examples of spontaneous regression of cancer have been recorded from time to time, but many of these are based on inadequate evidence." And many clinicians have shown an unwillingness to report their cases in the medical literature, not infrequently because of fear of criticism from their peers.

Still, reports exist, though we sometimes had to scour the back shelves to find them. In the Stanford Medical Library, for example, in a musty archive that looked as if it hadn't been opened for decades, we retrieved a behemoth leather-bound volume of a 1907 *British Medical Journal* containing an article with a promising title: "A Case That Seems to Suggest a Clue to the Possible Solution of the Cancer Problem," by one Dr. Charles MacKay. Thumbing the cracked, yellowing pages, our eyes fell on a passage that spoke to the heart of the matter:

> Occasionally a true cancerous tumour comes to a pause in its growth, when it seems in fact to have lost its power . . . It is reasonable to suppose that some agent must have been at work either as aiding the body tissues in their resistance to

4

attack, or acting in antagonism to the cancer cell . . . If there is such an agent, what is it? Is there possibly elaborated in the body of the patient a something which can . . . effect a spontaneous cure?

It was almost shocking to see the unanswered questions we were now posing mirrored almost ninety years ago. The case was that of a thirty-seven-year-old woman, her tumor so far advanced she had to be repeatedly "tapped" like a maple tree to drain fluid from her lung cavity. Though the physicians had fully expected her to die, she had unexpectedly recovered. Here, in the story of Miss XY, suffering a terrible "mammary scirrhus" in the autumn of 1904, we listened for the echo of an actual person: a person who, against all odds, had struggled, endured, survived. Miss XY's astonished physician had noted with clinical understatement:

It was found that the condition had entirely altered. She could swallow easily. The respiration had fallen from 44 to 24. The fluid in the chest was in greateer part gone. She gradually took food in fairly good quantity and improved in every way. Still more remarkable was the fact that the seat of the local disease . . . gradually underwent a change for the better quite as great as the general condition. . . . In some places the skin regained its original whiteness. . . . The diseased parts that had not been treated with the X rays have undergone an extraordinary change.

We would never know what happened to this woman born in another century, a narrow portion of whose existence could be prised from the dry maw of the stacks. We wanted to know how this woman had thought and felt as she battled from her bed, what her dreams had been, whether friends and family had helped her. Here the report was mute, though we could feel the woman's travail and the doctors' concern radiating from the pages like heat lingering in a stone.

Indeed, the older reports were striking in their greater attention to the unique "selfhood" of the patients. These were days when doctors wrote about how their patients lived from first-hand observation. It was a time of home visits, when physicians might share a dinner or a birthday party and had time to talk about their patients' hopes, fears, and beliefs.

A 1914 medical report of partial regression of breast cancer has a tone strikingly different from a typical report today:

> The patient rallied like a young man . . . In July she visited a sister in Denver and while there did a great deal of sightseeing . . . I shall not soon forget my feelings when, two weeks after I had been . . . to the home of the patient . . . [so] that her few remaining days might be as comfortable as we could make them, and listening to her: "How long do you think it will be, Doctor?" and our equally resigned assurance that we did not know, but not very long, and her final reply, "I hope not, I am so tired," she walked into my office, with a triumphant smile and the greeting, "I am getting better, Doctor."
>
> If I had signed her death certificate two weeks before I think the sensation would have been but little less delightfully confounding.

With the advance of technology, such intimate care has been supplanted by a more streamlined, mechanistic, and often impersonal style of treating disease. But even the modern reports are a treasure trove. We found hundreds of them languishing unexamined in medical journals. We decided to start our quest with decades-old reports, reasoning if their subjects were still alive, they would be an extraordinary demonstration of the longevity of some remarkable cures. We began to track down their authors. Retired doctors in their eighties wrote in elegant, spidery penmanship on the backs of our permissions slips how thrilled they were that someone, anyone, had even noticed. Other return missives were more than faintly maddening. One doctor who had treated a

cancer. His daughter remembers him saying, "If I ever have cancer, I don't want to live," which, she says, "is why my mother didn't want the doctors to tell him he had a terminal diagnosis. She was afraid he would go into a depression. I think that helped a lot with his recovery."

It has been proposed a terminal diagnosis can act as a self-fulfilling prophecy, and several cases in the literature suggest that withholding information may sometimes enhance a patient's survival. Dr. Charles Mayo, son of the founder of the Mayo Clinic, cites a case of incurable colon cancer in which the family elected not to tell the mother she was to die within months. Mayo included in his case report a letter he received from the woman's son twelve years later: "My mother is unaware of having had a cancer, and since she appears 'cured,' we think there is no point in telling her." It could be argued that telling a patient his "chances" could cause him to give up; on the other hand, the information may be just what another patient needs to rally his resources.

But what else might have helped Mr. Moore? The answers died with him on a dusk-shadowed street in suburban Daytona. "It's got to be in the auto-immune system," says Dr. Lowy. "If I had to do it all over again, I'd draw blood on him and put it away and freeze it." He says with a note of lamentation. "We were thinking about doing that around the time he got hit by the car.

"To me, spontaneous remission is just what it says," he offers with a shrug. "Spontaneously it just happens without cause or effect. But," he hastens to add, "I'm not gonna laugh at anybody's theory."

Dr. Lowy's is a common view both in and out of the medical world. After all, if a phenomenon is truly spontaneous—an unpredictable (and untraceable) bolt from the blue—there can be no controlled studies, no predictable results, no therapeutic model. Little is left for science, seemingly, save to swerve and take one brief glance in the rearview mirror at the receding profile of another phantom hitchhiker.

The willingness to look is the first bastion of science: Research Drives Practice is a cherished first axiom. New fields of scientific inquiry are founded as often by surveyors as by explorers; by men and women who measure the landscape of available information so that theorists and experimentalists can raise on the marked-off site a new edifice of knowledge—an edifice from which practitioners at last emerge to put discoveries to human use.

But remission research is something of an exception. Despite its vast potential importance, it has attracted little or no systematic attention. To the contrary, medicine often expresses a frosty disdain for one-of-a-kind anecdotal cases. One prevailing view has it that such cases are too few to be of value. The figures most commonly cited are one in 80,000 and one in 100,000. Such figures, however, are unsupported by scientific data, and may be too low. It has been estimated that only ten percent of remarkable recoveries ever appear in journals, and this, too, may be a conservative figure: Even preliminary research for this book turned up dozens of cases never reported in the literature. How many valuable stories of unusual healing remain locked in lateral files in medical offices around the world?

Some researchers suggest that many doctors are reluctant to report such cases because there is no agreed-upon scientific explanation. "The particular problem with case histories of remission," says medical journal editor Harris Dienstfrey, "is that no one knows what to do with them. In order for a given case to be published by medical journals, it needs to fit into an established theoretical context. But there is no theory yet, and context is only created by write-ups in the journals.

"The question becomes," he says, allowing himself a dry laugh at the scientific catch-22, "How does medicine communally decide what gets studied and reviewed? Or to put it another way, What is an acceptable level of mystery?"

Is spontaneous remission an acceptable mystery? Even if it were, how useful are existing case reports in studying it? The researchers Challis and Stam, analyzing journal reports of cancer remission from 1900 to 1987, note that although immunological and hormonal factors, operative trauma, and infection are all raised as possible causes, questions about the patient's personality and lifestyle never are. Current research suggests, however, that personality and lifestyle do have strong health significance. Challis and Stam speculate that the reason for this information blackout may be that "no physician was willing to risk his/her reputation by reporting a case of spontaneous regression he/she felt was due to a psychological method." Such omissions leave us to guess at the characteristics of people who undergo remarkable recoveries. Do they eat certain kinds of food? Do they have psychological, social, or spiritual traits that might help trigger remission? And how could we integrate such information into the medical system to give people the best care and support?

Though few if any members of the orthodox medical community could be said to specialize in the study of spontaneous remission, many clinicians readily confess their fascination with the subject. Dr. Tim Oliver is an oncologist at Royal London Hospital. An urbane and youthful-looking fifty, Oliver is on the cutting edge of conventional medicine. A specialist in testicular and kidney cancer, he is racing in his lab to discover how tumors manage to switch off normal cell defenses, hoping someday to "fire the missing genes into the tumor" and reactivate the body's natural self-protection.

Oliver is also a bit of a medical apostate. Noticing that aggressive treatment for kidney cell cancers was not particularly effective, he hit on a radical notion: He would treat those patients seemingly able to contain the disease with only "surveillance"—essentially no treatment at all, save "watchful waiting." To his surprise, out of a group of seventy-three patients, three had complete remissions, two had partial ones, and four had periods of prolonged stability of more than a year. (Of the three patients who had complete remissions, one remained so for at least six years.)

Certain of Dr. Oliver's cases have particularly strained his understanding of biological science. He fishes from a file cabinet the lung X rays of his "famous" remission, a woman he treated between 1981 and 1983. Her kidney tumor had metastasized to her lungs, and her prognosis was terminal. But Oliver found that her tumors waxed and waned not with the inexorable progress of kidney cancer, but with the ups and downs of her relationship with her physically abusive husband. Though she eventually died, her separations from the man, as far as he could tell, may have been crucial medicine.

Another patient with lung metastases, whose wife had died six months before, "went behind my back," says Oliver wryly, "and hired a psychic medium who proceeded to 'contact' the spirit of his deceased wife." The wife's purported shade told the man that crossing over to "the other side" would be a premature journey. "He ought to have died seven years ago," notes Dr. Oliver, "but he's still kicking around." Oliver, whose observations have led him cautiously to introduce the psychological dimensions of healing into his practice, estimates that what he refers to as his "optimistic brainwashing" of patients adds one to ten percent to their chances of improvement. Not a large percentage, he admits, "but in many cases that's all that chemotherapy adds, too."

As Dr. Steven Rosenberg wrote about the mystifying Mr. DeAngelo, "The single most important element of good science is to ask an important question." One question might be: Does there have to be a natural, inexorable progression of cancer, a doctrine that has long been an oncological article of faith? For most cancers, the answer can only be discouraging. A 1926 British study of 651 women with untreated breast cancer revealed an average duration of 3.2 years from onset to death, and a median (the point where half of the patients had perished) of 2.3 years. A Boston study a year later revealed an almost identical average of 3.3 years and median survival of 2.5. Five years later, another study revealed a median survival of 3.3 years. But this figure, the latter study casually mentions, was obtained by "omitting two cases of alleged duration of 40–41 years." These latter cases are what statisticians call "outliers," routinely omitted from calculation because they fall too far outside the boundaries of the statistical playing field. Thus out of a study of sixty-four patients, two exceptional—even revelatory—cases are dismissed with two flicks of a parenthesis.

It is something of an irony. Science in general, and the physical sciences in particular, have achieved their greatest successes through the study of rare natural phenomena—the examination of a few odd radioactive minerals altered history forever; Gregor Mendel's solitary wonderment at how pea plants with albion petals could produce offspring with purple ones—in effect, a spontaneous remission of white flowers—led to the feats of genetic prestidigitation that now astound our age.

If anomalies in the mineral and vegetable kingdoms can so profoundly change our world, how much more so exceptions in the human realm? "The treatment was successful, but the patient died" is both a jibe at the medical profession and a grim insider's joke. The more intriguing obverse—"the treatment failed and the patient lived"—is what we are determined to explore.

CHAPTER TWO

Defining the
Impossible

T HE RARE BUT SPECTACULAR PHENOMENON OF SPONTANEOUS
remission of cancer persists in the annals of medicine, totally inexplicable but real, a hypothetical straw to clutch in the
search for cure," wrote Dr. Lewis Thomas from his perch as president of New York's Memorial Sloan-Kettering Cancer Center.
His stance was in some ways typical of those in medicine who
profess an affable interest—at once embracing the phenomenon
nearer and holding it at arm's length, all without once defining
what in the world it is.

Even among the small community of world experts the definitions have varied. Tilden Everson and Warren Cole, the grand
old men of the study of spontaneous remission, defined it as the
partial or complete disappearance of a malignant tumor without
adequate medical treatment, though they do not equate it with
cure. The Japanese researcher Ikemi extended the definitional
umbrella to include long survival, even with the continuing presence of malignancy.

Some argue that rather than thinking of remission as a distinct state, one should instead speak only of "time to recurrence." In this view, all remissions are but a temporary respite from the inevitable return of the disease (although since little more is known about the natural behavior of remissions than the mating habits of the Loch Ness Monster, it is hard to say whether one class is permanent and another more transient).

Patients who have experienced recoveries rarely seem to find the term "spontaneous remission" very useful. "It's semantics," one told us. "For me, healing isn't sudden, it's a lifelong process. I work at it." Said another, "I never use the word 'remission,' because they say what I had never *goes* into remission. So I just say I had something and now I don't."

These points, raised by those in a good position to comment, are crucial ones. By remission, do we mean something temporary or permanent? By spontaneous, do we mean instantaneous? Of unknown causation? The label, at once mystical and meaningless, is a scant gesture of understanding. As one prominent researcher complains, "It has a suggestion of something happening without a cause. That, of course, is also absurd, for everything has a cause, apparent or inapparent."

How can we study something if we cannot quite define it? Webster's dictionary hints at a path through the woods. The original meaning of the word "spontaneous" (derived from the Latin *sponte,* "of free will"), has little to do with the suddenness, rapidity, or immediate change without cause which contemporary usage implies. The word, the dictionary reveals, originally had more to do with something occurring due to a "native internal proneness," a tendency to "act by its own impulse, energy or natural law." It implies a natural process that arises from within.

We believe the term "remarkable recovery" is more in the spirit of this root meaning. We propose this broader term to deliberately include more people, a need that became apparent from our research. When we first began asking doctors for cases of "spontaneous remission," most would insist they had never seen any, or perhaps "one in a twenty-five-year career, and I've lost track of them." But when we asked if they had ever had cancer patients who did extraordinarily well—a terminal patient who received merely palliative treatment but unexpectedly recovered; a person who had held off the progression of his or her disease years past all statistical expectation; someone whose tumor had partially regressed when its known natural history would have predicted inevitable growth—doctors almost invariably replied, "Well, of course, I've seen quite a few of *those*!" Not infrequently, a physician would put us in touch with someone who had an extraordinary story of unlikely survival to tell us.

We were forced to acknowledge a startling point: Because the prevailing definition has been so narrow, a phenomenon of critical interest to medical science (and ultimately to the patients in its care) has been slipping through our collective fingers. If a person survives long past his or her prognosis, even if he or she eventually dies of the disease, has not something worth investigating occurred? If someone treated by a protocol expected to grant him or her only six months of life goes on to live many years before succumbing, should we not be filled with curiosity? Certainly, some aspects of these people's bodies, minds, or even spirits must have accounted for the outcome. But we cannot begin to know if we do not designate such instances as remarkable enough to warrant further study, if we do not crack a very exclusive club to include people who had previously fallen into a medical gray area.

Indeed, we became convinced that these grayer areas contain keys to new strategies to prolong life, and can provide ethical hope to those faced with a terminal diagnosis. They may even reveal the properties of a heretofore unmapped system of the body and mind—the Healing System.

If there is anywhere we should find evidence for an intrinsic human healing system—which Norman Cousins saw as a "grand orchestration" of all the forces that move a person from sickness to health—it is in those cases we are placing under the broader rubric of remarkable recovery. We embarked on our journey in the belief that by casting the widest net, we stood the best chance of catching the Healing System in action.

Reports that indicate spontaneous healing had occurred following transfusion of blood from other patients in remission raise exciting questions about biological factors that may be isolated and cloned. Instances of remarkable recovery following infections and fever indicate bodily mechanisms that may amplify the immune response. Cases where meditation and hypnosis seemed to contribute to an unexpected medical outcome point to sketchily mapped mind-body connections.

A definition is a scientific tool, no less so than microscope or telescope, slide or cyclotron, for it gives us a new way of apprehending reality in hopes of learning something new. In this case, if we can discern patterns—any patterns—in people who do significantly better and live significantly longer than their conditions would dictate, then—whether they are simply "nature's own experiments" or the product of the biopsychosocial equation of their lives—we will find information of critical importance in the treatment of disease.

A cascade of definitions from many different sources has created a whirlpool of misunderstanding of remarkable recovery. The various terminologies reflect the general lack of knowledge about the phenomenon in the first place. But they also comment on the narrowness of traditional categories, which focus more on the behavior of tumors than on the behavior of people who make unique choices as they cope with disease. To understand the full spectrum of the healing response, and to put a wide-angle lens on the relationship among disease, treatment, and personal traits, we decided it would be useful to break remarkable recovery into six basic categories: 1) No Treatment: those cases where patients were properly diagnosed via X rays, biopsies, or other medical tests, had no medical intervention, and their disease just went away; 2) Inadequate Treatment: cases where diagnosis is followed by conventional medical treatment considered insufficient to produce either a cure or a remission—the physician gives up, yet the patient returns one or five or ten years later free of disease; 3) Equilibrium (or Delayed Progression): those people who show either a partial regression of cancer or who live with their disease in reasonably good health for long periods of time; 4) Long Survival, in which people undergo conventional treatment yet survive far longer than the statistics for their type of cancer and treatment would mandate; 5) Complementary Treatment: where patients have resorted to an often motley combination of traditional and so-called "alternative" treatments to get well; 6) "Miracles": so-called spiritual cures, such as the healings documented by the Lourdes International Medical Commission.

NO TREATMENT

How common is the disappearance of an incurable disease with no meaningful intervention? The impact of such an ocurrence on a physician can be felt in one 1910 medical report we found. A man had a cancer of tonsil, tongue, and voice box so advanced that there was a "foul discharge" from the growth on his throat. He was sent home to die. Wrote his doctor:

> I told him nothing could be done except treatment to re-
> lieve his suffering [i.e., palliative], and that he could not live
> very many months. . . . About eighteen months later the pa-
> tient came to see me. I did not recognize him, and was
> thunderstruck when he told me who he was, as I had
> thought of him as dead. He was in perfect health and the
> only trace of the growth was some smooth scar tissue. He
> told me that shortly after returning home and settling his af-
> fairs, the pain and discharge ceased, and the growth began to
> disappear. He had had no treatment except antiseptic gargles
> and sprays, and anodynes to relieve pain.

Clearly the enigmatic Mr. Moore, whom we met in the previous chapter, fell neatly into this category. So does a woman named Carol Knudtson.

Carol's early life had been uncommonly serene. She'd grown up on a small dairy farm outside Madison, Wisconsin, in a world sprung full-blown from the untroubled brow of Norman Rockwell. She'd lived on the very same street as the boy she later married and grew up listening to the Green Hornet on her Montgomery Ward transistor radio, hooking it up to the old-fashioned wall phone for better reception. There weren't many people to call anyway: When she'd married her husband in 1954, the town had a population of 303. Now, she thinks the place has "grown like crazy" because the populace has swelled to five thousand.

As a child, Carol dreamed of becoming an astronaut, or a missionary bringing the Gospel to the globe's distant climes. She used to wonder, she says, "if I was crazy because I felt so different. I'd ask my mother if I was adopted." Her active imagination was double-edged, sometimes tormenting her with the sense that something terrible was on the verge of happening. After the Japanese bombed Pearl Harbor, Carol, a willful eleven-year-old, refused her parents' request to fetch something from the barn, convinced the moment she snapped on the light, enemy bombs would home in on her.

One nightmare had started in grade school and continued through high school and beyond: "I was stepping off the curb and a big truck was coming. I was screaming bloody murder and I couldn't get anything out. Then I'd wake up just like that. It kept repeating over and over."

But if her childhood intimations of awfulness were suddenly to manifest themselves when she was fifty-two, surely they wouldn't be in this irksome feeling of a tiny barb lodged in the back of her throat. Most likely, she had thought, it was an errant hull left over from her usual "nightcap" of hot popcorn and TV. But the sharp sensation wouldn't go away. Her doctor suggested her house was too dry, and she dutifully bought a humidifier. But as Thanksgiving gave way to Christmas and then New Year's, the nagging thing only seemed to grow, till it felt "like a wooden stick reaching over and poking into the other side of my throat."

Then a lump appeared in her neck. A biopsy revealed a fast-growing lymphoma. Her fiendish nightmare truck, gears grinding and airhorn sounding, was at last bearing straight down on her.

21

The report on her case in the journal *Cancer* describes Carol's disease as an "aggressive histologic subtype" in which regression is "extremely rare." What subtype of person Carol fell into was irrelevant, her first doctor told her: " 'With this disease,' " she remembers him saying, " 'it makes no difference how old you are, what your skin color is, how much money you've got, or what you believe in—it's not good.' He painted it dark, and I could see all the doctors just looking at me feeling sorry." She contemplated dying then, trying to envision what would happen to her son, her little daughter, and to Dean, her husband of over twenty-five years. "Dean was very taken aback, but I didn't shed one tear," she says, curious now as she thinks back to her reaction. In shock, she could do little more that night than look out the window and stare, feeling "just like I was floating in outer space," refusing even to answer the telephone.

But her husband, she says, "didn't like the idea that bang, bang, bang, treatment was going to start Monday morning. Dean just plain got mad and said, 'That's it.' We're going to the Mayo Clinic for a second opinion.' " With her husband's action, she rallied somewhat. "I'd been really dumbfounded by the diagnosis, but then I remembered my mom always said the good Lord doesn't give you more than He knows you can bear." She and Dean drove up to the Mayo Clinic, where for a full week she submitted to bone marrow tests, CAT scans, and "the whole ball of wax." Dean, who was "crying practically all the time," insisted they go "down to the library and dig through everything, one book after another." During her week at the clinic, however, she became convinced her lump was shrinking. When she told her doctors, she recalls, "They just looked at me and laughed and said 'No, it can't get smaller.' "

Instead, the Mayo Clinic confirmed her original diagnosis and sent her back to Madison for treatment, referring her to Dr. Paul Carbone, now the director of the University of Wisconsin Comprehensive Cancer Center. Dr. Carbone, she says, "had compassion. He made you feel so good." But when he examined her, all he could observe was "a little raspberry." He referred her on to an ear, nose, and throat man who told her there was now no visible condition to treat. "The world for me went upside down and inside out a little," she says. Dr. Carbone's medical report catalogues the event straightforwardly: "Because of the apparent regression of the primary tumor mass, chemotherapy was withheld, and she was followed monthly with physical examinations by two physicians. The cervical lymph node regressed completely and the physical exam was completely normal by late spring 1982." In less than six weeks, every symptom of cancer was completely gone.

"I kept going back," says Carol, "and the doctors would just bring their students around to show them this amazing thing that had happened to me." Even at her most recent checkup, she says, "I had a young Indian doctor look at me just baffled. He just kept saying, 'Interesting, interesting.' "

For diffuse large-cell lymphomas whose survival is measured in months, spontaneous regressions are rare. The median survival after diagnosis is one year. What had happened? Carol had no treatment, nor any complementary health practices that might conceivably have affected her outcome. (A self-admitted junk food gourmand, she laughs. "Mom and I would drop off my daughter at school at eight o'clock in the morning, go down to the local A&W, and have hamburger steak and French fries for breakfast. My diet never changed. I'm still on hamburgers!")

Carol was always, however, an unusually strong believer in the power of positive thinking. She had been something of a fanatic as a child, diligently clipping out piles of Norman Vincent Peale columns from the daily paper and tucking them away in her bedroom. Religion, too, had been a vital force in her life ever since she'd gone to Bible school. In her home, the radio is tuned constantly to a religious station. During the illness, she felt fortified that her mother, sister, sister-in-law, and a church "prayer-chain" had implored God for her cure. She recalls feeling a small geyser of hope when a Catholic priest in the hospital had paused to pray over her: "I thought it was pretty wonderful that he would pray for me when he didn't even know who I was, and me being a

Lutheran besides. I think that had a little bit to do with it all turning out so well."

Carol's husband died of cancer a few years ago. She still wonders sometimes "why he didn't get out of it and I did."

INADEQUATE TREATMENT

O ne of the most puzzling categories of remarkable recovery, one that has too often flown beneath the radar of registry, are cases that shouldn't have caused a cure. There are examples of cancers disappearing after experimental protocols that later scientific investigation shows to be utterly useless; or remissions that follow so-called "palliative" treatment, where a terminal patient is given chemo or radiation with no hope of doing more than easing his or her pain.

Dr. Rose Papac, a leading Yale University oncologist, found one such case almost by chance while rummaging through her own back records. On a cold January morning in 1967, Edward Petrelle had staggered into West Haven's VA hospital with a dangerously high fever and a calamitously low blood count. Tests revealed that the fifty-two-year-old TV repairman was suffering from acute myelomonocytic leukemia, a rapidly fatal cancer of the blood in which abnormal cells choke the bone marrow. At that time, if untreated, the median survival statistic was only three months. Though Petrelle was labeled a "poor candidate for specific therapy," Papac nonetheless prescribed chemotherapy. The treatment order, however, was accidentally rewritten so the man received only a fraction of the standard dosage.

Nonetheless, Petrelle's case fell off the charts. His fever broke, his blood counts rose, color suffused his face. The microscope revealed that the abnormal cells had vanished. The spectacle of this Lazarus-like resurrection, Dr. Papac remembers, was "a once-in-a-lifetime experience."

We found Edward Petrelle living alone in a lower-middle-class suburban neighborhood in Denver. Now a wizened and gnomish eighty, Petrelle, who has also become a watch repairman ("Certified Master Watchmaker of the American Horological Society," he recited with pride), is at a loss to fathom what repaired his own intricate inner workings. Sitting on a piano bench with the sheet music for "I'm Always Chasing Rainbows" open behind him, he told us of being hopelessly sick, depressed; of how "they gave me some chemo, but it was no good."

"I'd stopped eating. Everyone was telling me I would die. I was like a vegetable. But my sister-in-law, she was siding with me. She refused to believe I had leukemia, no matter what the docs said. And Dr. Papac, well, I could feel she had a good heart, she was warm with me, there wasn't an assembly-line feeling."

Papac, in turn, remembers him as "a very frightened person, paralyzed by the thought of death." From all outward appearances, Petrelle *was* dying, slipping in and out of a near-coma. But as he recalls, "They said I was sleeping all the time, but I wasn't. I was fighting, fighting, as if I was sliding down a deep tunnel and would keep jerking myself back."

He was sinking, but then somehow he rallied. He thought back to how he had laboriously taught himself to snap his fingers again after a severe bout of arthritis, forcing one digit soundlessly to graze the other until he mastered the gesture. About his battle with leukemia he says, "It takes an awful, awful lot to get me mad, but I finally got mad at myself. I got disgusted I wasn't walking. I got up and walked down the hospital hallway, even though my feet hurt. I said to my feet, If you're going to hurt, you're going to hurt, but you're coming along with me anyway. I've got a very stubborn nature. I buck whatever goes wrong. I give it the business, even if it's cancer in my blood." Later, with his legs so weak and numb he could hardly stand, he made himself walk around the backyard. Then he forced himself to walk up to eight miles. "But I still walk five miles a day," he says. "I never felt this good before I got sick!"

Today, Ed lives with his grandson and spends his time tending his garden, complaining good-naturedly about "the poor soil." He credits much of his remarkable recovery to "how you take care of yourself. I know one thing—if you are going to sit in the chair all day long, you are just going to sit there and die." Twenty-seven years after they met in the Veterans' Hospital in West Haven, he and Dr. Papac still exchange Christmas cards.

EQUILIBRIUM (OR DELAYED PROGRESSION)

In a report entitled, "Long Freedom from Recurrence after Operation for Cancer of the Breast" in a 1925 issue of the *British Medical Journal,* a doctor describes the case of a woman who had been treated by mastectomy twenty-four years earlier "for a typical scirrhous cancer." Now, decades later, the woman showed up in his office with

> a small lump in the skin, two inches below the middle of the right clavicle . . . [T]he microscope showed typical breast cancer. A further examination while the patient was anesthetized revealed hard tumours in each ovarian region, and she died within a year. . . . The fact that the recurrence was in the skin of the chest and that it was typical breast cancer leaves no doubt that this was a case of genuine recurrence of the original tumour, and not of an independent new growth.

Cases like these, remissions pioneers Everson and Cole believed, were evidence for a natural, innate mechanism for the biological control of cancer, clear evidence that cancer's march through the body is not always relentless and preordained, but may sometimes halt for a lifetime. Pathologist William Boyd in his 1966 text defined remission as "a temporary amelioration of a condition, to be followed later by an exacerbation. When a tumor has been growing rapidly and then slows down or appears to halt . . ."

Time can be variable. "I've seen breast cancer cases that don't recur until thirty years later, says oncologist Dr. Leo Stolbach, "though for a majority of patients, a recurrence, if it is to happen, will be within the first five years." Even then, Stolbach told us, the course is not entirely predictable. He describes one patient who has survived five years after a recurrence but "still she works every day and she's doing fine. It's the kind of case you would have thought would be dead in a year, but it really doesn't have to be that way."

Dr. Hugh Faulkner, an eighty-year-old general practitioner we met, was in a better position than most to understand the significance of his own short prognosis: "They found a shadow in my pancreas—immediate operation was advised. On operation they found a tumor in the head of the pancreas the size of a tennis ball—on biopsy it proved to be adenocarcinoma. There was nothing further to be done, the tumor was inoperable." He looked up the epidemiology and found that he was unlikely to live more than four to six months, "I faced this as a doctor. I wanted to make the remaining time as pleasant as possible and to die with as much dignity as I could."

Dr. Faulkner remembered a friend who, while dying of lung cancer, had thrown a huge, lavishly catered party to go out with "a flair," surrounded by good friends, good food, and good wine. Perhaps, Faulkner thought, dignity wasn't everything, though flair for him meant ending his days in a comfortable hospice, but ironically even the thought of it made him feel better. "My physiology," he said years later, "got the message of hope before I did. I didn't even notice. My wife did."

Dr. Faulkner's wife, who believed strongly in the mind-body connection, induced him to try shiatsu and macrobiotics even as he was preparing to die. "I found that the first [shiatsu] treatment helped for pain and stiffness," he said. "But I knew shiatsu doesn't heal cancer." With his classic, dry British reserve, Dr. Faulkner, according to his wife, "found it very difficult to talk about his feelings, to talk about himself. He found it difficult to remember anything that happened to him that wasn't comfortable. I remember everything in great detail, but he would forget all the nasty things." But in some inexplicable way, his wife's love, belief, and spiritual faith seemed to help him survive.

Hugh Faulkner lived eight years past his terminal diagnosis before dying of a recurrence of his disease in 1994. To the end, he maintained the stance of the skeptical British doctor, still puzzling over the unknown forces that gave him back his life but beggared what he was taught in medical school. "I was conscious that I was doing something about my cancer even though I wasn't intellectually convinced," he had told a friend. "I still don't talk about cure, but I accept the fact that I have what Western orthodox medicine calls a spontaneous remission—which means, in other words, we don't know."

LONG SURVIVAL

To understand the full spectrum of self-repair, we realized we would have to include those who were conventionally treated but were living long beyond the statistical expectations. The healing system takes many forms. Perhaps for these people, medical interventions like chemotherapy functioned not only as external treatments, but somehow as ways to kick-start their own internal mechanisms of repair.

Christine Anderson had no reason to be anxious about her regular checkup. It was July 1989 and her life, if not perfect, had found its own gyroscopic center. A shy, thirty-seven-year-old brunette, she had a beautiful five-year-old daughter, Rachael, and a good office job at the 3M Corporation in nearby Atlanta. Her husband had died four years before of lung cancer, but Christine, who had worked in her father's Virginia tobacco fields since the time she could walk, had with signal grit and tenacity struggled back to her feet.

But a few months later, while taking a shower, she felt a lump. She, who had been so afraid of death since she was a little girl crying over her father's early passing, had what turned out to be a five-centimeter malignancy. Events progressed along a path all too familiar to hundreds of thousands of American women: Mammogram . . . biopsy . . . mastectomy . . . chemotherapy.

Christine had reacted badly to the chemo. She could live with the hair loss—Rachael had giggled at her funny wig—and even the griddle-iron fevers, but her second treatment caused convulsions and an alarming plummet in blood pressure that had required a transfusion. Worst of all, it was seemingly for naught: Lung metastases were discovered, their spread and size too advanced for surgery. The X rays had shocked her. "They looked like my husband's lungs when he died"—died when Rachael was five, the same age Christine had been when her own father had sickened away. Christine's doctor had offered to adopt Rachael "if anything happened," thinking it would ease her mind, but it was scant consolation. Her oncologist told her to come back after the first of the year and start a new series of treatments: She had only three months to live, but he wanted to make her remaining time as comfortable as possible. A second doctor confirmed the pitiably short prognosis, gently suggesting she not delay making out her will.

But looking at Rachael, thinking of how hard she had worked to come this far, Christine could not resign herself. She began to read books on healing, praying for a way back to life. She recalls a turning point just after New Year's. She got furious with her sister, whom she had been supporting as she lived with her: "I was fed up. The only thing I ever asked her to do was fix supper, I did everything else." Her sister packed up angrily and left. That Monday, Christine started work again. A few weeks later, she drove to Tennessee to climb Stone Mountain, "just to prove to myself I could do it."

Church had always been a central part of her life. She had run away from home when she was only twelve and was taken in by a minister and his wife. One Sunday at her Baptist church in Chamblee, she heard a doctor "give testimony" about his heart disease and receive annointment with holy oil. She decided that if a doctor could ask for divine aid, she too wanted to be anointed, embraced by the community of believers. All that month, every day, she wrote over and over in her diary her simple affirmations: "I know God can heal me . . . I know that God heals . . . with You watching over me. . . ."

The congregation gathered the last week in January and performed the ceremony for Christine. The next week, coincidentally, was her birthday. Her friends "were coming out of the woodwork," she remembers. She counted sixty-seven visitors, each one knowing it would likely be the last time they would share. Someone had baked an enormous cake and brought it in, its dozens of candles ablaze with cheerful ferocity. Ignoring the potential for the occasion to turn into a preemptive wake, someone shouted out, "Make a wish." Christine shut her eyes tight, sucked in as much air as she could hold, and soundlessly asked for a miracle "for my daughter's sake." Fortified by her wish, with Rachael's face uptilted in anticipation, she was surprised to find that she, whose lungs felt like antique, tattered bellows, had blown all thirty-eight of the candles out with a single breath. "I knew then," she says emphatically, "that I was going to live. I knew something had happened."

On her next checkup, amazingly, her lungs were clear. Not long after, her glossy, dark brown hair grew back in. Overcoming her shyness, she acquiesced to a friend's urging and went on a date with a church-going computer programmer who, five months later, proposed to her in front of everybody at choir workshop. Her oncologist, Dr. Jeffrey Scott, gave away the bride. The daughter he had once offered to adopt, now thirteen, was the maid of honor.

Her doctor's reports, though they take no notice of these significant inner and outer events, sketch out the tale: first we meet an "unfortunate thirty-seven-year-old white female" with a poor prognosis; then a patient "in complete remission" six months later; "a pleasant white female in no acute distress with clear lungs" shortly thereafter; two years later, a patient whose metastatic breast cancer had a "remarkable response" to repeated courses of chemotherapy; then, three years later, a "wonderful young female" who "has gotten married and seems quite elated" and remains "remarkably in remission."

The doctor's report notes with what sounds like a mixture of happy surprise and incomprehension: "Doing remarkably well considering the lack of historical cures or long-term survivors of such a problem."

Today, five years later, Christine's lungs remain cloudless. "I don't call it spontaneous remission," she insists. "I call it divine intervention." She now plans to become a psychologist counseling cancer patients. But again, what happened? Some might say her cure was a result of her surgery, or of some form of delayed reaction to several grueling rounds of potent chemotherapy. But survival of metastasized breast cancer is a very unlikely event. Dr. Scott, asked by a local journalist if he would class Christine a miracle, answered, "I wouldn't argue against it."

Did Christine's chemo have any effect? Perhaps, though the curative power of conventional cancer treatment may be in some ways more of a gray area than its practitioners generally admit. Current statistics suggest that with the exception of childhood cancers and certain rare forms of the disease, survival has not improved much over the last twenty years. For four of the most common cancers (colon, rectum, pancreas, and lung), there is, says UCLA internist Martin F. Shapiro, "no convincing evidence that chemotherapy offers any benefit whatsoever," though many patients receive the treatment.

In his comments on Everson and Cole's 176-case review of spontaneous remission, C. I. V. Franklin remarks that "Sixty percent of the regressions lasted more than two years, with many over ten years. If the same criteria were applied to regression following hormonal or cytotoxic chemotherapy, response rates may not be much greater than the reported incidence of spontaneous regression!" Writing in 1918, Dr. G. L. Rohdenburg raised an issue that today would be the ecclesiastical equivalent of uttering a heresy: "The occurrence of partial or complete spontaneous recession should make one very critical in judging new therapeutic procedures, that they may not be falsely credited with the results produced by forces of the nature of which we are for the present entirely ignorant."

Could remarkable recovery be more ubiquitous than we have previously thought, hidden beneath the statistics of conventional procedures? Even more radically, What percentage of medical cures may be instances of remarkable recovery mistakenly attributed solely to treatment? Since remission occurs with a yet unknown frequency, it can be convincingly argued that some of the apparent successes of conventional (as well as unconventional) therapies may be cases of remission that have little to do with the medicines themselves. It is an overlooked challenge: Could a class of treatment be in reality a collaboration between medicine and the innate powers of the healing system?

COMPLEMENTARY TREATMENT

S tories of remarkable recovery are rarely simple. A person is diagnosed, goes through chemotherapy, responds partially, and somehow gets well. Another responds not at all and walks out only to reappear like an apparition. Another has a biopsy, does some chemo, goes back for scans, drinks some herbal teas, takes up yoga, and heals.

Most of the things people actually do cannot be found in case reports. Some alternative forms of medicine, once seen as quack remedies, placebo nostrums, or at best unproven therapies may become the basis for tomorrow's "real" medicine. Today's "useless herb" may become, as have countless folk remedies in the past, tomorrow's miracle pharmaceutical. The National Institutes of Health's Office of Alternative Medicine is studying everything from "antineoplastons," protein components of human urine, to shark cartilage in its quest for effective anticarcinogens. Generally, only proven treatments are mentioned in medical case reports, omitting data that could help explain what made a given person the exception to the rule.

Even when it is duly inspected, however, the curative action of most so-called alternatives is a vast unknown. Witness, for example, the following case report from the literature of a man who had a remission of hepatocellular carcinoma (HCC), or liver cancer. Medical treatment had failed. But to his doctors' surprise, "Over the next six months, the liver decreased progressively in size. He informed us that he had been taking Chinese herbal medicine. When last assessed in late 1979, he was still working, asymptomatic, and apparently free from recurrence. His food habits were not noticeably different from before. The recipe of Chinese herbs that he took was subsequently tried by us on about 20 consecutive patients with HCC. No detectable regression of tumor was observed in any patient."

The difficulty of sorting out what may be a veritable cat's cradle of healing factors in remarkable recovery can be seen in the case of Suzanna McDougal. Suzanna had always thought she was the world's least likely candidate for cancer. She had been raised on a farm in the Midwest where her Scotch, German, French, and English ancestors had lived and farmed for two centuries. Her family had always grown vegetables, and her mother, a librarian, had once ceremoniously handed her a book, *One Acre and Security,* admonishing her to read it line for line. Suzanna later became the hardworking owner of her own one-acre "biodynamic" organic farm near Hamilton, Montana.

"I come from a long line of green thumbs," she says with a laugh. "People who believe humans were put on this planet to take care of plants." Suzanna had named her farm Lifeline Produce, and had been growing some medicinal herbs and collecting others from the surrounding woods to create "wild-crafted" tinctures and salves for naturopathic doctors.

Then, in February of 1987, she went in for a routine Pap smear. During her examination, an ovarian growth as large as a four-month-old fetus had been found. A sonogram revealed a lemon-sized "dark spot" in the center, an ominous sign. Despite her interest in alternatives, Suzanna had no hard-and-fast objection to conventional medicine—her grandfather and great-grandfather had both been MDs. Still, she decided she would wait before being treated, going on an herbal and dietary regimen and seeing a naturopathic practitioner every week. But when another sonogram revealed that the dimensions of the mass hadn't changed one whit, she scheduled surgery for that April.

Her gynecologist asked if she would grant permission for a hysterectomy if it proved necessary, but Suzanna refused. The surgeons removed a thirteen-centimeter cyst and an ovary. Two days later, her doctor told her everything seemed fine and Suzanna could go home as soon as she was able. "I don't see hospitals as healing places, so I was out of there in three days after major abdominal surgery," she says proudly. But a few days later, she received a call: The pathology report showed an aggressive, high-grade ovarian cancer. She would have to come back for an immediate hysterectomy.

Suzanna sought a second opinion, with the same verdict: If she didn't have the operation followed by chemotherapy, she wouldn't live a year. Leaving the doctor's office, "I cried, gave him a hug, thanked him for his advice, and told him I'd go home and think about it. When I got home, the first thing I did was drink three glasses of wine, turn up the music, and dance, cry, laugh, and sing. The next day I went to see a naturopathic doctor and decided I wanted to try to heal myself. I've never been afraid to do something on intuition."

"I believed in hard work," she continues, "so I began a regimen. I went on a macrobiotic diet, used a special herbal formula, got 'crystal washings' three times a week. I did massage, visualization, took herbs, meditated twice a day. People came to me with all kinds of alternatives and doctor recommendations. I had good food, good air, good water, space." Her eighty-six-year-old neighbor prayed for her every day. She did a lot of hiking and "climbed a lot of mountains." She found an African dance teacher and learned to drum and dance to the wildly complex polyrhythms. She took singing lessons. "When I was little, I would enjoy singing but everyone would tell me to shut up, that I couldn't carry a tune. All of sudden, when I got cancer, I realized I had to do it. I never thought I could sing a note, and now I'm in a wonderful choir."

But when she went back in to see her doctor early that fall, the prognosis was still grim. They detected another growth on her remaining ovary. "I redoubled my efforts," she says. Feeling she had reached a critical turning point, she went on a seventeen-day juice fast, tossing down handfuls of vitamin and mineral supplements, digestive enzymes, "fifty pills a day." She would go up to her friend's cabin to be alone, a respite from the parade of friends who sometimes made it impossible to concentrate. Her visualizations became more vivid. In one, she was on a beach where an old woman cradled her tenderly in her arms. In others, she would be riding a horse like the ones that used to graze in a neighbor's pasture when she was a kid. Sometimes it would even be Black Beauty, the Black Stallion, or Queenie, from her favorite books from childhood, hooves drumming sand into spray, her one hand buried in its mane, the other waving free.

On her next visit to the doctor, there was no trace of the tumor. Recently, she bought seventy-eight acres in the Bitteroot Valley, planting seven hundred trees "to give back to the earth." She plans to turn the land into a healing center.

What cured Suzanna? How can we even begin to evaluate relative efficacies and active ingredients? Conventional medicine is stymied, caught in a category confusion: Can only "real" medicine be curative? How do we decide, or is it even necessary? Suzanna did what she felt was most congruent with her own ability, experience, preference, and training. But anything she did other than recognized treatments *could* be judged a harmless placebo. According to common wisdom, placebos can't cure cancer; neither can juices, herbs, and vitamins. Though partisans of various alternatives would be eager to claim her cure as their own, even Suzanna is not certain which of the options she chose was effective. Wrote Suzanna's MD: "This patient is rational, intelligent, and quite set on pursuing alternative, unorthodox remedies for her proven ovarian cancer. Thus far she has been successful in that there is no evidence of recurrence. She is willing to accept the risks, and I have agreed with her right to decide her own fate."

MIRACLE

The earliest report of a miracle in a medical journal, titled "Spontaneous Regression of Cancer," was reproduced in an article by Dr. S. L. Shapiro for *Eye, Ear, Nose, and Throat Monthly:*

> Near the end of the thirteenth century a zealous, young priest of the order of Servites fell ill with a painful cancer of the foot. He bore his trial without a murmur and, when it was decided that amputation should be performed, spent the night preceding the operation in prayer before his crucifix. He then sank into a light slumber from which he awoke completely cured—to the amazement of the doctors who could no longer detect any trace of the disease. The holy man lived to the age of eighty and died in the order of sanctity.

The man was later declared St. Peregrinus, making the very patron saint of cancer a case of spontaneous regression. Dr. Shapiro goes on to summarize the famous case of Sister Gertrude:

> Sister Gertrude of the Sisters of Charity in New Orleans was admitted as a patient to the Hotel-Dieu Hospital in New Orleans on December 27, 1934. Her health had been failing rapidly for some months. On admission to the hospital, she was jaundiced and suffered from severe pain, nausea, chills, and a high fever. She was under the care of Dr. James T. Nix, who had previously operated on her for a gallbladder condition.
> A preoperative diagnosis of cancer of the pancreas was

made, and an exploratory laparatomy performed on January 5, 1935. The head of the pancreas was found to be enlarged to three times its normal size. The process appeared to be inoperable and the prognosis hopeless. A biopsy of the tumor was done and the wound closed. A diagnosis of carcinoma of the pancreas was made by three pathologists.

The sisters of the order interceded with Mother Seton, deceased founder of the order. In a series of novenas the sisters asked Mother Seton to spare the life of Sister Gertrude so that she might continue in service. She began to improve in health and made rapid progress. She was discharged from the hospital on February 1 and returned to her duties on March 1.

For seven and a half years after the operation she performed her arduous duties. She died suddenly on August 20, 1942. An autopsy was performed thirty-six hours after death in the laboratory of the DePaul Hospital in St. Louis, Missouri, by Dr. Walter J. Siebert. The immediate cause of death was ascertained to be massive pulmonary embolism. There was no evidence of carcinoma of the pancreas.

Another miracle attributed to Mother Seton was the case of Ann O'Neill. Ann still remembers being a frightened four-year-old hospitalized with acute lymphatic leukemia. It was Easter week in Baltimore, 1952, and at the time the disease was one-hundred-percent fatal (though today it is seventy-three-percent curable). The priest had given her a final blessing, and her aunt had already sewn her a tiny, hand-stiched burial gown out of yellow silk. But her parents bundled her up and took her out in the rain to the cemetery where, surrounded by praying nuns, she was laid on the tomb of Mother Elizabeth Seton.

A few days later, back in the hospital, blood tests had revealed an apparent miracle: There was not a trace of the cancer. Vatican investigators traveled from Rome to look into the case. Nine years later, the Church insisted that Ann submit to a painful bone marrow biopsy to confirm her cure (overseen by Sidney Farber, a

Harvard professor of pathology who had developed the first effective treatment for leukemia). The Pope declared her a miracle, and not long afterward canonized Mother Seton an American saint. Is there a scientific explanation? Ann's doctor, Milton Sacks, one of the country's foremost hematologists, testified at the Vatican tribunal that given the bloody sores on her neck and back, severe anemia, and 105-degree fever, she should not have survived a disease that was then "inexorably fatal."

If there is no medical explanation, could there be a psychosocial one? All who were there remember how fiercely devoted Ann's mother, Felixana "Sis" O'Neill, was to her dying child. The Sisters of Charity nuns who staffed the St. Agnes Hospital remember her shunting aside the head pediatrics nurse when she'd asked the little girl if she'd like to go to Heaven. "No, Sister," Sis had interrupted, steel in her voice, "not yet." Dr. John Healy, then a young resident on the pediatrics ward, had vivid recollections fifty years later of Sis's all-consuming faith. "She never even questioned for five seconds that this girl was going to get better." Pregnant with her third child, sponging her burning daughter with alcohol in a desperate vigil, Sis left her side only to give birth to the baby.

Or is there a biological explanation?

Ann, in the midst of her ordeal, had developed severe chicken pox and penumonia; several of her doctors had wondered if this had somehow stimulated her immune system, though no such remission had ever lasted. Whatever the cause, Ann is now a forty-six-year-old hairdresser, a grandmother who has had her share of troubles (most recently a divorce and the killing of her eldest son by a sixteen-year-old). She attends Mass several times a week, sometimes twice on Sunday. She says that when she goes to church services, her body feels as if it becomes electrified, filled with the Holy Spirit. But her life is otherwise ordinary, struggling. She professes to be tired of a lifetime of attention and publicity, of being a "walking relic."

The very existence of such cases—of any cases of remarkable recovery—confronts us in starkest terms with the notion of a healing "x-factor," a hidden variable in the mind–body–spirit equation that cannot be found on the medical charts. It poses an important question: How and why does this happen, how can we meaningfully study it, and what are the implications for restoring human health?

Our inability to define—and make distinctions between—various types of remarkable recoveries has up until now made their study and application impossibly rarified. Doctors are pragmatic people. To most, a "spontaneous remission" is an angel dancing on the head of a pin—almost never seen firsthand and impossible to quantify. The tiny circumference of definition has created an infinitesimal elite of unexplained (and unexplainable) cases that seem little more than odd medical curios. But by widening the aperture of exploration, by showing how remarkable recovery can be placed along a continuum of response, we believe the scientific and, finally, humanistic opportunities enlarge: It becomes possible to learn from people who have had a wide variety of healing experiences; to accumulate enough cases to look for meaningful correlation; even to apply what is learned in order to expand our repertoire of treatment. If human beings possess untapped powers of self-repair that can effect the dissolution of a tumor, the regeneration of various organ systems, or the healing of normally terminal conditions, then it is of vital importance to medicine that such powers be investigated in all their various guises. It should rightfully be part of our everyday understanding of how the human body heals itself—an understanding that has been the golden thread through all medical traditions since the dim beginning of the healer's craft.

It is unlikely that explanations for the phenomenon of remarkable recovery can ever be reduced to the microscopic maneuvers of "killer T-cells," or explained by genetic anomaly. Evidence is mounting that healing can be best understood within the totality of a unique individual life. But there is an emergent biology of remarkable recovery. Dr. Steven Rosenberg's encounter with Mr. DeAngelo, for example, was the start of a personal mission that led him, by the relatively tender age of thirty-four, to the position of chief of surgery at the National Cancer Institute. Several years ago, he devised a highly experimental treatment for advanced cancer using cells engineered to produce tumor necrosis factor (TNF), a potent enzyme capable of rapidly dissolving bulging tumors in test animals, and which might have been a factor in Mr. DeAngelo's astounding medical hat trick.

As Dr. William Boyd wrote in 1966 with some annoyance, "Perhaps it is time we stopped using such expressions as 'astounding,' 'incredible,' and 'unbelievable' when we hear of a case of spontaneous regression of cancer, and concentrate a little on the angel's crown, which is immunity."

Dr. Lewis Thomas, while averring that "no one has the ghost of an idea" of how remarkable recoveries occur, believed the biological mechanisms would some day be fully understood. "Some have suggested the sudden mobilization of immunological defense," he writes, "others propose that an intervening infection by bacteria or viruses has done something to destroy the cancer cells, but no one knows. It is a fascinating mystery, but at the same time a solid basis for hope in the future: if several hundred patients have succeeded in doing this sort of thing, eliminating vast numbers of malignant cells on their own, the possibility that medicine can learn to accomplish the same thing at will is surely within the reach of imagining."

CHAPTER THREE

*Powers of the Body:
Is There a
Biological Explanation?*

THE BLIND BIOLOGY OF CANCER MIGHT APPEAR TO RENDER any talk of remarkable recovery moot. Its malevolence knows no bounds. Although cancers of the lung, large intestine, and breast account for half of all occurrences, it can savage any-thing—liver and bone, ovaries and testicles, the brain, the nose, the tongue, the auditory canal, the salivary gland; eyelid and ejac-ulatory duct; heel and heart. When two normal cells come into contact, they politely stop dividing, a microscopic social grace called "contact inhibition." But for cancer, no such inhibitions exist. "The cancer cell," says oncologist Lucien Israel, "is a wild and totally asocial individual, programmed to proliferate without restraint, to compete with its neighbors for food, and in the end, to destroy the organisms at whose expense it survives."

Cancer's signal characteristic is not its rapacity, but its restless, seemingly unquenchable wanderlust. Normal cells are well rooted, possessed of a strong sense of place. Even benign tumors stay anchored in the locale where they were born. But cancer is nomadic. Through a process called metastasis, it invades neighboring tissue and organs one after the other, galloping wildly through borders of bone.

Cancer's growth follows a classic geometric progression, doubling like a zygote. After its thirtieth doubling, it reaches a centimeter in size, the smallest size at which it can be detected in deep organs. It is rare for it to go beyond its fortieth doubling—a ten-centimeter diameter composed of a trillion cells—before fatal complications set in. "That means," says one oncologist, "that for these tumors, we are at present able to offer treatment only in the last quarter of the evolution of the disease, which is terribly late."

But remarkable recovery proves that cancer is not always invulnerable. The body is sometimes able to control or even eliminate cancer. Surely there must be a pure biology of remission that can explain how an obdurate, deadly object like a tumor and its metastatic satellites can evaporate. Somewhere in the tangled web of bodily systems—immune, circulatory, respiratory, neurological, digestive, eliminative — or on a glinting speck of gene set like some improbable diadem on our twining DNA lies the secret to the trick.

Whatever the mechanism of remarkable recovery, the question of what helps, or even what cures, led us back to the earliest eras of medical practice and forward to the emerging medicine of the future. That people unexpectedly recover from cancer suggests there is a biology of remission hidden somewhere in the body's myriad systems. But where?

In their landmark compilation, the researchers Everson and Cole wrote: "The existence of spontaneous regression . . . supports the concepts of the biologic control of cancer and reinforces the hope that a more satisfactory method of treating cancer than surgery or irradiation may be found." Their epic text is a treasure trove, not just for its cases but for its inspired attempt to find a biological pattern. The authors had noticed, for example, that remissions tended to fall into certain types of cancers: kidney cancer; neuroblastoma (a childhood cancer); melanoma (a skin cancer that can spread to the lung, brain, and other organs); and choriocarcinoma (an aggressive cancer of the uterus).

The reports were intriguing: Some people recovered after a mere biopsy, indicating a possible rousing of the immune system to eject the unwelcome guest; some recovered following transfusions of plasma and blood, hinting at the existence of blood-borne components that might react against the invader; some recovered following infections and fevers. One woman with melanoma who had a severe infection at the site of her disease recovered after a partial removal of the tumor. Had the infection or the fever sounded an alarm that mobilized the body's natural system of self-repair? The remarkable recovery of the mysterious Mr. DeAngelo (chapter two) had another aspect. After doctors had first removed two-thirds of his cancerous stomach, he had suffered a serious infection and fever. Ten days after the operation, his surgeons had reopened the wound and found pus spread throughout the abdomen. Sometime thereafter, the cancer disappeared.

Clinicians have proposed a variety of other natural mechanisms that might be at work in remarkable recovery: hormones, allergic reactions, interference with the blood supply (and, hence, the nutrients) of a tumor, removal of carcinogenic agents, unusual sensitivity to usually inadequate treatment, severe shock such as coma or hemorrhage, and genetic factors.

The question of how the body fights cancer has formed the hidden backdrop for a long debate over treatment. On one side are strategists who attack the disease with surgery, chemotherapy, and radiation. But others, less heretical-sounding as time goes on, have focused on the possibility that the body's own defenses against malignancy might be augmented by the outstretched hand of medical science.

Nearly a hundred years ago Dr. William Coley, one of medicine's unsung heroes, observed that fever, the body's natural response to an infection, seemed to stimulate the remission of certain kinds of cancer. Coley, hailed today by many as "the Father of Immunology," is an example of how one individual's fascination with remarkable recovery mustered him to the front lines of medical understanding.

Coley was a novice surgeon in 1890 when he lost his first patient, the nineteen-year-old sweetheart of young John D. Rock-efeller, Jr., to a fast-spreading sarcoma. The tumor had begun its relentless gnawing in her right arm, and radical surgery had failed utterly to spare her life. Devastated, Dr. Coley scoured the records of New York Hospital (now part of Memorial Sloan-Kettering Cancer Center) dating back to the 1700s until he found several instances where patients had experienced "spontaneous regressions" of sarcomas and other cancers. One common pattern, he noticed, was that several had developed acute infections and fevers prior to being snatched from death's jaws.

He was elated when, examining later records, he uncovered one living survivor of terminal sarcoma. Tracking the man down and interviewing him, Coley learned that the patient had a severe streptococcal infection of the skin prior to his unexpected recovery. Deciding he had discovered the secret—that infection had mobilized an immune response which killed the cancer—Dr. Coley set out to devise a treatment based on artificially inducing infection and fever, which he surmised could prompt the body to attack the tumor decisively. First, he injected live streptococcal bacteria into the tumors with limited success. It was a risky procedure that was very difficult to control. Patients ran high fevers, with violent shaking and chills. Then Coley hit upon an idea that, like many advances in science, proved to be the crucial step toward a successful treatment. He added another bacterium to the brew and, to eliminate some of the risk of a too-severe infection, killed the two bacteria with heat.

His first experimental case with the mixed toxins, which would become known to the medical world as Coley's Toxins, was a nineteen-year-old boy who in 1893 presented himself with an inoperable sarcoma of the abdomen and pelvis. Dr. Coley injected him at the site of the tumor for almost four months, causing raging fevers that often reached 104 degrees or more. The boy received no other treatment yet had a complete remission, remaining in good health until he died of a heart attack sixteen years later.

Encouraged, Coley forged ahead. These were the days before the advent of antibiotics; the science of bacteriology was in its infancy. Sometimes the artificial infection would spin out of control; whereas other times, perhaps owing to the varying strength of individual immune systems, it proved difficult to induce even after repeated injections.

Still, Coley persevered. A portrait of him at the time shows a dashing young man with a walrusy moustache, pasted-back hair, and a determined gaze. With his erect carriage and noble demeanor, he could have passed for the Union soldier he so resembled in his militant devotion to his cause: "No one could see the results I saw," he wrote in 1909, "and lose faith in the method. To see poor hopeless sufferers in the last stages of inoperable sarcoma show signs of improvement, to watch their tumours steadily disappear, and finally see them restored to life and health, was sufficient to keep up my enthusiasm."

He was, in effect, inducing artificial "spontaneous remissions," and many for whom no other therapy was available benefited. In a summary of 210 Coley patients with inoperable disease, fifty percent of those with soft-tissue sarcomas survived five years or more. In the same study, thirty-eight percent of patients suffering lymph node cancers (lymphomas) achieved five-year survival. (In patients suffering from bone sarcomas, which often required amputation to stop the advance of the disease, Coley's treatment was less successful. In one analysis, only thirteen percent of those with inoperable disease survived five years.)

Eighty-six-year-old William Curtis is the second longest surviving Coley's Toxins patient (the other is ninety-one). When we found him, he recalled for us the summer of 1920 which he spent in bed sick, unable to eat more than crackers and milk, the doctors assuming he had scarlet fever. Back in school that fall he bumped his leg on a bench and was surprised that it quickly became hard and swollen. He was diagnosed with osteogenic sarcoma, and, as was the fashion at the time, X-ray treatment was administered and radium needles inserted directly into the mass.

But as the tumor increased rapidly in size, his condition deteriorated. During that time, one of his doctors, familiar with Dr. Coley's work, thought to administer the toxins.

Curtis vividly remembers "the chills, the burning-hot fevers" that lasted for twelve to twenty-four hours. Though the effects were not sufficient to prevent an amputation seven months later, they appeared to halt the progress of fatal metastases, saving his life. In 1921, osteogenic sarcoma had a five-year survival possibility of only one or two percent. Says Dr. Curtis, "In my case, the toxins had no visible effect on the primary tumor. But I'm eighty-six, so something must have helped me attain this venerable age!" Obviously, he says, "there were millions of sarcoma cells in my bloodstream, but none of them grew." He speculates that Coley's Toxins must have caused his body to develop antibodies to the cancer.

Curtis later attended Rush Medical School in Chicago, and was honored in 1933 at the city's National Bone Sarcoma Registry as "the only patient in its records ever to turn up alive."

A more bizarre incident two years later reminded him again how close he had come to death. In Seattle for his state medical boards, he was required to examine correctly a specimen brought in from a pathology museum. "When I came up to the table, they presented me with the leg of a boy. The diagnosis was easy—sarcoma—and I handed it back." The pathologist glanced at the leg's records and went pale. "Oh my God, I'm sorry, Bill," he stammered. "This leg is *yours!*"

Dr. Curtis laughs heartily to tell it. He never needed the leg during fifteen years of general practice, delivering 1,000 babies during the war while standing on his prosthesis. He's retired now, living at the Covenant Shores retirement community on Mercer Island off the Seattle coast, singing in the choir, playing the cello, riding a tricycle, painting watercolors of ships and sails and lighthouses.

When we asked Dr. Curtis what factors he thought contributed to his recovery, he listed "the moral and psychological support of my sister, X-ray and radium treatment, a stable and supporting family, and Coley's vaccine therapy."

Dr. Curtis, who practiced medicine in a time when doctors prescribed mustard plasters and onion poultices for pneumonia, has not kept up with the stratospheric new techniques of immunological medicine, but he feels such approaches are just common sense. He remembers a remarkable recovery from his own practice: "An ovarian cancer had metastasized to the lungs. No treatment seemed possible—she had a great, dense ball of metastases—so we'd just watch, take a picture every couple of months. One time they'd be large; next time they'd be small. I watched her for years, even took her X rays to a conference, where they were quite amazed but couldn't explain it. This person had an ability—which I think many people have—to control her cancer through her own immune system. Doctors these days concentrate so much on getting rid of cancer, cutting it and burning it and poisoning it, but it still keeps moving around the body. The solution's got to be in the person's own natural ability. If we could figure out what this lady was doing, we'd have it made."

Clearly, we thought, Dr. Curtis must be right. The immune system *would* be the first place to look for the biological mechanisms of remarkable recovery. Fever, for example, is an immune response. Higher temperature stimulates the activity of the body's white cells, allowing them to thunder to the site of an infection more rapidly and consume microbes more readily.

Many researchers remarked on the occasional occurrence of severe infections preceding tumor regression, a factor we, too, have found in a number of cases. Such infections are usually accompanied by high fevers. Cancer cells are more sensitive to heat than normal cells. Could it be that the heat of fever—or more likely, some more complex biological alchemy associated with fever—mobilized the body's healing system?

Fever is a theme sounded in many reports of remarkable recovery. One woman who underwent a round of chemotherapy that was not expected to help her recounted to us, "As the chemicals oozed into my veins, they seemed to make my skin hot night and day. Every night I would have high fevers. My husband would hold me in his arms, sponging my head and neck with cool water. I was perpetually cooking." Could the fever states as well as the chemo have contributed to her cure?

We tracked down a doctor who reported in 1964 "the first recorded case of complete regression of bronchogenic carcinoma that we can locate in the literature." He professed to have "no real explanation. [The patient] was just an ordinary guy, there was nothing special about him. Somebody got him to get out and work on a farm and eat a healthy diet, the old health cure." He paused, then offhandedly added, "He had a period of fever for four or five days which was really unexplained."

Dr. Coley did not believe fever could be the entire story in his own well-documented recoveries. "If high temperature alone were the sole cause," he wrote in 1931, "then all febrile diseases associated with . . . malignant tumors should show marked regression. Such we know is not the case." Rather, Coley saw the reaction as part of a wider healing system of the body, an idea that has been borne out by modern immunological research.

It is testimony to Coley's success that, during a time when the vast functions of the immune system were largely unknown, he had the participation of such a wide spectrum of the medical community. (Of the hundreds who were treated with Coley's Toxins, only a portion of the records bear his name; two-thirds of the cases were reported by other MDs.) It is also to his credit that by the mid-1930s, the American Medical Association listed Coley's Toxins as the only systemic treatment for cancer. But his were handcrafted remedies that worked best on a small subpopulation of patients (soft-tissue sarcomas comprise only 0.7 percent of all cancers). After his death in 1936, more broadly applicable techniques of chemotherapy and radiation had supplanted his oddly homebrew-sounding vaccine.

Coley's Toxins might have wound up consigned to the dustbin of medical history were it not for his daughter Helen Coley Nauts. Her dogged efforts to preserve her father's legacy helped lead to current understanding of the body's natural immune mechanisms.

Helen told us she didn't start out as a crusader. After her father's death, she had merely planned to write his biography for the family. But one day, she recounts, "I went to the barn and found a stack of papers." The stack was box upon box, filed in order of years since the turn of the century: 15,000 letters, diaries, and medical records.

"He didn't throw anything away." She laughs fondly. Going through them, she became convinced she had stumbled on an unknown archive that could have vast scientific implications. Before long, she had sold her father's rare-book collection to help finance what she began to refer to merely as The Work. Her husband soon cashed in his life insurance policy to stoke The Work's all-consuming boiler fire. She goaded oncologists in carefully modulated tones, refusing to listen when they told her that she should just drop it; that she, who had no degrees or stature in the medical field, would never get anyone to even read her conclusions; that her father's ideas were too archaic or, alternately, too wildly premature.

In person, Helen Coley Nauts is a dynamo, a single-purpose juggernaut with a quick wit and an Upper Manhattan gentility. She continues to caretake her data (70,000 references, mostly handwritten, on infection, fever, and remission) in a home office whose every square inch is crammed with boxes and files. At eighty-six years old, she is amazingly fit and utterly formidable, after a decades-long campaign to preserve and extend her father's legacy. She became a self-made scholar of medical history, consuming tens of thousands of articles, finding fascinating antecedents to Dr. Coley's theories. There was Schwenke's eighteenth-century report of a woman with inoperable breast cancer who had exhausted the remedies of the time. In her terminal stage, an abscess formed on the woman's leg. It grew, oozed pus, and, the more abundant the suppuration, the more the cancer diminished. The woman allowed the ulcer to heal, whereupon the cancer recurred. When her physicians opened a new "issue" at the site of the abcess and allowed it to again suppurate, the breast cancer once again disappeared.

Helen discovered that others besides her father had known infection could heal. Such paradoxes inspired physicians in the eighteenth and nineteenth centuries to induce "laudable pus, setons, or issues" in their inoperable cancer patients—in effect, the first immunotherapy. Helen Coley Nauts described one nineteenth-century experiment in a published monograph:

> A French physician, Dussosoy, applied gauze dressings soaked in gangrenous discharges on ulcerated breast cancers or inoculated "gangrene" in a small incision . . . [S]uccess was complete. The ulceration destroyed the entire tumour, which sloughed off on the nineteenth day. Dussosoy then concentrated on controlling the progress of the gangrene, succeeded in doing so, and in a few days the ulcer became bright red and covered with healthy granulations.

But Helen Coley Nauts did not stop at research. She was determined to bring back to life The Work itself, a task that sometimes resembled re-creating Pompeii from a few lava-scorched frescoes and inscribed pottery shards.

The technical obstacles alone seemed insuperable. Helen, with extraordinary patience and persistence, plowed through all the records to find the right instructions for her father's personally titered, mixed, and measured microorganisms: the dose, frequency, site, and especially the duration of treatment. "Coley," writes his daughter, "had no bacteriological training at all and relied on others to make the preparations." Dr. Coley, she writes, published 143 papers between 1896 and 1936 but failed to detail how, or how long, to administer the treatment. Even some of his contemporaries had not been able to replicate his work. Still, Coley and his colleagues, out of 523 inoperable cases totted up 238 successes—diagnosed cancers still alive after five years—and 285 failures, a stunning, near fifty-percent cure rate.

In 1976 Helen Coley Nauts contacted Lloyd Old, a prominent

physician and researcher at Memorial Sloan-Kettering Cancer Center, asking him to set up a study of Coley's Toxins using available modern laboratory techniques. Dr. Old breezily challenged her to bring him one hundred well-documented cases. She responded by carting in documentation for over a thousand into his office.

Impressed, Old undertook a study on mice, finding that the toxins stimulated the animals' immune systems to produce what is now known as tumor necrosis factor, or TNF. This chemical, produced by the immune system in infection and fever, has since been genetically cloned and used in patients in clinical trials—in particular by Dr. Steven Rosenberg, who, after witnessing the recovery of the irascible Mr. DeAngelo, had been spurred on in his own immunlogical steeplechase.

Coley's Toxins (now refurbished with the sleeker, more technocratically comforting term MBV, or Mixed Bacterial Vaccines) at last stood revealed as the seedbed for the current crop of therapies using "biololgical response modifiers"—substances, like TNF or the famed interferon, that are derived from the body's own immune system and that scientists hope to use as a new magic bullet against cancer.

Referring to Coley's pioneering work in immunotherapy, Steven Rosenberg writes: "Those who have scrutinized Coley's results have little doubt that these bacterial toxins were highly effective in some cases." In 1979, Rosenberg and his associates initiated a study combining Coley's Toxins and chemotherapy to treat patients suffering from non-Hodgkin's lymphoma. When evaluated five years later, patients treated with the Coley's Toxins/chemotherapy combination responded more completely and had longer survival than those treated with chemotherapy alone.

Rosenberg singles out the largely self-educated Helen Coley Nauts as one of the foremost scholars in the area of "nonspecific cancer immunotherapy." Building indirectly on William Coley's legacy, Rosenberg has inserted genes that stimulate tumor necrosis factor (TNF) into patients' lab-isolated cells then reinjected the modified cells into the body, achieving some notable remissions of advanced melanoma.

But other researchers suggest TNF is only a part of the puzzle. As one told us, "With Coley, tumor necrosis factor was only one short-lived piece of a cascade of effects orchestrated within the system. I'm not sure you can ever isolate some single active ingredient in the lab."

Coley's enumeration of the multiple effects of his treatment are a familiar laundry list to students of remarkable recovery: fever, inflammation, the regeneration of tissue and bone. We were curious to note that all are reminiscent of the most homely phenomenon of self-repair, the healing of wounds. Could the not-so-simple mechanism that heals cuts also be implicated in remarkable recovery?

Recall the patient (chapter two) who returned to his "thunderstruck" doctor after he had been sent home to settle his affairs and found his growth disappearing. "I had thought of him as dead," wrote his physician. "[But] he was in perfect health and the only trace of the growth was some smooth scar tissue." Scars are the mundane endpoint of a healing process that can be seen in any scratch, nick, or gouge that becomes infected.

Since ancient times doctors described the four stages as heat, swelling, reddening, and pain. We now know some of the mechanisms behind these observations: Increased blood flow creates redness and a sensation of heat; aggregations of white blood cells cause swelling and pain as blood plasma containing proteins and antibodies rushes to fight off outlanders and dilute toxins. Specialized white blood cells called granulocytes form the pus that collects in wounds. Finally, fibrous growth—scar tissue—forms a web in the wound, trapping blood cells and bacteria to contain the infection.

Compare this biological scenario to the observations of a doctor named Eugene Hodenpyl, who in 1910 conceived of the idea of injecting ascites (a fluid often collecting in great quantities when the body's normal "plumbing system" is clogged by cancer) from a case of "spontaneous remission" into other cancer patients:

The general effects of these injections in man has been nearly uniformly to induce a temporary local *redness, tenderness, and swelling* [our italics] about the tumors, which soon subside. Then occur softening and necrosis of the tumor tissue, which is now absorbed or discharged externally, with the subsequent formation of more or less connective tissue. In all cases the tumors have grown smaller; in some they have disappeared altogether.

Hodenpyl, who died before he could complete a detailed report of his findings, surmised that the body's production of ascites (or some substance contained within them) might not be purely pathological but instead be the body's last-ditch attempt to heal.

We found another hint of the power of whatever factors reside in ascites while reexamining one of the first case reports we retrieved from the archives—Dr. MacKay's 1907 report, "A Case That Seems to Suggest a Clue to the Possible Solution of the Cancer Problem." His patient (chapter one), a breast cancer patient, had come home from the hospital "in a hopeless condition, and for several weeks in December her state was one of semi-collapse." Her chest was discolored a deep blue. The left breast, "filled with malignant growth," was swollen and hard. "Swallowing anything," wrote Dr. MacKay, "even a teaspoonful of water was . . . sometimes impossible." The most he had been able to do to ease her suffering was to "tap" her lung cavity to remove some forty ounces of bloody ascites fluid.

One morning later that month, however, her condition entirely altered: "She was much better and felt comparatively comfortable. She could swallow quite easily." Coincident with this improvement, the fluid in her chest disappeared as the hard growth shrank away. No explanation is offered, but MacKay wondered aloud: "Is it too visionary to entertain the hope that a method founded on imitating what appears to have taken place in this case may eventually be possible?" Even before Hodenpyl, MacKay contemplated a similar experiment—injecting the ascitic fluid from a patient who had recovered into others with a similar disease—in an early insight into the potential of what we now call biological response modifiers.

In another early report of remarkable recovery from breast cancer, recorded by Dr. G. A. Boyd in 1914, it is yet again suggested that the body's ascitic fluid seems to have played some role in the healing process: "While the experimental evidence is against the ascitic fluid having any curative influence," he wrote, "it is hard to divorce in one's mind the sequence of events. . . . The ascitic fluid may have given rise to protective substances whether in the nature of antibodies . . . [or] enzymes . . . that, acting upon the tumor cells, may have caused the retrogression noted."

Like Dr. MacKay before him, Dr. Boyd had noticed how quickly the body had filled up with fluid, then how the fluid, its work seemingly done, had been rapidly reabsorbed by the body. He was struck by the inescapable image of a substance self-secreted by the body whose job it was to inundate—and through some corrosive power of the immune system, kill and dissolve— a deadly tumor. Boyd wrote, with a mixture of frustration and joy, "I feel that nature has flaunted her cure under my eyes and they have been too blind to see."

What these early experiments mean for cancer patients today is unclear. Perhaps there is not one "magic bullet" that will lead to the dissolution of a tumor. Perhaps a combination of different components working synergetically is required to eliminate cancer.

But the fact that the body, at least on occasion, has its own way of ridding itself of tumors has profound implications. The evidence gleaned from case reports of remarkable recoveries for the power of the body's own immunity has been for decades the leading edge of cancer research. A researcher at a 1974 Johns Hopkins conference on spontaneous remission—the only such conference ever convened—summed up the general consensus by announcing: "I'm going to put my money on the immune system. We've got a hobbyhorse—let's thrash it for what it's worth!"

Clinicians for the last one hundred years have commented on the relationship between the cancer and its internal environment, the human body. Surely, observed William Handley at the turn of the century, "The recorded cases of the natural repair of cancer, far from being anomalous and exceptional, merely illustrate more strikingly than usual the natural laws which govern every case of the disease. The order of Nature admits of no real anomalies, and is often best brought to light by the close study of apparent exceptions."

The "apparent exceptions" to the incurability of cancer—remarkable recoveries—have led researchers and physicians to study those cancers known to more commonly regress. The childhood cancer, neuroblastoma, which develops in the neural tissue of fetuses and often shows up as abdominal tumors in infants, has long been known to disappear with striking frequency. In fact, it is one of the only forms of cancer where, depending on its type, a remarkable recovery may be *expected*. Specialist Dr. Audrey Evans, a physician at Children's Hospital of Philadelphia, has developed ways of distinguishing a "good" type of neuroblastoma—which affects some seven percent of babies with the disease—from a more severe "bad" type. Only one in five children has recurrences in the "good" type, as opposed to ninety percent in the more aggressive "bad" kind. Using a formula that takes into account the child's age, the stage of the disease, and the level of a blood component called serum ferritin, she and her colleagues can predict the likelihood of regression with such accuracy that they do not normally treat infants who have the "good form" with anything more than surgical removal of some of the tumors.

"For a long time nobody had a spontaneous regression because neuroblastoma was so bad that nobody went without treatment," says Dr. Evans. "I'm sure there are far more cases of spontaneous regression than we see. We have a significant number of children that we treat with surgery alone. We know there is disease left behind after surgery. We may only get ninety-five percent of it. We don't do anything further, and the disease doesn't come back."

When Irene Markham's fourth child, Kendall, was diagnosed at birth with neuroblastoma, she was horrified. She was a divorced single parent wrestling with her own demons of alcoholism, poverty, and the aftermath of an abusive childhood. The fresh tragedy was almost more than she could bear. As Kendall's condition worsened, Irene—a full-blooded Eskimo and Jehovah's Witness—told the doctors she wanted to bring her son home to die.

"But a friend of mine came over and said some prayers with me. I remembered when I'd been little and very sick with an ear infection—I had a sore throat, enlarged heart, swollen joints—and my aunties prayed for me. I'd recovered because I was in this Eskimo house, and my companions were the stars in the sky. So my friend and I prayed, even though I expected to see Kendall dead in the morning, but his swelling went down and he was still alive."

The doctors had obtained a court order to transfuse needed blood to her son in spite of Irene's religious objections. "When I saw my baby he was so red from head to toe I didn't want to hold him, but the doctor got mad at me and told me to go be with my baby, that my love could heal him faster. It was really funny holding this baby with lumps the size of marbles. He had rashes and was so red and sore all over. But I stayed with him. We'd go through little conversations with each other. I'd say, 'Are you all right?' And he seemed to say, in between little baby gargles, *Yes, I'm all right*. 'Are you all right?' *Yes, I'm all right*. We'd carry on like that until we both fell asleep."

Kendall continued to improve. When he was two, a friend told Irene about the healing power of an herb called hyssop. Discovering that each time she administered it, his urine tests for neuroblastoma (vanillylmandelic acid) went down, Irene gave it to him every day as he grew up. When she first showed Kendall his "lumpy" baby pictures, he had told her, "Mom, I must have been a deformed seed," but today he is a healthy fifteen-year-old. Nearly all of his dozens of nodules have regressed, save a handful which Irene watches carefully under a doctor's supervision. Kendall, she says, is a typical rebellious teenager. "Sometimes he bugs me and drives me crazy. But he's all right." She repeats it like a well-worn prayer. "He's *all right*."

Irene has still not settled in her own mind the cause of her son's cure. "He didn't have any chemo or radiation. It was the transfusions in their book, sure," she says, referring to her doctors, "but to me, a part of it had to be the herbs, and especially the love. Love can be stronger than medicine." Hers may be an unscientific opinion, but the medical explanation for such occurrences is not entirely clear, even among the experts. Says Dr. Evans, who has seen hundreds of neuroblastoma cases and dozens of remissions: "Some immunologists disagree with me, but I think the immune systems of these babies are involved. If we can understand the role the immune system plays, we might be onto something. For example, it might be found that drugs depress the immune system, and we may not want to throw drugs around at people. We can only assume that the patient with a lot of disease who is handling it himself is mounting some sort of rejection response."

Other theorists have suggested that children's almost routine remarkable recovery from "good" neuroblastoma is caused by natural mechanisms of cell maturation. The various cells of an embryo normally develop from an undifferentiated "blast" form to highly specialized cells with specific functions—whether fingernail or eyelid, stomach or brain. Cancer cells, in effect, refuse to grow up. (In adults, cancer cells are "de-differentiated," almost embryonic versions of normal cells.) As Kendall matured, his remaining neuroblastoma cells may have matured at the same time into healthy, differentiated tissue. This would mean that all bodies contain self-righting mechanisms—in part, no doubt, genetic—that can make "immature" cancer cells grow into normal ones.

Dr. Evans believes that genes, too, may well play a role. She notes that in "bad" forms of neuroblastoma, chromosomal abnormalities in the patient are much greater in number than those in patients with the "good" form. Genetics may eventually provide a key to understanding how cancer can, seemingly of its own accord, sometimes go away.

Oncologist Wally Sampson told us, "The big news is that there are genetic programs built in to stop cell growth in general. One of the things that intrigues me is that kidney cells, once they're mature, tend not to reproduce. Maybe they know the secret of how to stop growing again. It's time we took a look at the tumors that are most likely to regress and see what they have in common, even if they're from different tissues." His surmise again raises a controversial question: Are some seeming responses to treatment actually part of a natural process of regression? Are certain types of cancer—the sarcomas, melanomas, and lymphomas, for example, which make up a large percentage of reported remissions (as well as Dr. Coley's and Dr. Rosenberg's cures)—genetically marked for sporadic recovery?

The map of the human chromosome and its genes is medical science's most bruited Grail Quest. The modern era began in 1970, when a Swedish scientist discovered that if cells were stained while in the process of dividing, each chromosome would display the dark and light bands representing its genetic pattern. Abnormalities in these bands—bands missing or broken off often correlated with human physical abnormality—would then be traceable. The search was impeded by at least one problem: Chromosomes have a consistency like undercooked transparent Chinese rice noodles. Rubbery and colloidal, they refused to lie flat. Their length could not be stretched out to reveal more than a paltry 640 bands of gradation, a tiny fraction of their informational wealth.

Enter Jorge Yunis, a fifty-one-year-old doctor who, after cobbling together a series of intriguing but unsatisfactory devices, finally perfected an oddly homemade way to read the chromosome like a large-type library book. Yunis's technique is to stand six feet above a slide placed at a twenty-five-degree angle to the floor, flicking bits of cell-bearing goo onto his target. The precise tilt of the slide keeps the chromosomes from being squished beyond recognition or slithering off the slide entirely. "I can usually score a bulls-eye from six feet away," he announces proudly. His technique immediately began paying dividends. In a series of stunning refinements, he detected almost 10,000 bands with an electron microscope.

Prior to his work, scientists thought perhaps fifty percent of cancers involved chromosomal defects. Yunis's high resolution analysis revealed a figure of ninety-seven percent. Moreover, it could now be seen that chromosomal rearrangements were indicators of how slowly or how aggressively a cancer will move through the body—knowledge of incalculable potential benefit in prognosis and treatment strategy.

Yunis also found that if a patient's cancer cells have an upside-down segment on the sixteenth largest chromosome, the chances of the patient's survival are excellent. Interestingly, he notes that patients with this chromosomal pattern are sometimes more sensitive to chemotherapy. Are there genetic markers that single out people prone to remission? Are these same people also those who do well in treatment? And most challengingly, are these two related: Are such people, in effect, already primed for healing, making their treatment as much a catalyst for their own innate self-healing mechanisms?

One participant in the 1974 conference on spontaneous regression, Dr. David Weiss, suggested yet another biological paradigm that might have implications for remarkable recovery: Cancer could be seen as a parasitic organism, literally feeding off its host. Tumors, like any other living tissue, need to eat to live. Perhaps, he suggested, when the nutrient environment became less hospitable, the cancer might find it difficult to grow. Perhaps there would be nutritional ways to change the balance of the system back toward normal growth.

Special dietary regimens have been cited in a number of documented cases of spontaneous remissions, particularly in the older literature, though the sometimes improbable-sounding "menus" patients adopted may becloud more than they clarify.

In a 1887 report, a man with an inoperable "osteo-sarcoma . . . a tumor on his scapula, as large as a pint bowl" was instructed by an alternative medical practitioner to "take from the brook which ran through his native farm a plant which grew there (the adviser did not say what it would be), and use a weak infusion of it for his only drink every day until the tumor had disappeared. His diet, besides this, was to consist of bread alone. This advice was strictly followed; the plant he used was 'water dock.' " When the man returned to his physician two years later, his physician "found the tumor had nearly disappeared, there being apparently only a trifling thickening of the skin."

In a report of lung cancer in 1984, the physicians state, "The patient's general condition by then was very poor (general exhaustion and loss of eight kilograms of weight within three months). The patient started a diet free of fruit, potatoes, sugar, animal proteins and animal fats. Within a few months, his condition gradually improved." In another lung cancer case, the physicians noted the patient "took two halibut liver oil capsules daily for a considerable period of time, four vegetable compound tablets daily, an occasional barbiturate for sleep, and vitamin B1 tablets. The vegetable compound tablets were analyzed and were found to contain asparagus, parsley, watercress, and broccoli."

The dietary practices we discovered in the case literature have ranged from herbal therapies; to eating large quantities of meat; to eating no meat; and, for a woman with malignant melanoma, eating "nothing but grapes." Researcher Harold Foster, who reviewed 200 cases of remarkable recovery, found that nearly eighty-eight percent reported making substantial dietary changes, "usually of a strict vegetarian nature" prior to their healing.

How or if a diet might affect the body's ability to recognize and eliminate a tumor is a difficult question to answer. A poor diet may reduce the amount of oxygen available to the body's tissues, making them vulnerable to attack. (Since cancer cells can survive more effectively than healthy cells without oxygen, poor nutrition may allow cancer cells to proliferate.) A diet that brings increased oxygen to the blood and tissues may be the stimulation the immune system needs to finally be able to attack and eliminate a tumor (or, in Dr. Weiss's earlier mentioned formulation, make the environment "inhospitable" to the disease). Though many dietary practices are acknowledged in Foster's analysis of 200 cases, one thing is clear: Many people make profound changes in their eating habits when diagnosed with cancer, for reasons ranging from medical (or quasi-medical) theory to plain common sense.

"They tell me there are leukocytes in my blood, and sodium and carbon in my flesh," wrote George Bernard Shaw. "I thank them for the information, and tell them there are black beetles in my kitchen, washing soda in my laundry, and coal in my cellar. I do not deny their existence, but I keep them in their proper place."

A similar attitude of pragmatism was embraced, with characteristic enthusiasm, by Norman Arnold. At fifty-two Norman was happily married for twenty years with three growing sons. He was president and CEO of one of the ten largest liquor distributors in the country, a philanthropic pillar of his community who had headed the local chapter of the Boys Clubs, the state Children's Bureau, and the Governor's Economic Task Force.

But in that crisp Carolina fall of 1981, Norman felt a sharp, persistent pain in his lower back. Though the preliminary diagnosis was gallstones, he had an uneasy feeling. "What's the likelihood of you finding something else?" he'd asked his doctor the night before surgery, reassured to hear the chances were nil. But the next day the surgeon, a friend who had been at Norman's Fourth of July barbecue pitching horseshoes weeks before, found a tumor brooding on the head of Norman's pancreas, with metastases to lymph nodes and the liver. The pathology report read, "metastatic adenocarcinoma of the pancreas, with documented nodal metastasis and isolated metastatic disease to the liver."

His wife, Gerry Sue, was the first to hear the news. She saw the ashen look on the doctor's face, heard the dread word pronounced. "I remember saying to him, in shock, just on automatic, 'You know, we're supposed to go skiing at Christmastime.' And he said that would be OK. And I said, 'Well, our twin boys are having their Bar Mitzvah in April.' And he said, 'Can you move it up?' It was then I realized the time frame he was talking about."

Pancreatic cancer is a virulent, almost invariably fatal condition for which there was no successful treatment; ninety-five percent of all cases die within six to eight months of discovery, 99.7 percent die within eighteen months. Norman, after a brief period of depression—"I was hoping to have a little more time to see the kids grow," he told Gerry glumly—didn't let it get him down for long. "That's what they say," said Norman. "Now let's see what I can do."

In the hospital, thumbing through the August 1982 issue of *Life* magazine with Marilyn Monroe gazing sultrily from the cover, he'd spotted an article about an MD who had reportedly cured himself of cancer with a "macrobiotic" diet composed largely of vegetables and rice. Norman felt a rush of hope. An early contributor to Vitamin C pioneer Linus Pauling's work, Norman had "always been kind of a health nut with things I understood, like exercise," though he admits, "I ate very badly. I thought meat three times a day was necessary for someone with my body type. I didn't think anything of eating a half gallon of chocolate ice-cream at a sitting."

Now, galvanized by the article, Gerry Sue hired a Japanese couple who specialized in macrobiotic cooking to meet them at home the day Norman came back from the hospital. They showed Gerry Sue how to prepare brown rice, seaweed, and adzuki beans. "They believed in it so strongly," Norman says. "It was the first thing that made sense to me—the idea of getting well, not just buying time."

He had found a paperback book written by a woman whose husband, a university professor, had pancreatic cancer and was reportedly healed by macrobiotics. Norman immediately picked up the phone and called her. Her husband was dead, she said. "Well, that didn't sit too well," said Norman wryly. "But he died of the flu," she added helpfully, seven long and fruitful years after he'd been given only weeks to live.

Elated, Norman phoned the popularizer of the diet, Michio Kushi, at his home in Brookline, Massachusetts. Informed that Kushi was leaving the country that same evening, Norman was undeterred. "I want to see him today," he insisted.

"Can you be here by five?" asked Kushi's secretary.

Norman promptly chartered a plane, arranged for a car at the airport, and within hours was at Kushi's door, still bearing drainage tubes from his operation.

It was a different world. The big stone house with its imposing portico reminded him of the Addams Family. Neat rows of shoes sat outside a marble foyer filled with benches of people waiting, hushed and orderly "like in churches or synagogues." But Norman and Michio Kushi hit it off famously. When the self-effacing Japanese philosopher told the hard-driving businessman that he could recover, "I just grabbed him in a bear hug," Norman says. "Everyone else had told me all I could do was buy a few months. He was the one who said I could beat this thing."

Norman knew if he was to have any future it would depend largely on macrobiotics. He asked his lawyer to go to Boston to pore over Kushi's records for any cases of pancreatic cancer. The man's search eventually took him to Minnesota, where he found a retired airline pilot who had recovered from pancreatic cancer, then found three more living cases. "Good," Norman told him, when he received the report. "Now I can have some confidence in this thing."

Norman began subscribing to medical journals, newsletters, computer information services. His cousin, an expert in immunology and allergies, became his "quarterback for the medical side of this thing," directing him to leading oncologist Dr. Phillip Schein.

Schein, whom Gerry Sue Arnold remembers as "a wonderful doctor and a wonderful person who just had this way about him," told Norman he'd managed to keep some patients alive up to eighteen months with chemotherapy. Norman, who had been given only a six-month prognosis, decided to chance the aggressive regimen because he was impressed with Schein. After the first treatment, "including a chemical they call the red devil, the one that makes your hair fall out," Norman had gone home and collapsed. After his second treatment, he refused to lie down; he spent the rest of the day working in the yard. "I think he felt that if he went in and lay down," says Gerry, "he'd never get up again."

Meanwhile he continued his search for alternatives. He consulted a physician who used imagery exercises, went to a hypnotherapist, and finally, after his fifth chemotherapy treatment, flew down to *Getting Well Again* author Carl Simonton's center in Dallas. "It was a scene." Gerry laughs. "We traveled with our macrobiotic cook, who looked like a Sixties hippie. Norman bought the ugliest rubber plant you've ever seen because Michio Kushi told him he needed 'green oxygen' in his room. He got so attached to it we had to bring it home on the plane."

Sitting in a circle the first day, each patient was expected to introduce himself and tell his life story. Norman got up and left, saying he had to go to the bathroom. "I'm kind of a loner," he explains. "Listening to other people's deep feelings made me uncomfortable. It was like peeping through a keyhole." When he didn't come back, someone was dispatched to persuade him to return. Back in the circle, Norman began to feel a sense of commonality that was, he says, "a big turning point for me." He began trying to change "from being a type A-plus twice over to at least an A-minus."

The visual imagery he chose for his cancer was idiosyncratically his own. Refusing the standard exercise of "little white dogs eating bad cells," he imagined "strong, potent, virile blood was working on this tumor like muriatic acid eroding cement. My kids drew pictures of it with me, too. It was a total family effort."

The strict macrobiotic diet proved a catalyst that would affect every part of his life. "It was like I was on an umbilical cord. I had to be home for lunch, or carry my lunch with me. I couldn't just jump on a plane and go to New York." Everyone in town by now knew that Norman had pancreatic cancer ("It was a shock to the community," Gerry says. "He was so visible and relatively young"), and that he and his family were following a stringent diet. Some friends stopped inviting them to dinner; others were tolerant of the special food they brought with them. Some restaurants cooked special meals for them. Still, remembers Gerry Sue, some people "just laughed. 'It's so pitiful,' they would say, 'that this dying man is so desperate he'll try anything.' Everybody was looking to see what would happen next."

So was Norman, who was improvising the game plan as he went along. Through his cousin he located a research institute in Philadelphia that was carrying out a pioneering study in monoclonal antibodies. Gerry Sue recounts: "Norman didn't fit into their program. But he went into a meeting with them and made himself look so strong and healthy. He said, 'I'm a winner, I can do this.' I think they felt anybody fighting that hard should be given a chance." A month later, he received a dose of mouse monoclonal antibodies in a protocol that called for a single shot.

As his regular chemotherapy ground on for five treatments, his weight plunged from 160 to 112 pounds. He was becoming despondent at what even his doctors said was only a stay of execution, not a cure. Finally, over Dr. Schein's strenuous objections, he decided to quit. "If you let this thing get ahead of you," Norman remembers his saying, "you'll never catch up again. It'll finally get the best of you."

The Arnolds went on a long-anticipated vacation in the Bahamas, renting a little house on one of the outermost islands. Norman would sit and look at the water, listening to his visualization tapes. The family would play Monopoly, swim, take boat rides. When they came back home, Norman declared he could feel himself getting better.

A few months later, he went back to see Dr. Schein. "You look really great," the doctor enthused, assuming Norman had continued chemotherapy. Norman confessed he had stopped treatment. Gerry remembers, "I thought the doctor was going to drop his pad and paper, he was so shocked. 'Well, what have you been doing?' he demanded. 'You look better than I do.' "

"I've been on this diet," Norman offered, "and doing mental imagery."

Gerry remembers the doctor turning to her and shaking his head. "You know, the patient always knows before the doctor when he's getting better."

According to Michio Kushi, the meals of unrefined grains, beans, vegetables, and occasional fish allowed the body to throw off accumulated poisons and flooded tissues with oxygen and nutrients. He reassured Norman that the odd effects he was experiencing—everything from passing flu symptoms to seeing his tongue turn a disconcerting black—were a typical "discharging" of built-up toxins. Norman began to feel more vital than he had in years.

Macrobiotics, say the Arnolds, was more than a diet, it was a way of life. Kushi, a philosopher not a scientist, continually stressed that macrobiotic living encompassed good family relationships, exercise, and a positive outlook. Norman realized "one of the strengths of macrobiotics is not just the regimen but the fact that you are reminded every time you eat, five and six times a day, that you're doing something helpful. It inspires your optimism, makes you feel you're in control. No one shows up to tell you, 'We're going to do this procedure to you,' or 'Now, take this pill.' "

Seven months after diagnosis, an ultrasound scan of Norman's abdomen showed a normal pancreas and "no evidence of metastatic disease to the liver." In another six months, all evidence of tumor was gone and blood, ultrasound, and other tests showed no sign of the disease. Years later, on his sixtieth birthday, Norman climbed Africa's 19,600-foot Mount Kilimanjaro.

What cured Norman Arnold? Monoclonal antibodies have shown essentially no effectiveness against pancreatic cancer, and only limited effectiveness in most other cancers. It is hard even for him to venture to what extent it was the food, or the regimen, or the mental imagery and meditation. "I think the most important thing was it all gave me a psychological and emotional lift that strengthened my immune system," Norman says. When we asked Norman to draw a pie chart showing the relative percentages of factors he felt were crucial for his cure, he responded: "will," 10%; diet, 9.999%; medical treatment, .0001%; and "unknown," 80% (see appendix three, page 320).

Gerry Sue recalls a conversation she had with a group of doctors shortly after Norman's recovery. "One doctor looked at the other and said, 'Oh sure, it's called instantaneous remission.' And I said, 'Isn't it funny that nobody ever told us that was an option?' I mean, when he was so sick, we kept asking is there any hope? Is there anything good that can happen? No one said, 'Maybe there'll be an instantaneous remission.' "

One of the astonishing properties of living systems is their ability not only to reproduce themselves, but to repair themselves, to self-organize. Said microbiologist René Dubos: "You could guess that in all living things, human beings included, there must be some mechanism for spontaneous recovery, because if there were not, no living thing could survive the constant insults from the environment."

Whatever the mechanisms of remarkable recovery, it is evident that self-healing mechanisms may be as complex as the people to whom they belong. The body's own healing system encompasses more than genetics or biochemistry. A biology of remarkable recovery would include the immune system, cell biology, biochemistry, genetics, and host-parasite relationships—the areas most frequently studied by the exceptional scientists who felt that within the body's systems of self-repair hid the answers to fighting disease. But medicine is now beginning to include in the equation the uniqueness of the individual—the individual who disappeared from the medical literature so long ago.

How people grapple with a fatal disease is not a linear process. Many who experienced remarkable recovery describe undergoing profound psychosocial changes—changes that new studies tell us may powerfully affect the functioning of the immune system. When it comes to the complexities of healing, the more limited and prosaic our questions, the fewer—and poorer—our answers may be. Asking the right question, however, can be the first domino that topples a row of black-and-white preconceptions. We decided to start with the simplest, and the most profound: Would you mind telling us your story?

CHAPTER FOUR

To Weave a Tangled Web: Is There a Mind-Body Mechanism?

E VEN WHEN IT HAS ACKNOWLEDGED THE PHENOMENON OF remarkable recovery, medical science has shown little interest in the notion—put forth almost unfailingly by patients—that thoughts and emotions could have something to do with it. But the people we spoke to insisted that how they got well, perhaps even *why* they got well, included their beliefs about themselves, feelings about others, and relationship to the world—often in proportions greater than they allotted to treatment. It quickly became clear to us that to come to grips with the mystery—and the reality—of remarkable recovery called for a fresh conceptual framework, new research techniques, and eventually, perhaps, a new form of medicine. If there are mind-body factors associated with the disappearance or arrest of a tumor, they might well form the basis of new, multipronged programs of prevention and treatment of disease.

Can beliefs affect a rapacious disease, or is it just New Age folklore? Take a famous case from the 1950s, of a patient suffering from terminal lymphosarcoma known to posterity by the pseudonym "Mr. Wright." He had "huge tumor masses the size of oranges throughout his body," wrote his physician, Dr. West, requiring an oxygen mask to breathe as his chest was filled with "milky fluid." He was too far gone for the treatment of the time, nitrogen mustard and X ray. But, said West, the patient still clung like a drowning sailor to a single flotsam of hope: Krebiozen, then trumpeted in the popular press as a wonder drug, was coincidentally to be tested at the clinic.

Unfortunately, Mr. Wright didn't qualify for the experimental treatment. Patients had not only to be beyond the reach of standard treatment, but had to have life expectancies of at least three months. "To give him a prognosis of more than twelve weeks," wrote Dr. West, "seemed to be stretching things." Besides, the clinic had been allotted enough supply for only a dozen patients, and the slots were filled. But Mr. Wright's "enthusiasm knew no bounds," the doctor wrote, "and as much as I tried to dissuade him, he begged so hard for this 'golden opportunity,' that against my better judgment, and against the rules of the Krebiozen committee, I decided I would have to include him."

The shots were to be administered thrice weekly. The bedridden, gasping Mr. Wright was given his first injection on a Friday. Returning to the hospital on Monday fully expecting "he might be moribund or dead by that time, and his supply of the drug could then be transferred to another case," Dr. West was shocked by a recuperative miracle. While all others who had received the drug were unchanged, Mr. Wright was strolling around the ward, "chatting happily with the nurses and spreading his message of good cheer to any who would listen." Upon examination West found, in a now-celebrated observation, "The tumor masses had melted like snowballs on a hot stove, and in only these few days, they were half their original size."

Within ten days, Mr. Wright was discharged with nearly all evidence of disease vanished. However, after two months of virtually perfect health, Mr. Wright read that all of the clinics testing Krebiozen were reporting dismal results. He began to lose hope, and relapsed to his former condition. It was at this moment that an audacious idea seized Dr. West. He saw an opportunity to investigate how "quacks" were sometimes able to get curative results with seemingly useless medical procedures: "Knowing something of my patient's innate optimism by this time, I deliberately took advantage of him. This was for purely scientific reasons, in order to perform the perfect control experiment which could answer all the perplexing questions he had brought up. Furthermore, this scheme could not harm him in any way, I felt sure, and there was nothing I knew anyway that could help him.

"Deliberately lying," wrote Dr. West, "I told him not to believe what he read in the papers, the drug was really most promising after all." When the patient logically asked why he had relapsed, West temporized that "the substance deteriorates on standing," but that a new "super-refined, double-strength" product would be arriving on the next day. West's dissimulations went so far as to delay the fictional shipment's arrival so that his patient's "anticipation of salvation had reached a tremendous pitch. When I announced that the new series of injections were about to begin, he was almost ecstatic and his faith was very strong.

"With much fanfare, and putting on quite an act (which I deemed permissible under the circumstances)," Dr. West administered an injection consisting of nothing but fresh water. Mr. Wright's second recovery from death was even more dramatic. The masses again melted away, the fluid in the chest vanished, and he became "the picture of health" until two months later, when the final AMA report came out showing Krebiozen to be worthless. A few days later he came back to the hospital, his symptoms in full, malign flower, and within two days of his return was dead.

To answer the mystery of what had occurred in this forbidden experiment is a complex task. Some might say it was merely a wild coincidence—some tumors are known to wax and wane as part of their biological process, though very rarely and seldom dramatically timed to placebo injections. Sarcomas and lymphomas are cancers upon which the fever-inducing Coley's Toxins had once proved effective. Was there fever? Dr. West reports he had indeed left his lymphosarcoma patient "febrile" on the Friday he received his first shot.

On the other hand, Dr. West's extraordinary experiment was perhaps the only such pure placebo experiment—an experiment based solely on the patient's belief system—ever admittedly and deliberately performed on a cancer patient by an MD.

Classically a simple sugar pill masquerading as a pharmaceutical, the placebo was once an integral element in the physician's little black bag. Describing his education at Harvard Medical School earlier in this century, Boston doctor Richard Cabot wrote: "I was brought up, as I suppose every physician is, to use placebos, bread pills, water subcutaneously, and other devices of acting upon a patient's symptoms through his mind."

One memoir of the turn-of-the-century doctor Sir William Osler recalls the great physician's visit to the bedside of a boy afflicted with very severe whooping cough and bronchitis. In this pre-antiobotic epoch, weapons against such now prosaic-sounding diseases were few and recovery seemed unlikely. The dying boy, writes the memoir's author (who was also the child's older brother) was "unable to eat and wholly irresponsive to the blandishments of parents and devoted nurses alike."

Dr. Osler made his first house call to the boy dressed in the magnificent, scarlet academic robes of an Oxford don. "To a small child this was the advent of a doctor, if doctor it in fact was, from quite a different planet," reads the account. "It was more probably Father Christmas. After a very brief examination this unusual visitor sat down, peeled a peach, sugared it and cut it into pieces. He then presented it bit by bit with a fork to the entranced patient, telling him to eat it up and that he would not be sick but would find it did him good as it was a most special fruit."

At the door, Osler took the father aside and pronounced with uncharacteristic dolor that the boy's chances of survival were slim. But the doctor continued to visit daily for over a month, never failing to don his majestic robes in the hall before entering the child's sickroom, always offering the boy nourishment with his own two hands. Here is the inconceivable picture of one of London's busiest and most celebrated doctors attending a patient for forty consecutive days just to administer a placebo. But this "inspired magic, independent of higher degrees and laboratory gimmicks," helped catalyze the boy's unexpected and complete recovery.

Once again, the medical literature pointed toward a potentially valuable clue. While it was clear to us there must be a biology of remarkable recovery, we wondered if the anecdotally celebrated power of the mind over the body could also be significant. It would not have been an alien notion to doctors of an earlier era. But somewhere along the line, the power of the placebo—the power of belief—to influence anything but the most benign "psychosomatic" conditions had been utterly dismissed.

To understand why, we might take a brief overview of a battle that seesawed throughout the previous century. In 1845 four leading German physiologists (Helmholtz, Ludwig, DuBois-Reymond, and Brucke) swore a celebrated oath to account for all processes of the body in purely physiochemical terms. Though the German school's influence rapidly expanded (15,000 American doctors traveled there to study laboratory experimentation), it was in direct conflict with a style of medicine that had existed for centuries, if not millennia—a medicine which believed that the patient's inner life and social being were vital components of all diagnosis and treatment.

We can still hear the echoing cannonades of this epic contest for the heart of healing, a civil war that until recently had sundered the North of the head from the South of the body. On the materialist side, one nineteenth-century theorist quipped that the mind's influence upon the body was nonexistent, the mind being no more than "the steam-whistle which accompanies the work of a locomotive engine but cannot influence its machinery." On the other side, in a paper read before the Alabama State Medical Association in 1895, New York doctor W. L. Conklin proclaimed, "As well might the balance wheel be left out of account by the machinist who would acquire a thorough knowledge of an intricate piece of machinery, as that the mind be disregarded or little thought of by the physician."

Physicians like Conklin who believed medicine should take into account not only biological, but behavioral, moral, psychological, and spiritual factors had come to their position from close clinical observation of the patient. But such models and methods began to fade by the end of the century, as a patient-specific model of treatment gave way to a disease-specific one. Any reported relationship between mental states and bodily functions was deemed biased, subjective, nonmeasurable, and thus scientifically unreliable. Proper research could only be conducted in laboratories on isolated constituents—microorganisms, components of blood and urine, tissue and organ—to devise universal remedies independent of individual patients.

This approach has left modern medicine in the odd position of having to relearn something it knew a century ago: Belief, thoughts, and feelings affect physiology. Harvard cardiologist Herbert Benson, famous for demonstrating in the 1970s the objective therapeutic effects of "the relaxation response," points out that by the 1930s there was not a single article in *Index Medicus* discussing effects upon the body of mental states, as this was now considered impossible. The maximum effects of placebos were considered trivial, perhaps useful in altering a patient's subjective experience of pain, but not in curing a disease. Critic Dr. Norman Sartorius of the World Health Organization wrote: "The healing process has been relegated to the position of a disturbing effect, summed up under the name 'placebo,' equated to some kind of noise in the system."

But, as clinicians for the past several decades have begun to realize, that "noise" can sometimes be almost deafeningly loud: The placebo response may powerfully affect the body in ways that cannot be accounted for by medicine alone. For example, hidden in the background noise of a 1983 *World Journal of Surgery* article on a chemotherapy trial for gastric cancer, buried as a single numerical entry in a single chart, is a fascinating notation: Nearly one-third of a control group—a group that received only a salt-water placebo in place of powerful chemicals—had experienced "alopecia." Alopecia—mirror-avoiding, clumps-on-the-pillow-every-morning hair loss—is a side effect well known to cancer patients who take powerful drugs. The control group had taken, in essence, nothing at all, yet they experienced a marked physiological alteration.

Perhaps, then, it is in the placebo effect that we may find an explanation to a baffling case report we found in the medical literature. A forty-six-year-old man was admitted to the Portland Veterans Administration Hospital on March 12, 1956, complaining of a lump on his right ear. The final pathology report revealed malignant melanoma of the ear with metastasis to one lymph node. Nine months later, the report reads,

A five mm. deeply situated subcutaneous nodule was noted just posterior to the angle of the mandible. . . . The patient was in considerable pain but refused hospitalization and was given a prescription for pain medication. The patient did not return for subsequent follow-up examinations and it was suspected that he had died. He reappeared thirteen months later, however, on July 15, 1958, in apparent good health. . . . The patient was carefully questioned about his course during the past thirteen months. He had received no medical advice or treatment but had applied Vaseline and compresses to the area of his tumor. . . . He attributed his cure to prayer. . . .

It is not likely that the Vaseline-and-compress cure would make it into medical annals as a cure for terminal cancer, any more than would prayer. His case has all the earmarks of a placebo cure, though the power of suggestion—in this case, self-suggestion—is not generally considered a factor in cancer remission. But the power of suggestion has been implicated in several cases that appear in the medical literature.

Take, for example, the following report drawn from an era before the widespread use of ether, when the medical use of hypnosis for anaesthesia was still in vogue. In the 1846 "Report of Tumor Remission Associated with Hypnosis," a woman diagnosed with breast cancer was hypnotized by La Roy Sunderland (1804–1885), a clergyman who developed a method of hypnosis that he termed "pathetism." Mr. Sunderland worked with the woman, who had "a tumour bigger than a hen's egg," for several days as preparation for complete anaesthesia during her upcoming surgery. He accompanied her to the operating room and performed the hypnotic induction, but to a surprising effect. Here, verbatim, is his testimony in the case report:

> At the appointed moment I had Mrs. Nichols spellbound in the position directed by the surgeon. Her whole muscular system was in a state of cold rigidity resembling the sleep of death. Four surgeons were waiting below, and now, upon notice which I gave them that all was ready, they came up into the room where the patient was entranced. They instantly spread their surgical instruments upon the table, which was supplied with water, sponges, and all the implements necessary on such occasions.
>
> The first thing Dr. Walker did was to search for the location of the cancer. After manipulation for some minutes, he turned to the surgeon who stood nearest to him, and said, "The bounds of the tumour do not seem to be well defined." He then left, and the second surgeon tried to find the tumour; but in a few moments he gave it up, and was succeeded by the third and the fourth. Then Dr. Walker examined the patient once more, and began to look somewhat embarrassed. Each one of the surgeons now examined the patient over again, and twenty minutes more they spent in searching for the tumour, for which one of them had been treating that same lady for a year and a half. The surgeons now left the patient, and putting their heads together in a corner of the room, they whispered something I could not hear; when Dr. Walker said to them, "We have concluded

75

it best not to operate," I asked, "Why not?" and he replied, "We do not find that there is any tumour there."

With this statement, the sticking plaster, the scalpel, and other instruments disappeared, and now my attention was given to the restoration of the patient. . . . During the few days she had been Pathetised, the tumor and the pain had disappeared as if by magic, and as they have now been gone for fourteen years the presumption is that she may be considered cured . . . I give this as a remarkable case of self-induction, and the self-healing energies of the human organism.

What healing energies? Did the hypnosis itself, simply by overthrowing the domination of ordinary waking consciousness, allow some deeper mind-body process freer rein? There has been an increasing number of modern studies that indicate hypnosis has the power to directly affect the immune system, surely a key biological component in remarkable recovery.

In one study, Japanese researchers selected thirteen high school boys known to be highly allergic to a certain plant. In the experiment, they were told to close their eyes and then were touched on the arm with the leaves of a harmless plant while being told, "This is the poisonous plant." All thirteen broke out in reactions—from simple redness to swelling and blisters.

Next, the researchers reversed the procedure. This time when the boys closed their eyes, they were brushed with the poison ivy–like plant that had on other occasions caused a reaction but now received the suggestion that the plant was not poisonous. Only two of the boys developed a skin reaction to the plant.

The study (which has been variously cited as a hypnosis experiment and a placebo experiment) has vast implications for immunology, for it indicates that at least some immune responses may be much more influenced by emotions, thoughts, or beliefs than previously thought.

One leading theorist (and passionate experimentalist) in this area is Dr. Theodore X. Barber. Barber began his career when, as a graduate student in 1950s, he happened upon a case report by Dr. A. A. Mason in the *British Medical Journal* describing the use of hypnosis for a skin condition called congenital ichthyosiform erythrodermia, or "fish-skin disease." It is a hideous, generally incurable affliction in which the skin thickens and blackens, taking on a fingernail-hardness that cracks and oozes when bent. But Mason had in his first hypnosis session told the boy to feel the skin on his left arm becoming normal. Within five days, the hard skin softened and fell off. Initial gains were equally rapid: Both the boy's arms, ninety percent of his back, and fifty to seventy percent of the skin on his buttocks, thighs, and legs were miraculously restored. Five years later, the skin that had been cleared remained so, while that which had not was unchanged. It proved, Barber was later to write, that "at least in some individuals, abnormally functioning skin cells begin to function normally when the individual is exposed to specific words or communications."

Mason's report convinced Barber that hypnosis was "the royal road" to solving the mind-body problem. But along the road to the palace, Barber became a bit of a heretic, contesting the widespread view that hypnosis is a special state of consciousness that must always be deliberately induced and that produces abilities not available to people in ordinary waking life. Rather, he says, it is simply a heightened state induced by a belief in a particular set of suggestions.

He lays down a slightly bellicose gauntlet to his colleagues: "[I]nstead of asking the vague question, 'How does hypnosis alter "unchangeable" bodily functions and processes,' we can ask the more precise and more productive question, 'How do suggestions to let go of extraneous concerns and to feel-remember-think-imagine in new or unusual ways lead to the cure of warts, the amelioration of incurable skin diseases, the production of skin inflammation and blisters, the inhibition of allergic responses. . . .'"

There have been numerous debates over what exactly constitutes a state of hypnosis. Stanford University psychiatrist Dr. David Spiegel demystifies the word by breaking it into three discrete components: One is *absorption:* "the hypnotic state is like a telephoto lens: one sees a few things with great detail and clarity but loses the broader perspective." Another is *suggestibility*, "a heightened responsiveness to environmental input . . . the narrower the focus of attention on an instruction, the less likely is the person to evaluate critically . . . making response more likely." The third is *dissociation*, as when we daydream while driving and then "wake up" miles past our exit (so-called "highway hypnosis").

Dr. Spiegel notes that "hypnotic phenomena such as dissociation are intrinsic to the experience of trauma." A number of researchers have suggested that the diagnosis and treatment of cancer itself may be sufficient trauma to induce such dissociative states. Certainly, dire disease is a moment of shocking dislocation, when suffering or annihiliation seems inescapable. Clinicians specializing in post-traumatic stress disorder (PTSD), note that trauma creates altered states that seem to short-circuit rational thinking patterns of the cortex and process information directly in the limbic system, the seat of the emotions and many autonomic functions of the body. Could trauma act as a stimulus to trigger the mind-body mechanisms we believe are integral to the healing system? Many cases we found offered tantalizing glimpses into this possibility.

Cindy Zeligman was living the upscale, exurban good life in Evergreen, Colorado. She was an executive "headhunter" in charge of U.S. operations for an international personnel firm, an ex-model with a beautiful young son and a husband who ran his own lucrative construction company. The couple were impassioned skiers, taking helicopter trips into the backcountry to whoosh along white-powder bowls, relieved the plumes of pristine snow feathering behind them obscured the growing rockiness of the marriage.

One Friday evening, Cindy and her son went to the cellar to feed a mewling litter of newborn kittens. The five-hundred-gallon propane tank that was a necessity of mountain living had just been filled, but Cindy thought she smelled gas. Turning off the pilot switches on the hot water heater and the furnace, she hurried back upstairs. Her husband met her at the basement door. Waving off her concern, he suggested she start a cheery blaze in the fireplace while he trudged down to relight the pilots.

"My God, no," she remembers shouting. "It'll explode."

"Oh, it will not," he said, teasingly tugging his Bic from his jeans pocket and flicking its small fuse to show her.

The world exploded in a searing bellow of flame. Cindy sensed more than saw the bluish fireball that momentarily lifted their house from its foundations. Then she was a bright torch, her nylons burning like napalm. She rolled on the ground, ninety percent of her body's surface already scorched, half of it with third- and fourth-degree burns. She enfolded her burning son's body in her own barely extinguished one, smothering his flames; then with an eerie calm used an index finger charred to the bone to dial 911 for a Flight for Life chopper. She had the presence of mind to enumerate her own and her son's allergies to penicillin, and to call a neighbor who was a nurse. Then she passed out.

She was awakened when the emergency van scooped them up, screeching around hairpin mountain curves looking for a spot below the mountain fog line for a helicopter intercept. All the while Cindy was clinging to life. "I was keeping Zach very calm, telling him, 'Fight for your life, little one; you fight for your life. Hold a picture in your mind of all of us together happy and having fun, you and Mommy and Daddy and you just keep that picture. Promise Mommy you'll keep that picture.' And he said, 'Yes, Mom.' "

She remembers "doing great" until they pulled her stretcher from the van toward the chopper, and she heard her son screaming, " 'No, please don't take my mommy away from me, please don't take her away.' That's when I lost it."

She died then, flatlined, the emergency techs losing her heartbeat for two minutes and thirty-two seconds as the helicopter's metal wings scythed toward the lights of Denver. But she was already somewhere else, looking down in pity at a badly burned body. "I knew it was me. I was watching them fight to save my life, but I felt like I was in this light, being held by two hands, so warm and loved and at peace that had I not had a child, I would have let go."

Whether due to religious experience or a spontaneous state of hypnosis in response to massive traumatic injury, Cindy somehow knew she was chosen to survive. Later, she read the terse report stating there had been no expectation of getting mother or child to the hospital alive. Her husband, who had been separately rescued, had sustained second-degree burns, but she and her son had extensive, critical injuries. Despite the frenzied catheterization, oxygen, the nasogastric tube, and IVs, too much time had elapsed. They had too much trouble running a line to pump precious fluids into their bodies. Cindy said a silent prayer, giving her life up as no longer her own, asking to be guided. "I remember just saying, 'God, please! I have to raise my son and I haven't been with my grandmothers enough and I haven't been happy. Please give me another chance, please let me live, please!' "

Then the helicopter landed and she somehow returned. "I snapped back into my body and I remember opening up my eyes and just knowing, *I'm here, I'm here.*" She came back into a body whose every pore was igniting with fresh agony. The morphine they gave her while they debraded her raw flesh and rasped exposed nerves didn't take the edge off the unending conflagration. Cindy entered a state of dissociation. "The pain was so intense that I spontaneously took my mind to a cave by the ocean. I imagined walking on a beach with Zachary while they scrubbed my body with steel brushes twice a day."

Cindy had learned to dissociate early in life; learned as a child how to survive when the searing anguish was incest, her abuser's large hands on her, forcing her down. "He was taking my body for his own pleasure against my will, and the only way I survived him touching me was to 'leave.' I would float up to the corner of the room and just watch what he was doing, but it wasn't me." As a child, this ability preserved her sanity. As a burn victim, depending on how much we choose to credit mind-body factors, it may have saved her life.

When her new suffering became unendurable, Cindy would again feel as if she were leaving her body, traveling out through a series of tubes and tunnels, seeing the striated grain of the musculature, hearing the *shoop-shoop* whooshing sounds of her blood, "my physical doors shutting off behind me until I was out, *whew!* totally free." She was in a coma for ten days. She could see her relatives crying, her grandmother and mother already in mourning, her brother pleading for her life as doctors gently urged them to say their good-byes. She weighed seventy-two pounds, a skeletal, ruined mannequin with burning blue eyes. She was given a one percent chance to live.

Infections raged as she drifted in and out of consciousness. No sooner would the doctors identify one strain than another untreatable bacterium would ravage what was left of her flesh. Nothing worked. "Then all of a sudden," she says, "it just started getting better."

Her team of thirty physicians was amazed. But she knew why she survived the tongues of flame and the twenty-seven operations in two-and-a-half months. Secretly, guided by some instinct, she was discovering mind-body switches, flipping circuit-breakers, turning her life-force back on. "I would always, always, always see myself healing, I would mentally send emeralds, diamonds, rubies, and sapphires shimmering through my bloodstream. I would dispatch Pac-Women—never Pac-Men!—through my body, to cleanse and eat and attack all of the bad infection.

"I would imagine this jet-black stuff coming out of me during what I called my 'flush,' starting from the top of my head and going down through my body pulling out poisons and toxins. Then I'd refill my body with white light and I would have such peace. I'd make myself stay there, to rest, to heal."

Today her skin has healed beyond anyone's expectations, though it still shows the fire. "They would love to keep working on me, but I'm just going to keep my little topographic maps. I'm not worried about the scars. We all have painful scars on the inside that no one can see, I just wear mine on the outside now."

Today Cindy is president of the Zach Foundation, an organization that provides support for severely burned children. "I've dedicated my life to this work," she says. "That's my passion and my fire. Now I say I'm well-done. Burnt to perfection."

Though some people require an external influence to enter hypnosis—a charismatic physician or a ceremonious injection of saltwater—Cindy, who had learned the skill early, was able spontaneously to enter a mental state that some researchers believe is intrinsicly healing.

Hypnosis, whether spontaneous or induced, has been shown to cause accelerated wound-healing, inflammation, increased or decreased blood supply, and increased temperature, all factors implicated in remarkable recovery. One study showed how with minimal training, subjects could quickly raise or lower the temperature of specific areas of the skin by eight to fifteen degrees Fahrenheit.

These phenomena have been noticed and used to measurable effect in the treatment of severe burns, where blood flow to affected areas can make a critical difference in the healing process. Cindy's instinctive inner healing techniques, for example, would have been familiar to New Orleans burn specialist Dabney Ewin. Dr. Ewin, founding president of the New Orleans Society of Clinical Hypnosis, observed that trauma seemed to throw a patient spontaneously into "a state equivalent to trance, i.e., his perceptions will be imprinted and acted on in a manner similar to post-hypnotic suggestions." Ewin, a surgeon, advises that a burn therapist "insert himself into the patient's spontaneous trance, establish rapport, teach the patient to control his pain, and then direct him through guided imagery"—in other words, to utilize the patient's own power of belief as a healing force.

Ewin suggests to patients that they mentally go to a place very much like Cindy's imaginary "cave by the ocean," a place where he or she will feel relaxed, peaceful, pleasant, fun, and totally free of responsibility. He gives the folk-tale example of Brer Rabbit's "laughing place" and tells them this is where their injured areas can be soothed. Dr. Ewin has noticed that there is often less edema and sometimes no scarring where it might otherwise be expected. He first used his technique on a twenty-eight-year-old worker in an aluminum plant who had stepped knee-deep into 1750-degree-Fahrenheit molten metal. Ewin gave him suggestions that his leg was cool and comfortable and would continue to feel that way until it healed. The man became ambulatory and was discharged from the hospital just nineteen days later.

Ewin's observation that the timely use of hypnosis can prevent or limit the progression of inflammation from burns has a history: In 1887, Belgian scientist, philosopher, and hypnosis aficionado Joseph Delboeuf made two small burns on the skin of a hypnotized patient with a red-hot iron bar. He then suggested that one would be painful and the other not. The outcome was a dry scorch mark with no scar on the side he'd suggested would be painless, while the other side produced a suppurating blister with subsequent scarring. As with Dr. Ewin, suggesting away pain early seemed to decrease inflammation and increase the healing process.

The mechanism of pain has provided fascinating clues to investigators of the mind-body healing response, though it has sometimes confounded as much as clarified. One small landmark study appeared in a 1978 issue of the British medical journal the *Lancet*. Dental patients suffering the aftermath of an extracted tooth were given a sugar pill and told it was a powerful painkiller. They reported significant pain relief, a well-known placebo effect. But experimenters then added another layer: a separate group of dental patients was given along with their placebo the chemical naloxone, a substance known to block the action of the brain's own painkillers, or endorphins. This second group experienced significantly less pain reduction than the first.

Here was a study, then, that indicated a specific mechanism for placebos—endorphins—without which the magic effect would not occur. Some scientists believe that endorphins mediate *much* of the mind-body effect, whether that effect is triggered by trauma, placebo, hypnosis, or anything else. Certainly, hypnotic suggestion and placebos ("suggestion given physical form," says one researcher) seem to have similar outcomes. Warts, for example, have been proven to be equally susceptible to both hypnotic suggestion and placebo "drugs."

But the picture is not entirely clear. Two separate studies found that the endorphin-blocker naloxone failed to prevent pain reduction in patients under hypnosis as it had for patients who took a placebo. And in yet another placebo study, pain reduction occurred even *with* the endorphin-blocker. One explanation is that other forms of endorphins may stealthily bypass the naloxone blockade. There are likely many mind-body routes, many mechanisms to create the same effects. It may then even be that different states of mind affect the body along different pathways. Or that the same substances have multiple effects: Relief of pain may also stimulate immune function, since pain-relieving endorphins are key messenger molecules that also talk to the immune system.

Messenger molecules, formally known as neuropeptides, have been found in both brain and body, making them prime candidates for a variety of links among thought, emotion, and healing. If anyone can help explain how such linkages actually *work,* it is Candace Pert, former chief of the Brain Biochemistry Section of the National Institute of Mental Health and the co-discoverer of endorphins.

"This is my brain on a Swedish MRI scan," she tells a crowd of pharmacology students at a lecture. She points proprietarily behind her to a giant MRI image of an ovoid ringed in electric blue, a Fabergé egg with a crenelated gob floating in the center. The signals passing between mind and body, she informs the students, are drugs churned out by the body's internal pharmacies: everything from stimulants to depressants, antibiotics to insulin. "Dangerous drugs," she jokes, like the testosterone and progesterone that saturate an adolescent's every perception. Drugs that alter consciousness; drugs that change physiology; and mostly— *definitionally*—drugs that change both.

Neuropeptides and their receptors are usually described as lock-and-key mechanisms: Only a peptide of a particular shape fits a particular receptor. But Pert urges her audience to imagine a more fluid situation, "big long proteins all wiggly, dynamic, changing shape. In one shape, they may turn on some process in a cell, in another turn it off. All of these messenger molecules, changing from second to second, keep us buzzing and humming. We're no more than a big signaling factory."

Given the current state of our science, we can only wonder if Cindy Zeligman, as she imagined "flipping on circuit breakers" in her scorched body, was also signaling some inner switchboard to direct her healing. Perhaps her trauma-induced dissociative state allowed neuropeptides to slide more readily into particular receptors; her belief that she would live may have ferried a coded survival message to her body; the intensity of her emotions may have sent a specific internal healing "drug" surging along the yet-unknown pathways of remarkable recovery. A lot of the brain's signaling, Pert is convinced, is emotional. The little wriggling neuropeptides, she points out, can reroute blood flow, creating "the flush of love" by regulating which blood vessels are open or constricted. It is hard not to hear the clicking of locks to our postulated biological mechanisms of remarkable recovery.

Immune cells, as it turns out, all have neuropeptide receptors, which means, Pert explains, "the biochemistry of emotion is mediating the migration of natural killer cells through the body." Even tumor cells have such receptors, she adds; emotions may mediate *their* movements as well. "It's not far-fetched to think," she says, "of cancer treatment based partly on emotional intervention. Maybe that's the reason emotional catharsis seems often to precede healing; it's like kicking an old TV set stuck on vertical hold."

Michael Ruff, Pert's husband, is a youngish neurochemist whose somewhat scruffy, laid-back mien belies his responsibility for the essential discovery she refers to—that the body's immune cells are equipped with receptors for endorphin molecules. The implications are striking. The emotion of joy, for example, is associated with endorphin secretions. The same secretions/emotions (at this biochemical level, the terms are almost synonymous) could activate the immune system toward remarkable recovery.

Ruff suggests one scenario whereby cancer cells could receive messages that would cause them to die off: All cells are programmed to receive signals to activate encoded programs that lead to their death. This sort of cellular *hara-kiri* is for the overall benefit of the body. "When the immune response is activated, various cells multiply to fight off infection. But you also need a regulatory mechanism to shut things down, so that the extra cells die off once they've done their job." He pauses for a moment, running his fingers ruminatively through his beard.

"Maybe remission is cancer cells getting that same die-off message. A cancer is as vulnerable as a normal cell to the chemical message that activates genes that cause its DNA to dissolve, its chromatin to condense, and the cell to just sort of melt away."

Ruff thinks it entirely possible that emotions could well have a role in the death of a tumor. He gives the example of standing in front of a runaway truck, feeling a surge of terror that activates every fiber in the body to jump instinctively to the side. Powerful feelings, particularly those pertaining to survival, might similarly stimulate a healing response. "Maybe it doesn't even have to be that massive. Cancer is a major aberration, but it's the result of subtle alterations over a period of time. Healing may also be a subtle shift, like a seesaw swinging back again. Maybe the seesaw could be tipped by the molecules of emotion."

He paints a picture of the body's defenses not unlike the famous if apochryphal example from chaos theory of a butterfly's wing stirring the air in Tokyo causing, through some incremental escalation of step-up effects, a typhoon off the California coast. "It's a cellular cascade. A cell is affected by a peptide that causes the cell to release ten peptides that change another ten peptides, and suddenly there are a hundred peptides. Cancer is a screw-up in the activation of this cascade. Healing may be getting it going again."

Contrary to the conventional view, in which psychological forces are too small and weak to affect cancer's *anschluss*, the mind-body is a microworld where victory goes not only to the strong, but to the smart; where information is power. The brain is ripe with receptors for molecules associated with emotion, the same molecules that wind up on the front lines against disease. Immune cells are ever mingling with the brain as they circulate through the body, giving reports, receiving instruction, rushing to other bodily sites with communiqués, taking matters in hand to heal wounds. Remarkable recovery suggests that under certain circumstances, cancer may be less an unbreachable fortification than an elaborate house of cards trembling before a gust of informational wind.

Wally Shore (not his real name) always thought he was invincible. He'd held a belief all his life, he says with a chuckle, that "nothing could ever hurt Ethel Shore's little boy." After all, he'd survived the Normandy invasion. Later, he'd been on a ship headed for the Pacific theater when the captain announced the Bomb had been dropped on Japan, whereupon the ship turned safely back toward New York.

So Wally remained certain his stomach pains were nothing serious until his physician informed him he had colon cancer. Though his doctor recommended a surgeon, Wally, who prides himself on his independence and resourcefulness, decided to find his own. Cold-calling Memorial Sloan-Kettering, he managed to get a surgical nurse on the line and asked her, "If your brother had colon cancer, who would you have remove it?" The nurse was reluctant to make a recommendation, but Wally persisted. " 'Listen,' I said, 'do you know my name?' She said, 'No.' I said, 'Do I know yours?' She said, 'No.' 'Well,' I said, 'I'm in deep you-know-what and I need your help.' " She finally recommended a surgeon.

A few days after his 1982 surgery, Wally was already "slogging down the hall in my slippers," cheerfully dragging his IV cart. He stopped short when he encountered his surgeon and took in the bad-news expression on his face. The doctor was blunt: Though he had managed to remove the tumor, it had inoperably metastasized to the liver. Wally spent most of the day anguishing over how to break the news to his wife and three daughters. Sunk in despair, he experienced an event which he believes changed his odds of survival: A seventy-two-year-old hospital volunteer wandered in and gave Wally a copy of *Getting Well Again*.

Thumbing through the bestselling book on visualization and healing by radiation oncologist Carl Simonton and psychologist Stephanie Simonton, Wally felt on familiar ground. He'd always been fascinated by the mind's mysteries, as a child essaying dime-store techniques to "hypnotize everybody in sight, especially," he says with a wry wink, "when I wanted my friend's kid sister to play spin the bottle." But finding the guided imagery in the Simontons' book "too simplistic and passionless," Wally instinctively summoned up images fraught with emotional power. He recalled his fear during the Normandy invasion, when a bullet sang past his ear and killed the man next to him. He conjured up his repetitive postwar nightmare, the one in which he was lowering 4,000 pounds of ammunition by crane to a landing craft in choppy seas, terrified he'd crush the soldiers below. He remembered, incongruously, the precise sound of the jungle drums in old Tarzan movies, their every thump a war cry, like they were saying kill, kill, *kill!* He was sure certain emotions could affect the body, remembering a newspaper story of "some ten-year-old kid who lifted a car off his father," and a "little guy" in the army who when deliriously drunk required all the men in the squad to hold him down. Wally fixated on "how I would feel if somebody were to come at my children with a knife—I would tear his heart out!"

During that long night, he came up with his own program of psychoneuroimmunology: "I decided I needed to combine the imagery, which is about killing the cancer, with a method of stimulating the adrenaline flow, like you would when you get yourself ready to do a karate chop." He visualized his cancer as a helpless jellyfish, "those obscene, hateful little things with rainbow colors that wash up on Long Beach." Then, he called up his rage. "It was like an out-of-body experience," he says, peering intently from behind dark-rimmed glasses. "I went through the ceiling with fury, because I wanted to live very badly. I was sixty years old. I'd just had my first grandson, and his birthday was coming up." His fists clench, as if in memory of iron-clad determination. "I wanted to get the hell out of that hospital. I wanted to be well. I wanted to see the end of my movie."

The Simontons' book suggested exercise, so Wally pulled on his tennis shoes and began hiking through the halls of Sloan-Kettering. "You should have seen me," he says, with a gleeful chortle. "Here I was, IV in my arm, tube like a bamboo shoot stuck down my throat, trailing a catheter. I was quite a sight, but I didn't care." Calculating that each floor tile was one foot square, he paced out a mile and then began determinedly trudging exactly three miles a day. "The way I saw it, I was in a fight," he says, "and I decided I would train more than any fighter in history." Ever curious, he read magazine articles about endorphins and learned how exercise released substances "that fight depression and make you high."

He soon became a welcome spectacle in his ward, cheered on—"They'd yell, 'Go, Wally, go' "—by everyone from nurses and doctors to the people who mopped the floors. A relentless, impassioned talker, he finagled other patients into lacing up their tennis shoes and pacing him on his improvised track. He was strong enough to leave the hospital in time for his grandson's first birthday.

From his first day at Sloan-Kettering, Wally, a gregarious, warm man with a gift for instilling confidence, began counseling other people with cancer. Some, he commented, had "no glow in their eyes. They're leaning back. They're weak. But when I start telling my story, I see a light come on behind their eyes, and then all of a sudden their whole body posture changes. I talked to this one guy who hadn't been out of the house for a year. We talked and talked, and the next day the guy joined a health club."

Within a month his surgery, Wally had started on a chemotherapy his doctors told him could do no more than slow the cancer's progress, but he says, "I was going to do anything that might help turn the thing back." He kept on doing his vivid imagery five times a day and stuck to his own health regimen, playing six hours of tennis every day "except only three hours the third day after the treatment." After his wife and children bought him a dog, he insisted on walking the little schnauzer five miles daily, their six legs churning through rain or snow, winter or summer.

After a year of a treatment that was only expected to postpone Wally's inevitable demise, his doctor was visibly shocked to find the tumors had vanished. After a few months' more chemo, with the scans still negative, Wally simply stopped the treatment. "My wife and I decided I was cured," he says, adding emphatically, "not in 'remission,' that horrible word that denotes it's going to come back." Wally hasn't been back to Sloan-Kettering since 1985. Every year, the hospital sends him a questionnaire "to see if I'm still alive. But, you know," he says, "no one there ever asks me why."

"Why" is to some extent anyone's guess. We can only imagine the biochemical tumult in Wally's body as he unleashed his free-for-all of ever-changing images and urgent emotions upon his cancer. Did his "pumped up" feelings mobilize neuropeptides to augment his immune system? Did entering a highly absorbed state of self-hypnosis five times a day somehow alter the blood flow or temperature around his tumors, drying them up like beached jellyfish? Whatever he, or Cindy Zeligman, or any of our dozens of other cases of remarkable recovery did, seems a unique outcropping of their own deepest belief systems and most profound life experiences.

But we wondered if there were ways to deliberately stimulate mind-body mechanisms for remarkable recovery. The Simontons' *Getting Well Again,* which had galvanized Wally Shore on his journey, has become something of a cancer patient's bible. Stephanie Simonton recalls all too well how she and her husband reaped the whirlwind upon its first publication.

"We had made the theoretical leap of applying behavioral medicine strategies to cancer and then made our work public," she told us. "It created a *firestorm* of controversy. It was the first time anybody credentialed within oncology—Carl was a radiation oncologist—had suggested the psyche could positively affect cancer outcome, and practices like visualization and biofeedback might be beneficial. Even though there was a psychoanalytic theory indicating that the mind might play a role in sucepitibility to cancer, we were one of the first to hypothesize that the mind could be harnessed positively to aid cancer recovery."

In a preliminary study, Simonton gained impressive results teaching imagery to cancer patients, who showed a forty-seven-percent increase in immune function after only three weeks of twice-weekly classes. Writes Simonton, "The forty-seven-percent increase in immune function we observed was both statistically and physiologically significant, as it is estimated that it takes at least two years for the immune system to recover from radiation therapy. Our star patient, who was seventy years old—an age when you expect the immune system to be much more sluggish—had a 300-percent increase."

Simonton notes that there was even a "dose response." The more often patients listened to the imagery tape, the more immune system enhancement there was—"just as if they were taking a medicine." But she learned the most from one of her "failures," a man whose immune system "did not increase with the imagery treatment. He had been diagnosed with an advanced cancer and had a very poor prognosis. However, after his diagnosis, he literally transformed his life. He ended an unhappy partnership, cut back on his work commitments, and devoted more time to his family and the activities that brought him pleasure. He lived a very high quality of life for over three years and was walking and jogging regularly until the last few months of his life. Even though his immune system was not enhanced through the treatment intervention, his lifespan was significantly longer than expected, and the quality of his life was beyond what we would have expected medically."

Simonton's conclusion is that "the whole issue of healing is a complex business. There are multiple mechanisms. I don't think only one thing affects it." Imagery practice itself, she notes, may have many effects besides any direct influence on physiology. She writes, "It may give the patient a logical basis for being more hopeful, which may enhance mood and result in immune and neuroendocrine changes. When you visualize, you may also be creating a relaxation response, reducing stress and allowing the body to enhance lymphocyte proliferation. Just the act of creating pictures in your mind's eye in a trance state may affect brain function in ways that have direct biological impact." She recites a number of other factors that might contribute to healing: nutrition, prayer, social support, fun, physical exercise, even "having a kind of emotionally delicious quality of life day to day."

But there are indications mental imagery in particular can have highly specific effects. A recent article in the *International Journal of Neuroscience* describes a fascinating experiment in "cyberphysiology" (*cyber* from a Greek term meaning "that which steers," or more simply, "the helmsman"). The article was entitled "Voluntary Modulation of Neutrophil Adhesiveness Using a Cyberphysiologic Strategy." (Neutrophils are immune cells that defend against infection and heal tissue damage in inflammatory responses.)

The experiment had proceeded as follows: The students in the experimental group were taught self-hypnosis and visualization, then given a description of neutrophils' special functions and properties. Each subject devised his or her own highly personalized imagery to attempt to increase the cells' property of adherence. For example, one imagined her neutrophils as Ping-Pong balls with honey oozing out onto the surface of the balls, causing them to stick to whatever they touched.

The training lasted two weeks, and saliva and blood samples were compared with blood samples drawn before the training began. They were then tested for immune components like neutrophils, lymphocytes, monocytes, and platelets. Amazingly, the only statistically significant change in the immune cells was the neutrophils' ability to stick to foreign objects. Even the total count of neutrophils remained identical for both groups.

Wally Shore envisioned killing cancer jellyfish, with his kill-kill-kill jungle drums as a sound track. Cindy Zeligman saw healing diamonds, rubies, and emeralds flowing through her system, closely followed by an armada of Pac-Women. Each of them believes the same strange premise suggested by the neutrophil experiment: Images in the mind may sometimes alter physiology in specific ways.

It would not seem strange to Tibetan monks, who for centuries have been using elaborate religious visualizations to produce startling, measurable effects on their bodies. Nearly a decade ago, Harvard cardiologist Herbert Benson, author of several bestselling books on the medical effects of meditation, became intrigued by accounts of monks who could wrap their naked bodies in sheets dipped in icy water and then dry them in frigid weather using only a special "psychic heat" generated by their own bodies.

With the Dalai Lama's blessing, Benson flew to India, trekking from a Raja's palace that boasted the world's highest cricket field to Himalayan valleys, wiring up monks with electronic measuring devices while they performed their spiritual exercises. He found to his amazement that some monks could raise their skin temperature as much seventeen degrees above normal in near-freezing weather, even though the body would normally route blood *away* from the skin toward the core organs to keep warm. "If an ordinary person were to try this," says Dr. Benson, a short, square man with steel-gray hair, gold-rimmed glasses, and a stolid twinkle, "they would shiver uncontrollably and perhaps even die. But here, within three to five minutes, the sheets started to steam and within forty-five minutes were completely dry."

Here, perhaps, is a clue to hypnotherapist T. X. Barber's earlier-posed riddle of how some people can "feel-remember-think-imagine" in ways that can markedly affect blood flow, temperature, immune response, and perhaps even the progress of disease.

The most notorious, most homely, and most medically unequivocal instance of the mind curing the body is the lowly wart. Generations of internists, dermatologists, and their wise grandmothers have known these blemishes, tough as box turtles, can be mentally zapped out of existence if the patient can be induced to believe. In one study reported by Dr. Lewis Thomas, fourteen patients literally covered with the growths were hypnotized and told that the warts on one side of their bodies would go away. Within a few weeks, all or nearly all the warts on that side of their bodies disappeared. The warts on the other side flourished as brazenly as ever.

We might ask, So what? A wart is an unsightly but harmless condition, not a fatal disease. But Dr. Thomas, the late president of New York's Memorial Sloan-Kettering Cancer Center, heralded the wart's potentially epochal significance. Warts, he pointed out, are the defended, turreted castle of a virus, an entity that often defies conventional medical treatment. Though a wart's structure is dense and hard, often harder than a tumor, it can be ordered into oblivion by mere hypnotic suggestion. Warts may undergo, in other words, a remarkable recovery, based solely on the powers of the mind.

At first, Dr. Thomas thought, such wart cures might be affected by a change in blood flow that shut down the precapillary arteries in and around it "to the point of strangulation." But then the viral etiology of the wart became known, and with it the "plausible notion that immunologic mechanisms are very likely implicated." If the warts-be-gone mechanisms were immunologic, he reasoned, then there must be some unknown aspect of mind capable of directing the impossibly complex molecular traffic of B-cells and T-cells, suppressor cells and killer cells. The biological pirouettes the body must accomplish to rid itself of one homely toadstool of a wart stagger the imagination:

> [A]ny mental apparatus that can reject a wart is something else again. This is not the sort of confused, disorderly process you would expect at the hands of the kind of unconscious you read about in books, at the edge of things making up dreams or getting mixed up on words, or having hysterics. Whatever, or whoever, is responsible for this has the accuracy and precision of a surgeon. . . . Just think what we would know, if we had anything like a clear understanding

of what goes on when a wart is hypnotized away. . . . It would be worth a War on Warts, a Conquest of Warts, a National Institute of Warts and All.

Dr. Thomas's magical-realist institute never materialized, though there has grown up in its stead a sort of invisible college of wartologists, researchers helplessly fascinated by these lowly carbuncles of the flesh. As in everything pertaining to the healing system, the mechanisms of wart disappearance have been debated. At least two researchers, Thomas Clauson and Richard Swade, lose no time linking a homely affliction to a deadly one: "We see in warts a model for metastasizing tumors." They note that warts spread over the body, though presumably by viruses, not malignant cells, and that, like tumors, they are nourished by capillaries whose blood flow, if stopped, may bring about their destruction. By suggesting that patients focus on mentally diminishing the amount of blood reaching the wart, Clauson and Swade found that within a period of a few days to two months, the warts "simply diminished and disappeared, shriveled up and left." Blocking the process by which tumors compel neighboring tissue to construct blood-vessel aqueducts to nourish them is an anticancer strategy currently being investigated by the National Cancer Institute.

When it comes to investigating the barely delineated realm of mind-body medicine, there is no cut-and-dried methodology. Even accomplished Tibetan yogis like those studied by Dr. Benson leave leeway in their colorful descriptions of how mind might affect anatomy. These yogis, one Western scholar explains, report that their stylized visualizations "are not solid realities which one can point out like in the physical body, in spite of the fact that people often try to make exact identifications." While the images are highly elaborated and exact, "the variations of their description point to the fact that the meditator or adept has to find them for himself."

In this last sentence, perhaps, is one of the great secrets to unlocking the resources of the healing system: No one's key is identical.

We found it common for patients to attribute their survival to the often highly individualized things they did for themselves. Their efforts are often dismissed in the medical community as fantasy, an example of the patients' need to assert an illusory control over the blind predations of biology.

But then what are we to make of Garrett Porter? When Garrett was only nine, he began to experience numbness on his left side. His parents, concerned, took him to the doctor, who diagnosed an inoperable malignant brain tumor. Garrett began receiving radiation, but also started psychotherapy with a woman named Pat Norris.

With her halo of fluffy silver hair and benign, cornflower-blue eyes, Norris resembles a vinegar-free Auntie Em from the corner of Kansas most closely abutting Oz. She is the daughter of famed researchers Elmer and Alyce Green of Topeka's Menninger Institute, who virtually invented the field of biofeedback. Biofeedback is based on the idea that bodily processes ruled by the autonomic nervous system—housekeeping functions like heart rate, skin temperature, and respiration, long considered automatic—can be brought under a degree of conscious control. Using instrumentation attached to the body that makes visible or audible any variations in these physiological activities, people can learn, by literally seeing or hearing what their body is doing in "real time," to reduce high blood pressure, eliminate migraine headaches, control irregular heartbeats, increase and decrease blood flow, and even, in some reported experiments, control the firing of a single nerve cell. Pat had witnessed her father's experiments with a Hindu yogi named Swami Rama, who demonstrated through instrumented measurement he could preferentially heat just *half* his hand, calmly set his heart to fluttering, and perform feats that knocked every then-extant view of control over physiology into a bejeweled turban.

But Pat was more concerned with application than theory: How could all this autonomic training *help?* She began doing work with prisoners trying to enhance their self-image through the magic of voluntary hand-warming, proving to murderers, junkies, and thieves that if their thoughts could control their bodies, "they weren't someone else's puppet, and so maybe could embody more of their humanity."

She'd been raised to believe people could master their own fates down to the jot and tittle. When as a child she'd gone to her parents with a stomachache, she was told, *"You're* the boss of your belly." So when she met Garrett, a suffering, bulldog-determined nine-year-old with preternatural self-possession and a talent for imagining, she knew what she had to do. "If you tell your white cells to congregate in a spot," she told us, "maybe they do. I'd never worked with a cancer patient, but I believed Garrett could somehow mobilize his defenses and win."

When radiation failed to shrink the tumor, Garrett stopped treatment but continued on with his biofeedback. He had first learned simple autogenic training: "I pictured holding my hands over an open campfire, and the biofeedback device showed that the blood rushed to my hands." It was a beginner's technique, Garrett told us, "like picturing cutting into a lemon, seeing the juices fly, and taking a mental bite. If you're any good, you salivate. It's not a big thing. But it shows your body doesn't control your mind, your mind can control your body. By warming my hands, I was telling the blood where to go."

After a while, Garrett found the exercises too boring. "I saw my brain tumor as an invading planet in innerspace," he says, "so I thought, why not have white cells I could fire at it from a space-ship?"

Pat tailored Garrett's visualizations to his fascination with "Star Wars" and "Battlestar: Galactica," weaving elaborate story lines in which his T-cells were space ships and the tumor, an alien invader. She would put him into a relaxed state, directing him to travel through his body from head to toe. A photo in the book they later wrote together shows a tableau of loving concern: Garrett lies on a couch with Pat's hand resting gently on his shoulder, her face filled with quiet concern, emanating support. Their visualization sessions, the book makes clear, were theatrical affairs filled with high emotional drama. A sample:

Pat: All right, ease in the throttle and take off. Let's keep in voice contact as you go. Your planes are rising nicely on the radar. It's approaching target. Now, as you get near, tell me what you see. Tell me when you see anything at all.
Garrett: I see some kind of round ball, sir. Calculators say that it's the target. . . . It's a round-shaped, dumb-looking thing.
Pat: All right, prepare for attack. Ready laser gun number one. Ready laser gun number two. (Sound effects)
Garrett: Ready, Sir.
Pat: Now, fire!
Garrett: Commencing firing, squadron. (Sound of missile being sent and hitting.) Hit, Sir!
Pat: A direct hit! a direct hit! Excellent, excellent! Do you see something dissolving?
Garrett: Yes, Sir. The side of the thing is dissolving. Stand by for releasing shells with those body white cells in them.

Garrett would practice his visualizations every night. But one night, as his T-cell space cruisers were exploring the alien territory, they couldn't find the tumor. He scanned all over, but could only come up with a small white dot. He ran to tell his father, who was skeptical. But, a few months later during the course of a CAT scan it was discovered that the tumor had indeed disappeared, with only a single white spot remaining.

Pat expands: "I have had physicians ask if it was not wrong, cruel, and unethical to suggest to patients that they might be able to alter the course of their own illness with visualization. But there can be no failure in trying. Everyone can be a success at trying, and trying brings strength and energy of its own, which is a healing force."

"It's completely natural to heal," she maintains. "Spontaneous remission is too mystical-sounding; it's like the medieval term "spontaneous generation," when they didn't have enough science to see germs. Doctors think psychophysical factors are a very minor part of curing cancer. But patients who heal say it's major. If our culture supported it, I think a lot of people could get over cancer partly by bolstering their own immune systems."

But how? In their own way, Garrett's visualizations were scarcely less detailed than those used by the sheet-drying Tibetan monks, who develop mental pictures of thousands of supposed psychic "nerves"; five-colored light beams emanating from numerous tiny triangular-shaped thunderbolts. But the mechanisms whereby such imagery might translate into significant physical effects are not yet known.

Perhaps an illustration of how messages travel between mind and body—if such linear terms even apply—may be found in a neuropeptide called angiotensin. Angiotensin is a sort of thirst-molecule. Inject a bit of it in a rat's brain—even a rat that has already drunk its fill—and the rat will furiously begin to lap up water. Angiotensin receptors are found not just in the brain, but all over the body. If some of the substance is drizzled into a rat's lungs, the lung tissue will retain water rather than allow it to be exhaled with the breath. If angiotensin is placed in the kidneys, they too will adamantly retain water within their domain.

Angiotensin thus seems to relay the same billboard-like message wherever it appears: Need Water. The same molecule is perceived analogously in different systems of the body. Is it similarly possible that the human neuropeptide associated with, say, blazing joy translates into vastly improved morale when it lands amidst the defending forces of the body? Does a feeling of fighting spirit call up molecules that then infuse fighting spirit in massed armies of T-cells? Do the powerful emotions reported in some cases of remarkable recovery become molecular winds that fill the sails of immune armadas?

For that matter, why should the sources of "healing information" be limited to information molecules? The environment, too, conveys information into the body. A diagnosis once uttered becomes an image or an emotion that may somehow transduce into neuropeptides in the patient's immune system. Encouragement from a friend or family member is transduceable information: a vivid statement of the human healing potential by a psychotherapist; a belief system imparted by a spiritual preceptor; a cultural attitude; a ritual; a loving touch; a story; a piece of music or art; love itself—all may travel in the form of peptides through the body's healing system. The famous remissions researcher Yujiro Ikemi proposes a model: "All levels of organization are linked to one another in a hierarchical relationship, so that a change in one necessitates a change in others."

Garrett Porter's story, for example, reveals the wide spectrum of potential stimuli to the body's innate healing system: Relaxation and self-hypnosis; vivid visual imagery; the emotional punch of dramatic fantasy; the love between a healer and a very sick boy; a strategy congruent with a specific life passion. Garrett, once considered terminally ill, is now twenty-three years old and an elementary education major at a university in Hays, Kansas. He has some physical as well as emotional scars from his bout with cancer—he's confined to a wheelchair, has learning disabilities, and a permanent bald patch from radiation. Now engaged to be married, he's trying to put the past behind him.

Garrett remains enamored of all things airborne, continuing to construct model airplanes in a room in the back of his house. He has joined the United States Air Force Auxiliary's Civil Air Patrol, flying as the backseater/scanner in a Cessna 172, helping to spot downed aircraft. Contacted recently by a nearby family whose five-year-old son had an inoperable brain tumor, Garrett for months spent his spare time encouraging the boy until one night a call came that the boy was dying. Garrett dressed up in his Air Patrol uniform to say good-bye.

When we talked with him about what helped him in his own fight against cancer, he cited his doctors, the devotion of Pat Norris, and the support of his parents, both social workers. ("They were terrific. They were always analyzing everything. It was like having Freud for parents.") He also believes in his biofeedback and visualizations.

But in the end, Garrett says, he attributes his healing to "the power of the human spirit."

Medically speaking, we can as yet scarcely guess what this power might be, though it was invoked again and again in our interviews with remarkable recoveries. It can safely be said at this point in our scientific knowledge that we simply don't know. Trying to encompass the power behind the mere banishing of warts, Dr. Lewis Thomas took on the slightly dazed tone of a man whose skull has just encountered a brick wall. "There almost has to be a Person in charge," he wrote, "running matters of meticulous detail beyond anyone's comprehension, a skilled engineer and manager, a chief executive officer, the head of the whole place." But so far, he adds, the "whatever, or whoever, is responsible" eludes comprehension.

Dr. William Osler, one of the outstanding scientists and clinicians of an earlier era, would have agreed. Eloquently summing up the placebo's power, Osler wrote: "Faith in the gods or saints cures one, faith in little pills another, hypnotic suggestion a third, faith in a plain common doctor a fourth. . . . The faith with which we work . . . has its limitations [but] such as we find it, faith is the most precious commodity, without which we should be very badly off."

CHAPTER FIVE

In Search of the Miraculous

THE FURTHER WE EXPLORED REMARKABLE RECOVERY, THE
more it seemed that belief—whether in a treatment, a person, a setting, or a system—was a key variable in what we began
to think of as a mind-body-*spirit* equation. But talk of a spiritual
realm often seems flailing and abstract, beyond the measurement
of science.

The spirit moves us all differently; it is revealed to each of us in
varying contexts of belief. A spiritual experience for one person
may be gazing awestruck over the edge of the Grand Canyon,
feeling nature's grandeur swallow up the small, discursive ram-
blings of the mind; for another, it is a short daily prayer. Someone
may find epiphany in the ordinary—"the universe in a grain of
sand"; another in mystical experience that seems to pour down
from on high; for yet another, true transcendence resides in a tender moment with a loved one.

But one thing is certain: The spirit is made evident in how it
actually touches us. Just as a single molecular neuropeptide can
appear in different parts of the body carrying the same basic mes-

sage, so does the spirit announce itself in multiple aspects without being confined to any one of them. Whether it is experienced as a fullness of heart or an exhilaration of mind, a rush of endorphins or a mobilization of white cells, it is not so much what spirit is—an ineffable question—but how it manifests in each individual life.

When we first began our study, we thought it might be best to marginalize those remarkable recoveries most associated with spirituality—the so-called miracle healings. But whatever we may think of them, however much they may strain our credulity or joust with biomedical canon, reports of miracles—occurrences that seem beyond scientific law—just won't go away.

In a 1910 article for the *British Medical Journal,* Dr. William Osler saw no reason to reject such claims: "Literature is full of examples of remarkable cures through the influence of the imagination, which is only an active phase of faith. . . . Phenomenal, even what could be called miraculous cures, are not very uncommon. Like others, I have had cases any one of which, under suitable conditions, could have been worthy of a shrine or made the germ of a pilgrimage."

There is no culture on earth bereft of shrines and sites of pilgrimage, of places to petition the divine when all other recourse has failed. The historian Diodorus of Sicily took note of the many cures attributed to the Egyptian goddess Isis, who was said to heal the blind and the maimed. Islamic pilgrims venerate the waters of Zam-Zam at the shrine of Mecca, where many such cures are recorded. The Greek shrine to Asklepius, it is thought, once housed a sacred spring from which sufferers reverently splashed the healing elixir. The Mohawk Indians tell the story of how their chief Nekumonta located a place of healing waters that miraculously cured his plague-ridden wife.

But the waters of Lourdes are surely some of the most bathed-in, imbibed, and celebrated in history. The purported healings in this town in the French Pyrenées have undergone extensive attempts at documentation, not only by the Catholic Church, but by the doctors of an official medical commission.

The story of Lourdes began in February 1858 when, while out gathering firewood, fourteen-year-old Bernadette Soubirous had a vision of the Virgin Mary. The vision, dressed in a white garment with a blue sash and speaking the local peasant patois, reappeared to her eighteen times, revealing to her the location of an underground spring. Bernadette dug into the earth with her own hands until water appeared. Within a month, though the apparition had made no reference to healing, "three miraculous cures" had occurred at the spring. Rome was at first deeply skeptical of miracle reports emanating from the provinces, but in 1862 a commission of inquiry accepted Bernadette's vision as authentic. A huge basilica was built over the cave, and Lourdes quickly became Christendom's preeminent healing shrine. Bernadette herself was to die at the age of thirty-five of what has alternately been reported as bone cancer or disseminated tuberculosis.

Though the church has recognized only sixty-five miracles in over a hundred years, millions of pilgrims—one in six of them officially registered as sick—stream in during the peak season, seeking healing in a place that is part holy shrine, part sanctified tourist trap. Skeptics may dismiss Lourdes, wrote Ruth Cranston, author of *The Miracle at Lourdes,* as "a gigantic hoax, a marvelously planned propaganda piece . . . cleverly conceived by astute ecclesiastics to lead erring followers back into the fold." But Cranston was deeply moved by her experiences there, and eventually became a believer. She describes first arriving in 1955 on a packed pilgrimage train, where "from every window faces looked out, filled with hope and expectation, greeting their promised land." Its mostly ailing passengers broke spontaneously into "Ave Maria" as they neared the station, the hymn catching fire from car to car until "the whole long train rang."

Lourdes may be a sort of religious theme park, but the constantly echoed theme is healing. It is a place designed down to its smallest particulars to stimulate the innate healing system; to dispel doubt, overwhelm the senses, still the chatter of reason and kindle a soaring devotion. Each pilgrim who wishes it receives individual care and attention, largely from devoted, unpaid volunteers. The ill are pulled in small blue carriages, past thousands of flickering candles and mounds of white flowers, through crowds hoisting symbolic banners, beneath a clock that strikes "Ave" every hour. Statues of St. Michael crushing Satan loom over street processions in which ordinary folk mingle with Swiss pastors, English curates, Italian *monsignori,* and African bishops. Wrote Cranston: "This is a city of . . . people who have come from the four corners of the earth with but one purpose: prayer and healing."

Like all religious shrines, Lourdes moblizes at every turn what psychologist Jerome Frank calls "expectant faith" whose efficacy, he says, is determined by the "congruence of the belief system" between pilgrim and place, sufferer and healer.

Medical scientists earlier in this century professed an acute interest in Lourdes, if only as a laboratory of mind-body phenomena. Faith healing was viewed with an ambivalent mixture of fascination and skepticism. The contents of the 1910 *British Medical Journal* where Sir William Osler uttered a famous pronouncement on faith would be shocking to most doctors of the late twentieth century: Here was the world's preeminent medical publication filled with articles titled "Considerations on the Occult" and "The Interactions of Mind, Body, and Soul."

"Even as we write," offered one distinguished doctor and medical professor, "religion and medicine are kissing each other." Then, as now, it was for many doctors a reluctant display of affection. The patients who flocked to Lourdes were characterized as unusually suggestible people, "sentimental neurasthentics" in the grip of "hysteria" and "self-hypnosis," their apparent cures based upon false diagnoses. Cancer specialist H. T. Butlin, president of England's Royal College of Surgeons, derided "the large army of 'sofa saints,' neurotics, and neuro-mimetics of every degree and kind. How easily some of the people lend themselves to a cure by faith!" He cited a case he himself knew, of an elderly woman whose emotional shock at seeing her grandson fall in front of a passing train had made her deaf. Although the boy was discovered unharmed a few hours later, the woman did not recover her hearing until six months later. "It came back as suddenly as it had left her. Had she been on a pilgrimage to Lourdes at the time, what a splendid example of spiritual healing hers would have furnished!"

However, after describing a case he witnessed in his own practice, the "spontaneous" healing of a recurrent cancer for which multiple surgeries had been unsuccessful, he poses a question that those who study remarkable recovery today still struggle to resolve:

> When we see the extraordinary influence which is exerted on the body, on its blood and tissues, by fear, by hope, by love—how, on the one hand, the individual fades and wastes and even dies; how, on the other hand, appetite is restored, sleep returns, the blood grows richer and redder, and a kind of resurrection of the body is effected—is it unreasonable to assume that this resurrected body may sometimes differ from the former body in some fine chemical changes which science is not yet able to measure or even to discern? And if this can be induced by other states of the mind, why not by faith?

The Lourdes Medical Commission, however, insists that it bars cases of spontaneous remission when it deems they could have resulted from natural biological processes rather than divine intervention. The theological standards for miracle cures were set in 1734, when Cardinal Lambertini (later to be named Pope Benedict XIV) promulgated a canon that required the illness be dire; its healing medically well-documented; no treatment of any potential efficacy be used; and that the cure be complete, final, and definite, and of supernatural rapidity. Adds current Lourdes Medical Commission director Dr. Roger Pilon, "It is absolutely necessary that the healing be extremely fast [no more than seven to ten days] otherwise it is as banal an occurrence as any doctor can witness."

Doctors have also witnessed rapid remarkable recoveries in

nontheological contexts. Recall the entirely secular case of "Mr. Wright," whose tumors melted away when, in an atmosphere of expectant faith in his doctor and Krebiozen, he was administered a placebo dose of distilled water. Though Mr. Wright's remission was not permanent, one scientist notes that "the incredible rapidity of his healing also suggests that his autonomic and endocrine systems must have been responsive to suggestion, enabling him to mobilize his blood system with such amazing efficiency to remove the toxic fluids and waste products of the fast-diminishing cancer."

And commenting on the Lourdes miracles, psychiatry professor Jerome Frank writes, "The processes by which cures at Lourdes occur do not seem to differ in kind from those involved in normal healing, although they are remarkably strengthened and accelerated." He adds that although there may be "a sudden and . . . immediate improvement in function . . . , actual tissue healing takes hours, days, or weeks . . . and gaps of specialized tissues such as skin are not restored but are filled by scar formation as in normal healing." We began to question how impermeable the barrier is between miracles and the sorts of mind-body effects we have seen in other cases of remarkable recovery.

In his independent study of healing reports from Lourdes, physician Donald J. West observed that many cases were diseases known to sometimes undergo remission; they were "potentially recoverable conditions." He gives tuberculosis as an example. Twenty-seven of the sixty-five official Lourdes miracle cases— fully forty percent—were of tuberculosis. Once considered completely incurable, a scourge to the nineteenth century as cancer is to ours, TB is now known to be containable, and on rare occasions even curable, by the body's own immune system.

Still, there is a French saying: "It is easier to be canonized in Rome than deemed a miracle in Lourdes." Only about 2,000 out of millions upon millions of Lourdes pilgrims have been deemed by the various medical committees to be medically inexplicable cures. Only sixty-five of these have been adjudged outright miracles. And even the pool of candidates seems to be drying up.

There were 1,536 inexplicable cures examined during the twenty-five years (1892–1917) Dr. Boissarie was president of the Lourdes medical bureau. By contrast, during outgoing president Dr. Mangiapan's eighteen-year tenure, there were only three.

An article portrays Dr. Mangiapan as being not a little anguished. "I passed my life at Lourdes saying that we are facing a total penury of inexplicable cures," he told a journalist. Mangiapan believes that the Church's 250-year-old requirement that no potentially effective treatment can have been given may be a sieve of too fine a mesh in an era in which most people who are diagnosed get some form of treatment. Though he called for a loosening of the rules to allow for changing times, the Vatican has remained adamant.

In 1993, Catholic doctors came to Lourdes for a conference titled "Cures and Miracles" to try to sort out the differences, in effect, between remarkable recovery and miracle healing. The air was charged with speculation and not a little anxiety. A French newspaper wondered if the conference was a harbinger of a "devaluation of the very notion of miracle"; if progress in genetics, immunology, and psychosomatic medicine would explain away the cures. Even Dr. Charles Chassagnon, who heads the Lourdes International Medical Committee, has commented, "In fact, it's difficult to affirm that any cure is medically inexplicable. A doctor is by definition a scientist. The miracles of Lourdes are, in the strict sense, a little old-fashioned."

In fact, it took thirteen years of investigation to ratify the most recent and, so far, the last of the Lourdes miracles—the case of Delizia Cirolli. In spring of 1976 Cirolli, a twelve-year-old child from a village on the slopes of Sicily's Mt. Etna, was admitted to the Orthopedic Clinic of the University Hospital in Catania with a painfully swollen right knee. X rays and a biopsy showed a bony metastasis on her right tibia which was diagnosed as neuroblastoma. The surgeon advised amputation, but the family, aghast, refused. Palliative cobalt radiation was prescribed although, like the proposed surgery, it was not expected to substantially extend her survival. When she was transferred to the radiotherapy unit, she was so manifestly miserable that her parents, wishing her to spend her final days surrounded by family and friends, took her home untreated.

That August, her village raised money for a pilgrimage to Lourdes. Delizia and her mother spent four days attending the dramatic processionals and being bathed in the waters, but no improvement resulted. Indeed, X rays in September showed extension of the growth. Her mother began to prepare Delizia's burial clothes according to local custom, still giving her water from Lourdes daily. The villagers continued to pray for her cure. Shortly before Christmas that year, Delizia suddenly said she wanted to get up and go out. She weighed only forty-nine pounds, but, though extremely weak, she was able to hobble without pain. Her knee swelling disappeared within days, leaving her with greater freedom of movement. Her general condition returned to normal within a few weeks.

"This is a golden, marvellous case, a case one could show to any skeptical doctor and be assured he'd find it incomprehensible," enthused orthopedist and bone cancer specialist Dr. André Trifaud at the 1993 "Cures and Miracles" conference. However, Dr. Trifaud, one of Delizia's examiners for the Lourdes International Medical Committee, delivered a distinctly mixed message. "I don't want to cause you pain," he told his audience, "but perhaps one day we will have an explanation of her cure, thanks most notably to recent work by . . . researchers in this area."

It was Delizia's mother who insisted a miracle had occurred. The Vatican report notes that the woman returned to Lourdes the year after the healing, "vehemently" insisting the bureau's doctors examine her daughter for signs of God's intervention. Delizia's right knee joint was visibly deformed, but X rays clearly showed the disappearance of the lesion and bone repair. She was reexamined on subsequent annual pilgrimages and in 1982, members of the Lourdes International Medical Committee declared her cure (by a two-thirds majority vote) to be medically "inexplicable." The Church granted her miracle status in 1989.

The decision was not without ambiguity, however. The cure,

which was written up in the *Journal of the Royal Society of Medicine,* had not been instantaneous. Nor had it been perfect: The girl had been left knock-kneed and required subsequent operations to correct the leg deformation. Cardinal Lambertini's centuries-old rules in this modern Lourdes miracle were, as one participant put it, "nuanced." The medical committee decided, after much deliberation, that she had not had a neuroblastoma as originally diagnosed, but a Ewing's sarcoma. Although the reports note no unusual bouts of high fever, her two-week recovery period is consistent with Dr. Coley's observations of the rapidity of regression of sarcoma resulting from his deliberately induced fevers and infections (at most "one to two weeks").

And though no psychological profile is cited, there is the possibility that proposed mind-body mechanisms of remarkable recovery were also at work. Dr. Trifaud mentioned at the Lourdes conference the curative power of emotional "upheavals" *(bouleversements)* and psychological change *(réorganisatrice du psychisme)*. He is obliquely seconded by current Lourdes medical director Dr. Pilon, who told us diplomatically, "We must admit that today the frontier between the domain of pure organic and the psychosomatic manifestations of rather intense mental states has become blurred."

To understand what mind-body forces might have been at work in Delizia's recovery, it might be useful to compare it with a similar case reported by Dr. Johannes Schilder, a physician at the Helen Dowling Institute in Rotterdam who has been studying the psychosocial components of spontaneous remission. Dr. Schilder's "Patient S." was ten years old when he, like Delizia, was diagnosed with a malignant giant-cell tumor on his tibia. As with Delizia, the orthopedist bluntly told the parents he would have to amputate, and similarly, they refused, telling him, "He's our child, and you haven't got anything to do with this. We will find a way." The family doctor unexpectedly sided with them, at one point illegally removing the boy's X rays from the hospital file and referring them to a doctor in Germany.

Again, as in Delizia's case, the entire village rallied. Rather than take a trip to Lourdes, however, they arranged for a car to drive the boy on a pilgrimage to the door of a rather eccentric German physician, who prescribed a protein-rich diet, massages, and as much daily play as possible. The man was the first expert to state the boy would be cured, though he uttered what struck Schilder as a rather fairy-tale prognosis: "Your boy's going to make it because of his blue eyes and blond hair."

Back home, Patient S., like Delizia, was surrounded by a powerful circle of caring. As Dr. Schilder describes it: "The boy is given the front room of the house, all sorts of toys, and full attention of the family, classmates, and fellow villagers. When the whole village gathers in church for nine consecutive days to pray for the boy, the pain in his leg disappears. Diets, massages and full attention are continued for more than a year. Since he cannot yet walk, he builds himself a cart which is pulled along the roads by the family's dog." And like Delizia, though the tumor disappeared, the boy's leg grew crooked and later required corrective surgery.

What we see in both cases are powerful stimuli to the mind-body healing process—parents' unceasing concern; the tangible social support of an entire community; unconditional love; vivid and powerful stimuli to the imagination; reinforcement of self-worth; collective spiritual invocation; and positive pronouncements from a respected and apparently charismatic figure of authority.

The presence of these mind-body factors, of course, make Patient S.'s and Delizia's cases no less extraordinary. Still, it becomes tempting to view many of the Lourdes healings as relics of bygone days when diagnosis was less definitive, analysis of cases less incisive and secular, and the power of the mind over the body cast in theological terms. Biblical-level, impossible-sounding cases of the lame rising from their wheelchairs are today usually chalked up to observers' psychosomatic naïveté. After all, the poet Elizabeth Barrett was confined to bed with paralyzed legs for twenty years until her elopement with fellow poet Robert Browning enabled her to escape her tyrannical father. A year later, she climbed mountains in Italy with her new husband; two years afterward, she gave birth to a son. Her miracle stemmed from a change of heart and circumstance. Her paralysis, it is now assumed, was "functional," not organic.

Still, we came across two supposed miracle cures where there was enough serious organic damage to make us heed the great psychologist William James's famous injunction against "premature closing of our accounts with reality." One of these was the astonishing story of Leo Perras.

We decided to pay a visit to Perras, who lives in a converted farmhouse a few miles from the upscale, college burg of Northampton, Massachusetts. It's just a little way down Route Five, but the road signs plunge to the edge of the rural abyss: Fruit, vegetable, and fudge stands segue to the Oxbow Sport and Package Store, where slats hanging like the bellows of a played-out accordion advertise Live Bait, Guns 'n' Ammo, and Mom's Broil-o-Dog.

When we pull up to his house, Perras is standing on his front porch scanning the traffic, a man in a neatly pressed tweed sport coat, upright and narrow as a two-by-four. It's a house he has lived in for the past fifty years.

"You thought I was a big guy, right? It's the phone voice," he says proudly. "Everybody gets fooled." In fact he's small, but with a booming, tough-guy croak. Over his cardinal-red tie is a very large black-and-gold crucifix with a bas-relief of the suffering Christ. Perras wears it like a Purple Heart, and in a sense it is, earned in a lifelong battle for body and soul that began on Christmas Eve 1939.

Perras was an agile young kid working overtime in the town textile mill when a factory handcart laden with 300 pounds of uncut cloth toppled onto his back. An operation for a herniated disk followed, then a sacroiliac fusion followed by ten years in a heavy steel brace, gulping painkillers, and undergoing yet more operations. Over subsequent years, his situation progressed from catastrophically bad to worse. Finally, doctors in Boston decided to do a "cordotomy" to remove tissue that was pressing on the spinal cord. Leo woke up with no sensation in the lower two-thirds of his body. Later medical examinations revealed he had no deep tendon reflexes. His spine had been in large part transected.

Perras's struggle with despair was epic. After he had withdrawn into silence in his room, sinking fast, his wife had driven him in his wheelchair to the center of town and simply left him on the sidewalk. Realizing, as people walked past him unseeing, that he would have to make his own inner decision whether or not to go on, he chose life. Throughout his decades of travail, he managed to do volunteer work at local hospitals and in groups for the disabled. He even continued with his carpentry work, jerry-rigging a complicated hydraulic contraption that enabled him to almost single-handedly build a house for his daughter and son-in-law.

But after nearly twenty years in a wheelchair, Leo had given up all hope of recovery. His wife heard that Father Ralph DeOrio, a well-known Catholic priest, was holding a healing service in nearby Worcester. Knowing he'd be reluctant to attend—"If God wants to heal me," he'd told her the last time she'd suggested it, "he can do it right here"—she got one of his friends to convince the skeptical paraplegic, then bundled him into the back of a van and got him there in time for the service.

All afternoon, for five hours, Leo Perras sat listening to the service, which was conducted at the high emotional pitch of faith healing everywhere. He was about to ask his wife to wheel him out when the six o'clock bells began to ring. "All of a sudden Father DeOrio stops," Leo recalls. "He turns around, crosses the sanctuary and comes right up to me. He blesses me with holy water, puts his hands up and says, 'In the name of Jesus Christ, rise!'"

Though it's obvious he's recited his story dozens of times, Perras's eyes mist. "I didn't realize I was standing until I was face-to-face with him," he says in a choking voice. "He never touched me. It felt as if I'd been picked up out of the wheelchair by a pair of invisible hands. I didn't even know what had happened because I still didn't have any feeling in my legs. Then I just looked down, and my God! I'm standing. He says to me, 'You and I are going to walk down the center aisle of this church to the front door.' "

Leo walked—*walked!*—through a pandemonium of flashing cameras and well-wishers into his van. After hours of stopping off triumphally at friends' houses in what soon became a caravan, he pulled up to his doctor's house. It was nearly midnight, and Dr. Mitch Tenerowicz, chief of staff at Northampton's Cooley Dickenson Hospital, came to the door barefoot and blinking. "When he saw me standing there," Leo says, "he just yelled 'Omigod!' I could see this cold sweat just rolling right off of him."

Neurologically, his doctor told him, nothing in his condition had changed. He still had no reflexes. "His muscles are totally wasted. His calves are the size of my wrists. Why he is walking I don't know," said Dr. Tenerowicz, who had been treating Perras for ten years. Leo's limbs, he noted, had been "so emaciated . . . that, anatomically, they shouldn't have been strong enough to support him." Even a simple broken leg, he added, requires at least five weeks in a cast, crutches, and physiotherapy before it can be walked on again; here was a man who hadn't walked in twenty years.

So thoroughly had Perras lost sensation, Tenerowicz observed, that a few months previously the carpenter had failed to notice a nail embedded in his foot until it became visibly infected with "this tremendous abcess." Leo, in fact, claims he did not regain feeling in his legs for three months after the healing, despite his newfound mobility. "I felt like I was somehow just floating along in midair, like a torso with nothing underneath. I used to have to look down to check where my feet were." He leans back in his orange BarcaLounger, chain-smoking Raleigh filters, crossing and uncrossing his legs in an extravagant arc, his mirror-finish patent-leathers shooting out light. He's showing off a little; he still can't seem to get over it.

He yanks a thick photo album off a shelf and ceremoniously dons a pair of gold-rimmed bifocals, leafing through yellowing newspaper clippings and snapshots till he comes to a picture of himself coming down some stairs, his expression the one that must have been on Neil Armstrong's face when he took his first jouncing step on the moon. It's a look of great bemusement, one foot on the stair, the other floating toward the ground, his arms spread a little as if afraid of teetering over and shattering his miracle on the sidewalk like a borrowed china plate.

We ask him if he'd roll up his trousers so we can feel the miraculous limbs. Crouching at his feet, it is possible to almost wrap one hand around his calf, which nonetheless feels hard and muscular. It is difficult to imagine what they must have looked like before his perplexing resurrection—according to Dr. Tenerowicz, his leg muscles tripled in size within months of his healing.

In the back of the house, Leo's built a small chapel with two pews. By the door sits his battered wheelchair with its peeling American flag decal; the room is dominated by a life-sized plaster figure of Saint Joseph scavenged from a torn-down church. He slings his arm familiarly around its shoulder. "God uses the simple things of this world," he says, beaming, "to confound the wise."

Indeed, a variety of observers maintain that those most likely to experience supposedly miraculous healings do not interpose much critical thought between themselves and a higher power. Such people, it is thought, are more likely to be powerfully affected by the charisma of the healer and the atmosphere of the healing ceremony, itself designed to still the inner critic.

Magician and debunker James Randi criticizes such ceremonies with a singular vehemence, dubbing DeOrio a "Vatican-Approved Wizard," accusing him of making inflated claims, neglecting to supply serious researchers with documentation, and elevating psychosomatic cures to divine intervention. Counters the local bishop's representative, "Sure, some [cures] are psychosomatic, and some hysterical, and some can be explained through natural reason. I didn't have a problem with that, because they're still real. . . . God is working throughout a person's life. It's not that important to prove it's extraordinary or divine intervention."

Like Deliza Cirolli and Patient S., Leo Perras was surrounded by strong psychosocial influences: His doctor had obtained for him the tickets to the service; his best friend insisted he attend; his wife kept up a steady drumbeat of enthusiasm; there was a buildup of intense expectation. Writes psychologist Paul Roud, who also studied Perras's case: "The scene at the church—people fighting to get in—was entirely alien to his experience. Leo states he couldn't believe it. . . . Many events nurtured the suspension of his belief system. . . . After spending twenty years in a wheelchair, Leo was accustomed to second-class treatment. Maintaining respect from others was a constant struggle. At the church, however, he was suddenly treated like a guest of honor; a path was cleared for him and he was ushered to the front."

We visited one of Father DeOrio's weekly events, which are held at the Worcester Memorial Auditorium, a cavernous hall with faux-Grecian columns just across the street from the town's Boys' Club. The Sunday we were there, the place was packed to its soaring balconies. Embroidered banners proclaiming, "I Am the God Who Heals," "Be Careful of Your Soul," and "Heal Us Wounded Healer" hung from the rafters. There was a plangent, echoing murmur, like the building anticipation of a pregame basketball crowd. Light glinted off the spokes of dozens of wheelchairs lining the lip of the stage as a choir sang rousing spirituals. Father DeOrio, a short, balding, ordinary-looking man in a clerical collar, was transformed during the service into an orator fully capable of bringing his congregation to a near fever pitch. Like a hypnotherapist, he encouraged his audience to let go of their ordinary awareness, suggesting their bodies might begin to feel very light, that there might be direct contact with an infinite source of power.

Stepping off the stage to wade into the aisles to perform hands-on healing, DeOrio keeps up a constant stream of suggestion through his hand-held microphone: "Medicine is just a tool, and so am I. I'm only God's light switch. I'm not the juice. My destiny is to bring you into contact with your own supernatural, spiritual self."

As we have seen, the healing system may be activated by a strong emotional charge, amplified by the presence of people of like minds, by the power of ceremony, and the stimulus of expectant faith. But we also found that beliefs seemingly powerful enough to produce spectacular healing can be internally generated, or stem from sources we find it difficult to explain. Such was the case with a science teacher and former nun named Rita Klaus.

When Rita Klaus (née McLaughlin) was nine years old, she had a near-death experience while almost drowning in the deep end of a swimming pool. Going down for the third time, she'd had an apparition of "Jesus, Mary, and St. Joseph in a big, white light. They were standing before a vast number of people. I was off to the side, yelling, *I'm here! I'm here!* Finally Mary turned and just smiled and shook her head." The next thing Rita knew, she had been fished from the water and was lying by the side of the pool being frantically resuscitated.

She later told her younger sister about her vision, who just "laughed and screamed and hollered. She thought it was the funniest thing she ever heard in her life." Embarrassed and angry, Rita didn't tell anyone after that. "I just made up my mind that I wanted to go to this beautiful place I'd seen called Heaven. Since the holiest people I knew were nuns, I decided I was going to be a Sister."

She announced her plans to her parents, and then stubbornly, uncompromisingly pursued them. She tried to enter a convent when she was fourteen, but was turned down as too young. The next year, making an unusual exception, the Church allowed her to enter the Novitiate. At only seventeen, she received the veil. A picture of her at twenty shows an alluring young woman, her flawless complexion framed by a white wimple, a fully ordained nun of the Servite Order—the order of St. Peregrine, patron saint of cancer.

That same year, Rita discovered she had multiple sclerosis, a chronic, slowly progressive disease of the central nervous system that causes a wasting of the nerve sheaths of the spinal cord. It typically progresses in fits and starts over several decades of life, causing crippling degenerative symptoms in almost every system of the body. Finding herself no longer able to manage the rigors of convent life, Rita was given dispensation from her vows. After finishing her college degree in biology, she settled down as a junior high school science teacher in a suburb of Pittsburgh.

But her initial symptoms receded, as they are known temporarily to do in many multiple sclerosis cases. Rita began to think she'd been misdiagnosed. Though she still wore orthopedic shoes for some residual problems, she told anyone who asked her the white lie her doctor had suggested, that she'd had childhood polio. Soon the stunningly beautiful former nun became a blushing bride. Three children followed in quick succession.

But even as she resisted the small telltale signs, her disease was returning. One day her arm suddenly went numb and she dropped her baby, who, cushioned by his comforter, was luckily unhurt. A few days later, as she was about to get out of her station wagon in the shopping center, she found herself temporarily paralyzed from the neck down. Alarmed, she went to the doctor, who confirmed it: The multiple sclerosis was back, now with a sere vengeance. After she had confessed her long-hidden illness to her husband, he sat in stunned silence, then angrily stormed out, only to return contritely to tell her, "I'm no saint. But we'll try."

It often seemed that sainthood would be a minimum requirement. The disease rapidly progressed. Rita's cane gave way to a walker, then to leg braces and crutches, and finally to a wheelchair. The MS caused complete paralysis of both feet and ankles. Spasticity and contractures of her leg muscles led to structural deformities and intractable sciatic nerve pain. Her doctors, reasoning she would never walk again, finally performed a radical retinacular release to relieve the pain and pressure, cutting the tendons that hold the kneecap in place. Rita was permitted to "walk" short distances in her house with the aid of full-length steel leg braces and forearm crutches, but most of her day was spent confined to her wheelchair.

She had tailspun into an emotional aridity; felt her religious faith curdle, become ashes. She felt bitter toward the God who had led her first to the convent, then to married life, only to abandon her. "I hated my body, I hated myself, I hated my family," she told us. In the midst of her despair, her husband urged her to attend a healing mass. At first she refused. "I'm a science teacher," she said angrily. "It's a bunch of malarkey. God does not intervene in the natural order. Every time I see these televangelist creeps, I feel like puking."

But she yielded to her husband's entreaties, allowing herself to be "shoved into a church pew" with full-length steel braces on. The most humiliating moment came when she was suddenly "grabbed from behind and hugged by this priest who prayed over me while all these hallelujah people waved their hands in the air." But her indignation gave way to "the strangest experience. I didn't see the people anymore, I didn't feel the priest there. There was just this white light, a feeling of absolute love like I'd never felt coursing through me. I felt forgiven and at peace. I wasn't physically healed, but had peace of heart, of knowing I was loved and could weather anything."

She would need all the spiritual resources she could find as the disease continued its progress. Her doctors told her there was no hope of improvement: The damage to nerves and tissues was irreversible. But as hard as the coming years would be, she had again found her faith: "I went back to my life of prayer, but one based not on books or scriptures or tradition but a personal relationship with Jesus. It was a more mature faith, a working faith: I stopped thinking about myself first all the time. I started looking at people who were worse off in a thousand different ways, if not with disease then with family problems, alcoholism, drugs, depression. I couldn't help them physically, but at least I could be supportive, listen to them, and pray."

That same year, just after Christmas, Rita had had a vivid dream. "I dreamed I had gotten a personal written invitation from Jesus. I could actually feel the texture of the paper—it was so *white*—and the calligraphy was so beautiful. It said, 'Dear Rita, you're invited to come to my church where my Mother is appearing.' Then I found myself in this big white church with this big white arch. I heard a roaring like the wind, and in the wind came this cloud, and in the cloud came Mary. And I woke up. It was so clear, I thought it was real."

Not long thereafter, somebody gave Rita a gift book with pictures of Medjugorje, a town in Yugoslavia where six youths claimed to have seen visions of a beautiful woman who called herself "Blessed Virgin Mary, Queen of Peace." Their visions had made the area a site of healing pilgrimage until civil war later shattered the country. As Rita thumbed through the book on her lap, she was startled by a photo of the Medjugorje church. "It was all white, unadorned, with white windows, white arches, no painting on the walls, no nothing," she explained to us. "It was exactly the one in my dream."

Six months later, after eating a late dinner in bed at the end of a sultry June day in 1986, Rita was completing her rosary and waiting for her husband to finish watching the eleven o'clock news. She suddenly heard "a very sweet voice that seemed to be inside me, outside me, all around me, yet there was nobody there. I very distinctly heard the voice say, 'Why don't you ask?' "

She was dumbfounded. Ask for what? She hadn't prayed for physical healing since her experience of "beautiful love" had restored her faith. "I had already said, 'Lord you can have anything you want from me,' and couldn't just go back and say, 'Now take away this disease.' I had just accepted it and tried to make the best of the way I was."

But now she found an unfamiliar prayer rising unbidden to her lips—a plea to Mary to give her the faith that Jesus had said could move mountains. She instantly felt "a sudden surge of electricity down the back of my neck and into my arms and legs . . . pins-and-needles . . . a sparkling feeling of effervescence, like bubbly champagne. It went through the right side of my body, which was most affected."

The next thing she knew it was morning. She had slept through the alarm and had to rush off to her scriptural studies class at the local college, oddly amnesic about the strange occurrence the night before. But during class that morning, she suddenly noticed "a rush of heat that was like fire, starting at my feet and roaring up through my body. It was uncomfortable." The next thing she knew, her legs began to itch unbearably. She bent over to scratch at the heavy cotton stockings she wore to keep her braces from rubbing sores on her skin and realized she had sensation in the lower part of her legs. More shockingly, "I could wiggle my toes, something I had not been able to do for over ten years. I just sat there and felt my toes going up and down inside my big orthopedic shoes. I thought I was having some weird muscle spasm."

She didn't hear what the theologian conducting the class was saying, though she was later told that ironically, he had been arguing forcefully against the existence of miracles. "He was saying there is always a natural physical explanation. I'd been so obsessed with what was happening to me right then, I hadn't heard a word he said."

When she got home, Rita felt hot and bent down to remove her leg braces, then realized her leg "looked strange." Her right kneecap, which since the tendons had been cut had migrated into a deformed-looking, sideways-facing position, seemed somehow back in place. "I just remember screaming, 'My God, my God, my leg is straight!' " She slid off the remaining braces, tore off her long socks, tucked her big blue skirt into her waistband, and said to herself, "If I am cured, I can run up the stairs!' And I ran up all thirteen steps, reaching the second floor landing." Now beside herself, she tore out the front door, ran down through the woods and jumped across a creek, shouting thanks to the sky, grateful that "we had a couple of acres here so nobody came in a white coat to take me away."

She called her priest, bellowing into the phone, "I'm healed! I'm healed!

" 'Who is this?' he kept saying, but I kept yelling, 'I can run, I can run, I can run!' Finally he said, 'Is this Rita?' He said, 'I want you to sit down, calm down, take some aspirin and call your doctor.' He thought I'd gone nuts."

Still babbling and crying, Rita hung up and called a girlfriend, who found her standing in the living room barefoot and di-sheveled, "a bawling mess," her muddied dress still tucked into her waist, a nest of leaves and grass in her hair. The two women grabbed each other and danced wildly around the room, finally collapsing in a heap on the hearth.

When her husband Ron, a public school teacher, came home, he recalls being more terrified than elated. He knew Rita's mus-cles had atrophied; her bones were deformed. "I felt panic-stricken," he said. "She used to have short remissions where she'd feel a little sensation for a week or a month, but the doctors had said that was all over now, and not to encourage false hope."

He and Rita went to the rehabilitation hospital that Monday. The doctors who convened to examine her were flabbergasted. As the nurses scurried for her charts and patients gawked and craned, the doctors' reactions tellingly varied: "One of my doc-tors saw me and started to laugh. He thought I must have had a twin who I'd brought in to play a practical joke on him." Her neurologist, she says, was "so angry! He said there is no cure for MS, no such thing as miracles. He even called people at the hos-pital and told them I was a fraud and a fake." Her orthopedist kept shuffling her X rays, unable to comprehend what had hap-pened. Her urologist, who had last seen her with her bladder swollen to many times normal size and incontinent, retested her and confirmed the organ had returned to normal. "He said there was no way he could explain it, that it was the most beautiful thing he'd ever seen in all his years of practice, and then he cried."

We obtained one of Rita's neurological reports, dated June 23, 1986, which reads, "Totally independent of any equipment. . . . She has regained full strength of both lower extremities. . . . Her deep tendon reflexes are all symmetrical and normal. . . . A tremendous recovery, I am not sure where to place it in this short period of time. The patient did not get tired of demonstrating to me how good she was. . . . I am very happy and . . . just stress to them to maintain sobriety."

After examining her, Dr. Donald Meister found no trace of

MS. "Spontaneous remissions of multiple sclerosis are possible," he affirmed to a local newspaper. "The only thing that doesn't fit here is that usually the permanent damage that had occurred up to the point of the remission does not go away. In Rita's case, every evidence I could see would suggest that she is totally back to normal."

But there was nothing normal about the year following her healing which was, Rita says, "Horrible. People think a miracle would put you on cloud nine, but my whole life had radically changed." It was hard for Ron, who had been "more caretaker than husband" to adjust, and he and Rita began fighting. "He's a very private person, and we were really coming unglued trying to fend off the tabloids."

Her kids, Rita told us, "had become absolute undisciplined little monsters" during her years as an invalid. She has pictures of herself, she says, "pulling out plates of moldy food and mildewed towels from under their beds." Her children also suffered in the aftermath of the miraculous. "Teachers would call them aside and tell them their mother was greatly exaggerating. Other kids would taunt them, saying, 'Your mom talks to aliens.'"

Rita now teaches science in a parochial school where she never speaks of her healing. "The school has gone to a New Age catechism. It's really a social justice book on ecology, full of Indian legends, Mahatma Gandhi, Vincent Van Gogh, the Sierra Club. There's no mention of Mary, or the angels. It's all about living and acting globally and responsibly. That's very important, but that's what we always cover in science class."

But science class cannot explain Rita's experience. "I believe that there's a scientific explanation for everything that happens to the human body," says Dr. Meister. "Whether it's divinely inspired or not, is not for me to decide. I'd love to know how this happened. I have a sister sitting in a wheelchair with multiple sclerosis in Philadelphia. She's fifty-seven. She's had it for seventeen years. Tell me how this happened. I'll use it again."

His poignant question cuts to the heart of the problem: Can we ever fully understand the underlying mechanisms of "miracle" healings, let alone reliably apply them? Rita's story contains tantalizing clues to the possible multiple pathways of remarkable recovery. Certainly in evidence are the episodes of psychological dissociation and absorption we have seen in a number of other cases. (Writer Ruth Cranston, collecting the subjective testimony of both official and unofficial Lourdes healings, noted that many spoke of a sense of "unawareness," of being transported beyond themselves, absorbed in thought, oblivious, "dazed," all subjective reports of dissociative states.)

Rita's sensations of intense heat are also intriguing. Physicians have often noticed that the return of sensation to nerve endings is accompanied by feelings of painful burning, indications of a physiological process. Sensations of heat, as we have suggested in previous chapters, can also be produced by psychosomatically mediated alterations in blood flow. Lourdes miracle Vittorio Michelli, cured of a sarcoma that had literally disintegrated his hip, reported a sensation of heat moving through his body immediately upon entering the holy spring. Medically inexplicable Lourdes cure Fernand LeGrand, suffering from extensive paralysis and gangrene as the result of polyneuritis affecting the spinal nerves and spinal cord, described "a great warmth through all my body" after being immersed in the bath.

Ruth Cranston reports on two unofficial cases: one cured of stomach cancer who described a painful "terrible burning"; another, who had the "sensation of being put in boiling oil" the moment she was immersed in the cold Lourdes spring; and Abbé Fiamma, who described a sensation "like the insertion of a red-hot iron under the skin."

Such experiences are not limited to Lourdes. Father DeOrio intimates to his parishioners they may experience "electricity going right through you right out of my body. Heat. A jolt of lightning, so to speak." Indeed, such phenomena seem to be cross-cultural. The !Kung bushmen of the Kalahari talk about a healing force they refer to as "boiling energy." Cardiologist Herbert Benson, trying to explain the measurable heat generated by Tibetan yogis, speculated to us that "by our calculations of the calories of heat generated, there must be an energy source in the body other than the ones we're currently aware of."

In a case cited in the *Journal of Medicine and Philosophy,* a middle-aged businessman named Mr. Jacobson who, diagnosed with an intractable hiatal hernia, decided to attend an Episcopal healing service. He had gone even though, he said, he took faith-healing "as a joke." Indeed, when one of the ministers laid his hands upon his head and prayed, he felt nothing whatsoever. But Mr. Jacobson says:

> [Later] on the way to my car I thought, "I wonder if I got healed? How are you supposed to feel when you get healed at one of these things?" And then I thought, "Well, it doesn't matter. Whether I get healed or not, I won't lose faith in God." Then suddenly, I felt like *high voltage* touched me on my head and I had a feeling that I can only describe as *like bubbling, boiling water* [our italics] rolling to my fingertips and back up . . . I knew I had been healed.

He returned to his doctor and asked that another upper gastrointestinal tract series be done. The next morning his physician called to say, "I can't explain it, but the X rays are perfectly normal."

Reports like these sound in some ways like indications of unusual nervous system activity. Writes British doctor Daniel J. Benor, who has enthusiastically taken up the study of healing phenomena, "Objective measurements of heat during healing do not demonstrate a rise of temperature. This seems to suggest a synesthesia, or crossed-sensory perception. Nerve endings which perceive heat may be stimulated by healing energy of some sort which is different from heat, but which overlaps with it in some manner to stimulate the nerves."

The possible role of the nervous system has occurred to earlier researchers. After personally witnessing a spectacular Lourdes cure earlier in this century, Alexis Carrel, a Nobel Prize–winning surgeon from New York's Rockefeller Institute, concluded that here was "a place where things of the utmost medical importance were undoubtedly occurring, things . . . which could throw a wholly new light on . . . the mysterious role of the nervous system." Rita Klaus's subjective impressions of "electricity," in fact, are intriguing indicators of possible unusual nerve activity pertaining to the healing of MS, a nervous system disease. Ruth Cranston quotes Brother Leo Schwager, a lay Benedictine and wheelchair-bound multiple sclerosis sufferer, who similarly described "something like an electric shock" immediately before getting up from his wheelchair at Lourdes.

Subjective descriptions of unusual forces or energies crop up in many cases of both "miraculous" and remarkable recovery. Millennia ago, Hippocrates recognized that the sensations of heat and tingling that accompanied a laying on of hands were often followed by a relief of symptoms. Though we might attribute these to mind-body mechanisms we have previously discussed, he believed they were produced by a vital force, the *vis medicatrix naturae* (the healing power of nature), and that the physician's function was to discover what blocked the individual's access to this force and to restore its flow.

Similarly, Chinese medicine is based on a belief that the body has a kind of internal wiring system designed to conduct the life-giving energy they call *chi*. It is composed of "meridians," which are said to function something like transformer stations. Though certain medical effects of acupuncture on these meridians have been documented, they do not correspond to any known nerve, circulatory, or other physiologic pathway in Western science. When a needle is inserted into a meridian, patients often report a sensation like an electrical charge, which Chinese physicians claim is a release of *chi* energy to heal an ailing body part.

It may seem a naive fixation on semantics to ask whether the feelings of "electricity" sometimes described in healings might have literal meaning. Lively discussions on this subject had taken place in earlier days of modern medicine, then faded away. In the June 1910 issue of the *British Medical Journal,* one physician wondered if human beings were "the keyboard of an electric installation . . . an Aeolian harp which discloses the motion of winds which we cannot see."

But such quaint-sounding inquiries should perhaps not be entirely dismissed. Bioelectrical energy does play a role in human metabolism. The body, primarily composed of saltwater solution—an excellent conductor of electricity—can be viewed on one level as a battery, with positively and negatively charged ions, conducting mild current through the water-bathed tissues. A small, measurable electric current shoots across the space between two nerve cells, or neurons, to signal them to fire.

One distinguished contemporary medical pioneer in this area is Dr. Björn E. W. Nordenstrom, the former head of diagnostic radiology at Stockholm's Karolinska Institute. Nordenstrom, the chairman of the Nobel Assembly (which picks laureates in medicine) and the inventor of the percutaneous needle biopsy method of diagnosing lung tumors, had been puzzled to note that on X rays such tumors sometimes exhibited radiating, sunlike streaks he named a "corona complex." Could these odd exposures indicate, he wondered, that tumors had special electrical properties? He eventually found that tumors frequently showed positive charge compared to surrounding tissue.

Realizing his biopsy needles could double as electrodes, he began using them to apply a minute positive charge to tumors, amplifying their natural signal. He discovered to his gratification that such signals seemed to provoke the body into routing a variety of tumor-fighting immune factors to the site, including a "massive accumulation" of white blood cells. The cause, he hypothesized, was what biologists refer to as an "injury current," a difference in electrical potential that arises between injured tissue (or a tumor) and the surrounding healthy flesh. Scientists had long accepted it as a given, but few if any had tried to understand its implications.

Nordenstrom's work revealed that this energy was part of the body's very own electric circuitry. Such circuits, he showed, affect everything from the activities of immune factors to the circulation of blood through capillaries (two mechanisms frequently

127

proposed as conduits for remarkable recovery itself). Relatively weak electromagnetic fields—which have been shown to speed up the healing of fractures, affect cellular metabolism, and even contribute to the "spontaneous necrosis" of tumor tissue—could be viewed, he writes, as an "extrabiological guiding principle."

The significance of his ideas has not been lost on colleagues in scattered corners of biological research. A recent scientific review paper, noting the "extreme sensitivity to electromagnetism" of cells and organisms, suggests how only minute amounts of energy could stimulate the body's natural propensity to self-heal:

> I propose that the process of healing is initiated whenever sufficient energy is captured to push the system to the point from which it naturally evolves to the self-organized critical state. A small disturbance allows the appropriate cells to overcome some energy barrier, similar to a ball needing a slight push to get over a hump before it rolls down to a valley.

Dr. Robert O. Becker, a New York orthopedic surgeon, has been called "the father of bioelectromagnetics." He points out that man-made electromagnetic fields (EMFs) have been shown—in even minuscule, barely detectable strengths once regarded as too low to be anything but benign—to affect dividing cells, immune system function, and neurohormones. EMFs, says Becker, are clearly capable of producing "a cascade of changes" in the body. "It was simply assumed," he says sardonically, "that the laws of physics guaranteed there could be no interaction between unseen fields and living things. It's not true." Such weak EMF fields are believed by some scientists to be responsible for the clusters of cancer cases that show up in residential areas too close to transformers, power lines, and electrical substations.

But that which hurts may also heal. While chief of orthopedic surgery at the Veterans Administration Hospital in Syracuse, New York, Dr. Becker became fascinated with how salamanders regenerate lost limbs. He discovered that the "control system that started, regulated, and stopped . . . their healing was electrical." His discovery, he says, pointed to a system that operated "below the central nervous system, along a common pathway regulating healing and growth through an intricate transfer of electromagnetic information."

Over the years, his work has led him to conclusions others might find metaphysical but Becker considers within the eminent domain of science. "Perhaps people who seem to be able to heal through 'laying-on-of-hands' are putting out electromagnetic fields within a certain special frequency range that affects the body's own fields, and through them the cells of the body itself."

Olga Worrall was perhaps the most studied purported healer of modern times, producing intriguing physical effects on living and inanimate systems under experimental laboratory conditions. Robert N. Miller, an industrial research scientist, found that water "treated" by Worrall revealed, when examined by infrared spectrophotometry, changes suggestive of an alteration in hydrogen bonding, an effect almost identical to that obtained by immersing magnets in water for several hours.

Worrall, herself, who believed prayer to be a form of "attention" that created "a carrier wave" for healing, staunchly maintained that "the body is not what it seems to be with the naked eye. It is not a solid mass. It is actually a system of little particles or points of energy separated from each other by space and held in place through an electrically balanced field. When these particles are not in their proper place, then disease is manifested in that body. Spiritual healing is one way of bringing the particles back into a harmonious relationship."

Dr. Elmer Green, director of the Mind-Body Lab of the Menninger Clinic and a pioneer of biofeedback research, conducted a set of experiments to see if healers' claimed ability to sense and convey "energy" was, in his words, "a bunch of malarky or something that could be proven." Using a highly sensitive electrical measuring device, he found that some healers' bodies emitted startling momentary surges of 80, 100, even on occasion 200 volts during times they stated they were sending out their healing energy. "That's not possible," Green says mischievously, "except it happened. Nobody knows what it means. But we saw the electrical side effects."

But the side effects of what? Green, like Becker, thinks it may be a form of "information" that somehow sets off a biological cascade within the body. In an attempt to define the phenomenon, the journal *Advances,* which specializes in the frontiers of mind-body medicine, offered a definition that expresses as much bafflement as insight: "Healing is the direct influence of one or more persons upon another living system without using known physical means of intervention."

Whatever it is, more than one patient we interviewed turned to it when all else had failed. Jeanne Stone had done everything medicine had to offer to treat the follicular lymphoma in her right calf. But after several surgeries, radiation treatment, and four grueling rounds of chemotherapy, she awoke one morning to find that a miniature phalanx of new tumors had grown up like dark mushrooms, arrayed at her original surgical site. Some were the size of fingernails, others little larger than a pinhead. Horror-struck, she grabbed a ballpoint pen from her nightstand and circled each one, counting no fewer than twenty-four lumps poking up from her skin.

A doctor's diagnosis confirmed it: Her lymphoma had recurred. But deciding the last-resort experimental treatment her physicians suggested seemed to have too many risks and too few benefits, Jeanne turned in another direction. She had for years been deeply immersed in armchair metaphysics, trundling back and forth from the library with armloads of Shirley MacLaine books and subliminal tapes on weight loss and "past life regression," finding in them "glitches and glimmers" of unexplored inner lands. When a friend who knew of her health predicament told her about the New Agish Healing Light Center Church—run by an "energy healer" and former atmospheric physics researcher named Rosalyn Bruyere—"I decided to take a leap of faith," Jeanne says. Her friend had suggested to her with an aura of certainty, "If you go, you will be healed," and as with many a

Lourdes pilgrim with little more to lose, Jeanne found even a rumor of healing sufficient.

Jeanne had been a Presbyterian for fifteen years, teaching Sunday School and singing in the choir. But she had quit years before. "My image of God was much bigger than what I was being taught theologically. It was not the God I knew." Her visit to the Healing Light Center Church was confusing, foreign, exciting. "They didn't tell me what they were doing, just laid me on a sort of a massage table. First they said they would 'read my aura' by running their hands back and forth above my body. They began to work very extensively around the abdomen. They didn't even touch the leg where the tumors were." Still, she experienced strange sensations from the healers' odd ministrations. "After the second treatment, I felt this surge that was coming up from the abdomen area, right up the center of my body. I would feel a pulsation like a sudden rush of adrenaline." She found herself so "highly energized" she couldn't sleep. She went downstairs to the motel pool, marveling that she could swim lap after lap whereas the day before, "If I'd gotten halfway across the pool, I'd have been lucky."

Her healers also asked her to talk about her life, in order to "discharge" any emotional trauma from the years prior to her illness. Under their floating hands, she talked about the pain of losing custody of her children through divorce; the suicide of her second husband; finally finding herself over fifty, working three part-time jobs and being on food stamps; moving with her youngest son to her parents' house in Lincoln, Nebraska, only to have her mother and father die one day apart; finally being forced to declare bankruptcy. Her tears flowed freely in an overwhelming sensation of release.

Her stay at the healing center, she told us, was "life-changing, a tremendous spiritual experience. They treated me for an hour each day for five straight days." She also learned relaxation techniques, and ways of contacting her "inner guides": "The healer did a guided visualization with me to introduce me to a 'helper.' I had expected someone very much like the pictures of Jesus, long flowing gown and surrounded by a halo. But instead, I got a clear picture of a guy dressed in Reeboks and jeans and a sweatshirt whom I named 'Jaime.' And the first thing Jaime said was, 'I love you, I have always loved you, and I always will love you.' When I came back out of that altered state, I cried and I cried and I cried. I felt so blessed that there was someone, even if they weren't in my normal reality, who really cared about me."

What Jeanne calls her "heightened sense of perception" continued for a period of months after she returned home. But even more surprising was the effect on her tumors. "Every one of these tumors had been in a place where I could watch it, touch it, feel it, look at it, and see the progression one way or another. Well, they flattened out after the first treatment. Five of them were completely gone by the end of my fifth session. The rest of them continued to smooth out and just eventually disappear over the next month or two after I got home."

She found a surgeon who, though puzzled by her unconventional activities, shared her enthusiasm for what had occurred. "He looked at my leg and he looked at me and he said, 'Well, by golly! They're gone!' I've had a good feeling with him ever since." When shortly thereafter, a small lump arose on her thigh, she sought treatment from another healer, "a delightful person," finding to her amazement that the lump "got very red and inflamed. After the swelling and the redness disappeared, the lump disappeared, too." A subsequent lump that did not go away was surgically excised.

Here, then, is a complex picture of one person's confrontation with the mysteries of the healing system: Jeanne had a disease, lymphoma, that researchers have noted seems biologically to regress more readily than other types of cancer; she used some conventional medicine; she also turned to a therapy that involved powerful emotional catharsis, imagery, a pilgrimage to an exotic but supportive environment, and feelings of unconditional love. In the reddening, inflamed swelling of her tumor sites prior to healing, we again see physiological mechanisms we have noticed in a number of cases of remarkable recovery, perhaps stimulated in part by states of absorption, dissociation, and suggestibility.

We were interested to note, in fact, that healers themselves seem to enter into these very same states. The late M. H. Tester, a purported British healer, wrote: "My conscious mind shut itself off as the power flowed through me. At these moments, I lose an appreciation of time. I had no idea if I had been 'out' for a few seconds or for many minutes. Later, I realized it must have been quite a while." An American physician writing under the pseudonym Rebecca Beard describes in her 1951 autobiography how her remarkable recovery from an untreatable and potentially fatal heart condition led her to make a "transition from *materia medica* to spiritual therapy." Beard's description of her state of mind when she transmitted healing energy included, in one researcher's words, "meditative prayer during which attention is directed away from one's self; and reduced discursive and analytical thinking, resulting in a 'stilling of the mind.' " Another researcher's study of "transcendent" states described by healers and mystics includes "states in which elaborate and seemingly real images are experienced" and "altered states of consciousness in which forgotten experiences are remembered in elaborate detail." The realm of the spirit seems to include many of the mental and emotional phenomena we have previously noted in remarkable recovery, though it may not be limited to them.

Traditional cultures have spent millennia studying the many dimensions of the healing system, using their own versions of microscope and flask to discover not only pharmaceutically active herbs, but potent "medicines" of music, dance, prayer, imagery, altered states, and social support. Rituals once viewed by science as superstitious wrapping paper of ingenious jungle drugstores are now being recognized by medical anthropologists as "active ingredients" of healing—the same ingredients often seen, under different labeling, in remarkable recovery. Unfortunately, traditional healers do not write up case reports in a *Journal of Shamanic Medicine,* compelling us to rely on direct observation.

Our search to understand the spiritual aspects of remarkable recovery took us to the city of Salvador in the Brazilian province of Bahia, where the Afro-Brazilian rituals of Candomble *(cahn-dom-blay)* are still practiced in their pure form. The population is seventy-five percent black or mulatto, the descendants of slaves once belonging to tribes like the Yoruba, whose belief systems can be traced back to Egypt and India. Even the baroque Catholic Bon Fim (Good Hand) Church, its walls festooned with crutches and other evidences of purported healings, is also filled with references to African iconography—a Virgin Mary with wings and a mermaid's tail, bare-breasted and pregnant as a fertility goddesses, carved by slaves in rock-hard jacaranda wood.

Candomble is a religion that believes strongly in the unification of mind, body, and spirit. Its doctrine holds that reality is composed of two worlds—the *Aye,* or physical world, and the *Orum,* or spiritual realm. Usually, the worlds are separate. But in ceremony, they are united, which practitioners believe generates powerful forces of healing.

At the annual ceremony in honor of Oxumare, the god of transformation and healing, the crowd files in and fills up the benches and bleachers. Three drummers take their places on the platform. They set up a throbbing beat as a dozen women, ranging in age from fourteen to sixty, shuffle out to begin a rhythmic circling, arms floating gracefully, elbows bent. They are dressed in lace headdresses and white blouses and African hoop skirts. They circle languorously, the older women as graceful as the young girls, bare feet whispering over brick. The lead drummer, a powerful-looking, jet-black man with the face of an ecstatic, makes his instrument sob and rejoice. Singing floats over the music, lifting and falling like oar strokes.

The women, growing wilder in the absorption of trance, approach the seated spectators, some ill and seeking healing, embracing some while others hold their hands, palms outward, like heliotropes imbibing some invisible energy. The dancing, drumming, and expectant prayer of the congregants produce a profound sense of healing, a palpable energy that can be felt in body and in soul.

A man glances sharply at the tears streaming down his neighbor's face. "The gods are very beautiful, yes," he says, himself far away, his voice warm, drowsy, syrup-thick. The room seems filled with what the Japanese call *aware,* the bittersweet, elegiac joy that encompasses both beauty and its passing; the poignancy of knowing that this moment is what it is like to be fully human, and that we must inevitably return to a narrower existence. We watch the women whirl regally in their gowns of aquamarine and orange and green, their brass crowns gleaming, the gods spinning them as they dance, re-creating the world before the world was sundered.

The case of Muriel Bourne-Mullen, a feisty, seventy-one-year-old geriatric nurse living in England, would seem to have little in common with practitioners of such ceremonials. But Muriel, who grew up in the mysterious India of the 1920s and '30s, the daughter of the British Army officer who'd arrested Mahatma Gandhi, was weaned on folktales of Ram and Sita and stories of Hindu mystics. After marrying a police official who'd risen in post-independence India to become special protection officer for Indira Gandhi, she traveled into the interior of the country, often witnessing moving tribal religious rituals.

Muriel has tried to understand all spiritual faiths, though she has been a devout Catholic all her life. She had always prayed with fervor, but in 1987 she discovered she would be needing intercession, a lot of it, if she was going to live more than six months — the median survival time, her doctors told her, for her untreatable metastatic liver cancer. They'd tested, poked, and prodded for weeks, then "came to my bed, pulled the screen around, and said, 'We're sorry, your cancer has spread to the lungs,' and told me that treatment would be quite unnecessary."

Muriel had been a cancer ward nurse. She had seen people perish of every dread permutation of the disease. She at first took the news of her own illness calmly, then sank into a bleak depression, staring out the window mentally saying good-bye to life—good-bye to the gentle waving of the leaves, good-bye to her husband of forty years, good-bye to her children, and worst of all, to her adored grandchildren. But after her entire family gathered around her that Christmas, crowding into her council flat from as far away as California, she felt heartened and began to rally.

As she had all her life, she turned diligently, passionately, to prayer. She beseeched St. Jude, patron of lost causes. She recited, with the ardency of the parochial schoolgirl she once was, the lovely, yearning litany to the Mother of God, the one that began, *Remember, oh most loving Virgin Mary, that it is a thing unheard of that anyone who ever had cause for your protection or implored your help or searched for your intercession was there forsaken.* She prayed to be forgiven, prayed for the return of health, prayed for the cancer to "disappear and go away."

It was an outrageous requisition, even to the divine, but Muriel Bourne-Mullen was no stranger to marvels. She hastens to add that she's "open but not gullible"; that she "looks into things" before coming to a conclusion. "But I have so many stories of things," she says, "that I actually saw." She talks about a yogi employed by her husband's police colleagues who was reputed to have the power to heal poisonous snakebites at a distance. "If someone was bitten by a cobra, it was government-approved policy for the police to spend the money to send a telegram to this man. He was very religious, said his prayers six times a day, wouldn't step on an ant or eat meat. If the telegram carrier walked in wearing leather, he'd get a tight slap! Anyway, this yogi would say a prayer—a *mantra*—and go into deep concentration for a few minutes. And the person far away was always cured. This fellow would even predict the exact words the victim would say when he came round. There are things you can't explain. Sometimes truth is stranger than fiction."

In Muriel's case, her doctors were forced to agree. After Christmas, she inexplicably began gaining weight. Her tumor shrank down, then finally disappeared, a fact confirmed by X rays, biopsies, and scans. Her lungs completely cleared. The tumors that had occupied both quadrants of her liver were mutely attested to by scar tissue.

Seemingly anxious to drag her confounding case back inside medical boundaries, her doctor urged her to undergo a liver transplant, a proposal she'd indignantly turned down flat. "I was perfectly hale and hearty, love. I told him there was now nothing the matter with me and that would be quite unnecessary." Then she giggles like a schoolgirl. She had received her "thing unheard of."

Cases of things unheard of are rarely written up in medical journals. The Vatican-investigated "miracle case" of Ann O'Neill—the four-year-old whose healing from leukemia was attributed to Mother Seton (chapter two)—has never appeared as a case report in the literature. Hematologist Dr. Milton Sacks told a *Washington Post* reporter in 1993, "The only reason this case has not been written up is that I have been afraid to."

Muriel *was* written up, but her actual story disappears between the lines of her medical report. In the journal *Gut,* cases unfold with no more charm than the blunt prosody of its title. In the 1990 write-up of Muriel's almost unprecedented story, her human dimensions are reduced to zero. We fleetingly encounter "a sixty-three-year-old white woman with a four-month history of abdominal discomfort and bloating after eating" who then vanishes in favor of more elaborately sketched "pleomorphic" tumor cells with "bizarre giant nuclei." The report confirms the original diagnosis of metastatic liver cancer, and reiterates that since "no treatment was considered worthwhile, the patient was discharged home with no drugs." It notes that there have only been two published reports in medical history of a regression of primary liver cancers, and only one, from China, of a metastatic condition. It recites a litany of possible mechanisms—endocrine, immune mechanisms, disruption of the tumor's blood supply—but seems to spread its hands helplessly as to how, or why: "The patient received no treatment for the tumour, and regression therefore can be truly described as spontaneous." There is no mention of Muriel's spiritual experiences and beliefs, or of the fervent prayers that fit no therapeutic schema.

But it is hard to ignore the fact that cases like Muriel's often include what we call, with a certain imprecision of language, prayer. Take the 1964 medical case report from the previous chapter, of a man with a "massive recurrence" of metastasized melanoma who had applied Vaseline and compresses to his tumor and attributed his cure to prayer. Assuming Vaseline is not some unknown, panaceaic agent, could his attribution of his recovery to "prayer" mean anything at all? And what *kind* of prayer are we talking about? The report tells nothing of the man's religion. He might have been imploring the omnipotent Allah of Islam, Buddhism's compassionate Avalokitesvara, the Native American Wakantaka, or the ineffable Tao. His prayer might have taken one of the forms exactingly spelled out by theologians—petition, intercession, confession, lamentation, adoration, invocation, thanksgiving, or any of the contemplative practices in our globe's spiritual cornucopia.

It is interesting to note, however, that prayer often involves the very states we postulate are associated with healing: absorption in a single focus; the relaxation response; emotional catharsis; a humbling of the reasoning cortex; visualization; active imagination; coherent intention; to say nothing of possible unknown energies or, some would maintain, higher powers. Prayer, in other words, seems almost designed to stimulate the healing system.

We also began to wonder if there were personality factors conducive to "miraculous" remarkable recoveries; some special receptivity that enabled prayer to work. Leo Perras, for example, had a highly artistic personality (his meticulously carved, woodcraft bas-relief of "The Last Supper" is a masterpiece of folk art), a trait often associated with hypnotizability. He had an unusually willful personality; a strong, active desire to help others; a refusal to allow handicaps and obstacles to disengage him from life; and, like Rita Klaus, a quality of not so much hope but what might be called "creative surrender."

In Muriel, we also found a person of stubborn life force. She scarcely seems like a grandmother of twelve. It is easy to see traces of the hellion she had been in her youth, when she was a semi-professional dancer who tangoed to big band music (averring she's "no prude," she expresses dismay at "present-day head-banging music"). She recalls with a hint of pride: "I was argumentative. If I saw something was wrong, I expressed my opinion whether anybody liked it or not. I used to shout and throw things. I had a mind of my own."

Her mind was an unusually open one. Though she'd enjoyed a cossetted life in the self-contained British community, with its own dancehalls and cinemas, mansions and servants, imported gramophones and lipstick consignments, she was never quite comfortable with aloof colonial grandeur. "It was like South Africa. We weren't allowed to learn the local language or even talk to the servants."

After Indian independence, when her family fled back to England, she had remained behind, fascinated by the ferment of "a country that needed its freedom." Her father had arrested Gandhi enough times to get to know the nonviolent hero, often telling her the Mahatma was "a wonderful man who has done nothing but peacefully struggle for his country." Now, at last, she could explore the colorful world outside the colonial quarantine.

She pursued what she calls a "checkered career." With her husband, she'd roamed "from one end of India to the other, north to south to east to west." She'd braved Hindu-Muslim riots, joined the women's auxiliary during the war, met Mother Teresa ("a very tiny, frail old lady who emanated this unreal power"), and raised donations for leper colonies. Through it all, Muriel's faith sustained her. "I don't walk around with the Bible," she says. "But every time I've been in trouble, God sort of lifted me out of it. I believe he answers prayers. When one door closes, He's opened another for me. So my faith is very, very firm and very, very deep."

Her faith includes a skepticism of mere trappings. "I mean, let's be honest. All religions are peaceful, but I saw Hindus and Muslims slaughter each other in the name of religion. Same as the Catholics and Protestants in Ireland. No religion tells people to shoot people in their beds, put bombs under somebody's car. It's all how you interpret it." Muriel's interpretations are those of a person whose spirituality transcends organized religion. "We've got the Virgin Mary; Hindus have the goddess Durga, who sort of helps you out. And they've got special shrines people with sick-nesses go to to be healed, just like Lourdes."

Muriel is apparently able to enter states of high absorption, say-ing her prayers with a mantralike intensity. She has had at least one outright visionary experience, "a very queer dream a few days after my husband died. I saw him standing in the doorway. He was real. He had on his long trousers, but his top body was bare. Suddenly he raised both his hands to me, and he had the marks of the crucifixion on them, and the scourge marks were on his back. And then he just faded. I felt that he was trying to say something, maybe that his suffering was over."

Whether in their private spiritual experiences or in the midst of a healing ceremony, whether conventionally religious or not, many who have experienced a miraculous recovery spoke to us of a sense of a divine presence we are hard-pressed to scientifi-cally quantify. Here we reach the edge of knowledge. Often, the most we could do was listen intently to individual testimony, marvelling at how powerfully a spiritual experience may at once transform and confirm someone at his or her deepest level of being—something that may create physical healing.

The beauty and idiosyncrasy of such experiences can be heard in the words of a man we met named Frank O'Sander Juliano, Jr. In June of 1983, Juliano, then a twenty-three-year-old heavy-equipment foreman, was operating a 6,000-pound backhoe to help carve out subdivision development in upstate New York. It had rained the night before. The ground gave way, the machine rolled on top of him, and, as Frank puts it, "crushed me in my pelvis."

Trapped beneath the behemoth that had nearly torn him in half, he screamed for help, clawing at the damp ground, trying to pull himself free. The weight of the machine had sheared his sacrum and lacerated both major arteries in his leg, a condition that is often fatal within minutes. Though not particularly reli-gious, Frank says, "I turned to God. It was like my last breath, so the only thing I got out was, 'Father.' But mentally I completed the sentence and said, 'Father, help me.' And I remember that it was like the whole earth got quiet and peaceful—you could hear a pin drop. It was as if God sent his holy spirit to me, a giant swish of love like warm melted butter. I knew right away, though it wasn't very logical, that things were going to work out."

Frank was rescued by a quick-thinking coworker. Precious minutes elapsed before they managed to drive madly to the emergency room, where doctors immediately put Frank in inflatable pants to stanch the bleeding, and, unable to find a pulse, plunged a catheter into his vein. While blood poured into the leaky vessel of his crushed body, Frank was prepped and sedated.

While on the operating table, he died. What followed, in his own estimation, was an encounter with divine grandeur that he described for us.

"I remember sitting up, and seeing my body lying on the operating table. One of the things I was scared about was, I was looking down into my face, and my eyes were closed, and I remember saying in my mind, 'How come I can see and my eyes are closed?' After that, I was drawn away from the scene, like at the very end of a movie, before the credits, when they just pull the camera back. I thought I was heading in the direction of the operating lights, but then I realized it was taking a long time to get to something only forty inches away."

Continuing to travel toward the mysterious light source, he encountered what he calls a "guardian angel." The figure was indistinct, he says, "like on TV when they put someone behind a screen to disguise their identity." He and the misty figure climbed upward. When they reached the top, "this angel bowed at this kind of altar, then did a very crisp about-face. And when he did, that strength that he had given me to walk was gone like someone threw a light switch off. I went down like a bag of potatoes. I remember noticing I wasn't breathing like you do when you're alive. I was just lying there on my back, all helpless out in the middle of nowhere.

"And then I remember the presence of God coming, like a

tidal wave coming into a beach. At first it was a big swell. And then all of the sudden, it's like this big wall of water. And here you are, about the size of a little pebble. I remember spiritually gasping and saying to myself that I was glad that I was dead, because it was just so awesome. The magnitude was as if you were lying on a sidewalk, and somebody slid a skyscraper like up to you, and stopped it right at your nose.

"And so there I was, really at God's feet, maybe ten inches of space between us. That space was the most painful part spiritually, kind of like if you were a little kid and you approached your mother, and there was a moment expecting to be instantly picked up, but you weren't. I think it was only like two or three seconds. But it was just so agonizingly painful, those seconds of separation.

"And then I remember God bending over, so to speak, to scoop me up just like a loving parent would pick up a newborn. I was in God's arms, the size of a baby even though I'm like twenty-three years old. And God hugged me. And when He hugs, He hugs *through* you. It was like warm water being poured into a bigger basin of warm water. It was still me, but I was all part of that. I was mixed in with God like the chocolate in chocolate milk. The milk's the milk and the chocolate's the chocolate, but now it's all together.

"From this safe place, I watched my operation. I saw and heard the doctors and nurses, but I could also hear what was going on in their minds. I could see tears in this particular nurse's eye, and I knew she was really crying in her heart that I was dying. And God and I were conversing. When God and you speak, it's like turning a page in a book. Everything is a conclusion, a revelation, an exclamation point, like, *Oh wow, oh wow.*

"The conclusion that God was saying to me was a lesson about being judgmental of others. And God was saying to me, 'Look how much she loves you,' and the conclusion was, 'And she doesn't even know your name.' And He was also saying, 'Look at how much *I* love you,' which was a revelation like a thousand times a thousand, and then another thousand thousand times that of the nurse's love."

The next thing Frank remembered was waking up in intensive care. He went on to have a highly unexpected recovery from his injuries—despite the prediction he would never walk unassisted, his faith spurred him through years of therapy that led to his being nearly completely ambulatory, even able to ski.

At the heart of a cure, says current Lourdes medical director Dr. Roger Pilon, is the relationship with "this God who is Love." The most profound secret of Lourdes is the revelation that, as Père Henri Joulia puts it, "God loves me personally, not just in a general sense. God loves me, even if I'm a ne'er-do-well, even if I'm a poor specimen, even if I'm disabled or on drugs or have AIDS, even if I'm reduced to the simplest circumstances, even if I'm a criminal—God loves me. When I've discovered that, I've discovered a reason to live."

Dr. Pilon is a soft-spoken man with dark skin, graying hair, and Eurasian-looking features, and the measured caution of his words is belied by the passionate expressiveness of his gesturing hands. In deference to several Tibetan lamas in attendance at a 1993 Montreal conference on healing, he interspersed his lecture with comments about "the interior vision of Tibetan mystics, recognizable to the great Christian mystics" and the similarity between Buddhist and Christian notions of compassion.

Though he never tires of reemphasizing that the signal characteristic of a miracle "resides in the incredible acceleration of the processes of physiologic regeneration," he stresses that "today one does not come to Lourdes for physical healing, but for the heart conversion. One does not need these extraordinary events to be ravished." What he is referring to is perhaps the most mysterious factor of all in remarkable recovery: the force said by religious mystics to permeate all things—the energy of love. It is what the Tibetan monks report they feel when they practice their extraordinary production of body heat, which they say dissolves the duality between self and other in the blazing psychophysical heat of compassion. Said purported psychic healer Agnes Sanford, "Only love can generate the healing fire."

A miracle is by definition an irreproducible experiment. The healing system's manifestations are infinitely varied, not just from religion to religion, or from place to place, but from person to person. The various mind-body-spirit factors that seem to contribute to remarkable recoveries are unique to each human personality.

Looking at so-called miraculous healing, the religious among us might be inclined to say, "God did it." But it is incumbent on us to ask, "What, then, is God?" The spirit infusing a place? An "extrabiological" energy? The selfless love of another? The healing system is accessed along myriad pathways, "God" being, depending on one's beliefs, one or all of them. A miracle will always be something of a mystery—not because science cannot draw progressively closer to understanding, but because each person's soul can never be plumbed, nor the mysteries of each heart completely fathomed.

CHAPTER SIX

Is There a
Recovery-Prone
Personality?

W HEN WE DECIDED TO INVESTIGATE CASES OF REMARKABLE recovery, we were both hampered and exhilarated to find ourselves in uncharted research waters. Remarkable recoveries have been a phantom population, never adequately defined and so rarely singled out for study. Our predecessors, Everson and Cole, had never asked about the singular characteristics of the people whose "spontaneous" remissions they had diligently compiled. And as we have seen, the average medical report rarely goes beyond age, diagnosis, and treatment.

We spoke to a large number of remarkable recoveries, many of them verified in the medical literature. It made sense to try to determine what, if anything, they might have in common. In our search for similar threads within the different stories, we had considered mechanisms of biology, aspects of the mind-body connection, even spiritual beliefs. But the more interviews we conducted, the more we were struck by the sheer force of individual personalities, by how people's approach to healing had been a reflection of their own unique selfhood.

Given the innate complexity of human beings, what we might mean by selfhood is not easy to pin down. *Webster's* defines personality as "the totality of an individual's behavioral and emotional tendencies . . . character traits, attitudes or habits." Personality has been alternately framed as an individual's predominant mood state (optimist or pessimist); his or her "coping strategy" (passive or aggressive); style of relating to the environment (Jung's introvert/extrovert); by early childhood experiences (Freud's oral/anal/genital "fixations"); or temperament (considered primarily genetic by some, socially acquired by others).

We tend to adore and abhor typologies. We enjoy it when the astrology column in the newspaper holds before us a pleasantly vaporous mirror and tells us we are thus-and-such; but we do not like to be fixed, narrowed down to thus-and-such and no more. What might be called the "personhood" of an individual—at once unique and universal, fluid and inviolate, well concealed and open to inspection—is an ever-prismatic mixture that transcends artificial limitation.

Still, how we respond to a dire emergency like severe illness cannot help but be based on our particular temperament and talents; on what we celebrated and suffered as we grew; on the tenor of our relationships with others; on our beliefs about ourselves and the world at large; on how we have learned to navigate the vessel of the self around (or over, under, or through) life's obstacles. Perhaps, we reasoned, there might be specific personality factors correlated with the phenomenon of remarkable recovery.

Psychologists have long been interested in whether disease could be linked to personality factors. Though many researchers remain skeptical, a body of evidence has emerged over the past decade or so for Type A (heart-attack prone) and, more recently, "Type C" (cancer-prone) personalities. One preliminary study by researcher Lydia Temoshok, who coined the term "Type C coping style," found that melanoma patients who rated higher on a scale of emotional expression had less aggressive tumors and stronger T-cell immunity. But Dr. Temoshok stresses the importance of avoiding rigid categories that mandate one emotion or personality type over another. "The cancer patient who keeps up a false front in the name of 'positive attitude' is doing himself a disservice," she says. "He's cutting himself off from emotions—fear, anger, sadness—that are necessary in the healing process."

The variations in emotions, attitudes, and personality types observed in extraordinary healing are amply illustrated by a case we found in a 1952 paper on forty breast cancer patients. The researchers cited a seventy-eight-year-old woman who had unexpectedly survived for ten years without surgery or adequate radiation. Refusing treatment on religious grounds she had, as the report puts it, "developed a strong paranoid reaction shortly after the onset of the cancer. She 'didn't need treatment because God was saving her.' She was vituperative in the expression of her rage. What role could this character structure have played in her 'miraculous' span of life with cancer?"

It is a question we asked ourselves as people shared their often deeply emotional stories. Not all of them had peaceful, loving, trusting dispositions—that was clear. Some were downright ornery. But over and over we took note of a certain quality that we came to call "congruence"—an impression that these people, in the midst of crisis, had discovered a way to be deeply true to themselves, manifesting a set of behaviors growing from the roots of their being. We were interested to find that a colleague, Dr. Johannes Schilder of Rotterdam, had chosen the identical term after an initial study of seven cases of spontaneous remission. These patients, he observed, had emerged from their experience with "a stronger congruence among emotions, cognitions, and behavior."

"I've had three tapes of interviews judged by peers," he told us, "and they agreed most unanimously that this one characteristic—congruence—was the most striking." Similarly, Lawrence LeShan, a psychotherapist specializing in cancer who has seen his share of remarkable recoveries, believes that "a person who is singing their own song in life, creating it in ways that fit their personality structure, may well stimulate the body's self-healing abilities."

LeShan's emphasis on "ways that fit their personality structure" is a key comment. Though all men and women may be created equal, we each respond to the world in different ways. When confronted with a challenge, some of us approach it head-on, some of us step around it, some seesaw back and forth in an ongoing balancing act. There are those of us who apprehend the world emotionally, those who analyze it intellectually; those who act impulsively, others who tend to deliberate. Such differences have been considered since ancient times to have medical implications. In the fifth century, for example, Hippocrates based his treatments in part on his patients' temperaments, which were thought to be linked to various body fluids or "humors": the sanguine (optimistic and energetic), the melancholic (moody and withdrawn), the choleric (irritable and impulsive), the phlegmatic (calm and slow). Each of these personality types, it was believed, had its own characteristic physiological patterns.

At first, we had wondered if the group of some fifty cases we studied would reveal a set of common traits associated with the physiology of remarkable recovery. We had at the outset of our work taken particular notice of the mechanisms of the placebo effect, considered to be a factor in at least some of the Lourdes miracles. We had hypothesized that many of our cases might turn out to be people unusually open to suggestion, an oft-noticed concomitant in placebo healing.

Recall, for example, the case of Mr. Wright (chapter four), whose advanced lymphoma had responded so markedly to the apparently worthless Krebiozen, and subsequently to a placebo of distilled water. Dr. Bruno Klopfer has suggested that Mr. Wright's personality—his capacity for an "enthusiasm that knew no bounds"—may have contributed to his dramatic if temporary recovery. Klopfer says of people like Mr. Wright: "When they get under great stress, symbolically speaking, their ego seems to pull up its roots and float on the tide." In other words, Mr. Wright, says Klopfer, did not have a securely rooted form of "ego organization," evidenced by "the ease with which he followed the . . . suggestion of his doctor without any sign of defensiveness or even criticalness."

We reasoned that we might find among our remarkable recoveries people who were particularly susceptible to suggestion, absorption, and dissociation, all components of the hypnotic state. Deciding to pursue our hunches wherever they might lead, we contacted Dr. Herbert Spiegel, a former clinical professor of psychiatry at Columbia University and one of the world's leading authorities on hypnosis, and asked him to formally evaluate our cases.

Dr. Spiegel's office is under the shadow of New York's Guggenheim Museum, its uncoiling spirals an architectural rumination on the layers and levels of the modernist psyche. But Spiegel, a psychoanalyst who sports what he calls a "Yul Bryner haircut" and who was trained by the field's greats—from Harry Stack Sullivan to Eric Fromm—does not favor the lengthy journey of long-term therapy for most of his patients. Spiegel, one of the key consulting therapists in the case of multiple personality known to the world as Sybil, cuts through the mind's maze-like twists using a ten-minute assessment technique.

He begins with a short verbal test to ascertain how easily a person can enter trance, a trait he feels is a key to personality itself. Ability to enter trance reveals how a person fundamentally relates to the world. "As you concentrate on a movie or a play, do you get so absorbed you lose track of where you are?" he asks today's patient, a soft-faced young blond man in a pastel sweater and rumpled white Arrow shirt. "Do you focus more on the past, present, future, or all three?" he asks, glancing at his checklist. "When you're learning something new, do you critically judge first and accept later, or the other way around?" Then, quoting the philosopher Blaise Pascal ("The heart has a mind which the brain doesn't understand"), he asks the young man whether he thinks more with his head or his heart.

Dr. Spiegel moves on to the next part of the procedure, the so-called Eyeroll Test. "Without moving your head, look up as far as you can," he instructs, and the man's eyes whir up like white roll-up window shades, evidence of a propensity for trance which studies indicate has a biological basis. Spiegel moves seamlessly on to a final segment, the Hypnotic Induction Profile (HIP), a quick procedure to determine how effectively a patient might respond to therapy while under hypnosis. In a soft voice, he guides his patient into the trance state. "Imagine you're floating, very pleasantly, like an astronaut weightless above the earth, your left hand light and buoyant." His manner is disarming, casual. "When you open your eyes," he continues, "you'll find your arm floating up all by itself, and you'll find this rather amusing." Moments later, the young man opens his eyes and, just as Spiegel suggested, guffaws amazedly to find his arm wafting upward like a helium balloon.

In four minutes and twenty-six seconds, the assessment is complete. "You were just in and out of hypnosis," he tells the man, complimenting him on his "good natural endowment. You didn't go to sleep, you didn't blank out. I just helped you learn a method of concentration." The man, Dr. Spiegel says, is on the high end of his scale. He gets totally absorbed in movies, is extremely trusting of others, accepts before judging, leads with his heart.

Dr. Spiegel, after fifty years of work with thousands of patients, has developed criteria he uses as a "guide and predictor of how the person negotiates experience." He has conceptualized three clusters of personality traits—or as he prefers to call them, "mind-styles"—named after figures in Greek mythology. The low-hypnotizable, or Apollonian (after the Greek god of reason), is guided more by rationality than passion, has limited dissociative tendencies, and has a sharply focused attention. The Odyssean, after Homer's journeyer Odysseus, is what Spiegel calls "a wanderer of fluctuating moods," a moderate dissociator who can shift between mind and heart, seeking to balance internal stability with outward receptivity to change.

The Dionysian (named after the Greek god Dionysus) has "an extreme propensity to dissociate and a marked ability for total absorption." Dionysians, he notes, are more prone to everything from post-traumatic stress to multiple personality. Their bias is toward feelings over logic. They show an acute sensitivity to the nuances of the environment, and a pronounced vulnerability to persuasion.

Both Dr. Spiegel and his wife and colleague, Marcia Greenleaf, see an important practical application for this schema: utilizing mind-styles to augment each individual's healing response. Marcia, a former modern dancer with big eyes and a soft voice, spent years developing techniques of mental rehearsal and body imagery for athletes and dancers. Her own performance career, she says, made it seem an "ordinary truth" that the mind influences the body, though she adds with a warm laugh, "I also knew you couldn't execute a double pirouette just through the power of positive thinking." Marcia soon realized she had a talent for placing people in trance states, which she believes can not only promote self-discovery, but provide direct contact with the parts of the brain regulating physiology.

"The sooner we have a sense of people's way of processing their world," Greenleaf believes, "the more respectfully we can help them with the appropriate style of medical intervention." She demonstrated this in a groundbreaking study. Greenleaf found that patients with different "mind-styles" had measurably different rates of recovery from cardiac surgery. The highly hypnotizable Dionysian types required more time to stabilize their blood pressure after surgery, a critical factor since hypertensive blood flow can rupture newly grafted blood vessels. The reason, she concluded, was that the Dionysians, with their "readiness to respond uncritically to new signals, especially under stress," were reacting with more pronounced agitation to the atmosphere of the intensive care unit, with its beeping monitors and constant aura of emergency. Their personality styles were actually affecting—in this case, adversely—the physiology of healing. (When they were moved into more sedate private rooms, their recovery times improved.) The mid-range Odysseans did better, she says, because they could use critical judgment to screen out disturbing signals, yet were still receptive enough to incorporate positive ones, thus exhibiting more "adaptive and versatile responses." The Apollonian low-hypnotizables, on the other hand, tended to be less responsive to outer influences in general, whether negative stimuli *or* external help. Their approach was more self-contained, analytical do-it-yourself. "Each 'mind-style' has different optimum requirements," sums up Greenleaf. "It helps to remember it's not just people who start out with 'white-knuckled positive' attitudes who heal."

In our quest for an understanding of how personality style might affect remarkable recovery, we asked Dr. Spiegel to conduct his ten-question interview, called the AOD (for Apollonian, Odyssean, Dionysian), with our sample of nearly fifty remarkable recoveries. Not surprisingly, we found that the capacity for recovery can be found in all personality styles, and that it may be more a matter of finding an individual "right path" than having the "right stuff."

Once upon a time, in the kingdom of England, the whole of the known universe bifurcated with an earsplitting crack. On one side of the great divide were the fans of John, Paul, George, and Ringo with their Dionysian dreams of yellow submarines and marmalade skies; on the other side of the chasm were aficionados of the defiantly earthbound Rolling Stones. It was rose-colored glasses vs. skeptical squint; get high vs. get real; "All You Need Is Love" vs. "Streetfighting Man."

Lesley Bermingham, who tested at the Apollonian end of the AOD scale, was a hard-core Stones fan from the get-go. "They were the first time I had anything that looked like a hero," she says. Born in 1947 in the heart of the boomer demographic, she was named after Forties leading man and matinee idol Lesley Howard. "When I popped out as a female child," she says with a laugh, "my dad wasn't too enamored."

She'd worked as a hairdresser and cinema usherette before marrying young. "I didn't have enough brainpower to enter into government or anything." But if Lesley, a straightforward woman with a straightforward shock of gray in her strawberry blond hair, sounds any isolated false notes, it is a false modesty: After marriage and kids, she ran for district council, won, and became an effective local representative and finally a town deputy mayor. Her administrative style was pure Apollonian: no sweeping visions, just a methodical, hands-on approach to problem solving, cobblestone by cobblestone. "Rather than go to the committee and say, 'Mrs. Singer keeps getting broken into, what are we going to do?' I'd go straight to the housing officer, and say, 'Look, these people are in great distress, so let's do something.' Not, 'What about that hole in that road?' but bustle off on my little motorbike to the highway officer. I hardly dealt with the councils, which rattle on for hours and decide absolutely nothing." She describes herself as "very practical, mentally independent, and very much a controller."

Even her views of relationship are light on the romantic frosting and heavy on the *quid pro quo:* "Reciprocation's the main thing: If you don't get something back, well, stiff cheese!"

In the AOD schema, the Apollonian style is "highly organized, directive, judgmental, takes an analytical approach to problem solving, is consistent, vigilant, self-assured." The low-hypnotizable Apollonian "will not readily take in new stimuli, but will be most influenced by his own pre-existing beliefs, opinions, and private agenda." Apollonians tend, Dr. Spiegel adds, to give very accurate descriptions of their symptoms, unamalgamated with metaphor. Thus, when Lesley began to notice a persistent pain in her side, she brushed it aside until "it kept on and on hurting. So I went to my doctor and said, 'Look, I keep getting this bloody stitch in my ribs.' " She was surprised when her doctor informed her that her left lung was three quarters full of fluid. She had rationalized her "little breathlessness" going up stairs as " 'Well, you're getting old, dear,' even though I was all of thirty-something at the time!"

Lesley's doctor made her cancel her council meeting and book herself into a hospital for a lung aspiration to clear it of fluid, a painful procedure. "God help me, I wasn't polite. I suggested the doctor's parentage wasn't what it should be. I insult everyone equally!" Unwilling to docilely follow instructions, she demanded to be part of her own care. "My husband always says I jump in with my size 6's. You either put up or shut up, and I haven't yet shut up."

In hospital settings, in fact, Apollonians are often labeled resistant patients because they ask so many questions. But, notes Marcia Greenleaf, "If you spend a half hour talking with them, letting them participate in working out their care plan, they are wonderful both on their own behalf and also to the staff." Transferred to another hospital, Lesley says, "I bumped into a nice doctor and we sort of sat down and spoke about it. I was very chatty. I wanted to know everything about everything. And he agreed to keep me informed."

From then on, she was a full partner in her own treatment. The lung aspiration had revealed a cancer which further examination showed had metastasized from a kidney tumor. "The doctor told me he'd found a nasty, then said to the nurse, Get Mrs. Bermingham a cup of tea. And I thought, *Oy loy oy, I would have preferred a gin and lemonade.*

"I did have a bit of a weepy session," she says, "but then I just got on with it." She had the kidney surgically removed, then went home. She did her own form of meditation, though she doesn't choose to call it that. Unlike the elaborate visualizations reported by some patients, she started "a little private regime. You just lie there very still, and you just say, 'I've got cancer—get the hell out of here.' Really and truly." She prayed, too, after her own fashion. "I'm not the kind of person that asks for things. I don't, you know, *winge, winge.* It was more just a request, really." Meanwhile, local nuns prayed for her. She received "just sacks" of mail ("The local councilor's the bee's knees," she says with a wink).

By her next X ray, her lung metastases were gone. Her doctor, she says, was "gobsmacked."

Lesley's trials were by no means over. She later developed a tumor to the brain, which she managed to view optimistically with the concrete logic of an engineer: "Those little nasty pieces had made their way up to the top block, which I said to myself was good, actually: As long as it's gone up there, it can't go anywhere else." She was subsequently irradiated (after she had "very cheekily" requested the radiotherapy be postponed four days to allow her to complete her final district election). She responded favorably to what her doctor calls "a mild dose" of radiation and has been cancer-free for over ten years.

Lesley had a moment—several moments—when she flirted with religion. Marcia Greenleaf notes, "An Apollonian in acute situations can be motivated to take on the characteristics of other types," and Lesley seems a case in point. "After you've had a threatening salvo shot at you," she says, "you get very close to your Maker, promise to do this, that, and the other. But after a period of time you revert back." Asked to account for her survival, she says with an emphatic toss of her head, "Sheer bloody determination."

We had each of our cases submit a questionnaire (see appendix three). A look at Lesley's results is revealing. She checked very few of the factors labeled "contributed significantly to your recovery"—only five of thirty-five possible items—typical of the Apollonian's go-it-alone approach. (Asked to mark off personal traits she thought were significant, the only one she double-checked was "independent.") Her choices from a list of possible psychospiritual factors were for the most part those that implied active grappling: seeing disease as a challenge, belief in positive outcome, sense of control, taking responsibility for disease, fighting spirit, renewed desire and/or will to live, positive emotions, and a commitment to living.

On the "pie chart" we asked each person to proportionally fill in with what they thought was most important in their healing. Lesley, using a ruler, sliced the chart precisely into two-thirds and two-sixths (see page 322). In one large slice she wrote, "Family is very important. Unfortunately they don't always have a clue what to say. Just show them you are not a victim anymore." On one of her two sixths, she said, "I will not be told I can't do it." On another one-third she penned a rational, unsentimental recipe for dealing with medical settings: "When in the hospital look around. You will always find or hear of someone much worse off. Use technology as you would a weapon, and enhance it with your thoughts of recovering. Work with the doctors 50-50. They can't heal you if you have already given up."

One of Lesley's doctors was Tim Oliver, an oncologist at Royal London Hospital. Referring to her case, he notes that "surgically removing a cancerous kidney may cause regression of distant metastases by removing the bulk of the tumor burden from the body." The mechanism of how the body can defeat the remaining cancerous tumors, he admits, is still not understood. Overall estimates of prolonged regressions of kidney cancer have ranged from .5 percent to twenty-four percent of cases (though death can occur from recurrent tumor a decade or more later). Skeptical of "media-led hype of miracle cures," Dr. Oliver is nonetheless intrigued by the possibility that psychosocial factors may on occasion influence the behavior of cancer. His broad, thoughtful-looking face exudes caring. Drumming his fingers on his folded arms, he says, "It is vital that doctors give patients a minimally realistic, faint concept of hope. I communicate some enthusiasm about at least the possibility of cure in a desperate situation. Regressions tell us there are things beyond our eyes that we cannot know." Then he smiles. "Of course, I am expressing a slight heresy."

Dr. Larry Norton wouldn't find it heretical. Had he been Lesley's doctor, he might have made deliberate medical use of her personality in his treatment. When he was in medical school at Columbia University, Norton took Dr. Spiegel's postgraduate class in medical hypnosis. As chief of Breast and Gynecologic Cancer Medicine Services at Memorial Sloan-Kettering Cancer Center, he uses Dr. Spiegel's assessment techniques to determine the mind-styles of his patients. "It gives me a method," he emphasizes, "to determine the proper way to explain something to a given patient, the proper way to develop options, and the proper way to help them handle difficulties that arise in treatment."

Dr. Norton has observed that people who are low in hypnotizability (Lesley is a good example) "tend to be very concrete. They don't like ambiguity. They want a lot of hard facts. They like to make their own decisions and restrict surrendering control to anybody—physicians, especially. They are very precise when they report their symptoms, down to the minute they felt a pain, or what they were eating when they felt nausea."

At the other end of the scale, Dr. Norton sees people who "tend to be more poetic in their description of symptoms. They have a greater tolerance for ambiguity. They also tend to be very suggestible. Every doctor," he explains, "has a patient to whom he or she has suggested a symptom—poking the patient's belly, for instance, and asking, 'Are you sure you don't have a pain there?'—who then develops that pain. I've seen patients wind up in surgery because a certain symptom was repeatedly suggested to them."

Here we approach a realm of personality explored earlier in this book: Researcher T. X. Barber's category of people who can "feel-remember-think-imagine" in ways that markedly affect blood flow, temperature, and immune response (chapter four). Barber has noticed that perhaps four percent of the highly hypnotizable population exhibit a particularly strong "psychosomatic plasticity," an unusually powerful ability to transform thoughts and feelings into physiological facts.

Similarly, researcher Ian Wickramasekera of the University of Virginia suggests, "There is growing evidence that such people's psychosocial and physiological functions—if you will, their software and hardware—are closer together in an almost topographical sense." Noting that such topography might be treacherous in terms of psychosomatic disease-proneness, Wickramasekera— whom we also enlisted in our psychological testing (see appendix four)—speculates it might be more easily traversible in terms of healing. He writes that a doctor or therapist might "reverse the direction of activity of one of the very mechanisms (high hypnotic ability) generating psychophysiological disorders . . . turning it around and using specifically that ability to make them well." We wondered if such a hypothesized mechanism might have played a role in the healing of a young woman named Geertje Brakel.

Geertje Brakel lives in a little white row house in Rotterdam, a Dutch port city guarded by sentinel windmills and teeming with bicyclists and yellow-faced trolleys. The house is adrift in a sea of plants—pot upon pot, from robust philodendrons to effusive bursts of spiky chrysanthemum. Her small outdoor terrace is an urban Tuileries of greenery whose chlorophyll embrace threatens to obscure the house from view.

Geertje, an attractive fortyish woman whose tinted prescription glasses border on rose colored, sits on her couch thumbing through a scrapbook of the person she once was. A succession of black-and-white photos show a pretty twenty-seven-year-old woman with a pixie haircut and deep-carved lines under her eyes, part Siren, part wounded sylph. In one shot, she is draped in a long black coat, her face beneath windblown hair an impassive mask, a dead ringer for the young suicidal poet Sylvia Plath.

Plath was one of Geertje's idols. "Like me, she found the world an ugly, painful place," she says. Geertje's friends became accustomed to her sitting spookily in a corner without saying a word, taking long, shuddering drags on a cigarette. For years, she had thought of suicide almost daily, passing her life, she says, "in my own fantasy-world." But one day a yet harsher reality penetrated her self-oppressive atmosphere. A routine checkup revealed enlarged ovaries. Exploratory surgery showed a fast-growing, inoperable cancer. She awoke to find a doctor sitting by her bedside, his mouth grimly set, explaining they could perhaps lengthen her life with chemo, but not save it. "It was in his eyes that I'm going to die," she told us in halting English. "Instantly I decided I would make myself well because they could not. The strange thing was, I felt good. There was a feeling of pure life inside of me from that minute on."

She declined chemotherapy and asked her boyfriend to look up books on alternative cancer treatment. She quickly decided to follow a stringent vegetarian diet she'd read about. Her doctor called it "useless self-punishment." She saw it as much of a ritual as a regimen for health. "I would say to myself with each bite, 'I eat this for my life. I don't have to die. It's only some cells of mine doing strange things they are not supposed to do. I have a big, strong body, and it can make them go right again.'"

But it was the sudden change in the very fiber of her existence that amazed her as much as those around her. "I thought, well, if I only have months to live, I would be completely crazy to just do what society or my parents want from me. It's no longer necessary I do things I hate; it is necessary I do things I love." What followed was an overnight transformation. She had been miserable; now "I felt very happy within me, laughing a lot." She had been afraid of meeting people. Suddenly, she says, "I felt connected to people for the first time in my life, like a dream coming true." Whereas she had been silent, now she "was talking very much, telling my girlfriends and my boyfriend I was convinced I didn't have to die. And they told me, 'Whatever your decision is, we will stay behind you.' They believed in me. And we developed a deep trust. Everything I sent to them, they sent back to me, and that made me stronger."

Geertje tested at the Dionysian end of the AOD scale. Perhaps because such people tend to be highly influenced by their surroundings, Geertje cut herself off from her parents, who had begun a sad deathwatch apparent in every nuance. Illness seemed to make her threshold of receptivity even more acute: "I became all at once sensitive to smell. I could not bear any perfume, or the feeling of jewelry on my skin. I couldn't stand the sound of automobiles. I was walking outside and sometimes shouting at cars because they made such a noise and such a bad smell. I found I could only love the smell of nature, the sounds of the birds, sea, wind, rain." She sought out positive input, spending her days dancing to her favorite music and reading her favorite books.

She was also buffeted by unpredictable outbursts of emotion.

"Two or three times a day, I was screaming in rage," she recalls. Her boyfriend chalked it up to anxiety, but an alternative healer she began seeing encouraged her to "express my emotions, whatever they are. I didn't feel guilty from that time on, and screamed and yelled when I felt like it."

For some reason, before her doctors' uncomprehending eyes, monthly ultrasound scans showed that her cancer's march had slowed and then halted. The scans, which Geertje used almost as a form of biofeedback—"a way to know when it's going wrong and when it's going right"—documented that after nine months, the cancer had diminished by a third. Finally it dwindled away entirely.

She celebrated her wellness; perhaps overexulted. She bought "very strange clothes, like stepping out of a Fellini movie." She stayed out dancing all night, coming home at noon to lie in the sun, sleep, and then wake up to go out again. But after two and a half years of health, Geertje discovered her cancer had regrown and spread. Her doctors operated and removed both her ovaries, informing her that even with chemotherapy she would have only a twenty- to thirty-percent chance of living five years. Geertje again declined to take "the chemicals." But she felt blackly depressed, suddenly depleted of her will to live, uncertain "whether I can do this again."

Lying in her hospital bed barely eating, she was assailed by frightening visions that she saw "with my eyes open, like a color TV set." She saw her beloved blue sea freeze over and towering frozen mountains spring out of it. In the frigid wilderness, she saw "a strange thing coming toward me, a devil that wanted to kill me." What followed was a terrifying hallucinatory encounter: "It grabbed me, but I had a knife and managed to kill the thing. More devils came, and I fought them on the ice, in dark holes, and then—my God!—I saw them coming through the windows of the hospital." She fought desperately. Each time she killed one, it would be transformed into "an innocent creature, sometimes a cat, sometimes a spider."

Her girlfriends, dismayed at her despair and mental disorientation, decided after consulting one of her doctors to try a shock tactic. They had been painting Geertje's house as a homecoming present. "They told me, 'Well, we have decided to respect your decision to die, and don't see the necessity for painting your house anymore. We're preparing for your funeral instead.' This very much surprised me, shook me up. In the deep, dark hole, I suddenly remembered I really want to be fully alive—good, bad, or in between. I said to my girlfriends, 'Well, now, bring me some food; bring me something to drink.' They looked in my eyes and saw the same thing they'd seen seven years before. So then they painted the house."

She decided not to continue her diet. Whereas an Apollonian low-hypnotizable might have seen a regimen as concrete nutritional medicine, for Geertje, "it had been more a process of mind, a symbol, a way to connect the outer with the inner." When a friend recommended a psychologist who was also a hypnotherapist, she leaped at the chance. On meeting him, she felt an instant sense of "one-hundred-percent trust. For the first time, somebody totally accepted me for who I was. He never told me, 'You must do this or you must do that.'" For two years, she traveled five hours round trip every two weeks to see him. "He knew exactly what I was thinking. We were two persons on one line." (Geertje repeatedly cites positive reinforcement from others as a healing force. Perhaps for those on the Dionysian end of the spectrum, who find it difficult to filter out unwanted stimuli, other people provide a much-needed buffer.)

Geertje again felt the volatile moodiness, with sudden outbursts of temper. And again, she was swept up in personal change. She began wearing the glasses that, despite her nearsightedness, she had always kept in their case in her purse. "I had thought, well, I don't see well without spectacles, but the world is too ugly to see. But I did put on my spectacles and thought, my God, there are beautiful things!" She began riding a bicycle—"very strange, because I hate going on the bicycle."

She had left the hospital with three tumors of several centimeters each. "After ten months, all together, they disappeared. And then I thought, I am better."

Her doctors concur. Dr. Hans A. Wynen of St. Clara Hospital, lowering his bifocals closer to the center of his good square Hollander features, says, "I thought her chances of being alive after ten years were just about zero." Adds pathologist Marco DeVries, who first examined her slides, "She is probably the best medically documented case of spontaneous regression I know of in the world."

Dr. DeVries invites Geertje to peer through a dual eyepiece microscope at her old pathology slide, pointing out the swollen purple nuclei of her cancer cells. It takes no knowledge of cell anatomy to pick out the horror. Some look like malign toadstools, some like night-blooming orchids, others like the speckled eggs of a flesh-eating prehistoric bird. "Now it is fourteen years and here you are sitting across from me." He is obviously moved. His eyes grow tender behind his outsized glasses. "If I really believed the pathologist in me, I wouldn't believe my eyes." Geertje beams at her ally.

Geertje continued going to the hospital every six months, a ritual she follows to this day. "Two years ago they saw markers in my blood that there was more cancer cell activity. I told my doctor, 'I'll come back in six weeks and you can look again and it will be better.' Six weeks later, the tumor markers were gone. The doctor was deeply puzzled. "He asked me, 'What are you doing to reverse this?' " Geertje pauses. "I said, it's just a feeling, something I know instinctively, from the inside. The emotions come up, and something happens in my body because of them, but I don't have words for it. It is just a big, big trust."

If Geertje can't explain the "something that happens" inside her, how can we account for her healing? Clearly, she exhibits Dionysian traits. Her hypnotherapist, she says, told her she was the best patient he'd ever had. "Many times of the day, I'm in a little trance. It's very easy for me to do."

She describes the enlivening (though sometimes painful) sensory acuity that seems to be one of the hallmarks of altered states. She has vivid childhood recall "from when I was one year old." She had imaginary playmates, she says, "all the time. I was always dreaming, living in my head." Her inner fears were equally vivid: When she was seven, she once clearly saw "a monster's hand" grab at her from under her bed, and thenceforth refused to sleep with the light off. (In this and other ways, she fits psychologist T. X. Barber's criteria for the "fantasy-prone personality," who have "real"-seeming daydreams and childhood experiences with imaginary playmates as well as "bogeymen and monsters." Such people, Barber says, also tend to exhibit pronounced mind-body plasticity).

Indeed, Geertje reports some of her fantasies are accompanied by powerful physical sensations, suggestive of psychologist Ian Wickramasekera's comment of "having software and hardware closer together." In one archetypal encounter, she says: "Just as if there were two persons in the room, I saw Death standing next to Life. The stronger Death became, the stronger I could feel the energies of Life rushing through my body. The heat was so strong that when someone was sitting next to me, they asked me, 'Are you a stove or a heater or something?' " During her remarkable recovery, her emotions, too, created noticeable physical sensations: "I was very fast irritated, and my head was red and hot all the time."

In filling out our form, Geertje checked off so many traits she felt described her that she omitted only eight out of sixty. The blanks themselves suggest a pattern: She leaves out well organized, neat, hardworking, pragmatic, rigid. She is also the only one who wrote, entirely *outside* the circle of her pie chart (page 321): "The source [of healing] was the switch from death to life, the movement of jumping out of the dark into the light, but in the end I have no words for the movement."

Most of us, statistically fifty percent, are in the Odyssean or mid-range segment of the mind-style scale. Odysseus was not a Greek deity but a mortal man, wandering between the Apollonian and Dionysian poles. Such people are adaptable, able to utilize both concrete thinking and abstract fantasy, depending upon the situation at hand.

Inge Sundstrom, who scored as an Odyssean, is a sturdily compact woman whose tousled shock of blunt-cut reddish hair makes her look like a mischievous middle-aged boy. "A hundred-percent Swedish," she jokes, "but zero percent tall, blond, and good-looking." Her husband, Eric, gives her a fond look. Eric is tall and silver bearded, his owlish glasses giving him a pastoral mien. They laugh easily, clearly in love, freely telling stories about one another.

"We're both know-it-alls," Inge offers. "So our deal is, we take turns being totally right. On even-numbered days, he gets to say the picture's hung too low, and that's that. On uneven days, I get to say it's too high. That keeps it equal."

"Except when we arm-wrestle," Eric says, as Inge laughs and reddens slightly, knowing what's coming. His wife, Eric explains, was once the formidable and much-feared women's state amateur wrist-wrestling champion "until one day she accidentally broke a young lady's arm."

"But that was it," Inge interjects. "After that, I stopped."

It was just a year after she and Eric were married that her gynecologist discovered what he diagnosed as a benign tumor in Inge's uterus. At first she'd resisted the idea of a hysterectomy: When the brisk young surgeon had told her she'd have to lose her ovaries—"It won't make any difference, you don't need them," he assured her—she had responded tartly, "Doctor, if we cut your balls off and put you on male hormones, would *you* know the difference?"

In the end she'd acquiesced, and quickly recovered. A year later, in 1991, while working in her garden, she'd noticed a painful swelling around her ear. *Bug bite,* she thought. But when she developed a high fever, her doctor sent her to the hospital for intravenous antibiotics. A routine chest X ray revealed shadows on her lungs, and the subsequent CAT scan ratified the unthinkable: "Out come these pictures filled with dozens of white spots that make my lungs look like a star map," she says. "Like somebody had shotgunned her with tumors," Eric adds.

Her doctors sawed off a section of her rib, like tree surgeons trimming an elm, to pluck out one of the gumball-sized growths for biopsy. The word came back from the pathology lab: leiomyosarcoma, a rare, slow-growing cancer with no effective treatment. Her oncologist—whom she remembers as a "little, sad man"—told her the news.

"Will I live a couple of years?" she asked.

"No," said the sad man, shaking his head. "Not that long."

"A year?"

"Six months," he replied.

Inge was incensed. "It was like putting the evil eye on someone." But even worse than dying was the thought "that the disease is going to steal your air." Inge flashed back to when she was five years old and had nearly asphixiated from whooping cough. Or the time she sucked a rolled-up slice of salami into her windpipe and her father had turned her upside down, her jaws clenched tight and eyes rolled up in her head, until his frantic efforts dislodged the obstructing delicacy. It had left her with a lifelong fear of choking—"If one of my kids coughs during dinner, I'm flying out of my chair ready to give her the Heimlich maneuver."

Now she lay in the hospital, feeling a crippling despair. How had this happened? She'd always been pragmatic about her health—had never smoked, had eaten fresh fruits and vegetables, exercised. She thought, incongurously, how she loved to thrift-shop, how "finding a forty-dollar silk blouse for three bucks would make my day. But having cancer made all the silk blouses in the world seem like dust." She resolved to kill herself if the pain became insufferable.

But then something in her rallied. She wrote in her diary: *"No, we are not supposed to die as the doctors say. I refuse to sit in death's waiting room, refuse to prepare for my own cremation. I am not one of the people the statistics spoke of. Even if 999,999 die, I am the one that beats the odds, the one in a million."*

A day after her lung biopsy, Eric remembers, "She was up and on her feet, pushing the IV stand. She told me, " 'I'm not just going to lie there. I need to get up and use my lungs.' "

A few days after she went back to work, a customer stopped in with a wool coat to shorten for Christmas. "This will be my last Christmas," Inge blurted out, and broke down in tears. The woman, shocked, returned the next day with a glass jug brimming with brown liquid, which she proclaimed was a "black ash brew" her seventy-five-year-old mother took daily in a shot glass. It consisted of boiled bark, twigs, and leaves supplied by an eighty-year-old Norwegian who vouchsafed it as a panacea.

Inge thought back to her own parents, hardy, self-reliant homesteaders who'd settled in Saskatchewan, her father trapping muskrats during the Depression when the food ran short. "They were a day's ride in horse and wagon from a doctor. They believed you had to mend yourself." She remembered her mother's home remedies—the spring tonic of stinging nettle soup that tasted better than spinach, an infusion of garlic oil for ear infection, a pillowcase filled with oatmeal for her father's aching shoulders.

In classic Odyssean style, Inge was able to draw on a variety of resources from both the outer world and the inner, picking and choosing practically between options. She had taken to waking up in the middle of the night, so she took her herbal potion in a wee hours ritual "instead of lying there and worrying." She'd make herself think of things that made her happy and "send that smile through my whole body." Or she'd do "an inventory check," first telling her heart and her lungs, "Thank you for working so well," then taking mental excursions "up into my brain to see if I can pull some switches in there for well-being." Sometimes, in sleep, she'd have flying dreams as she did when she was a girl, soaring over the deciduous northern trees, her flannel nightgown billowing, her hands outstretched and glazed with moonlight.

Other times, if she couldn't sleep, she'd practice breathing in, slowly and deeply past the unwary tumor sentries, inhaling delicious air for five, six heartbeats, visualizing her immune system destroying her cancer. An accomplished artist, she painted her white cells as tough-looking creatures with strong arms "bristling with power," swimming among her red blood cells hunting down cancer cells, "breaking off bits of them, squeezing them into smithereens, tearing them down, liquidating them."

Her diary tells the tale of her struggle for survival:

"Hello! Hello! Where are you?" I shut my eyes and search desperately for my immune system's main office. "Why do you have an unlisted number? We need to communicate. You—my body—we're making a big mistake. The doctors call our mistake leiomyosarcoma, and they don't have any cure or medicine to help. If we don't get it corrected and eradicated, it's the end of us."

She drew strength from memories of her grandmother, the one who laughed "like a loon" in public and unabashedly smoked men's cigars, "going *poof, poof, poof* through the house, 'to make it smell nice.' " Inge danced around the house with her seven- and eight-year-old grandsons, "playing follow the leader, doing goofy things to peppy music," momentarily feeling again like the child she once was—an energetic tomboy "with freckles, fire-red hair, and scabs on the knees" who lived on a dead end by the river where neighborhood kids danced in the street in the early evening.

She did yoga every day. She rode the kids' sleds down the hill behind the house, zooming over the crusted whiteness. She went on a "vitamin kick" at the urging of "an old flower child from the Sixties," drank water from the reverse-osmosis system her husband bought her, and avoided "any hair dye, antiperspirant, perfume, toothpaste that I wouldn't stick in my mouth and eat."

She stayed away from "people who give off bad vibes," stopped watching the news ("the world seemed too cruel"), and decided to forgive Ronald Reagan for his political sins ("you can't have bad feelings eating on you"). She sought her own modicum of balance. "You can't dwell on the negative," she says, "but you can't be a Pollyanna either."

One day, on a visit to the doctor's office, opening the envelope whose contents were usually an Academy Award from Hell, she savored a surprising victory: Rather than the steady growth and spread of tumors her doctor had predicted, the constellation of spots was noticeably smaller.

Inge was exultant. She brought her films and medical records to the university hospital at Madison and delightedly, a little defiantly, showed her CAT scans to the surgeon. "Look, they're shrinking," she said, pointing to the dwindling blobs of light.

He responded curtly, "We don't believe in Santa Claus."

"How about all these little ones that aren't there anymore?" she urged, a little crestfallen. He assured her that since scans were taken at five-millimeter intervals, they "could easily fall on a place where you can't see the tumors." The oncologist, however, was more encouraging, telling her, "You're doing better than we can do for you. Just go home and keep doing it."

Typical of Odysseans, Inge was able selectively to screen out one doctor's dim view and drink in another one's enthusiasm. Inge's pie-chart slices (see page 321) depict the adaptability often seen in the Odyssean personality style, the ability to combine a variety of beliefs and behaviors in response to crisis. "Love and support of family and friends" occupies the largest slice. In approximately equal importance, her pie contains "yoga, meditation, relaxation, stress reduction, visualization, planning to live to ninety, eat well, walks, be outside every day, avoid dwelling on horrible things, painting, doing creative things, dance, laugh, sing."

Somehow, Inge feels, she learned "the ungrowing of cancer tumors," though she isn't quite sure how. "When my husband puts his loving arms around me, is that strong happy feeling a direct line to my immune system?" she wonders. Or was it her "superstitious" yelling at her disease *Leiomyosarcoma, get out of there, get out of there*"? as she took her cherished morning walks, remembering her mother's admonition: "What you believe, will be"?

Today, says Dr. Meyer, her family physician, "It appears she doesn't have any active tumor. There are still a few small areas on her CAT scan, but my assumption is at this point these are all scar tissue."

He shakes his head in sincere puzzlement. "Here's someone we'd diagnosed, convened a tumor board to discuss her case, and finally decided there was no good treatment, no chemo or radiation, that would be good for leiomyosarcoma metatstatic to the chest. I have not one clue, at least not a scientific one."

Inge puts on her Russian fur hat and turquoise down jacket, slides her blue-tick hound, Shiloh, into a red warmer vest, and sallies forth into the champagne-glass chill of a Wisconsin morning for a "walk around the block"—three miles through seldom-traveled roads, cutting through farms and fields, running under ramshackle wooden covered bridges, their breath making fat, steam-locomotive clouds in the frozen air.

About twenty minutes later, big, fat flakes laze from the sky. "When you go under the big power line, you can hear the snowflakes hissing and frying overhead," she says. When she is out of range of houses and people and the occasional car drifting to work, she sings, loudly, first the innocent songs of her childhood—"The Happy Wanderer" and "Beautiful May, Welcome"—and then a boisterous Swedish drinking song, delivered like a Judy Garland belter. "You gotta use your lungs," she says with a grin.

You gotta use your lungs. Inge's personal watchword for seizing life is a fitting metaphor for a trait we noticed frequently in our study. To the Greeks, the lungs were the seat of inspiration, of *pneuma* or life-force; the region of the *thymos,* the blood-soul, the essence of selfhood. The lungs engage in active exchange with the environment, taking in, giving out, *working* at the task of survival. Similarly, it is not just who we are but how we enact ourselves in the world—our behavior—that carries us through life.

The preliminary results of our study show there is no fixed set of behaviors leading to remarkable recovery. But Inge Sundstrom, with her "leiomeyosarcoma get out of there!" attitude, her absolute *insistence* on survival, exhibited a major common denominator of our sample. Over seventy percent of our cases checked off factors that connoted an active grappling with illness—self-attributed characteristics such as fighting spirit, seeing disease as a challenge, taking responsibility, and the highest score (seventy-five percent), "belief in a positive outcome."

We borrowed the term "fighting spirit" from Dr. Steven Greer, who used it in a 1977 study to define a factor he found in longer-term survivors of breast cancer. Greer and his colleagues delineated five separate categories of psychological response to diagnosis: denial, fighting spirit, stoic acceptance, anxious/depressed acceptance, and helpless/hopeless response. At five years after biopsy, seventy-five percent of those patients who showed denial or fighting spirit were still alive versus thirty-five percent of those patients who exhibited either stoic acceptance or helplessness/hopelessness. At the ten-year follow-up, Greer and associates found that, though their population had shrunk due to mortality, the same approximate 2:1 ratio of survival still obtained.

We, too, noticed a quality that might be categorized as constructive denial in our subjects. Though Geertje Brakel checked off "acceptance of the disease" on our list, she also penciled in, "not accepting the connection cancer = death." In the same spirit, Lesley Bermingham's stiff-cheese, just-get-on-with-it approach included telling herself, "I've got cancer—get the hell out of here." Inge Sundstrom, against all odds, proclaimed herself "the one-in-a-million" who was "not supposed to die" of her disease. "Denial," writes Dr. Marco DeVries, "provides the time and space necessary to mobilize internal and external resources for the reorganization of life and for personal transformation. When they recognize that denial is a creative stage, health professionals may come to respect its positive aspects. . . ."

Between sixty and seventy percent of our subjects attributed their survival to what might be called "receptive" factors like faith, meditation, and prayer. Again, this finding was in accord with several previous researchers: Spiritual beliefs were a common theme in a 1975 study of five cases of spontaneous remission by Dr. Yujiro Ikemi. Though Ikemi noted that each person seemed "to have overcome cancer by accepting responsibility for resolving such a crisis for themselves," nearly all possessed a passionate religious faith.

Most intriguingly, we had asked a catchall question to see if some of the unusual, even "far-out" experiences that had cropped up in our interviews were at all common: "Have you ever had feelings or experiences (physical, psychological or spiritual) for which there seemed to be no logical or rational explanation?" We were a little surprised when nearly sixty percent answered in the affirmative, the great majority of these respondents falling either in the Odyssean ("mid-range") or Dionysian ("high") range. (Most, though not all, of our Apollonian "lows" answered the query with a simple "No.") Inge Sundstrom wrote, "I have vivid dreams in which I spend time with long-dead family members and wake up feeling their love." Geertje Brakel reported when she took ballet as a child, she would have the strange sensation of "going up to the ceiling looking down on myself dancing. This feeling of being out of my body was like paradise," a sensation she still has when she dances. Wally Shore (chapter four) told us: "Just after D day in Normandy I had a vivid dream of my maternal grandfather . . . I found out after the war he had died just at that time."

Others described feelings of being "spiritually directed," or having "ESP kinds of experiences." Sometimes these experiences were life-altering. One wrote, "In the hospital one night when I felt a ball of fire in my chest and I thought I was dying. Instead I realized that the message from my Higher Power was that I would survive. I felt healing from that moment on. How would I live the life given me? I must change, and I did."

It is hard to know how to interpret these results, for here we tread on unmapped terrain. We can report preliminary findings, but can only offer raw conjecture as to their relevance, if any, to the healing process. As such self-reports surfaced throughout the researching of this book, however, we found ourselves wondering whether such unusual experiences could betoken alterations in physiology conducive to healing. The fact that such a large percentage of our cases were capable, at least on occasion, of what appear to be states of dissociation or absorption might mean they were also susceptible to the placebo effect.

As we have speculated earlier, the ability to enter altered states—which cuts across personality styles—may enhance psychosomatic healing. In one famous experiment in psychoimmunology, five people, including two who were considered "deep-trance subjects" (the approximate equivalent of our Dionysians) and two classified as "medium-trance" (i.e., Odysseans) were injected with a purified protein derivative of tuberculin. Four exhibited the expected skin reaction of reddening and swelling as the immune system rushed to the area to combat the bacterial agent. However, after being placed in trance and given a suggestion that they would not respond, the four who had previously shown a positive reaction now did not. Their immune systems had been disarmed, so to speak, by a suggestion.

The report quotes the suggestion they were given verbatim: "You are now different—you will no longer react to the injection as you did before . . . your skin is now different, your left arm is now different, you are now different."

This emphasis on "differentness" presented us with an interesting paradox: On the one hand, we had been interested in the healing power of what we refer to as congruence—of being and acting in accord with the deepest self. However, it has been noted by a number of researchers that extraordinary healing is often preceded by profound personal change, sometimes even what seems like a startlingly different personality.

Our curiosity about how different personality types might be related to different physiological patterns led us to look for clues to remarkable recovery in the world of so-called multiple personalities (now classified as "Dissociative Identity Disorder," or DID). We came across a psychiatrist's report on a patient who was normally allergic to grass, as evidenced by her wheezing response to allergens and by skin reaction to a standard "scratch test." But when she was required to mow the lawn, the girl would switch into a "boy alter" personality who displayed no such symptoms. Like the tuberculin test, the scratch test is a measure of immune system response, which must give us pause when considering how the immune system might rally to cause the disappearance of cancer. Can it rally, too, in response to an alteration in what we call the personality?

The body of data for shifts in physiology correlating to shifts in personality is impressive. One recent paper sums up a raft of psychophysiological studies of DID (though cautioning that most of the studies did not rule out "spontaneous self-hypnosis and hypersuggestibility"). Clinically significant differences were found in eyesight variables like visual acuity, manifest refraction, color vision, muscle balance, pupil size, corneal curvature, keratomy, and intraocular pressure corresponding to shifts in personality. The paper cites another study which found consistent variations in levels of thyroid hormone (T4) in different personality states. A 1984 study found each "personality" had distinctly different central nervous system functioning. Another paper remarked upon differences in blood pressure between each personality. Most of the mechanisms so far implicated in remarkable recovery—immune and nervous system functioning, hormones, blood flow, and inflammation—all seem to be affected.

DID—what is popularly called multiple personality disorder—afflicts perhaps one-half of one percent of the population. Sarah Clauson (not her real name), a bright, articulate, resourceful, middle-aged technician at a Midwestern hospital in an inner-city area, is one. Sarah is a patient of Dr. Bennett Braun, founder and medical director of the nation's first in-patient unit for dissociative disorders at Chicago's Rush Presbyterian Hospital.

Braun had warned that Sarah often greeted strangers as "Sentinel," a tough, streetwise "subpersonality" who acted as gatekeeper to her emotional barricades. But watching Sarah tenderly affix paste-smeared electrodes to an elderly man with Alzheimer's disease, we saw no sign of this sometimes belligerent fragment of self, or of her other "alters": "Mona" (whom she describes as "the ultimate courtesan—she recites French poetry and sings Edith Piaf") or the other fourteen personalities she is integrating, under Dr. Braun's guidance, into a more coherent identity.

Eleven years ago, Sarah was diagnosed with diabetes. Her blood-sugar level is far higher than "Sentinel's" and she must adjust the dosage of her insulin injections accordingly. Here is a detail of great potential significance. The science of endocrinology was virtually founded around the substance of insulin, until recently thought to be produced only in the pancreas. (It has since been discovered that some areas of the brain contain more insulin than the pancreas itself.) Diabetes is a disease, which we normally conceive of as a fixed condition. But the radical implications of Sarah's case are hard to overlook: Apparently, diabetes—at least in some rare individuals—is not just a disease but a state of being, a particular refraction of personality modulated by a previously unknown neuroendocrine connection.

So-called multiple personality disorder is a painful, pathological state. But perhaps a far milder fluidity of self, a change from a monochromatic personality pattern to a fuller blossoming of selfhood, is conducive to remarkable recovery. Several researchers have noted sudden psychological turning points (in Ikemi's words, "existential shifts") preceding remarkable recovery. Dr. Marco DeVries and his associates found that a group of spontaneous remission cases they studied all showed a relatively sudden change toward increased autonomous behavior, and significantly altered attitudes toward illness, treatment, relationships, and spiritual beliefs.

Certainly, we saw this in many of our own cases. Inge Sundstrom not only changed her behavior, going on a "vitamin kick" and drinking her "black ash brew," but allowed more aspects of herself to emerge. She became a playful child, dancing and sledding and doing "goofy things" with her grandchildren. Lesley Bermingham, on the Apollonian "low" end of the scale, refers to alterations in her sense of self in her precisely demarcated pie chart: "If it helps, pretend you are someone else. Ask the questions someone else who has had all the tests would ask. Someone else can take it all in and give you strength."

Dr. Marco DeVries' sometime patient, Geertje Brakel, reported to us many instances of suddenly feeling like another person whose approach to life was 180 degrees different. Dr. Johannes Schilder, who along with Dr. DeVries has followed Geertje's case with interest, theorizes that a crisis like illness can summon forth parts of the self suppressed earlier in life, parts that may seem almost like different personalities. They are recruited with all their drives, resources, and skill sets, showing up in unusual behaviors and activities. Logically," he adds, "you'll also see manifestations of pain and distress attached to that wounded part of personality that was so long unexpressed."

Dr. Schilder has followed a circuitous path before arriving at the study of remarkable recovery. Asked how he got interested in the subject, the thirty-seven-year-old Schilder, who scarcely looks old enough to have completed a medical degree and a PhD, let alone scoured the world for miracles, answers playfully, "Ask my mama." Fascinated since childhood by New Testament healing accounts (even after, as he puts it, "I dropped my faith"), Schilder traveled to Africa to look for miraculous cases among missionaries, hoping to discover unknown psychobiological principles that could explain the mystery of remission. Schilder, whose towering frame is topped by a sunlit thatch of blond hair, was hard to miss as he strode into bush outposts on what ultimately proved a quixotic search. "I came back with empty hands to Rotterdam," he says, "only to have my mentor, Dr. DeVries, tell me, 'If you're looking for miracles, sit down. I've found a few here in your own backyard.' "

Schilder performed an initial study of seven cancer patients who had spontaneous remissions. All, he found, had a jagged "fracture" in their lives that had somehow been reforged in the crucible of mortal crisis. This had happened when a "mobilizing event" had pushed them "beyond the pale," causing them to "regain access to something essential to them" and become "more autonomous." What appeared to be a radical change to others—even an eruption of crude emotional behavior—was a reclaiming of this more congruent selfhood that had been lost. As one of his patients observed emphatically: "I resumed myself."

Schilder cites a woman with ovarian cancer metastasized to the uterus who "had a shift at the moment of diagnosis when told she had four months to live. 'That's absurd nonsense,' she said. She began stealing food from the kitchen, smuggling wine into the hospital, making jokes with her doctor, a completely different person than she was the year before.

He also reports the case of a carpenter, who just before undergoing a spectacular (but unfortunately, temporary) remission became, according to his wife, "very rebellious, pigheaded, dreadful in a way he had never been." He had had fits of anger and weeping in which he would bang his fist on the table. His every act and attitude broadcast the message, his wife told Dr. Schilder, "that 'I have very little time left, and I will have things the way I want them.' "

Dr. Schilder refers often to the work of Italian psychiatrist Roberto Assagioli. Assagioli believed that the notion of an immutable, indivisible selfhood was an illusion. We are each made up, he said, of a constellation of attitudes and self-images, all possessed of their own distinguishable "body postures, gestures, feelings, behaviors, words, habits, and beliefs." He referred to these "continually scuffling" parts of the self as "subpersonalities."

Dr. Schilder often was struck that "before the remission, there was access to only a certain group of personalities, but afterwards more are allowed to express in daily life." Indeed, Geertje Brakel's life is resonant with this struggle for expression of a fuller, more multifaceted personality, a struggle further catalyzed by (or coincident with) her remarkable recovery. On one guided meditation, she described to us meeting two inner selves: an "inner sister" who was "very straight, very conventional" and an "inner child" who somersaulted and turned cartwheels like "someone from the circus" and had "all the freedom in her." It struck Geertje: "These two figures, two opposites, together they are strong, and they made me better." She asserts that her healing came most fundamentally from what she calls "becoming true." Her comments suggest the form of selfhood Assagioli maintained is the healthiest: one that integrates "expressions of vital elements our being, however negative they may seem to us at first."

Dressed casually in a light yellow oxford shirt and pants a bit too large, Dr. Schilder is used to leaning over to talk to most people he meets. The effect is one of overarching protectiveness, as if one is standing in the rustling shade of a sturdy, paternal elm. A furrow of concentration creases his forehead when he speculates on his study's implications. Drawing himself up to his full height, he leans back, waving his hands in emphasis when he talks about future research plans, then bends close, his gaze piercing: "You know, it's not what they do, I think, so much as who they are. But in these patients, the self who begins is a different self than the one who comes out of it."

These cases point to a way of looking at selfhood that goes beyond any personality typecasting. Surely, for most of us, the thought that any battery of psychological tests could encompass who we are fills us with the same dread once expressed by the nineteenth-century poet William Blake:

Why wilt thou examine every little fibre of my soul,
Spreading them out before the sun like stalks of flax to dry?

Simplistic personality typologies may even have adverse health effects. One striking example was revealed in a study of Chinese men and women born in years culturally believed to presage a weakness in a particular organ system. Though there is clearly no mechanism for calendar numerology to directly affect an organ, self-beliefs can act as powerful psychosomatic triggers. Those who were born in so-called "fire-years," thought in Chinese folklore to carry greater risk for heart conditions, died of heart diseases at a greater rate than the general population, apparently affected in some way we do not understand by associations reinforced over a lifetime.

But when we look more deeply into Oriental typologies, they do not tend to be hard and fast. Rather, they point to the transformative potential inherent in each person's way of being. Every yin has its yang, every quality implies its opposite. There is no "good" or "bad" typology; each has weaknesses to be compensated for as well as strengths that can be cultivated. In the Chinese, Tibetan, and Indian Ayurvedic medical traditions, as it was for the Greek Hippocrates, typology is not a way to delimit a person, but to point to his or her healing potential. Beyond simplistic ideas that conventionally "negative" traits can make us ill and "positive" traits heal us, every "type" of person can find his or her own unique direction to recovery.

Perhaps the paradoxes of congruence and change were best expressed by theologian Paul Tillich: "In order to be healed, the spirit must be grasped by something which transcends it, which is not strange to it, but within which is the fulfillment of its potentialities. . . ." Such moments—Dr. Schilder uses the Greek term *kairos* (roughly, coming into a new state of being)—seem most often to occur in crises, junctures when our very survival hangs in the balance; when everything we are, have been, and hope to become must be marshaled in service of life. In the process of remarkable recovery, the organism's longing for wholeness is nowhere more evident; so is the equally self-evident fact that no two people's wholeness looks alike.

CHAPTER SEVEN

The Miracle of Survival

T HE WOMAN AT THE CANCER RETREAT RAISED HER HAND. Pen poised over her small notebook, she announced, "Okay, I'm ready—tell me everything I need to do to survive!" The hope that glimmered in her dark eyes belied the anxious pull at the corners of her mouth. One of us, Caryle, had just completed a talk on spontaneous remission and felt a slight flush of discomfort. She gave a sidelong, help-me glance to the medical director sitting to her right on the dais, but the doctor only smiled a faint smile that seemed to say, "Well, well, let's see how *you* handle this one."

Caryle had noticed the woman during the talk furiously writing, looking up occasionally to assure herself she hadn't missed some critically important nuance. Looking out over the small group, she wondered, echoing the woman's query, What makes one person survive and another die? Are survivors the happy, enthusiastic types of current mind-body fable, or just the beneficiaries of a dumb-luck roll of the dice? How can people know until they are told "You have cancer" whether they will respond with despair or challenge, denial or attack?

She slowly turned back to the woman and said the first thing that came into her mind. "What you do must come from what you believe. I could give you every study, every list of everything associated with survival, but—" and here she hesitated, groping for the right admixture of kindness and caution—"these are still other people's solutions."

Pausing to observe the effect of her words, discomfited by her own parsimony of prescription but knowing she was saying what was most true, she continued, "I will give you that list, and you may find your answer. Or you may find it's like wearing someone else's well-worn shoes—they only *sort of* fit."

The woman nodded, though her face betrayed a fleeting disappointment. But standard advice, no matter how careful or kindly, is of dubious value. Thinking of that roomful of people who were either doing well, wished to, or might not, we began to wonder again about patterns: What is it that enables a person to survive great trauma, whether cancer or a life-shattering event? Crises come in many forms, whether illness, injury, war, imprisonment, or abuse. The situations that overwhelm us may arise from within our own bodies, from the environment outside or, perhaps inevitably, from both.

One day we are whole. The next moment, all control is torn from our grasp. We may be flooded with fear of mortality, anger, or the strange, crystalline calm of severe shock. But after shock ebbs comes a frightening burden of choice, made of equal parts instinct, experience, and knowledge. A terminal diagnosis may be the end of the world to one person, a time to surrender to God for another, a call to battle for yet another. Crisis arouses the resources of the healing system, like a clamoring bell that awakens the sleeper; but such resources are channeled into different coping styles, whether inborn or learned. The goal, no matter what, is to gain mastery in a situation where lack of it could mean loss of life or sanity. The primeval urge to survive at almost any cost is at the root of the organismic response to challenge.

Researcher Susan Kobassa has noted that "stress-hardy" individuals are characterized by a coping style she calls the "Three C's": challenge, commitment and control. In a study of executives, she found that those who were stimulated by challenge, were meaningfully committed to their work, and those who felt they could exercise control over their lives and jobs were by and large healthier, a formulation that has also been applied to cancer survivors. Similarly, psychologist Al Siebert has moved his focus from people suffering the normal stresses of work and home life to those who have faced direr conditions—in this case, survivors of combat, imprisonment, and holocaust. "I had been in the paratroopers, and all of our training cadre were combat survivors," he told us. "I wanted to understand people who had been through far worse things than having been spanked as a child, or having had an alcoholic father. I wanted to look for a 'survivor personality,' which to me is an operational definition of a mentally healthy person."

A paradoxical pattern emerged from his research. Survivors, he found, were flexible, adaptable, resilient. In a great onslaught, they can bend like bamboo nearly to breaking, then spring back after the storm has passed. They had what he calls "biphasic" personalities: At once loving and angry, selfish and unselfish, self-confident and self-critical. His model is less concerned with what a person is like, than with how he or she responds when faced with unpredictable circumstances.

To better understand how people cope with traumatic experiences, we interviewed a famous Vietnam-era POW named Gerald Coffee. Coffee was a Navy pilot on the aircraft carrier USS *Kittyhawk* off the coast of North Vietnam in 1966. On his second mission, his plane was hit with antiaircraft fire. He and his crewman were forced to eject at an altitude of 3000 feet going 620 miles per hour. Gerry regained consciousness in the water a half mile from the beach, his broken right arm floating uselessly in front of him. "The culmination of all my training came to bear during those few minutes," he told us. "Once I hit the water, I did the mental and emotional preparation I needed to do to survive."

A firefight followed between the North Vietnamese sent out to retrieve the fallen airmen and the Americans trying to prevent their capture. His crewman was slain. Gerry, pulled onto a North Vietnamese patrol boat within minutes of his splashdown, was almost killed when American planes mistakenly opened fire on it, sending a bullet careening off his helmet. Seconds after reaching the beach, the boat was blown into splinters.

Gerry had been an art major in college, but he had received a draft notice with his diploma. Deciding to take control of his fate rather than passively accept the inevitable, he chose Naval aviation for no better reason than "it looked exciting. The recruitment posters were all beaches and Pepsi Cola."

Now, being force-marched northward, Gerry felt strangely detached, as if he were watching himself in a surreal black-and-white movie. "I couldn't remember how I got there. I replayed the whole battle scene, being chased on the beach, seeing the bodies washing in and out. Meanwhile, I was being marched through a gauntlet of villages, people with shovels and rakes and hoes, threatening, beating. I was seeing it from a distance, like it wasn't happening to me, like I shouldn't be there." He remained in the shadowy twilight state of shock for days.

After one failed escape attempt, he was stood before a firing squad, his arms tied behind him around a tree. "I told myself they were bluffing and at the same time thought, 'What a shitty way to die.' " The soldiers went all the way through "ready-aim-fire," then five of the six rifles clicked on empty chambers. "They were trying to break me, not kill me—but one kid forgot that his rifle wasn't supposed to be loaded, and his bullet cracked into the wood right above my head."

Gerry was taken to the old French fortress of Hoa Lo, an infamous part of the Hanoi prison system that became known in the media as the "Hanoi Hilton." The living conditions were "beyond spartan." Torture was frequent and harsh, and there was virtually no medical care. Gerry's broken arm had swelled to enormous size; the bone wasn't set for over a month. The thirty-two-year-old airman, who had been a "church-going but not necessarily religious man" with a "Heinz 57" spiritual background, turned to prayer. His entreaties, he says, changed from "Why me, God?" to "Show me, God, how to use this experience." Like many survivors of disease, he found a personal meaning in suffering that kept at bay the encroaching chaos.

He spent a long time in solitary confinement in a tiny cell. "They only began putting us together when they ran out of space. They decided we were more vulnerable alone and they were right. Once we were together, we cared more about ourselves *and* each other." As with so many cases of remarkable recovery, social bonds became powerful forces for life. "Our motto was Unity over Self."

If someone wasn't eating, the first sign the survival instinct had begun to wane, the coded tapping on the walls started. "It was, 'Hey, buddy. Hang in there. We've all been there. We've all tried. We know how you feel. Don't get down on yourself.'"

The men filled the emptiness of their lives with ever more elaborate "tap code" communication. A frequent debate over this crude prison telegraph concerned who was best equipped to survive the Hanoi Hilton—an engineer or a liberal arts major? Talking to him today, we almost hear Gerry, the art major, furiously rapping his argument on the wall. "I think we're far more able to survive if we develop the ability to live with ambiguity and uncertainty, to be creative in the present, to know we can't control the future."

His days of confinement—he would wind up spending seven years and nine days—became oddly fulfilling. Communicating with men on either side, composing a poem, designing and building a house in his mind, remembering restaurants, capitals of states, even learning French—Jerry's days were so full he often didn't accomplish all he had mentally planned. "Anyone who had any knowledge or expertise would pass it on, and everybody in the cell block would study it. I was like a sponge. I wanted to somehow maximize the positive aspects of the experience." One exercise that filled Gerry's days in isolation was "a long, long process of mentally reliving my life, and remembering details I'd long forgotten."

(Colonel Robert Sawhill, shot down in 1967, tortured, beaten, kept in solitary, told us he also created inner visualizations. "I played a lot of mental golf," he says. "I was never more than one or two over par." When he and other prisoners were allowed in a room together, they would spend time creating multi-course fantasy meals replete with appetizers, soup, wine, dessert, and brandy, elaborately describing each imaginary detail of its preparation.)

These days, after Gerry Coffee gives a speech, people sometimes come up and hesitantly, embarrassedly, confess to him they feel a stab of envy for an experience that had stripped him to the core of his being yet revealed hidden strengths. He doesn't find this odd: "What they're talking about is a rite of passage, something that forces you to discover yourself, your connection to other people, your relationship to spirituality. Anything that helps us do that is conducive to survival."

We saw these same survival characteristics in many remarkable recoveries. Francis Martin Killeen starts the story of his battle with cancer where he first learned to fight for himself, on mean streets where "you had to be tough, and you couldn't afford to be afraid. It was a New York thing," he says with a look that is half-wry, half-rueful. "Put me anywhere and I'll survive."

Killeen has a ready, shadow-chasing smile and a nose that looks like it might have been broken more than once. Self-avowed "one-hundred-percent Irish," he gives the impression of a genial, balding leprechaun with a slight middle-aged paunch. He was born in the Bronx two days after the bombs whistled down on Pearl Harbor. His earliest memories are of being hoisted on his father's shoulders in his Sunday best, watching the Liberty Ships steam home. "There must have been thousands of them," he recalls, a child's breathless wonder creeping into his gravelly voice. His cousin Billy was on one of those triumphal vessels. For years, his family had grabbed at every scrap of war news, and Marty, vigilant to everything in his surroundings, was fascinated by the emerging tales of brutality and heroism. His heroes were soldiers, or cops like his Uncle Mike, who gave him his first glass of beer and took him riding down Westchester Avenue, once pointing out a gas station where he'd killed three men who had attempted armed robbery.

Treasuring his cousin Billy's gift of his battle helmet "with a bullet hole two inches long," Marty had dreamed of being a marine. Instead, he became a journalist and television producer on the front lines of breaking news. When he was a little over forty, he moved to Atlanta to work in documentary television. The job was challenging and creative, but also entailed a rough relationship with a difficult boss, long hours, extensive travel, and separation from his family. Incrementally, the trickle of stress became a steady stream.

It was a hot Georgia summer and Marty was outside working on his house when he first noticed something was wrong. A man with a penchant for endurance, he felt weak as a kitten after a few hours. He ignored it. Soon thereafter, he developed bronchitis, began to lose his voice, and developed a pain in his shoulder so sharp it brought tears to his eyes. He figured it was his smoking and promptly quit.

But the pain kept ambushing him. After months, at last unable to endure it, he went in for X rays. When his doctor said evenly, "Why don't you put on your shirt and come into my office?" Marty was hoping for a take-better-care-of-yourself lecture, though something told him it was worse.

The doctor began slowly, measuring every word, "I may be wrong, so I don't want you to panic. I once had a patient commit suicide." Marty didn't have trouble fast-forwarding to the last word, "Cancer?" His doctor nodded, pointing to a dark dot on the chest X ray.

Outside the office, the word still reverberating in his head, Marty thought, irrationally, "No point quitting smoking." He bought a pack of Luckies, jumped in his car, and drove to a "little park with a creek, a peaceful little Civil War battle site." Sitting on the lawn, he looked at the cigarette he had just fired up, asking himself if it was worth it. "Yes, by God, it was! I always liked to smoke, since I was little. In one sense, crazy as it sounds from a guy who'd just been diagnosed with a lung tumor, that was the beginning of healing, because I took responsibility."

After the biopsy, the surgeon told Marty it was a small cell carcinoma. "He says, 'Ninety-five-percent fatal.' He doesn't say, 'Five-percent survival.' It hits you like a sledgehammer." Marty spent the rest of the day and night crying. "It wasn't like I needed a handkerchief, I needed a towel. There was a nurse on my floor, an angel, who would come in and hold my hand."

He awakened the next morning to a world unexpectedly glistening with snow. "God had played an April Fool's joke on Atlanta that day," he says. He took the blanket of purity and magic coating the town as a personal omen. He thought about his two young daughters, who "didn't sign on for a dead dad." His sorrow turning to anger, the streetwise Marty began demanding straight answers. "Where do they get these numbers, ninety-five-percent fatal?" he thought, bridling. The night before his surgery he had glanced into hospital rooms filled with cancer patients so ill they could no longer walk. The still very ambulatory Marty asked his doctor, "Do you count those people in your statistics?" When his doctor assented, he burst out, "Well, shit, my odds just improved."

Marty was already exhibiting a coping strategy Dr. Joel E. Dimsdale, who has studied survivors of Nazi concentration camps, calls "differential focus on the good." Survivors who were able to achieve a "mobilization of hope," Dimsdale observed, often reached back to "a pre-existing mode of belief . . . that ultimate outcomes must be benign, that suffering can be endured." Marty reached back to his wild hellion days for survival strategems. "I remembered one piece of advice from an old motorcycle rider: 'When you're in a jam, don't hit the brakes or you'll crash and die. Look for a gap, throttle as far as you can, and try to shoot through the opening.' "

Marty's opening came from a most unexpected direction. His five-year-old daughter was in a Montessori school. Every afternoon her class would "form a love circle where each kid sent love-thoughts to someone. After my biopsy, these three-, four-, and five-year-olds decided to collectively send me their love. And I swear to God I felt it, as if it came right in the window."

The next day his doctor gave him a revised diagnosis. It wasn't small cell but large cell carcinoma, which meant his chances had gone from ninety-five-percent fatal to eighty-five or ninety percent. Marty was exultant: From his "differential focus on the good" perspective, he reasoned, "I'd just doubled my chances!"

Energized, he was now anxious to begin treatment. One positive event followed another. He met a radiologist he really liked, who told him about someone else with the same kind of cancer still alive more than five years later. Marty began a torturous round of radiation. "It burned my shoulders black. I had to lie down twenty-eight hours a day. I got to where it would take me two hours to choke down a small plate of spaghetti. But I stayed at it." The physicians told Marty he would never talk again—the tumor was compressing the nerve to the vocal cord. But, sometime during the first week of radiation, lying alone inside the lead-lined room, he heard a silent voice inside say, "You're not going to die. You're not through. You've still got work to do."

Marty exhibited another characteristic often seen in survivors: affiliation. Like POW Gerry Coffee, he was able to find emotional sustenance in others. Marty is gregarious, always ready to crack a joke or laugh at one. "I made friends with all the nurses, the radiology technicians. I actually had fun most of the time." He made friends with the patients, too, though he was disturbed by how many had given up hope. Stopping as if to mentally re-create their faces, he says, "You could look around and actually see who was going to die. Their heads were down, they accepted the sentence they were given."

Marty rewarded himself after each treatment. He bought a pack of cigarettes, took out one and threw the rest away. He would plop down at a table in a little Italian cafe, order an espresso and something sweet, delightedly smoking his cigarette and reading the *New York Times*. To his doctor's surprise, while most radiation patients weaken, he kept getting stronger. He forced himself to play golf. "At first, I could go three holes before I lost it." Slowly he built himself to a full nine holes, overjoyed at his accomplishment.

He read every book he could find about people who had survived terminal cancer, saturating himself with hope. During one of his "twenty-eight-hours-in-bed days," he put his baby daughter on his chest and began to meditate. Holding the sweet, gently breathing infant, he was overwhelmed with an almost mystical sense of connection with "every other human being, flower, plant."

His family was having a harder time than he was believing he would live. His older daughter came to him in tears. "Dad," she wept, "I always thought you were going to be with me forever." His heart torn, Marty replied, "I will be, forever, if I'm dead or alive." He hastened to tell her, wiping her eyes, "But I'm going to live." He was moved by his family's feelings, but he also had to level with himself: The turgid atmosphere of inconsolable grief and fear was suffocating him. There were times he looked in their eyes and felt he was already the dearly departed.

Partly to spare them pain, partly out of his own instinct to survive, he announced he needed time alone. He encouraged his wife to take the children on a vacation. With his family gone, Marty blasted rock and roll through the empty house, practicing using his voice. "I remember when out of my mouth came this long AHHHHHHH, the first clear sound I'd made in months. I wandered around in incredible joy making these noises."

He continued on the unusually aggressive course of radiation, visualizing the invisible rays as "a golden, healing light" flowing through his body. He experimented with different colors, finally deciding he was most comfortable with the pale purple he still visualizes in his meditations. At the end of twenty treatments, whether it was the radiation, the prayers of his cleaning lady (who had fasted one weekend for him), his children, his attitude, or his imagery, the tumor virtually disappeared.

Marty's medical records tell the tale. In April 1987, when his cancer was first discovered, his doctor, not expecting much result, wrote to a consulting colleague, "I am very sorry this young man has this disease at such a young age with two children. I hope that he will receive significant palliation with the radiation therapy." His radiologist, noting he would be using the maximum dosage, hoped for no more than "a higher level of local control and possibly a decrease in the metastatic rate." But then, to their surprise, Marty "had a very good response with near clearing of the right upper lobe lesion. His hoarseness has nearly gone away. Strength is returning. He looks good in all ways."

Overjoyed and feeling he deserved a formidable reward, Marty ran out and bought his dream car, "a cool, cool, *cool* turbocharged convertible that could go 160 miles an hour." His wife thought it was crazy, but Marty decided if he died he wanted to be buried in it: "Just leave the top down when they shovel in the dirt."

He still felt he needed to get away for a while. So with his new car loaded with fishing rods, golf clubs, "a change of clothes and some cowboy boots," he waved good-bye to his family, telling them, "I'll be back. I don't know when." After a trip to New York to visit his father, he pointed his so-brand-new-it-didn't-have-plates, shiny black dream machine at the George Washington Bridge and never stopped. He dashed cross-country, climbing into the Rockies at a hundred miles an hour "with 'Graceland' blaring as loud as the speakers could crank and me screaming at the top of my lungs." After three weeks on the road, he pointed his car east and headed for home.

Driving through New Mexico he ran into an "amazing storm, one you see maybe once in five years. Off to my left is this big mesa, like a lightning rod. Constant thunder and lightning." Marty in his black chariot and "a big Cadillac with Texas plates" raced the storm and each other through New Mexico and Texas, the little towns along the way becoming a blur.

Back home, reality struck. He had no cancer, but now he had no disability payments. He had to go back to work. "Sure enough, it was like committing suicide. Ten or eleven months later, I noticed I was having trouble as I was driving to work. The car seemed to veer off to the right. My wife was saying the side of my face looked odd."

"Mr. Killeen unfortunately now has metastatic tumor to the brain," began his doctor's letter to a colleague after Marty came in for an examination. His hospital admission report reads, "Very poor prognosis attendant to central nervous system metastasis."

His doctor leveled with him. "I know you're a special case," Marty remembers him saying, "and you beat the last one through whatever means, medical or something else. But you can't beat this one. Don't even go for extended treatments or experimental therapies. Nobody survives. Get your affairs in order. You've got a couple of months."

Determined not to accept the prognosis, Marty convinced his radiologist to give him a maximum dosage. He also decided he wouldn't go back to his old job, ever. His medical report months later reads, "I can't believe how well Martin has done. He really is thriving." One day while having his now-traditional after-treatment sweet, cigarette, and coffee he happened across an article about cancer survivors. "Anger was good for you for the first year," he remembers reading, "but after that you need to find peace and joy." It made sense. He sold his house, packed up his family, bought a farm in Pennsylvania, and took his wife on a much-needed vacation.

But Marty began losing his voice again. When he returned to Atlanta, doctors found a tumor on his vocal cords. There could be no more radiation—he'd reached his lifetime limit. His medical team suggested implanting radium pellets in the tumor. Marty, still undaunted and ever ready to battle, enthusiastically agreed.

After surgery, with bandages swathing his neck like a grim gentleman's scarf, he asked the surgeon how the operation had gone. Had he gotten the pellets in? The surgeon shook his head no. "I went ballistic!" says Marty. "What the hell was going on?" His surgeon broke into a wide grin. "We couldn't find any cancer!" he shouted. Today, Marty Killeen grouses he is "the owner of fourteen hundred dollars' worth of radioactive pellets which I can't sell to anybody."

There are many forms of inescapable threat—a terminal disease that keeps returning, like a monster in a horror movie, just when we think we have killed it, or the capricious, brutal whims, passions, and hatreds of our fellow human beings. In both cases, the only way to survive is to go deep into the storehouse of who we most fundamentally are—our beliefs, sense of connection, unique talents and past experiences, hopes and dreams. Dr. Viktor Frankl, a psychiatrist who survived four concentration camps, writes, "Even the helpless victim of a hopeless situation, facing a fate he cannot change, may rise above himself, and by so doing change himself."

In our search for the keys to survival, we turned to the survivors of the Nazi camps. We were intrigued to discover that those who miraculously emerged with their health and/or sanity relatively intact shared traits similar to those of survivors of cancer.

Like Marty Killeen, Frankl showed, from the beginning, Dr. Dimsdale's "differential focus on the good." When the train pulled into Auschwitz and a detachment of prisoners stormed inside—members of a privileged camp elite who were rewarded by the Nazis for performing some of the cruelest and most odious tasks—Frankl took heart. They at least seemed well fed, they even laughed. *Who knows?* he had thought, before encountering the skeletal citizenry who lived in the charnel ground called Auschwitz.

Frankl marveled grimly at the resilience of the human organism in the midst of torment:

The medical men among us learned first of all: "Textbooks tell lies!" Somewhere it is said that man cannot exist without sleep for more than a stated number of hours. Quite wrong! . . . If someone now asked of us the truth of Dostoevski's statement that flatly defines man as a being who can get used to anything, we would reply, "Yes, a man can get used to anything, but do not ask us how."

The horrors of Auschwitz: marching over frozen ground for miles in bare feet to the labor sites; living on a daily piece of bread and a pint of watery soup, the body devouring its own subcutaneous fat till only a thin cloth of skin cloaked the bones; enduring beatings or torture as a constant plume of death rose from the crematoria.

Frankl witnessed, experienced, endured. In the camps, he would practice a crude form of psychotherapy to prevent suicides (a danger Marty Killeen's doctor, too, indicated he was well aware of). Frankl remembers counseling two prisoners who had determined there was nothing left to expect from life that "life was still expecting something from them." This made them rally: One man thought of the child whom he adored and who was waiting for him in a foreign safe haven; for another man, a scientist, it was a series of books that could not be completed by anyone but him. Frankl realized that the key to maintaining even a thread of health was "the uniqueness and singleness which distinguishes each individual."

He discovered the physiological power of hope and despair, observing that those who became depressed to the point of apathy tended to succumb (a factor, interestingly, noted in a recent study by Margaret Kemeny comparing long-term AIDS survivors with their shorter-lived peers). Frankl wrote of a friend who had dreamed that he would be liberated on March 30, 1945. On that very day, when it was clear their liberation was not at hand, the man suddenly became ill, ran a high fever, and died. Frankl attributes the man's death to his severe disappointment, which "suddenly lowered his body's resistance against the latent typhus infection." (We cannot help but speculate about the similarly negative immune system effects of a forcefully delivered "you have three months to live" medical prognosis).

It is important to note, in fact, a firm linkage between the innate human healing system and survival in the camps: Survival was often synonymous with each prisoner's level of immunity. Disease was ever rampant. The unhealthy prisoner who could not perform work details was selected for the ovens, if he didn't die in his cold, crowded bunk, or on forced marches, or in the midst of backbreaking labor. The body's resistance to disease—a resistance we know to be modulated by the mind-body factors of psychoneuroimmunology—was thus paramount.

Perhaps there is a profound clue to the inner mechanisms of the healing system in this fascinating observation by Frankl:

> Sensitive people who were used to a rich intellectual life may have suffered much pain (they were often of a delicate constitution), but the damage to their inner selves was less. They were able to retreat from their terrible surroundings to a life of inner riches and spiritual freedom. Only in this way can one explain the apparent paradox that some prisoners of a less hardy make-up often seemed to survive camp life better than did those of a robust nature.

Frankl also enumerated other familiar stimuli to the healing system—love and social support; humor; belief; idiosyncrasy; flexibility; will (and reason) to live—all notable in the remarkable survival of psychologist Edith Eva Eger.

It took Edith over thirty years to talk about her childhood. At a meeting where she was to give an address, she was presented as an Auschwitz survivor. When the moderator asked how many in the audience had heard of Auschwitz and only four people raised their hands, she decided she owed it to her family who had died in the camps to break her silence. Now she weaves the subject into every speech she gives.

With her short white hair, wide smile, and quick wit, it is hard to imagine that the stylishly dressed Dr. Eger is the same woman who lived through the nightmare of the Holocaust. She was raised on the Hungarian-Czechoslovakian border in an artistically talented family. Her middle sister was a child prodigy who could play the Mendelssohn Violin Concerto by the time she was six. Her older sister was the accompanist. No one knew Edith existed. ("Today, I pay attention when women introduce their husbands by saying, 'I want you to meet my better half.' I ask, 'What are you—a quarter?' ") Her mother, seeing young Edith's self-esteem withering away, sent her to dance school.

By ten she was training in gymnastics and ballet, hoping someday to become a member of the Olympic team. When the Nazi *anschluss* overran Hungary, she was told the most she could do was become an assistant to another would-be young Olympian approved by the Nazi Party.

When Edith was sixteen, her family—all except her sister Klara, who was studying music in Budapest—was loaded into a crowded, fetid cattle car bound for Auschwitz. Frightened, clutching her mother, she discovered that by some miracle, her boyfriend was in the next car. "Through the cracks he whispered, 'Whatever happens, I'll never forget your eyes and your hands.' I remember in Auschwitz walking around asking people, 'What *about* my eyes and hands?' It kept me occupied." As long as she could remember a time before Auschwitz, Edith could remain sane enough to survive.

At Auschwitz, in a long, silent line with the other women, she walked toward a "very frightening, very expressive-looking" man with "very piercing eyes" who with the flick of his index finger decided who went left, to the ovens, and who went right, to at least temporary life. The man was Dr. Josef Mengele, chief medical officer at Auschwitz and the engineer of the mad eugenic program to create an Aryan master-race. "Dr. Mengele pointed my mother to the left, and Magda and me to the right. But I ran after my mother. He came after me and told me I would see my mother soon. So you see," she told us, "the man who annihiliated my family also saved my life."

Day and night the smoke and flames belched out of the stacks across from her barrack, the black soot raining down in an unending precipitation of death. "I never cried in Auschwitz. I think I was afraid of feelings. I became numb." Like Frankl, like Gerry Coffee, like many remarkable recoveries, she found a secret inner refuge that dire circumstances could not crush.

She also clung fiercely to her most powerful social connection, her beloved older sister. She and Magda knew they would have to conceal their relationship. If the Nazis found out they were sisters they would be instantly separated. Eger recalls one time, her voice dropping almost to a whisper, they almost lost each other. Finding herself in a different line, she drew on her Olympian prowess. "I began to do cartwheels and splits and managed to get to my sister. We had to be quick decision-makers to survive. What was needed was to have someone to reach out for. We had each other."

Social support, the Nazis realized, bred strength; stoked the counter-inferno of the will to live. The concentration camp was designed to destroy every mechanism we have come to associate with remarkable survival—hope, belief, dreams, rage, joy, all shreds of coherence. But such things, as Edith proves, are indestructible.

She received her first survival lesson the very day she had joined her sister. A soldier came to her barrack looking for people with special talents because Dr. Mengele wished to be entertained. Many of Edith's schoolmates were with her, and knowing she was a dancer, "they 'volunteered' me. So I danced for Dr. Mengele." Finding a place deep inside that could not be touched, far from the pall of her mother's ashes pirouetting in the foul, hot updraft, she danced. "And when I was dancing, I closed my eyes and imagined the music was Tchaikovsky and I was in the Budapest opera house dancing 'Romeo and Juliet.'" After her performance, Mengele threw her a crust of bread.

Eger in retrospect has often wondered how she could have remained in many ways unscathed, sheltering her selfhood in her soul's deepest storm celler. "I could make a very good schizophrenic," she says with a sparkling laugh. "Maybe good survivors need to be." Edith had not only determined not to give up and die before the Nazis killed her—she had decided, above all, she was not going to let them twist her spirit. "I began to pray for the guards. I thought they were more imprisoned than I was. I changed my hatred into pity, because I was innocent whereas they would eventually have to deal with their consciences."

In the fifteen months before liberation—"when the saints came marching in," as she refers to her American liberators—she and Magda were moved to different camps several times, but fortunately they remained together. They were subjected to grueling hours of lining up to be counted and cleaning barracks; a monotony where every moment was saturated with fear of death and every day began with the showers, "never knowing whether water or gas was going to come out." But still there was imperceptible, improbable room for life-promoting humor. "I remember we had a 'boob contest,' " she told us, a smile playing on her lips, "and I won and got another piece of bread." Eva was also nourished by abundant, vivid dreams—dreams of dancing the ballet before an adoring audience, and dreams of someday meeting a man she could love.

In the spring of 1945, the Nazis knew their defeat was rapidly approaching. The Americans were marching toward Germany from the west, the Russians from the east. "But they told us they were never going to allow us to get out." Twice Eger was in line for the crematorium and was reprieved. The Germans were on the run, with no direction safe, trying to cover their atrocities. Eger was forced to join the Death March from Mauthausen, Austria, to Gunskirchen, Germany. Edith, the extraordinary survivor, had finally grown too weak from hunger and illness to move a step further. If anyone paused on the march, they were killed immediately, so "the girls formed a chair with their arms and they carried me. Imagine! That's why I'm saying that the worst can bring out the best in us."

On that march, with people starving and in some gruesome instances turning to cannibalism, Eger refused to be defeated. With almost every choice gone, she ate grass, carefully choosing among the infinite selection of blades like a gourmet.

The Death March ended for Eger in a forest near Guns-kirschen. The Nazis had placed a bomb in each barracks wired to one central lever. But before the fatal switch was thrown, the soldiers fled the advancing Americans. Walking through the landscape of unspeakable human desecration, a young American GI passing by a heap of corpses was startled to see a hand move. It was Eva. He pulled her from the pile. She was suffering from typhoid fever, pleurisy, pneumonia, and starvation. It had been two weeks since she had eaten.

Today, as a psychologist, Edith Eva Eger jokingly describes herself as a "cross between Dr. Ruth and Joan Rivers." She specializes in abuse survivors, people with post-traumatic stress disorder, Holocaust survivors and their children, and cancer patients. "Many people tell me cancer gave them life. If you want to see an honest person who looks in the mirror each day and says 'I'm beautiful,' it's a cancer survivor. They're real. They don't do what they don't want to do."

In recent years, Edith returned to Auschwitz. Though she was frightened, she says, "it was the most positive experience of my life. I wanted to tell my mother she was right. In that cattle car she told me 'Everything can be taken away from you except what you put in your head.'"

In Edith's story, we cannot help but notice some familiar factors we have seen in cases of remarkable recovery. Creativity. Dissociation. Belief. The power of even a single sustaining axis of relationship. The ability to find pattern and meaning—sometimes even a gallows humor—where others might only find random chaos. The will to snatch autonomy of action—even if literally only a blade of grass—from circumstances bent on crushing human freedom. (Similarly, while some patients succumb to the totalitarian imprisonment in their own bodies, others seek out even the smallest arenas of autonomy.) To be able to give to others in a situation where instinct would bid desperate grasping. (Indeed, among striking characteristics of remarkable recovery was an ability to place oneself in thought and deed within a larger context. We met many patients who turned to social service even as they were still struggling for their lives.)

Edith's husband of forty-seven years died recently of a recurrence of tuberculosis ("Hitler's Revenge," says Edith). There are now three generations of Eger's family. Her granddaughter is a ballerina. Edith Eva Eger wanted to remember in order to forgive, for she believes that only with forgiveness comes freedom. "What's the big deal about being Jewish?" she demands challengingly. "I am for people opening up communication with one another rather than tribalism. If you create an 'us' and 'them' mentality, you create another Auschwitz. It is important right now we create peace and love in the world."

At the Tenth International AIDS Conference in Yokohama, Japan, Rebecca Denison, founder of WORLD (Women Organized to Respond to Life-Threatening Diseases), shook hands with the prime minister of Japan. It sent shock waves through Japanese society. Rebecca is HIV-positive. Never had such a high official publicly touched a person with the stigmatized infection. Rebecca's picture was splashed on the front page of every newspaper.

Last Christmas Eve, Rebecca dreamed she was in the Holocaust. The nightmare was so indelible she was compelled to paint it, and has been unable to paint much since. In her dream, she had been flying, observing from above a horrifying scene: victims crowded into cattle cars, with no conductor and no soldiers on the train to keep the people in. It captured her feeling of the AIDS epidemic, "losing all these people and feeling powerless to stop this sinister occurrence."

It's a comparison made by many AIDS patients, who have seen loved ones waste into living skeletons that resemble the first images of the camps taken by army photographers. AIDS is a realm in which all who enter its gates seem to exit, as in Auschwitz, only as corpses. The ability to resist is destroyed: Opportunistic infections claim the body, and so-called AIDS dementia claims the mind.

"But in the Holocaust," says Rebecca, "you had people intentionally killing other people out of the vilest hatred. Most of the people with AIDS were infected in the process of loving or sharing something with another person. Also, with AIDS, you have all this rage but there is no Hitler, no way to say, 'Well, if someone would just take that evil little man, beat those Nazis, we'd be able to live.' That's why in my painting there's no conductor or soldiers on the cattle cars, yet they can't escape, can't stop the train. It's a different kind of powerlessness."

At the time Rebecca Denison tested positive, women with HIV were not just powerless—they were invisible. At many AIDS activist gatherings, she found herself the only woman present. "I felt uncomfortable being asked to speak about women's HIV issues because I didn't want to be a spokesperson for a community that didn't exist." Though she was first tested in 1990, Rebecca believes she was infected over ten years ago, when she was only twenty-one. She developed HIV-like symptoms two months after having unprotected sex with her college boyfriend: fevers, night sweats, exhaustion, excruciating vaginal infections, headaches, sores in her throat. The symptoms subsided in a few days, except for the lingering exhaustion. She, like many people, had yet to hear of AIDS.

She was only tested because she had volunteered to accompany a close friend who thought she had been exposed to the virus to the clinic to be tested. While she was there, Rebecca decided to have her own blood drawn. "We went back two weeks later for the results. What a shock! Hers were negative, and mine were positive. I had a lot of questions the counselor couldn't answer, like 'What was the chance I'd infected my husband? What was the chance that I could have a healthy baby?' "

The week after she found out her test results, she happened to walk into an AIDS demonstration in the street in front of her office. The demonstrators, members of the activist group ACT UP, were chanting, "AIDS is a disaster, women die faster." She looked at the flyers as she stood stunned in the crowd, shocked to read that many women with AIDS died within six months. "At the time, I didn't realize being HIV-positive was not the same thing as having AIDS. I started calculating, 'Let's see, today is June sixteenth so if I eat a lot of brown rice and broccoli, and take herbs and vitamin pills, maybe I can make it till Christmas.' "

Rebecca Denison, who remains asymptomatic, is not a center-stage activist, but a quiet, intent woman who simply didn't want to be alone. WORLD started as a newsletter. The day after a local paper printed an article about it, "we got thirty phone calls from women with HIV saying, 'I want to tell my story.' " Three years later, WORLD is in every state and about sixty foreign countries. Five thousand copies of the newsletter are distributed every month. WORLD is, in effect, a global community of women with HIV. "We do things like retreats where a hundred women with HIV go someplace really gorgeous and commune with na-ture, talk with each other, and laugh or cry hysterically. Most of the women who are active in the community live an incredibly long time."

If Rebecca's impression of longevity were true—there have been no formal studies—is it conceivable we can talk about re-markable recovery even in the context of what has been a nearly uniformly fatal disease? By virtue of its apparent incurability, AIDS has forced those desperately seeking a cure—patients and physicians alike—to travel to the far shores of the healing re-sponse. Margaret Kemeny, an immunologist at UCLA's Depart-ment of Psychiatry, has suggested that AIDS patients assessed with high psychological fatalism seem more likely to die quickly (though whether as a result of health-damaging behaviors associ-ated with such attitudes, a different, depression-causing neuro-chemistry of faster-progressing disease, or as a biological effect of emotional states is not yet known).

But in another study she uncovered clear immune system dif-ferences correlated with emotions. Grief, she found, may be a fa-vorable factor in HIV-positive people, whereas depression leads to greater immune system impairment. Here is a significant nuance: Grief may act as a powerful emotional catharsis, allowing someone to experience sadness and move beyond it, while depression could steadily sap the body's disease-fighting mechanism.

UCLA's Dr. George Solomon, psychiatrist, philosopher, and clinician, has also probed long-term AIDS survivors: Were they just random anomalies that statistically crop up at the far end of any "bell-shaped curve," he wondered, or was something else going on? In the 1960s while at Stanford University, Solomon had been one of the first to postulate a relationship among stress, emotions, and the immune function.

Solomon has been studying every aspect of long-term AIDS survivors, searching restlessly for common threads even as the epidemic relentlessly scythes its victims. Solomon, a wry man with salt-and-pepper hair and stylish eyeglasses, describes the striking differences he has observed between two doctor friends who are HIV-positive. "One went on disability, and now has around 300 T-helper cells and dropping," says Solomon. "He reads every article and is always bugging his physician for the latest information. He is obsessed with his health in a preoccupied, rather narcissistic manner." Dr. Solomon's other friend, he says, has a higher T-cell count now—over 500—than he did eight years ago. "He takes more time off than he used to, is knowledgeable but not obsessive about his health. He stays very involved in life, working, enjoying himself, doing things with people."

Among the characteristics Dr. Solomon found in a pilot study of long-term AIDS survivors was that they accepted their HIV status "without perceiving it as a doom-and-death sentence." To the contrary, survivors claimed they had found new meaning as a result of the disease. Many took up unfinished business, pursued unfulfilled goals, or found activities they were looking forward to in the future. Almost half had a prior experience with serious illness or accidents, perhaps giving them coping skills to draw on. Most had close friends with whom they could disagree openly and express negative emotions. They had altruistic involvements with other PWAs (People with AIDS), and good, if acerbic senses of humor. (One long-term survivor refers to himself as a "Jurassic Fairy.") They gave priority to their own needs, were assertive and didn't feel powerless or helpless, and did not act in either a defiant or passive mode when consulting with their physicians, rather seeing their doctors as partners. Long-term survivors felt they could influence the outcome of their illness, though each in his or her own way. "What's right for one person is not necessarily right for another," Dr. Solomon says, telling of a religious AIDS patient whose visualization was an image of Christ on a cross giving him a transfusion of healthy blood.

He pauses, letting his words catch up in the footrace with his thoughts. "There is the chicken-or-the-egg problem," he offers, "of whether these people are doing well because they are good copers and not insanely distressed, or because they're so thrilled that they're the exception to the rule that *that* makes them less distressed and better copers."

One of Solomon's studies was of nine asymptomatic HIV-positive gay or bisexual men with CD4 T-cell counts of less than fifty. Solomon relates an emblematic phone call he had from one of the men years later. "I said, 'How are you feeling?' He said, 'The same.' A little fatigue, but no illness. Then I asked, 'How are your counts?' He replied his last tests showed he now only had one T-cell. But then the man added, 'I'm telling you, it's the greatest T-cell ever. I've grown extremely attached to it. In fact, I believe I have the most powerful single T-cell in the whole world!' "

Before AIDS, there was hepatitis B, which by the 1970s had reached near-epidemic proportions in the gay community. In an effort to study the extent of the infection, the San Francisco City Clinic in 1978 began collecting blood from a group of over 6,000 gay and bisexual men, testing it for hepatitis, then freezing and storing the remaining portions. The blood languished, largely forgotten, until Paul O'Malley, the study's chief researcher, had an idea.

As news of a new epidemic affecting gay men emanated from

the Federal Centers for Disease Control (CDC) O'Malley turned to the frozen blood from the hepatitis B study for clues. In 1983, the San Francisco City Clinic, with money from the CDC, began to track down men who had volunteered for the original study. Extensive biobehavioral profiles and physical exams followed, and more blood was stored for future investigations. In 1985, when the HIV antibody test became available, researchers decided to ambitiously expand the project. They contacted as many of the donors of the blood specimens in the clinic's walk-in freezers as they could find, and got their permission to test their samples for HIV. Of 588 men whose stored blood tested positive, most had also developed the symptoms of AIDS.

But to the researchers' surprise, forty-two of these men, some more than fifteen years out, continued to show relatively robust immune systems. Their helper T-cell counts remained a normal 500 or above. Moreover, most of them had never taken the most commonly prescribed AIDS drug, AZT. Dr. Susan Buchbinder, chief clinician in the San Francisco Department of Public Health's AIDS office, has speculated these men may represent a subgroup of HIV-infected who, for reasons not yet understood, never develop the disease. She calls them the "long-term healthy positives."

Dr. Buchbinder, who works out of an elegant and imposing marble and granite edifice near San Francisco's City Hall, told us, "We began to realize we should go beyond the general studies of AIDS patients to try to discover what was keeping these people healthy." She is wrestling with a familiar conundrum of remarkable recovery: Are people at the far end of the bell-shaped curve simply random statistical events, or does something cause their unusual longevity? Surprisingly, she has not found any direct relationship among stress factors, exposure to drugs, alcohol, tobacco, or other infections. Her own sense is that it will be found that "there are multiple things that protect people. And that is good news, because it means there may be multiple ways of intervening against HIV."

Rob Anderson has been an artist since he could hold a pencil. His elaborate paintings of the human body bear mystical-sounding titles like "Awakening Man" and "The Herald." In one large canvas, a man in blue jeans and a turquoise pullover sits, head lowered, hands on the edge of a granite slab before a golden, flame-filled portal, either about to enter or just emerging from an inferno. Each piece, Rob says, is his way of expressing the "psychological realism" of his own struggle.

He is one of the "long-term healthy positives" of the original hepatitis B study in San Francisco. Dark-haired, bearded, with warm brown eyes and just the hint of a Southern accent, Rob clearly recalls receiving the news he was infected with HIV. One of the counselors "took me into his windowless little office cubicle, sat me down, leafed through his book till he got to my name, and he says, 'Well, our records show you've been HIV-positive since 1979.'" Rob was stunned. "I had never been particularly promiscuous," he says. "I immediately went home and asked my companion, 'Do you think I'm going to die?' He said, 'No.' I said, 'You're right,' and that's how I've felt since, with certain lapses and moments of doubt."

Rob's metaphysical beliefs have been critically important to his survival. He has kept up a regular meditation practice for fifteen years, which he says "helps me come to terms with obstacles in my past and gives me a better outlook," as well as inspiring his best paintings. His relationship with his partner of eleven years was "instrumental in keeping my attitude on-track." Though they have now separated they remain very good friends. When Rob found out his HIV status, he told only a few people. "I didn't want the negative energy of them worrying, of friends saying, 'You know he's HIV-positive. I wonder how long he's got?'"

He waited until an article about him was to appear in a San Diego newspaper last year before he told his parents he was infected, though they had known for almost twenty years he was gay. "I'm one hundred percent behind you," his mother had responded, while his father, a retired Navy captain and pilot, was quiet and sparing. "He's a nice guy, but uptight. I called him up and launched into this upbeat little trumpets-in-the-background, 'Hey, Dad! Guess what!' kind of spiel. He said, 'Well, this is a real shock.' Then he said, 'Well, let me get your mother.' "

Rob has photos of many of his friends who died of AIDS on the walls of his studio in his Victorian house in San Francisco's Potrero district. He speaks of them with soft remembrance: "I've realized death is not a finality. Although I'm losing friends, I'm not losing them in the long run. We're only separated by physical boundaries. If you're around people with AIDS toward the end, it's really sad; but you realize the body is just dropping away and there's still that spirit." After a moment of silence he adds, "I really feel there's a purpose in everything. I don't believe in victims." He classifies himself as "part dreamer, part realist, but always hopeful." He has never had an infection, and his T-cell count remains improbably normal.

Rob, along with James Russell (not his real name), is one of the ten longest-surviving "healthy positives" from the San Francisco cohort. In May of 1979, James gave his first vials of blood for the hepatitis B study. He had been living in San Francisco since the early Seventies, where he had been at first an active participant in, later a somewhat skeptical observer of, the city's fabled Castro district. The scene had exploded into public view when what had once been a tolerantly mixed neighborhood became a national gay mecca. Gray Line tour buses brought Middle America to gawk at a "gay Chinatown" of pulsing discos, iron-pumping health clubs, and growing social and political clout.

But something told James it couldn't last. He'd penned a prescient essay titled "The Castro Is Dead" in 1978, before the gale force of the AIDS epidemic hit. He noted "an uncharacteristic calm enveloping the two blocks. . . . Shadowy figures in doorways of closed shops give the scene a forlorn, even sinister edge. . . . The failure of the Castro was its inability to take care of its own."

James found himself in the eye of the storm in 1985, when he learned he was HIV-positive. "The test had just come out. I had done a pretty good job of convincing myself I would be negative, so when I found out I was positive, I was unprepared to deal with it. I felt like I had been punched. You have to remember that in 1985, the news was that being HIV-positive meant a quick death sentence."

About a year later he remembered he had been in the hepatitis B study back in the late seventies. He had his frozen blood checked and discovered he had been HIV-positive since May of 1979. "Frankly, it was kind of reassuring. Look how long I'd had it, and I was still perfectly healthy." James has maintained a good number of T-cells for over fifteen years. In some ways, he feels embarrassed about his healthy immune system. In his support group, he says, "people will come in with their latest T-cell counts exclaiming over having twenty-five new ones since the last time, or being really bummed out they lost seventeen. Some literally have none, or fifteen or thirty, while I most recently had nine hundred. When I get my results, I don't even talk about it." He hasn't had "a glimmer of a symptom," and has never taken any of the common drug regimens prescribed for HIV. His recently retired doctor, he says, "marvels over me. His attitude was, 'There's nothing wrong with you, so there's nothing to fix.' "

When James tries to understand his survival, his classically chiseled features grow pensive. He had chronic allergies as a child, he says, wondering if this means he has a congenitally "hyperactive immune system." He had grown up in a house filled with creativity and tumult. His mother, lovely, unstable, a talented musician, had killed herself on the evening she was about to be committed to a mental institution. He remembers her as "a figure of mystery and intrigue."

He took refuge by putting on elaborate marionette shows on a homemade wooden stage, writing plays like "The Monkey on the Moon," serving as producer, director, and impresario, charging the neighborhood kids a quarter for admission. He characterizes himself as something of a loner "prone to depression." He gives the impression of being at once a pragmatist and a romantic. He says he prefers napping to meditating, reading to jogging, and gardening to exercising, taking "countless" Polaroids of his flowerbed and sending them out as greeting cards.

"I think one of my survival mechanisms," he says, "is staying in the business of living a normal life, not having an existence dominated by this disease." The one characteristic he has noticed in his support group, he says, "is that we are all pretty strong-willed people. We are not shrinking violets. We are outspoken, stubborn, argumentative, difficult, crabby, grizzly old survivors."

He pauses for a moment, carefully considering his thoughts. Then he says, "If anything, the whole AIDS/HIV thing has given me a sense of the value of life. I tell myself, 'You are incredibly lucky. You have gotten to walk down this path all these years of the AIDS crisis untouched while vast numbers of people have died.' " He continues to draw hope from a chance remark one of his doctors had made which lodged firmly in his mind: "There's never been an epidemic in the history of the world that hasn't had exceptional survivors."

But why are these people still here? Dr. Jay Levy, an AIDS researcher at the University of California, blasts the random statistical anomaly theory, which he characterizes as an attempt to "minimize these cases through a mathematical formula. It is remarkable how some people can trivialize survival by labeling it mere chance. Nothing is chance. There has to be an explanation, and the answer will give us a way to help everybody." But he doesn't find any clear behavioral patterns. None of the long-term survivors he studies—he refers to them as "healthy non-progressors"—are on antiviral medications, but that is the only commonality he sees: "Some are on vitamins, some aren't; some are on herbs, some are not; some smoke, some don't."

Pressed to speculate on the root cause for long-term survival, Levy quickly adds, "I think it's genetic," citing survivors' high activity levels of immune cells containing CD8 receptors, which he believes may keep HIV locked inside infected cells in a latent phase. Certainly, if some genetic factor can be found in those who form the far end of the statistical curve, it holds out the tantalizing promise of treatment for the over eleven million infected worldwide.

Most researchers believe that the overpowering influence of biology far outweighs the influence of any psychosocial factors in HIV, where so many have been lost so quickly. But the survivors living in the often desolate heart of the epidemic wonder how much loss of life is hastened by society's widely reinforced belief that death will be swift and inevitable. Many say they have seen infected friends despair and, as did some Auschwitz inmates faced daily with the gaping crematoria, decide to curl up and die. One long-term survivor, healthy and HIV-positive since 1979, wrote us, "If I've had a remarkable recovery from anything, it's been from the overwhelming negativity surrounding HIV. I think the belief that HIV=AIDS=Death has taken many of my friends' lives."

All survivors are interlopers, confounding steep odds, defying neat theoretical formulas. In light of their often gripping stories, the "three C's" of challenge, commitment, and control struck us as inadequate, even tepid. In the face of what we have observed, the three C's could as easily be crisis, catharsis, and congruence; or caring, cantankerousness, and creativity. Looking through the lens of the healing system, we found common threads connecting those who had faced varying challenges to survival: a determination to live based on a belief in one's own value, a "differential focus on the good," an often rich inner life, which may yield the blessings of life even in a moonscape of death. The more research we did, the more complex the tapestry of the healing system became, interweaving the intrinsic and extrinsic, the self and others. The threads extend in every direction—but perhaps the strongest and most sustaining are the ties that bind.

CHAPTER EIGHT

The Social Connection

T HERE IS A HASIDIC PARABLE: A MAN IS VOUCHSAFED A VISION of the afterlife. He is first shown a great hall with a long banquet table filled with ambrosial delights. Each diner is equipped with a three-foot-long spoon, but no matter how much they contort their arms, thrusting their elbows into their neighbors' faces, their utensils are too long to maneuver even a single morsel into their gaping mouths. They sit together, opposite and side by side, in mutual misery.

"This," says the man's otherworldly guide, "is Hell."

The visitor is then taken to another place and sees an identical banquet table set with the same sumptuous viands and the same impossible silverware. Only here the denizens are well fed, utterly joyous, glowing with health and well-being.

"This," pronounces his host, "is Heaven."

The man is baffled. "What's the difference?"

"In Heaven," says the guide, pointing delightedly as a person lifts his long-handled spoon across the table to the parted lips of a neighbor, "they feed each other."

We live in a time of lone heroes; mock-heroes, really. Our collective imagination is saturated with individuals who attain pinnacles by dint of indomitable, solitary will. Not infrequently, cases of remarkable recovery are cast in the same mold. But deeper investigation gives the lie to the mock-heroic version of healing. Time after time, we saw the power of enduring marriages, devoted friendship, selfless acts, and indestructible love. One well-chosen utterance, one strongly conveyed belief, one palpable gesture from a friend or loved one often provided the hand that pulled someone from the abyss.

It has been the backdrop of nearly every story in this book: Garrett Porter's parents and a husband-and-wife team of therapists devoted themselves to his struggle. Geertje Brakel exulted in a virtual conglomerate of unexpected friendships and a therapist who understood her so well she barely had to speak. Wally Shore's wife of over forty years and an entire hospital cheered him on. Christine Anderson had the friendship and support of her oncologist and her entire church.

Whether the "Three C's" of remarkable recovery are conceived of as challenge, commitment, and control or, as we are more likely to maintain, crisis, catharsis, and congruence, there is a fourth C that forms the hub around which all healing seems to turn: Connection. Here is another dimension unexplored in the medical case reports, which tend to extract the individual from the web of social relations.

This "fourth C" may be the most universal and critical factor in remarkable recovery. As if we didn't experientially know, science is revealing on an almost daily basis how crucial it is to our health. Concludes one recent study: "The link between personal relationships and immune function . . . is one of the most robust findings in psychoneuroimmunology." Even the activation of microscopic lymphocytes has been shown to depend in part on the quality of interpersonal bonds. In general, according to the *Journal of the American Medical Association,* "married persons live longer, with lower mortality for almost every major cause of death, in comparison with single, separated, widowed, or divorced persons." (In one study of more than 27,000 cancer cases, it was found that unmarried persons had poorer rates of survival.) Over the last several years, an increasing number of such studies has indicated that the more a person is isolated from the social whole, the less healthy he or she is likely to be.

The implications are profound: If people without strong social support become sicker, then strengthening loving, supportive ties with others may be a means of stimulating the healing system. If separation and loss can lead to impaired health, then attachment and affiliation may help overcome illness. There is some logic in thinking in terms of a "two-way street," where the psychosocial routes toward illness may bidirectionally lead to the citadel of health.

We found in our own study of remarkable recovery that other people are powerful medicine. Most of our cases had been married over twenty years, and forty-one percent over thirty years, an unexpected finding for a sampling in this era of divorce. People in their lives often "came through" in the moment of crisis—or else new friends and allies surfaced to support them on their journey. Even those who attributed their recoveries to powerful inward experiences seemed to feel a deep personal connection with the imaginal figures or spiritual presence they encountered.

Sometimes, of course, it proved necessary for patients to reject old patterns of relationship. One woman who had decided to refuse a treatment for lung cancer her doctors admitted was likely ineffectual still had to face the anxiety and even the wrath of her loved ones: "I had to fight not only my cancer, but my whole family," she said ruefully. "I had to remind them it was *my* life." Relationships sometimes underwent wrenching change, often followed by renewal and growth. In most cases, people discovered enormous new capacities for loving, caring, and nurturing.

Patients often forged unusually strong relationships with a doctor, a therapist, a friend, or a support group. Over and over, we were struck by "the power of one"—how just one person's encouragement in the struggle against the most horrendous odds formed the pivot of healing; and how one remarkable recovery often rippled outward to inspire others—and sometimes, to affect society at large.

Even the most religiously tinged miracles, looked at more carefully, are woven into a rich fabric of social coherence. Conrad Hazen, a consummately upright man, had paid for everything in advance. He'd ungrudgingly scribbled a check for the funeral he'd planned down to the last pallbearers, chosen a coffin, composed his headstone, hand-picked the preacher, told his eldest boy just how much the bill should be to hollow out his resting place in the Florida earth. A final letter to his wife, Marilyn, and his two sons had been sealed, postmarked for posterity. Conrad, known to his many friends as Connie, had prudently sold off his thriving community dental practice. A devout Christian, Connie had determined Death would not find him unprepared but encircled by his family, at home, waiting.

It wasn't going to be a long wait. The malignancy in the upper right apex of his lung—a large cell, undifferentiated adenocarcinoma—was inoperable. Further surgical spadework had turned up the kidney tumor from which it had spread. His physicians had gone in, chopped out what they could, and sewn him up minus one kidney and a length of intestine, but the prognosis was shorter than a baseball season. The surgeons had been forced to leave a mass the size of a fist behind. "My doctor told me," Connie recounts, "that I'd better get ready to shove off."

"Before the cancer, I had been sitting on top of the proverbial mountain," he says, his voice seasoned with a slight, resonating Southern lilt. He'd had a good profession, a nice home, a comfortable income. An ardent family man who had grown up with ten brothers and sisters, he'd worked out with his son, played tennis with his wife, and at forty-six felt in the prime of life. He'd quit smoking ten years before, didn't drink, and was an active deacon and Sunday school teacher in his church. "I felt," he sums up, "that I was where the Lord wanted me."

Cancer had plunged him "from the mountain into the dark valley." Twenty-five radiation treatments had caused only minimal shrinkage. The large tumor enmeshed in his brachial nerve plexus became a supernova of searing pain. "I was numb. I couldn't pray. A hospital's a lonely place in the wee hours of the morning. I used to lie awake and wonder where God was." One day his body, overloaded with painkillers, lapsed into a coma from liver failure; became, he says, "like stone." The family was summoned to his bedside to say good-bye to the inert statue that had once been a husband and father.

But Connie Hazen wasn't gone, just . . . elsewhere. "I was in this completely real-seeming dream," he remembers. "I was lay-ing there in bed and everybody I'd ever known in my entire life was trooping in. Each one would come over and hug me. The door just kept opening and closing. Finally, the Lord, or Some-body, came in. He put a shining golden key in my hand and told me, 'This will unlock the secret of life, if you'll but look at it.' And I looked and exclaimed, 'Oh my God, it's so simple, why can't we see it?' "

It was around then, back in the waking world where his grief-stricken wife and kids wept, that the doctor came running in, white coat flying, and plunged a hypodermic into Connie's im-mobile body in a last-ditch effort to bring him around. Connie had bolted upright, still completely absorbed in his otherworldly sojourn, and with a blind and blissful urgency thrust the precious object only he could see into his wife's hand. "I don't need this where I'm going," he'd told her. "Where's that?" she asked. "I'm dying," he replied. Then he'd wrapped his arms around her and, still insensate, murmured, "I love you" over and over for two hours.

It was touch and go, but he had finally regained consciousness, only to find death sitting patiently in the corner. The doctors sent him home with a few weeks to live. The cancer had whittled his six-foot frame down to an 80-pound contraption of parchment flesh and balsa-wood bone. He contemplated suicide, horrified he might wind up a "parasite instead of a breadwinner," draining his family of their life savings. He refused to see his friends, not want-ing them to behold the emaciated and tortured POW he saw in the mirror. He was too weak to stand even for a shower. "Marilyn," he recalls grimly, "had to set me on a stool in the tub and run the showerhead over me, like bathing a dog."

But a fortuitous letter from a friend gently, decisively turned him back toward life. "I don't know if you are bothered when people see you in your condition," the man wrote. "But I do hope you remember there is no such thing as an ugly Christian."

"No such thing . . . as an ugly Christian," Conrad repeats today, his voice catching. "I'll remember those words until the day I die. They brought me back." The simple act of sincerity formed his fragile, swaying bridge back to the mainland of humanity. He announced to his family he had decided to fight, for their sakes as much as his own, "just so you all know I wasn't a quitter."

Marilyn chimes in, smiling at the memory. "All of a sudden one day, he stood up and he said, 'I know I'm going to die trying, but I'm going to try.' He started with little baby steps, couldn't even walk from the front porch to the end of the sidewalk." But one day, tottering, Connie made it. Not long after, he hobbled once around the block, then jubilantly phoned a buddy who goaded him into doing it twice.

Some weeks later, Connie was fully ambulatory. When he accompanied his wife to a mammogram appointment, the radiologist did a double take. "'Lord, what are *you* doing here?'" Connie recalls the man blurting out. "All I could do was just look at him and grin. It felt great to be around when everybody was sure you'd be gone."

"They decided to take a chest X ray on the spot," Marilyn continues. "When the technician brought it out, the doctor said, 'You've got the wrong X ray.' The man replied, 'No, this is Dr. Hazen's, I just took it out of the machine.' It showed the tumor had disappeared. There was nothing there except a dark line of scar tissue.

"It's as big a shock to find out that you're going to live as it is to face your death," Connie says wryly. He slowly regained his strength, starting a landscaping business with his two sons—

"being creative with bushes," Marilyn called it. "If I can pitch mulch for a year," he had told her, "I can take care of patients again." It's been fourteen years, and people are again filling his office to complain about their aching teeth.

Connie "witnesses" at his church sometimes, but says, "I'm not about to run up and down the aisle hollering Hallelujah. I don't believe He saved me to stand by the church door screaming hey-this and hey-that." When asked for advice by other cancer patients, it comes out in an earnest gush: "Cry if you want to," he tells them, "laugh if you want to. But mostly, hold each other, hold the people who are dearest in your life and tell them how much you love them."

Conrad had a vivid imagination as a boy, excelling at creative tasks such as drawing and woodcarving. He is easily able to enter states in which he "talks to God." He says, "I sort of just lie back and clear my mind of everyday, petty stuff. A lot of times I don't remember leaving the house and going to the office because I was talking to the Lord." His spiritual beliefs in an active, caring, loving God who intervenes benignly in ordinary life allow Conrad to follow inner cues, finding pattern where others might find mere coincidence. Connie would be unlikely to attribute his healing to the chance biological fact that kidney cancer is a disease known occasionally to undergo remission. Nor is it entirely clear he should.

But if a miracle was vouchsafed, it was also through the agency of other people—surely, the "golden key" of Connie's coma-induced vision. From the moment he was diagnosed, he was enveloped in a web of social support as strong as tensile steel. Marilyn slept and prayed on the floor by her husband's hospital bed. His oncologist, Alvin Smith, was one of his best friends—a man who had gone to high school with him, dated the same girls, and served as best man at his wedding. Connie's high school class had voted to hold their thirtieth reunion early just for him, "because they all knew that I was going to be dead, and wanted to tell me they loved me and would miss me when I was gone."

He found himself at the center of an extraordinary social outpouring. Says Marilyn: "Conrad's patients are from all walks of life, all over this city. We even would get letters from all over the United States from people we'd never even heard of, people who said they were praying for him. It was amazing how our lives touched so many other lives through word of mouth. It was like a prayer chain that reached to Timbuktu." But Conrad, in his moment of greatest jeopardy, had entrusted his golden key to Marilyn alone. "She's been with me every step of the way," he says when he gives occasional sermons at his church. "Through the portals of hell and back. She deserves these better days."

Conrad Hazen's case is reminiscent of healing practices in traditional cultures where the entire community rallies to pull a person from the jaws of death. Anthropologist Richard Katz describes the healing rituals of the African !Kung, in which tribal members will gather to clap, sing healing chants, and dance for hours, all the while pleading and arguing with the gods and ancestors not to take the sick one away. Katz paints a memorable scene of dancers pausing in their ceremonial circling to yell up at the sky to the spirits, "What business do you have here tonight! This man is not ready to go. He wants to remain with those who love him." Surely, Connie's high school class, congregation, friends, and family lofted similar requests heavenward.

Among the !Kung, too, the bond of marriage is a golden key to healing. "When I went back to the Kalahari in 1989," Katz told us, "I noticed something very interesting. Here are these men in the healing ceremony, utterly oblivious in trance, yet where do they fall when they fall down? Every one of them, straight into the arms of their wives. That's the place where, in the intimacy of this inner work, they're most understood and get the most support."

Loving relationships have measurable healing power. In one American study of leukemia patients preparing to undergo bone marrow transplants, fifty-four percent of those who said they had strong emotional support from their spouses, family, or friends were still alive after two years, while only twenty percent of those who said they had little social support had survived. In another study of over a thousand heart patients at Duke University Medical Center, researchers found that those who lacked a spouse or confidant were three times as likely to die within five years of diagnosis as were the patients who were married or had a close friend. A University of Nebraska School of Medicine study of 256 healthy elderly people found that those with confiding relationships had higher immune function. Dr. Blair Justice, a psychologist at the University of Texas School of Public Health in Houston, observed that it was this confiding quality, the level of intimacy and honesty, that determined whether social support also supported health. "It may be more important to have at least one person," he said, "with whom we can share open and honest thoughts and feelings than it is to have a whole network of more superficial relationships."

Such a relationship is not necessarily with a family member. We live in a culture where the nuclear family is on shaky ground. For many, special forms of extended family arose to support the process of remarkable recovery. Witness Daniel (a pseudonym), a young man who, according to the report in the *Journal of the American Academy of Psychoanalysis,* was "the first published case of 'spontaneous' recovery from cancer where the psychodynamics were known before, during, and after the incident." In 1954 Daniel, then a twenty-one-year-old struggling through Episcopal seminary, found himself in the midst of severe spiritual crisis. He had been single-mindedly bent on becoming a priest, but in his last year of training had been overcome with a great revulsion. He sought the help of therapist Gotthard Booth, who found the young man inwardly stalemated by a "powerful conflict between his preoccupation with sex and his ideal of celibacy." Daniel's mother, a deeply disturbed woman who had abandoned him at birth but remained an erratic, harassing presence in his life, had inflicted deep and enduring emotional scars. The case report noted, however, that Daniel was "flexible in thinking and imagination, emotionally responsive, capable of differentiated introspection."

He continued in therapy through the end of his seminary

years—years that were "a walking nightmare," says the report—finally refusing ordination and choosing a secluded, impoverished life as a New York City librarian. Growing uncommunicative with his first therapist, he elected to continue treatment with Margaretta K. Bowers, herself a somewhat unconventional personality who saw him in individual therapy and also placed him in a "strong, cohesive therapy group." Initially, Daniel barely participated, "seldom speaking and appearing not to listen." But soon a marked improvement was noted. He began to face fears of abandonment dating back to infancy and made progress toward greater trust.

Less than a year later, however, Daniel was diagnosed with testicular cancer. The subsequent operation catalyzed a powerful shift in which he acknowledged his need to give and receive love. He emerged from surgery certain for the first time that he truly loved his girlfriend, Constance, and wanted to marry her. Notes his case report, "Decisions to set one's life straight and come to terms with Fate following first knowledge of cancer often auger well."

But an ill-omened wind blew into his life in the person of his mentally disturbed mother, who vehemently maintained that Daniel's cancer was "punishment by God for *her* sexual sins." Daniel, unable to psychologically fend her off, succumbed to a psychosislike state in which he came to believe his disease was divine retribution and his medical treatment a form of crucifixion. He sank into a deep depression. Flat broke and unable to work, feeling bereft and alone in his plight, he told his therapist that he could think of only one thing that might help. He confided an almost desperate need to obtain a particular pet—a capuchin monkey he'd seen in an exotic animal store—so that, as the report reads, he might "cuddle and care for something or someone." Margaretta Bowers obligingly found a donor to help him purchase the animal, who then became a "significant friend."

Daniel continued to be emotionally unstable, however, sometimes experiencing great outbursts of anger. He hurt his hand once hitting a wall to keep from hitting Constance. While being treated for this injury, cancer metastases were discovered in his neck, chest wall, and lung. His chances of one-year survival were now placed at zero. He was administered cobalt radiation and nitrogen mustard therapy, the only treatments available in 1959, viewed at his stage of disease as mere palliation for a hopeless case. During this same period, his grandfather died. Daniel, who had been raised by his grandparents after his mother had deserted him, was deeply concerned about his grandmother's response to this crushing loss. With all his relationships in turmoil, the tumors on his neck swelled to the point where he had to hold his head so that it nearly touched one shoulder.

Margaretta Bowers bluntly informed him that his doctors believed he had only weeks or at most a few months to live. "What do you want to do before you die?" she asked. Abruptly deciding that only "living life intensely" furnished him any hope of survival, Daniel answered without hesitation: "I want to get married and be ordained." With mortality bearing down on him like a runaway freight train, Daniel commenced an extraordinary about-face in his long-shaky relations with the human race.

Constance, now also in Bowers's therapy group, agreed to marry him, and hurried arrangements were made for a wedding. The affair, which the group helped put together, was an extraordinary demonstration of social cohesion. Constance and Daniel, whose illness made him look like a "walking ghost," were joined in matrimony by the seminary ethics professor who had been one of his first therapists. The reception was held at Margaretta Bowers's house, across the street from the church, with his doctor in attendance. Despite his ghastly appearance, Daniel had known before he approached the altar something extraordinary, sudden, and wholly unexpected had taken place: Tests had revealed his large neck tumors had, by his wedding day, almost completely regressed.

Daniel, whom we found, after circuitous detective work, in a small southwestern town, recalls a time obscured by the haze of illness. "I remember leaving the hospital still labeled terminal, barely able to stagger onto my feet, getting straight into a taxi to get my marriage license." He then decided to contact the bishop of Long Island and, after some discussion, persuaded the clergyman to ordain him.

Margaretta Bowers stepped up his therapy to a daily schedule. She helped keep his erratic mother at bay. Bowers writes that she also used "age-regression hypnosis" to help Daniel relive the feeling of his adored grandmother's love. "After th[is] vivid and meaningful experience," she reports, "Daniel continued to have a consciousness of a very real, warm relatedness to the grandmother who loved him so deeply."

"Margaretta herself's very controlling and kind of far-out," says Daniel today, "but she's a very loving human being. She would put me into trance and give me all these suggestions of health and love and I'd drift off." Asked to recall the greatest moment of his journey, Daniel says, "The biggie was being told that my chest X rays were clear on my way to getting ordained." Tests done the day before had revealed a complete disappearance of his pulmonary metastases. The entire journey from death to life had been traversed between February and August.

Daniel's spectacular healing became a medical football. "Everyone wanted to lay claim to what had happened. The radiologist, who had admitted that even with treatment I had no chance, tried to insist it was the cobalt. Margaretta said it was her therapy. The bishop thought it was 'the grace of the sacrament.'" But Daniel himself attributes it to "being showered with a lot of love from Margaretta, from my wife, and from the members of the group."

This combination of love and therapy appears to have been the inoculation that enabled him to weather subsequent emotional storms, including the suicide of his mother and the death of his beloved grandmother, without a recurrence of cancer. Recent studies have shown, in fact, that the effects of even minimal "doses" of therapy can be powerful and long-lasting. (Dr. Fawzy in 1990 reported he had given forty newly diagnosed malignant melanoma patients six weeks of therapy aimed at teaching stress management techniques and effective coping skills. Not unexpectedly, among the immediate effects were increased vigor, more active coping, greater involvement in their own care, and enhanced natural killer cell function. But the great surprise was to follow: Six *years* later, members of the group that received intervention were three times less likely to suffer recurrence or death.)

Daniel finished graduate school in clinical psychology with honors. He went through a period of anger at Margaretta Bowers over his radiation-induced sterility, but later asked her to be the godmother of their first adopted child.

Daniel and Constance split up after eighteen years of marriage. A few years ago Daniel—who describes himself as "gray-haired, getting old, but still respectably attractive"—moved out of New York City, where he had worked treating heroin addicts. He now has a job "working with crazy folks" in a mental hospital. He has lost his fascination for monkeys—"they get very aggressive when they hit puberty"—and now owns several "good, well-bred," eminently sociable Irish setters.

His spiritual quest in the intervening years led him through humanistic therapy at the Esalen Institute, meditation with a Hindu swami—"I was a typical California seeker"—and finally back to an uncertain relationship to the Church. "I always recoiled from the idea that Jesus died for our sins," he says; now, after studying with "Benedictine meditation teachers, almost Buddhist-types," he continues to grapple with an uncertain faith, still mulling over the puzzle of his survival. Healing, he concludes, is "a crazy burst of uncontrolled energy. It's not following the rules but, as Joseph Campbell put it, following your bliss." But he keeps coming back to emotional bedrock: The roots of remarkable recovery, he says, lie in "the ability to love, to discover that your center is love, that everything is love."

Most of us learn love as infants, with the first blind gropings and nuzzlings at the breast. Premature infants who receive more tactile and kinesthetic stimulation have been shown to take more formula and gain more weight. The health benefits of the maternal relationship are incalculable.

Rocky Edwards and his mother's bond was tempered to indestructibility when he was diagnosed with leukemia at the age of three. After grueling courses of chemotherapy and radiation, the dragon in his blood was medically vanquished. But at age ten, not long after he'd pulled the sword from the magical stone of five-year survival, he began to have trouble in school. As Rocky, now eighteen, remembers it, "I wasn't functioning right. The work got harder and harder. I started losing my memory." He started staying home from school with headaches, closeting himself in his room with the curtains drawn because light had become a bright, unbearable flood.

Doctors discovered a melanomalike tumor growing in his brain and began immediate treatment. But within a few months the tumor doubled in size. An operation was performed, yet the tumor grew back. A subsequent operation removed a sizable portion, but also left Rocky partially paralyzed, deaf in one ear, and blind in one eye.

Rocky's mother, Terry, a customer service representative for a bank, was frantic. She had taken him from hospital to hospital, doctor to doctor, watching agonized and hopeful at each new procedure. Rocky says succinctly, "My mother was always there, from morning to night." Yet the tumor continued to grow. Terry became "obsessed with learning about his exact disease. Any book, any magazine, anything I could find on it. I had to gain some control."

But to no avail. When Rocky emerged from his fourth and final brain surgery, she recounts without a trace of sentimentality, "He couldn't even say Mommy. They gave him six months to live."

Terry took him home. He had gone from "a normal, nice-looking everyday boy" to a puffy-looking child with a droopy eye, numbness in his face, and a "buffalo hump" from the drug prednisone. As the swelling in his brain subsided and memory and language began to return, he grew more frustrated and angry at his disabilities. Rocky remembers his friends stopped coming around. "I guess it's just normal," he offers, "when kids find out you've got a disease, they think it's going to be catchy, like AIDS." But the hurt still lingers in his voice.

No matter how despondent Rocky became, or how much Terry Edwards' own despondency threatened to weigh her down, she kept cheerleading, cajoling, even browbeating when she had to, anything to keep Rocky from giving up. "He hated the wheelchair, so I'd get him out into the swimming pool with me, just to keep him moving around. Then I got him to walk using a cane, which he also hated. I had to be real rough with him sometimes. I'd say, 'You can't just lie there and die! Is that what you want?' And he'd say, "No.' Then I'd say, 'Then get off your fat butt and move!' "

It was a Sisyphean time, a time of small steps, of progress and regress, but eventually Rocky wobbled upright. Still, as Terry observes, "Cancer's hard on a family. My daughter kind of went her way and my other son went his. Rocky was giving up and watching TV all the time. My husband was having a hard time handling it. He started just staying away." It was around that time, in an example of the contagion of hope engendered by remarkable recovery, that Terry saw a boy on the "Oprah Winfrey Show"—a kid who had had a brain tumor, had done some crazy Star Wars-type visualization of space ships whizzing around in his head, and had miraculously gotten well. The boy was Garrett Porter (chapter four).

He'd gotten *well!* Terry was galvanized. Having no one to guide her, she immediately made up her own practices and exercises. "This may sound silly—I didn't know what the heck I was doing—but I'd place my hands over Rocky's head in the area of the tumor, and tell him we were just going to visualize together and see that tumor just coming out." She called a friend she had met at a local chapter of the Children's Leukemia Association, the Starlighters, and asked if she knew of any groups Rocky could go to.

"You mean a hospice?" the woman had asked.

"No—my son's not going to die yet!" Terry had snapped. But suddenly everything had seemed a dead end. She began to wonder if her efforts to save her son were "a selfish thing. Maybe because I wasn't ready to give him up, I was interfering with the way things were supposed to go."

One night, after an angry exchange with Rocky, she flung herself down on her bed, sobbing uncontrollably, her stoicism in shambles. "I was just sniffling and wiping my eyes when the phone rang. It was my friend from the Starlighters, telling me a speaker was going to be there that night from something called the Getting Well program." Scarcely knowing what it was, Terry was instantly energized. "I asked my husband; he didn't want to go. My daughter didn't want to go. My son didn't want to go. So I said, fine, I'll go." Listening to the talk, she says, "was like a weight lifted off my shoulders. When a woman got up and called it just another money-grabbing idea, I told her to sit down and shut up!"

Excited, she convinced a reluctant Rocky to travel with her to the center, which offered a "multimodal" program of psychosocial healing techniques. Says Rocky, "I went there for one day and decided it was pretty neat." His mother remembers how he immediately bonded with other members of the group. "It was Thelma, sixty-five, Kathy, a tad over forty, and this little kid Rocky," she remembers, laughing. The three of them became inseparable, she says, still amused. "Each of them would get depressed and refuse to get out of bed, but they kind of took *turns.*"

Terry went to each all-day session, doing every meditation and relaxation exercise with her son, egging him on as he made up images of Ghostbusters shooting "ray-guns of white light" at his tumor. The program even helped to repair the family's downed communication lines by counseling her husband and daughter.

Shortly thereafter, Rocky's MRI revealed his tumor had stopped growing. Says Terry: "The radiologist said to me, 'It looks like the radiation's working.' I said, 'He's not getting radiation.' That kind of floored him." Encouraged, Rocky redoubled his efforts. "He put so much effort into it," Terry says, "that I really believed he would get well. He would do it seven times a day, ten times a day, just continuously. We would still do it to-gether, the way that I'd started when I didn't know any better."

A year later, a new MRI revealed the tumor had "gone flat. It looked like a deflated balloon." Now, years later, Rocky still routinely pictures "a little white wolf who attacks tumors and keeps my system clean." But he credits his mother's unassailable devotion as the greatest healing force. He states it with the simplicity of the child he was: "When I said, 'I'm not going to get better,' she was the one who really fought to keep me. 'We'll find something,' she always told me, and she kept on looking." Asked to name a factor that accounted for her son's healing, Terry says without hesitation, "Belief. His, mine. The combination of us. We're *real* stubborn."

Stubborn would be as good a way as any to describe Grace Gawler. She had met her future husband, Ian, while working for him as a veterinary nurse. Shortly after they began dating, Ian had been diagnosed with bone cancer and had undergone a mid-thigh amputation of his leg. When she married him, doctors had given him two weeks to live. "It's a good thing he had attracted someone who believed he could be cured," she says, laughing. "I had no doubt of it, and I was absolutely not prepared to give up."

Grace's own background was not a seedbed of nurturance. "I had no real awareness of the importance of close family ties, relationship, and communication," she says. "I really functioned as an independent part of my family." She had thrown herself into schoolwork from the time she was ten, spending nights diligently wading through biology books. She had a passion, she says, for finding out how living things worked, already consumed with what she calls "the healer instinct."

She needed it to overcome Ian's scientific objections, the ones that told him he was a hopeless case. "My training in veterinary medicine said that osteogenic sarcoma could only progress toward death," he told us. "Grace's faith that anything was possible shifted me toward believing other things could make me well."

One of those "other things" was Dr. Ainslie Meares, whom he met a year after his leg amputation. Dr. Meares, now deceased, was a colorful collection of paradoxes, the freethinking offspring of a wealthy Melbourne family, a tradition-bound man who taught meditation yet remained a member of the city's most elite social clubs. Meares had devised a particular form of meditation he called "mental ataraxia," a deep, passive "inner stillness," which seemed to have contributed to several documented cancer regressions.

According to Meares's report in the *Medical Journal of Australia,* when he first encountered Ian Gawler, the "young man with an extraordinary will to live" was dying.

> He had visible bony lumps of about 2 cm in diameter grow-ing from the ribs, sternum and the crest of the ilium, and was coughing up small quantities of blood in which, he said, he could feel small spicules of bone. There were gross opacities in the X-ray films of his lungs. He had been told by a spe-cialist he had only two to three weeks to live, but in virtue of his profession he was already well aware of the pathology and prognosis of his condition.

Diligently practicing Meares's meditation, Ian and Grace contin-ued on their healing pilgrimage. They spent their honeymoon in the Philippines, chasing over the length and breadth of the coun-try for even a will-o'-the-wisp of healing. There Grace learned a special form of massage, and spent hours each day kneading her husband's dying body, whispering words of encouragement she believed even when he did not.

Their travels took them to India to meet a famous guru, and then finally to a spiritual community in Scotland. Remembers Grace, "I'd been giving Ian quite a lot of massage, and he had a very large bony tumor on his sternum the size of a saucer, stand-ing up a good half inch. I was massaging him one day and I felt a big chunk fall off inside. I could actually pick it up under the skin.

I had a really clear image of the whole thing disintegrating like coral.

"From that time on," she remembers, "it had just shrunk and shrunk. Ian occasionally coughed up bits of bone that did look like old coral. We still have them as souvenirs. It shrunk away until there was nothing left."

Dr. Meares, in his report, attributed Ian's cure to his inner state:

> He has developed a degree of calm about him which I have rarely observed in anyone, even in Oriental mystics with whom I have had some considerable experience. When asked to what he attributes the regression of metastases, he answers: "I really think it is the way we experience our life." In other words, it would seem that the patient has let the effects of the intense and prolonged meditation enter into his whole experience of life. His extraordinarily low level of anxiety is obvious to the most casual observer. It is suggested that this has enhanced the activity of his immune system by reducing his level of cortisone.

But the most significant factor in his recovery, Ian told us—one which Meares's report largely neglects—was "experiencing love, not only a feeling of love, but the manifestation of it, the care and attention Grace gave me." He discovered a "healing partnership," one that blossomed not only into a complete cure, but a healing movement.

After Dr. Meares's article appeared in 1978, the Gawlers were inundated with sacks of letters from around the world. Sorting them in the veterinary clinic every night, struck by the sheer pathos of people in desperate straits reaching out for help, they realized the need for a healing center. "People were going off and doing meditation, or pursuing diets or various therapies, but nobody was really tying it together," says Grace. "We felt there should be something that helped each person find their own key within a whole program. We decided to build a place that would give people the opportunity to search out what was right for them."

They purchased a forty-acre swatch of land outside Melbourne, dubbing it Rainbow Park. Ian and Grace lived in a small shed, anticipating they would build a house in six months. Instead, it took four years, during which time they had three children, each delivered in their ramshackle home. In 1981, they began a series of weekly support groups there for cancer patients. Today, with a staff of thirty, they run a residential care facility in the foothills of the great dividing range on Australia's eastern coast. Ian, ever the veterinarian, runs the center as an informal wildlife refuge, shepherding a herd of some fifty kangaroos, fretting about the effects of environmental pollution on his small population of koalas.

Of the ten thousand people who have passed through the center, six thousand have participated through weekly support groups. The reaction of the medical community has been mixed, Ian Gawler reports. "They recognize the groups and the techniques would naturally improve patients' quality of life. But when it comes to improving survival times, they're deeply skeptical." Referring to Dr. David Spiegel's landmark Stanford study showing that women with breast cancer who participated in weekly support groups had doubled their survival times, Gawler demands: "If a new anti-cancer drug was shown to double the life span of women with advanced breast cancer, wouldn't it be negligent not to recommend it?" (Concurs an article in the *New York Times,* "What has caught the eye of cancer specialists about the [Spiegel] findings is that the support groups added an average of eighteen months to the women's lives, appreciably longer than any of the chemotherapy medications they were also taking could have been expected to offer given the advanced stage of their cancer.")

Ainslie Meares's report failed to suggest another powerful social dimension often seen in remarkable recovery: the relationship with the healer. Meares himself was an impressive figure who stood six-foot-two and wore his long hair in a dramatically swept-back gray mane. "When you arrived at the group sessions," Grace Gawler remembers, "he'd first make physical contact. He'd lead each person in with his hand on their shoulder and sit them down. Then he'd go back and bring the next one into the room the same way. And he would walk around amidst people and make sounds—low, primordial grunting tones. It had a profound, almost hypnotic type feel about it. It placed you into a very deep state of relaxation. He had this enormous presence that just filled the room."

It is reminiscent of a recent description by ethnobotanist Mark Plotkin of a healing ceremony deep in the Central American jungle. The patient was a severely ill boy named Petrus. "The healer waved his hands in strange patterns just above and behind the boy's head, all the while moaning incantations in a low voice. After a few minutes of this, he started to massage he child's neck. . . . He began pounding a nail into a tree with a large rock and chanting the same phrase over and over—'Make this boy better.' " The man's presence was overwhelming, reports Plotkin, "like staring into a roaring fire at close range." After giving the child a drink made from medicinal plants, the shaman began singing; "as he crooned, he picked up his machete and started swinging it wildly over the boy's head." The shaman continued his ritual chanting in the pale moonlight. The next day, "Petrus came trotting down to the riverbank, smiling and laughing when he saw his father. The change in him was nothing short of extraordinary. His eyes no longer had their yellowish pall . . . I was stunned by the boy's recovery."

Ian Gawler himself cuts something of a figure. He wears a caftan, a wide-sleeved Middle Eastern–style robe, "for comfort and aesthetics." Tall and thin, his strong handsome face weathered and lined, he looks like a craggy extrusion of the land itself. When participants gather at the Jumbunna Lodge where the live-in seminars are held, they can glance over at him, his metal crutches neatly beside him, and take courage to live.

Gawler might be considered a classic "wounded healer," someone who in the course of his own recovery transforms his private quotient of suffering into an elixir for others. In mythology, the path of the wounded healer seems to wander in and out of the precincts of human fellowship. Oscillating between community and isolation, he returns bearing the boon of a new medicine. Similarly, we noticed that those who had undergone remarkable recoveries not infrequently had remarkable effects on the people around them, even upon society at large.

The story of Guo Ling is in many ways a Chinese parallel to that of Ian Gawler, the story of a patient whose own highly individual quest for healing almost inadvertently created a social groundswell. After the trauma of her father's death, Guo Ling was diagnosed in her thirties with a terminal gynecological malignancy. On the advice of experts in China and overseas, she underwent several operations, which proved unsuccessful. She was sent home and expected to die. Guo Ling had heard of Chi Gong, an "internal" martial art whose history in China can be traced back thousands of years to the monks of the Shao-Lin monastery. Reputed for its power to build up the "vital energy" of body and mind, it had never before been used to treat cancer, so Guo Ling decided to create a new form. Beginning her effort in middle age, she devised a Chi Gong style, which involved vigorous walking with the arms moving rhythmically in an arc around the body. After protracted practice, she had a remarkable recovery.

She then moved to Shanghai, a city where she knew no one. Gradually, through her initial followers, the story began spreading in the early 1980s that her techniques were effective with cancer. Guo Ling decided to found a club—a form of organization permitted by the government—and began to teach what is now known as Guo Ling Chi Gong.

The second member of her club, a man named Wang, was diagnosed with stomach cancer and after a course of chemo and radiation, was sent home from the hospital with three months to live. His wife had urged him to take lessons from Guo Ling, who she heard had miraculously recovered. He refused. But his wife badgered him until he showed up on Guo Ling's doorstep under marital marching orders. After three to four months, he began to feel better. His cancer disappeared and Wang, an engineer by profession, became an enthusiastic Chi Gong tutor.

Chi Gong, with its combination of visualizations, special movements, and purported psychophysical energies, may be well suited to stimulate the healing system. But Guo Ling's cancer club, which by the late 1980s began to grow and spread throughout Shanghai, provided cancer patients with a social support network as well as a healing practice. Cancer patients are shunned by many in China, who believe the disease to be contagious. Today, run by six unpaid administrators who have no office, the group has burgeoned into the 40,000-strong Cancer Patients' Recovery Club, visible in the hundreds of patients practicing Chi Gong in public parks, their arms windmilling slowly around them.

Even into her eighties, Madame Guo, a coarse-voiced, stockily built fireplug of a woman partial to brightly patterned muumuus, could be found leading classes of hundreds of people seven days a week, her short-cropped hair thick and black. She had hoped in vain that her apparent successes would be examined more rigorously in a clinical study.

But her grass-roots group represents more than just a healing methodology. It is an entire way of life. Madame Guo felt strongly that it was integral to an individual's recovery to give something back to society (a belief confirmed by several Western studies which cite "altruism" as a characteristic of those who recover from serious illness). When a group of actors put on performances to help raise money for the club's activities, members bought books for jailed youths. Madame Guo saw it as a way to spread the healing energy throughout society as a whole, as well as to increase her patients' ties to a wider social realm. The club in Beijing is named the "Cancer Patients' Paradise."

It shouldn't be surprising that various cancer self-help groups that have sprung up in recent years—many of them founded by former patients—would resemble healing communities and practices seen the world over. Patients often attribute their recoveries to an almost instinctive recapitulation of time-honored methods of stimulating the body's healing system. Many of the activities they chose would be recognizable to any traditional healer: meditation and imaginative exercises, purifying diets, music, dance, art, massage, group interaction, emotional "acting-out," even play.

The Bristol Cancer Self-Help Centre in England is perhaps the best known of such communities. The brochure lists individualized psychological and medical counseling; diet and food supplementation; breathing exercises; visualization; relaxation; healing ("nondenominational, only requiring a willingness to receive an input of energy"); creativity ("having fun, seeking uplift and inspiration through beauty, enjoying nature and visiting sacred places, following of our dreams, living out our unfulfilled ambitions"); shiatsu massage; music therapy; poetry; "voice work"; "whole food cookery"; and Chinese herbal medicine. Its goal, says cofounder and cancer survivor Penny Brohn, is "to provide an antidote to despair and a medicine for new life."

Penny is a proverbial ball of fire, an animated talker perpetually up in arms against "anything that strains toward mediocrity." She recalls a difficult childhood shot through with the "absolutely terrifying" presence of her lay preacher grandfather and an implicit requirement to be "the purest and most amazing and fantastic children" for her infinitely judgmental mother. She also recalls private mystical experiences, where "the only way I could cope with the stresses and strains of being alive was to lie in bed at night and just leave my body. I used to float up into the corner of the room and look down on myself and my sister and I had feelings of such bliss and tranquillity." These strange experiences left her with a "sloppy, humanistic Christianity" and a firm conviction that "we don't stop at our skins."

It was a belief she found of momentary comfort when, at age thirty-five, she was diagnosed with a breast tumor. It was 1979, and she was a freshly minted acupuncturist recently returned to England from her studies in Hong Kong. Still, Penny was not entirely surprised to find herself ill. Her social connections had fallen to tatters, leaving her alternately depressed, confused, and afflicted with a sense of groundlessness. Her father had died unexpectedly that year. Her mother, after announcing she couldn't live without him, followed him into death eight weeks later with a myocardial infarction. Penny's fifteen-year marriage had produced three children, but had made her "very unhappy for a long time." She had felt all that year that "something terrible was going to happen."

But when her doctors told her they were scheduling her for an immediate mastectomy with possible radiation and chemo as follow-up, she was appalled. "With the ink barely dry on my certification for holistic medicine, I just couldn't do it. My mother was one of these people who believed there wasn't much that cabbage-water couldn't cure, and she'd brought me up, for better or worse, with some wonderfully eccentric and idiosyncratic views about healing.

"Besides," Penny says, "I'd done a little research, and it looked to me that breast cancer statistics for conventional treatment were still not much better than they'd been in 1908." Gathering her courage, she told her doctors she wanted to first investigate alternatives. "I was so scared I was wobbling, because I faced a loss of approval and support, whereas if I just had the mastectomy everybody would have been nice to me." Her physicians were "completely horrified, coming into my room in threes and fours to persuade me till they couldn't all fit at the end of the bed."

Penny finally agreed to a biopsy under local anaesthetic, a procedure that proved longer and bloodier than expected when a much larger mass was discovered. When the pathology lab found it was malignant, hurried preparations for surgery were made. But Penny balked. "I was done with being a passive recipient that night. I would not be rolled over into taking this major step."

Penny had been a rebel of sorts in the Sixties. "I'd done all the usual things, telling people not to eat meat or use pesticides, sweeping around in long frocks feeding chickens and milking goats. But to take on anybody in authority directly and say No? Never. My husband, David, came to the hospital to pick me up and couldn't believe the change. He thought, 'Where is the woman who is such a wimp she'd say anything to please everybody? What has happened to her?' She was *gone.*"

At her insistence, she and David flew to Bavaria to investigate a controversial fixture of European alternative cancer treatment, Dr. Joseph Issels. Planning just to visit for a day, she was so impressed she decided to stay for the entire nine-week program. She submitted to a polyglot series of treatments which ran the gamut from homeopathy and naturopathy to fever-inducing immunotherapy.

But it was the center's more psychologically oriented programs that plunged Penny headlong into her own largely uncharted emotional rapids. When she was a child, she'd had a recurring nightmare: She dreamed of going into the basement and seeing a man with a guillotine and a boy kneeling before him. The man was going to cut off the boy's thumbs. She was next in line. Just as she would place her hands dutifully beneath the blade, she would wake up. It was a dream of utter powerlessness. Without thumbs, the hand cannot grasp and hold; it was a dream of life literally slipping through her fingers.

Now, with cancer's guillotine poised over her, she sought empowerment. "At Issels' clinic, I read a book that said cancer patients have 'difficulty expressing anger.' I thought, 'Oh well, not me' because I get angry about the whales and outraged over dolphins. Then I turned the page and the sentence continued ' . . . *in their own defense.*' And I thought Ah!" She makes a self-deprecating grimace. "Not too good at that." Then she grins. "So I then spent the next five weeks at the clinic stamping my feet and screaming, *Bugger!*"

In the first week, her friend Pat Pilkington showed up to lend moral support. Pat had used an inheritance to purchase a former nunnery in Bristol, gathering thirty or so people, and starting a small charitable foundation to explore meditation, yoga, acupuncture, and spiritual healing. Talking with her long into one night, Penny came to a sudden decision: "The hell with it, whatever else happened, if I lived long enough, I was going to set up a center for people who had cancer."

Pat remembers how Penny had set her jaw determinedly, a sure sign the deed was as good as done. "Penny kept wishing there was just one person who had healed in the way she was trying to, who could talk to her and hold her and encourage her. Suddenly the idea came to her that if she got herself well, *she* could be that person. That was her turning point. She had been quite low, but now, thinking of helping others, she was able to reenergize herself. She literally sat up and we began planning."

Whether it was Dr. Issels's medicines, her deep emotional explorations, mental imagery, her family, the loving support of a good friend, or suddenly having set her sights on a glorious goal, an alchemical event occurred: Penny's tumor, to her doctors' amazement, rapidly melted away.

Penny and Pat opened their center within a year of Penny's diagnosis. The house in Bristol was perfect: a rambling, Georgian-style former convent dating back nearly two centuries. Set amid large gardens overlooking a valley from the suburban Clifton terraces, it had thirty cubical bedrooms that used to be the nuns' cells, large meeting rooms, and a huge chapel. The program itself was improvised. Penny borrowed from her experiences in Germany and her Chinese medical training, setting out "the crudest three-legged stool of body, mind, and spirit. I'm not a scientist or a doctor, but in the valley of the blind it's the one-eyed man who's king."

The main purpose, Penny says, was "to unshackle patients from a self-fulfilling prophecy of death. If I could somehow show them that even one person in the whole wide world had managed to turn this thing around, it would give them hope. It seemed to me that nowhere in the hospital system was anybody getting the message that it might be possible to wrestle with terminal disease and succeed."

The center's one-day-a-week schedule became two and then three. Penny and Pat assembled a more structured but, from the patients' point of view, pleasingly hodgepodge program. There were relaxation classes, autogenic tapes, visualizations, nutritional instruction, even some volunteers from England's large Fellowship of Spiritual Healers. "Most important of all," says Penny, "we had group sessions where everybody sat around in a circle and talked."

When a popular television series focused on the Bristol center, it was, says Penny, "instant mayhem. We were inundated." The waiting list grew even longer when, in 1983, Prince Charles himself lent his support, citing the role the center had played "in influencing the way in which the whole community responds to cancer patients and their needs." Money began coming in from charitable gifts. Holistic doctors and nurses affiliated themselves. But then Penny, symptom-free for four years, experienced "a rerun of a bad movie." Two lumps appeared in her breast. One was surgically removed, but the cancer was found to have deeply infiltrated. It was too late for a mastectomy, though radiation held out a slim hope. Finding a radiologist who was willing to watch and wait, she decided to try yet again to cure herself. After a year, deciding that she'd been "a bit pig-headed and silly," she told her radiologist she was ready to undergo his treatment. "It was very funny," she says, "because he whipped out his plastic ruler, measured, and said, 'Well, you've taken me by surprise. Somehow you've managed to deal with this yourself.'"

Penny, now a two-time winner of a poor-odds lottery, was elated. She had written a best-selling book. The Bristol Cancer Help Centre had grown from "a front room in Downfield Road" to a complementary cancer care facility that had treated thousands of patients. Penny, a descendent of Baptist forebears, had taken to energetically pounding the pulpit worldwide, seeding new healing centers in South Africa, New Zealand, Hong Kong, and Zimbabwe. London's Hammersmith Hospital, calling Bristol "the gold standard for complementary care in cancer," set up their own groundbreaking multi-approach oncology unit. The "Bristol Diet," initially regarded with skepticism, became widely accepted for convalescents of every description. The residential program thrived.

Many of the Bristol patients had of course subsequently died, but it seemed clear that lives had been prolonged, and at a higher quality thanks to the center's programs. A shining cadre of "Golden Oldies," people who had come to Bristol in its first early weeks, was improbably still alive.

But in September 1990, the health of the center itself was nearly ruined when the preliminary results of a study were published in Britain's prestigious medical journal, the *Lancet*. The statistics were as startling as they were devastating: Women treated at Bristol, the study claimed, were three times more likely to suffer a spread of disease and twice as likely to die as women treated with orthodox medicine. The study, called the Chilvers Report, was the ultimate indictment: Alternatives, seemingly, were not just useless but actually abetted the progression of cancer.

The news came smack in the middle of plans for the center's tenth anniversary conference, turning a celebration into an uproar. As the press trumpeted the findings, the effects were instantaneous and far-reaching. Some cancer patients concluded, wrote one of the Bristol Centre's doctors in a rebuttal in the *Lancet,* "that activities such as relaxation or visualization may have seriously damaged their health."

However, amid a storm of subsequent criticism from peers and in the pages of the *Lancet* itself, the Chilvers Report researchers were forced to admit publicly their study had been fundamentally flawed. (One British paper called it "one of the most embarrassing episodes in British medical research history.") But the damage had been done, not just to the center but to Penny herself, for the relationship between individual health and the social environment is a two-way street. Penny had found the conflict an impossibly stressful time, though she was unwilling to "just quit and turn in my toes." The brouhaha, she believes, may have been a contributing factor in a third recurrence of her cancer.

"I kept plowing on in this typically self-sacrificial way. By the time I crawled into the hospital to see somebody," she says, "I had got such a big tumor in my spine that I could barely walk." She had an immediate course of radiation. "I could see that I had broken all my own rules and everybody else's. There was no way that I could sidestep some pretty confrontational treatment." Like the proverbial cat with nine lives, she recovered yet again, celebrating her healing by bicycling 200 miles from Moscow to St. Petersburg the following Easter. Her X rays a year later, her doctor said, were " 'not just OK, but brilliant.' He told me, 'You've rebuilt the bone, it's quite remarkable and I'm going to put the before and after pictures over my desk.' "

The jubilation again proved premature. Her travails returned with a vengeance, and Penny met them with her characteristic Perils-of-Pauline amalgam of pluck and luck. The tumor in her back had regrown, leaving the impacted neural connections on her spinal cord "hanging by a thread." The doctor told her he couldn't do more than try to dull the pain. "I thought, wow, this is it," Penny says. "But he came bounding back the next day and said he maybe could try a much longer, harder operation. He managed to get the tumor out and tossed it in the bin. Of course, my spine now looks like an Amnesty International candle with a wire wrapped around it and big metal rods to support it all, but I loved him. He had all the hand-dusting enthusiasm as if he'd only replaced my hip joint."

Her seemingly endless ups and downs have made her a survivor nonpareil. For her, the dividing lines between conventional and alternative medicine have blurred. "I will use whatever weapons I have," she says simply. "I've stopped beating myself up as a failure."

Besides, she says, very much in the spirit of the wounded healer, "my recurrences appear to have endeared me to more patients than any of my successes. Back when it looked like I was this kind of wonder woman who could do it all by herself, I was a hard act to follow. But as soon as I joined the rest of the gang, stumbling around getting it right one time and wrong the next, moving from enlightenment to confusion every five minutes, I think patients found me more accessible."

The staff at Bristol, as at most of the healing centers we found, strives for such human accessibility, based on an understanding that healing involves individual needs and potentials. Says Dr. Rosy Daniel, the center's medical director: "You can say something to one person, who's so ready to hear it they're like a ripe plum ready to drop from the tree, and their energy picks up and they take off like a rocket. Another, you say it three or four times, and nothing much seems to change. And then the sixth time, something will happen, whether it's a significant dream, an event in their life, or a breakthrough in communicating with their husband or wife. And you can see they've suddenly chosen life."

She has seen first-hand in her years at the Bristol Centre how a human connection, even one at the most basic level in the healing profession—the sharing of pain—can seemingly make a difference. She describes the first patient she saw at the center in 1986, a woman with widespread, metastasized ovarian cancer. "She was in agony, and I just didn't know what to do. So I said, 'Well, let's just feel this pain together,' and we ended up rolling around on the floor together for hours, just *being* the pain. She was screaming and groaning and ranting and raving. We laughed, we cried together, we ended up exhausted together. She left, and when I didn't hear from her, I suspected that she had died. But a few months ago, after eight years, she turned up here as a support person for somebody else!"

The role of the support person can be a difficult one. Says Penny Brohn's husband, David, "I once gave a talk at a group and someone asked me what it had been like for *me*. They usually ask Penny what it was like for *her*. And I answered that there were times that of course I was terrified she would die. But there were also times I was terrified she *wouldn't* die, because I wasn't sure how much more I could cope with. The thought of crying over the gravesite with everybody being nice to me was actually quite appealing at times. But I've undergone a terrific change, sometimes very much against my will."

Penny interjects, affectionately teasing her husband, "But we're together as a result of this passionate struggle and dance and fight.

Aren't we, sweetie?" She clasps his hand, their fingers interlacing. *"That's* the stuff."

The most fundamental denominator—the real "stuff"—of the social equation is just one other person. We saw again and again how crucial such a relationship is for remarkable recovery. For Connie Hazen it was his wife; for "Daniel," his therapist; for Rocky Edwards, his mother. We also saw, as the earliest tribal healers always knew, how healing is passed from hand to hand, from touch to touch, in widening concentric circles.

But there are many such circles to the healing process, overlapping in ways we do not yet fully understand. Bristol medical director Dr. Rosy Daniel enumerates what she says is only a partial list from her own experience: "Love, self-expression, communication, contact, faith, the rekindling of the individual spirit, the transformation of core values to the values of heart, a general connectedness to life." It is toward this "connectedness to life"—the most fundamental, and most complex, healing force of all—that we must next turn our attention; for at the center of its intersecting, weblike lines we found the crossroads of our central mystery: the human healing system.

CHAPTER NINE

The Healing System

MEDICINE HAS ADVANCED MOST DRAMATICALLY THROUGH a special form of epiphany: the understanding of whole systems. Science was not always aware, for example, that there was such a thing as a nervous system. Only when certain odd anomalies were noted and investigated—How could nerve damage in one place affect a distant part of the body?—were elements once viewed as separate revealed as a coherent, purposeful system. Entire specialities (and new cures) grew from the scientific equivalent of the old chorus "The hip bone's connected to the thigh bone."

Greek physicians dissected animals to learn how the arteries carried blood. But it took until the seventeenth century and the work of Dr. William Harvey to determine that the heart was a pump, that veins, arteries, and capillaries were connected to it for the purpose of moving the red fluid of life, and that the whole bruiting, biomechanical contraption was a *circulatory system*.

Medical understanding progresses from observation of effects, to structure, to function, to the divining of connections, and finally, to the proclamation of whole systems. Insights become more profound with each advance in means of investigation: The digestive system was first identified through observing how the mouth, teeth, tongue, and esophagus combined to chew, swallow, move, and dissolve food. But it took the principles of biochemistry to explain how the body turned dissolved food into the energy needed for growth and self-repair.

With new tools, the science of systems advanced. The idea that endocrine glands and their associated ducts might be systemic metabolic pathways was first postulated then proven. The nervous system's parts were diagrammed, models constructed, descriptive language honed and then, gradually, it was learned how messages of pain and pleasure traveled along the discernible pathways between nerves and brain. Lastly, some of the immune system's vasts and deeps were revealed.

It was only after a famous 1974 experiment by Robert Ader showing how a rat's immune system could be "conditioned" to respond to ordinary saccharine that three systems previously thought distinct—endocrine, nervous, and immune—were revealed to be an interconnected.

Ader's discovery, which heralded the new field of psychoneuroimmunology, or PNI, had ratified a system composed of other systems—what might be called a meta-system. The existence of this new axis, where nerve fibers talk to lymphocytes and endorphin molecules whisper to brain cells has revolutionized medical theory. We believe if there is one pressing argument for a thoroughgoing, urgent, and even passionate investigation of remarkable recovery, it is this: to discover, and utilize, the properties of another unmapped meta-system of the body and mind—the Healing System.

The late Norman Cousins once wrote,

I looked for "healing system" in the indices of medical textbooks and found nothing . . . I consulted the curriculum catalogues of medical schools and found listings for anatomy, physiology, endocrinology, pathology, psychology, immunology, physics, biophysics, and chemistry, but, again, nothing on the way the total organism is equipped to recover from abnormalities and illnesses.

The healing system, as we define it, performs three principal functions: self-diagnosis; self-repair; and self-regeneration. Usually these take place below the threshold of consciousness. Woe to the unwary cancer cell in a normally functioning body: It will be identified, destroyed, and disposed of, after which the body will immaculately refurbish itself. This is homeostasis, the healing system's constant, unobtrusive Acme Janitorial Service, on perpetual contract for health maintenance. It is the reason we don't need to think about cuts and bruises, keeping the surface of our eyes moist, or fighting the teeming bacteria our immune surveillance mechanism daily chops to bits.

But in serious injury or disease, an emergency mobilization becomes urgent. Norman Cousins referred to it as a "grand orchestration of all the body's systems enabling human beings to meet a serious challenge." Given that the immune system and nervous system (including the brain, the seat of thought and emotion) talk to each other, it is tantalizing to ask how many levels up the ladder of conscious awareness the healing system goes. It was long assumed, for example, that the autonomic system that controls basic bodily functions like heartbeat and temperature was purely self-regulating. But biofeedback and hypnosis proved that functions once thought to be beyond the reach of consciousness could be intentionally modified, often by entering into altered states of mind like meditative visualization, relaxation, and trance.

We began to wonder if, in a serious health crisis, the mind is summoned to the engine rooms of the body on an emergency basis, explaining some of the phenomena we have observed in remarkable recovery. It has begun to seem that only through a mind–body–spirit axis could such intangibles as will-to-live tangibly influence the course of illness. It might be said that the healing system comes fully into play when ordinary physiology can no

longer meet a threat, and the whole of what we are as human beings must be recruited to battle an adversary that will otherwise be
the end of us.

In mapping the healing system, we decided to heed the admonition of the late Buckminster Fuller, inventor of the geodesic
dome: *If you want to understand something,* he was fond of saying,
peering his through his trademark Coke-bottle glasses, *you have to
start with the universe.* The more broadly we looked, the more the
healing system seemed integral to the universe of stimuli that
comprise human life itself—seemed bound up with the elements
of our very selfhood.

A review of the people we studied in the previous chapter on
social support reveals the range of the healing system's complexity. All found strong social connections, and most had medical
treatment, though in most cases it had been deemed ineffective.
But Daniel also had psychotherapy, hypnosis, and a type of spiritual rebirth. Rocky did visualizations ten times a day and
participated in a multifaceted healing program. Ian Gawler
pursued yoga, acupuncture, meditation, a special diet, even
Philippine "psychic surgeons." Guo Ling did incessant Chi Gong
practice.

Their stories, like virtually all stories of remarkable recovery,
point to a constellation of factors that may trigger the healing response. We are not the only researchers to take note of this. A
sampling of cases from a 1977 medical journal article by psychologist Charles Weinstock entitled "Notes on Spontaneous Regression of Cancer" shows the tatterdemalion flag under which the
healing system operates:

Case Reports: 1. An aunt of mine was operated upon for
carcinoma of the colon twenty years ago. It was widespread
throughout the abdominal organs and cavity, and she was
closed up and sent home to die. However, this woman of
forty (who had lost both parents after long caring for them in
their old age) met a man who interested her just before the
cancer symptoms began. She was never told she had cancer,

and recovered rapidly as wedding plans proceeded. She is fine today after a rather good marriage. 2. Dr. Maurice Green, as an intern, observed the treatment of a physician with glioblastoma multiform. The operation was unsuccessful. The patient, however, had a regression rather than progression of symptoms and signs. Eventually he left the hospital completely well, indicating only that he felt differently about life after facing death. . . . 6. A male physician of 45 in South Africa was given up for dead with widespread cancer of the colon. He seemed particularly involved, however, in writing a book. He got better and lived 10 years at least. . . . 9. A woman of 51 had cancer of the bladder. This was unsuccessfully operated on. She had a religious conversion subsequently, and has been well for 10 years now. 10. A woman of 55 with terminal cancer of the colon was given two weeks to live. She was in skeletal condition. A grandchild was born. She gained much weight, lost all symptoms, and lived 14 months, helping much with the baby. . . . 12. A woman of 52 had carcinoma of the uterus (originating near or in the cervix). It had spread to the intestine and death was expected within weeks. But her much-hated husband suddenly died. Today a year and a half later she is entirely well.

The complexity of the healing system could be said to know no bounds—and respect no boundaries. The partial list of phenomena that may be integral to the healing system has grown throughout this book—from mechanisms of pure biology like wound healing, immunity, genetics, and neurotransmitters to emotions, belief systems, dreams and symbols, hypnosis, dissociative states, relationships, the power of love, visualization, art, biofeedback, nutrition, and even possible unknown "energy" effects. The study of remarkable recovery leads us, inexorably, to what Gregory Bateson once called "the pattern that connects."

But the pattern remains far from clear. We might take the hypothetical case of a cancer patient treated with a conventional regimen without curative result; who then tries an unproven alternative remedy; who does visualization, meditation, and prayer; who has several bouts of unexplained fever; who experiences a striking emotional catharsis; who has exceptionally loving, supportive relationships; who is adjudged to have a "coping style" marked by "fighting spirit"; and who then has a remarkable recovery. Explanations would fly fast and furious. Oncologists might speak in terms of an unexpected, delayed effect of chemo or radiation; geneticists of yet-unknown DNA markers predestining a cure; herbalists of the efficacy of red clover and chaparral tea. Neuroendocrinologists would suggest secretions of endorphins; immunologists a mobilization of Tumor Necrosis Factor. Theorists of mental states would point to spontaneous hypnosis or the placebo effect; theologians to spiritual intervention; social scientists to the salubrious effects of social support; epidemiologists to random statistical variations.

Remarkable recovery remains a continent of neighboring tribes inhabiting separate domains with scarcely a common language between them. The contending models and descriptions are worthy of the blind men and the elephant, each insistently disputing whether the whole of the beast is tusk, trunk, or tail. As with the attempts of early physiologists to understand other now well-known systems, we can only impute the healing system's existence from its appendages; collect such evidence (the alpha of all scientific theory) as we can; and hypothesize its mechanisms from the circumstances of inexplicable cures. Though our work necessarily remains speculative, we will take as our guidepost Einstein's dictum: "For the creation of a theory, the mere collection of recorded phenomena never suffices—there must always be added a free invention of the human mind that attacks the heart of the matter."

The story of a man named Peter Hettel is particularly rich with circumstantial evidence of the healing system, though, as is always the case, its threads must be teased out of the fabric of a lifetime. Peter's life up until the point he was diagnosed with cancer had been somewhat unmoored. Peter, who had tested as a highly suggestible "Dionysian" personality type on the AOD scale, often found himself strongly influenced by his surroundings. He had always felt conflicted between, as he puts it, "left brain and right brain stuff, logical and intuitive, self-suppression and self-liberation." Strictly raised as the son of an Army officer, he'd gone to prep school thinking he'd follow a military career and attend Annapolis. Instead, he fell in love with a "hippie girl" who had introduced him to the psychedelic world of the Sixties. The encounter had given him "philosophical insights" that eventually led to dropping out of college and drifting with a great amorphous tide of young pilgrims to San Francisco's 1967 Summer of Love.

But he was discomfited to hear the military scorned as "baby burners" at gatherings, troubled that he had joined the Love Generation at "the same age my father had been jumping out of DC-3's with the 101st Airborne over Arnheim and Normandy." Peter was soon drafted and wound up, as he puts it, "back in left brain mode." After basic training ("long hours in the hot sun thrusting bayonets into dummies yelling, 'Spear the bayonet—Kill!' "), he was assigned to military intelligence. There, he says ironically, "We practiced invading other countries and peeking into Johnny Carson's domestic surveillance file." He felt himself "being slowly ground up by the impersonal green machine." Once, on leave, he found himself at a hippie commune in West Virginia and returned "totally ruined as a soldier." He managed to leave the military "one step ahead of a court martial."

He went back to West Virginia where he lived idyllically for three years before switching "back to left brain mode," founding a computer company based on an innovative new operating system. He spent a year and a half, he told us, "in a closed office with a cigarette in one hand and a Styrofoam cup of bad coffee in the other, staring at a cathode ray tube twelve hours a day." Overstressed on the job, ignoring his own misery, he finally went to a doctor for a sinus that had been clogged for months. Polyps were discovered, and a biopsy sample taken on Halloween 1986 was diagnosed as cancer. (The pathology slides were sent to the chairman of the department of pathology at Houston's M. D. Anderson Cancer Center, who wrote back: "The appearance of the cells and the 'starry sky' look to fields lead us to consider it as an immunoblastic sarcoma that has likely evolved from a plasmacytoma.")

The cancerous mass was "debulked" with laser surgery but quickly began to grow back. The only possible treatment was so gruesome-sounding—removal of the sinus and pituitary gland, radiation, and possible blindness as a side effect—that Hettel refused. His diagnosis, he says, had sparked an incongruous reaction: "I felt like I'd gotten a hall pass from school. It was like, *All right!* This cancer may kill me, but no one's gonna be able to tell me what to do. No one can argue with fatality. I have an honorable way of dumping these self-imposed responsibilities. My attitude was, from now on, I'm gonna park my car wherever I want, when I want, because if I don't put myself number one, I might die."

Deciding that he could "always have them saw my head open as a last resort," he found himself back in the "venturesome mode" of his quasi-hippie days, times when he'd shoved a few bills in his pocket and hitchhiked off to parts unknown, "following my tendrils of intuition." It was this intuitive approach—perhaps, judging from Peter's Dionysian profile, his most native style—that now seemed to guide him. He adopted a stringent diet, laced with liberal quantities of carrot juice. "I'd been exposed to natural food from my commune days. It made sense to flood my body with high quality nutrients in the most digestible form." After extensive research, he decided on a natural health clinic outside of San Diego, well aware that tests showed his tumor was continuing to grow.

While his time shortened, a wild card turned up as he prepared to leave for California. Hearing he was ill, a woman he'd known vaguely in his commune days began a campaign of well-intentioned but irksome harassment. "She'd got it into her head that I had to come to North Carolina and meet some lady who was gonna heal me through 'brain balancing.' The whole thing sounded ludicrous. I tried to explain to her that I had my own plans. But she wouldn't let it loose." One day, after turning down a round-trip ticket his persistent acquaintance had phoned into the airport, "there was a pounding on my door," Hettel recalls, shaking his head. "There she was, frazzled. She had jumped into her car and driven all that way to fetch me." Feeling he was up against an irresistible force, Hettel acquiesced and got in the car. The next morning, he was taken to meet the woman's unortho- dox therapist, a "neurolinguistic programmer" who sat him casu- ally down, asked simply how she could help. "It blew me away. It was the first time anyone had asked me sincerely what *I* thought I needed." He found, to his surprise, his emotions poured out in torrents. "I was a mewling, existential mess of 'I've always tried to be a good guy' and 'Why me?' "

Patiently, softly, the woman asked him if he loved himself. "I heard this very small voice coming out of me, saying, 'No.' " Again Hettel broke down. In their next session, the woman began teaching him an assortment of purported "neurological repatterning" techniques—"cross-crawls" to coordinate the left and right sides of the body, eye movement exercises ostensibly aimed at "correcting" brain hemispheric dominance. There, on his hands and knees, crawling like a baby as the therapist tracked his eyes through a range of motion, Peter was suddenly plunged into a long-submerged memory:

"Right when my eyes clicked into one particular little place, I had a sudden, clear memory of being eight years old. We were living in the countryside. I'd woken up really early one morning before the rest of the family, and gone out all by myself. And there before me was a magical-looking field, with dewdrops like diamonds, and a grazing deer with its breath smoking from the cold. I remembered the sense of newness, of infinite possibility. Suddenly I was *in* it again, just exactly! I felt like I was a different person, or a person I'd once been but had completely forgotten. I started laughing, and just laughed and laughed, while my therapist burst into tears. I don't know how, but she'd managed to shift me from a despairing adult to this joyful little boy."

At her urging, he began to tell himself, "I love myself completely no matter what, I am an indispensable part of creation, valued, honored, loved." He went on an extraordinary healing journey. He kept up a rigorous vegetarian diet, gulped handfuls of vitamins, took up daily study of Zen and yoga with a meditation instructor who happened to live on the floor above his rented room.

He also devised a series of visualizations: "I'd imagine white immune cell bunny rabbits feasting on fields of orange cancer-carrots, which increased their energy and sex drive, which made them have sex and make *more* bunnies who were *also* hungry to eat more cancer." One morning, Hettel recalls, "I couldn't find enough carrots for all my rabbits. I thought, 'Gee, I hope my bunnies are all right.'" A week later, he began to experience "a lot of heat and pressure in my head. I knew something was radically changing. I was afraid that it was my cancer ballooning." Panicked, he reported to the hospital. But when he was told how low his odds would be with any available treatment, he walked out. "One doctor told me it would be my death certificate, but I realized that I had to decide to live or die according to what I felt comfortable with."

Shortly after that, he had a vivid dream. "I was standing in something like Carlsbad Caverns, with big, pink, bulbous stalactites hanging down. The pinkish ground was soft and spongy. Then there was an earthquake, and I had to run to avoid being squished by these overhanging things. They crashed down from the roof to the floor as I dodged through this kind of cave of flesh."

A few days later, Peter had a highly emotional phone conversation with his father. "My dad was a tough, blustering military guy, the spitting image of 'The Great Santini.' Now for the first time in my life, I told him exactly what I felt. I just openly and honestly expressed my anger towards him. He just slammed down the phone. It turned out to be the last conversation I had with him, because he died some months later."

A week after his blowup with his father, Hettel was doing a yogic posture called the Lion when "all of a sudden my nose erupted in this big nosebleed. I trotted off to the bathroom trying to staunch the flow of blood, snorting and hocking, and then began to spit up what seemed like pieces of pink rubber eraser into the sink." Probing the roof of his mouth with his tongue, he was shocked to find a big hole there instead of the tumor's familiar protrusions that had been there for months. "So I started hacking and spitting with religious fervor and spit out all of my tumor!"

"I ran to the doctor I'd been seeing and he was totally amazed. He ran a scope into my sinuses and said, 'Son of a bitch, no tumors.' Because he'd seen them there before, scanned them with an MRI, poked them." Hettel's doctor, University of North Carolina ear, nose, and throat specialist Patrick Browder, confirmed Hettel's story to us. "It was as if his body had rejected a foreign object, like a transplant rejection, just expelled it from his body. I can't account for it, other than he seemed to change his living habits dramatically, and adopted a take-charge attitude instead of just giving up. He began doing what he deeply wanted to do."

Peter's case contains familiar items on an emerging checklist of factors we believe deserve as much as tumor necrosis factor—to be called "biological response modifiers." But how many of these elements have to converge in any given instance before a meaningful correlation with a cure can be declared?

Certainly, the details of his journey span the spectrum: physical exercises to integrate mind and body ("cross-crawls" and yoga); personalized visualizations ("carrots and bunny rabbits"); a warm relationship with a sincere healer and a sympathetic MD; social support; emotional catharsis (his fits of weeping with his therapist, rage at his father); an existential shift ("a hall pass—no one's gonna tell me what to do"); healing nutrition through a regimen (a special diet); powerful transient mood states (recapturing joyful memories of childhood); an alternative diagnosis that implied an alternative healing strategy (his left brain and right brain needed to be "balanced"); a potent belief system ("I am an indispensable part of the universe"); the regaining of an essential, authentic part of himself (his "intuitive mode" from his younger days). All in all, Peter seems to have achieved a maximum congruence, a matching of inner being and outer circumstance. It is no wonder that when his doctor attributed his recovery to a "spontaneous remission," Peter expostulated, "Screw that! I worked my butt off!"

The concept of the healing system provides a window—more, a special lens—through which to look at cases of remarkable recovery in search of explanations. Still, no matter how we may try to present a coherent narrative, each report admits many versions of the same tale. In chapter three, we mentioned a man written up by his physicians as "the first recorded case of complete regression of bronchogenic carcinoma that we can locate in the literature." His surgeon, when we contacted him, could think of no reason for his cure—"just an ordinary guy, nothing special." The man had the worst form of the disease and had been sent home to die but had somehow rallied. His doctors, at a loss, had at least put in a few behavioral details:

> While at home the patient, who was fully aware of his disease and anticipated prognosis, states he learned that many patients who die of cancer literally starve to death. He subsequently developed a positive attitude toward survival and literally force-fed himself at every opportunity. He volunteered to do manual labor on a farm to be in the outdoors. During the subsequent 2 to 3 months he slowly gained weight and developed increasing strength and well-being.

The man had also, according to the report, spiked temperatures of 104 degrees over the course of weeks. An astute physiological detective well-versed in the lore of fever and infection-related remission might with due satisfaction pronounce the case closed. (One data analysis of 224 cases of spontaneous regression found fevers or infections in 62 of them.)

We, too, might have left it at that. But we thought that the patient himself, one Joe Mayerle, son of a Louisiana sharecropper and a devout Nazarene Baptist, should also have a chance to give his testimony. It took us several months to locate Joe, now seventy-three and hale as a woodlark. The search process was typical: We first located the author of his medical report, Dr. Bell, who referred us to Joe's surgeon. The surgeon never returned our calls, and Dr. Bell declined to call him on our behalf. But Dr. Bell's wife, who had been a nurse at the hospital, took it upon herself to send us a decades-old article she'd remembered in the *Saturday Evening Post*. The article written about this unusual patient mentioned the name of a town. By calling information, we found Joe's son, who, to our elation, was finally able to put us in touch with his father.

Joe Mayerle had grown up a farm kid, chopping and picking cotton. Like many in his generation, he had grabbed the escape route of the Civilian Conservation Corps at the bobtail end of the Depression. A card and a cutup, he'd taught himself the bugle while living in the forestry barracks, learning to jitterbug on the back of a moving pickup, and becoming an habitué of "this little old place outside Dodson where old guys would put nickels in the jukebox just to watch us kids dance."

Joe joined the Navy in 1942, serving on a "baby flattop" in the dark roller-coaster waters near the Pacific island of Attu, sneaking in a few choruses of "Sugar Blues" on his bugle when he had to sit up on watch. He was up there the day a plane roared through the barriers and slammed a friend one deck below with a wing, killing him instantly. The former local hijinks king had to play taps through the tears and whipping salt spray; but soldiering dutifully through the war's quotidian horrors, Joe had made his way back in one piece.

After the war, after stints as a bartender, truck driver, and heavy equipment operator, he'd settled in Washington State with his first wife, but the marriage went on the rocks. He met his second wife, Betty, at a dance joint where she worked. It was in the days before automatic jukeboxes, and Betty was a disembodied voice who cooed, "What number, please?" and spun the platters. Joe flirted with her over the microphone, finally sauntering into the back one night with a tray piled high with sandwiches for all the girls. It was, he says, "love at first sight."

Joe and Betty had been married only two years when, in February 1959, what Joe thought was only "a bad cold" that had filled his lungs with fluid turned out to be cancer. Betty was told the X-ray results over the phone. " 'Your husband won't live three weeks,' " she remembers one physician informing her "just like that."

When his wife came to him with tears in her eyes to tell him of the medical *pronunciamento,* Joe says, "I blew my stack. 'I've got one goddamn thing to tell you,' I said to that doctor. 'I'm going to live to piss on your grave!' " He allows himself a cackle of satisfaction; but back then he'd been scared, more scared than when the planes had screamed overhead and the flight deck had heaved and plunged in leviathan seas.

When he was admitted to the Veteran's Administration Hospital for tests, his weight was down by forty pounds. But he forced himself to be optimistic. The month before, Betty had told him that she was pregnant. Joe, who had adopted two daughters from her previous marriage, thought how fine it would be to hold a baby again—maybe even a son—and watch him grow. "Maybe there'd been an error," he thought hopefully. "Maybe an operation could borrow me some time."

But before the doctors could operate, Joe was stricken with violent, shaking chills. His fever shot up to 106 degrees. "The nurses stripped me butt-naked and wrapped me head to toe with alcohol ice packs. It seemed pretty funny at first until I thought I was going to freeze to death." His teeth chattering, he offered to "buy them the biggest steak in Seattle" if they would stop, but they continued their frigid mummification. The chaplain at the hospital prayed with him through the night. No one had thought he would last until morning, but when his wife arrived at 6:00 A.M., "I was sitting on the edge of the bed," he says with a grin, "smokin' a cigarette. Betty about had a fit."

The doctors puzzled briefly as to the cause of Joe's fever and the reason he had temporarily rallied, then decided he was at least strong enough for an exploratory operation. Surgery showed the lung was too far gone to do more than snip a biopsy sample from the mass. The medical report reads: "Left thoracotomy on this thirty-seven-year-old white man (JM) revealed an upper lobe tumor presenting on the visceral and parietal pleural surfaces. . . . No resection was considered possible. Frozen section was reported as a malignant neoplasm, probably poorly differentiated squamous carcinoma."

Joe lay miserably in his hospital bed, knowing he was on the brink of death. But then he felt something inside him sideslip back toward life. He found one unadorned prayer: "I only wished I could live long enough to see my new baby born."

For the next two weeks, Joe received a series of weak X-ray treatments for his chest pain. The pain subsided, but the cancer was unaffected by the palliative. "There was no response," the report in the medical journal read, "as judged by serial chest films." Joe returned home, plagued by intermittent fevers and one constant thought: how to stay alive until Betty gave birth. He had read in the newspaper that former Secretary of State and cancer patient John Foster Dulles had died not of the blight spreading through his body, but of starvation, so Joe determined he would force himself to eat. He also began to work outside (though the case report's mention of "volunteer manual labor on a farm" was actually, Joe says, "helping out my cousin in his trash dump").

When Joe showed up in the hospital six months later, he recalls, "the doctor turned as white as his uniform. He called over all the interns and nurses, and scooted me to the head of a line of patients waiting for X rays. When he was done taking my film, he pulled out the old X ray, which looked like someone had stood back ten feet and peppered it with buckshot, and put it beside my new one, all clean, and just stared." The doctor had wanted him to stay over that night, but Joe's wife was expecting. She gave birth to their baby, Joe Junior, his reason for living, that Friday. On Monday he got a call to report back to the hospital, where he found 200 doctors from Seattle had been assembled in full phalanx to hear his story. They listened to his physician, then heard him out, then were at a loss what to say.

"Do you still smoke cigarettes?" one of them ventured after silence and shuffling.

"Yeah, do you want one?" Joe had responded, bringing down the house.

For years afterward, the doctor would desultorily puzzle over him, prod him, jab and poke him for cell samples. Dr. Bell noted somewhat chidingly in a later journal article: "It is apparent that in our patient, who has continued to smoke for the ten-year period after disappearance of his tumor, there has been ample opportunity for a new tumor to present; that a new lesion has not developed suggests an acquired host immunity." Observing that animal experiments had revealed that "immunity after induced or spontaneous regression is more effective than that after surgical removal," Dr. Bell even went so far as to incubate some of Joe's lymphocytes, putting them in a Petri dish with another patient's lung cancer, and waiting to see what happened. While anyone else's white cells would have had as much effect as a flea on a junkyard dog, Bell noted with surprise that Joe's immune potion reduced the cancer cells' colony formation by more than half.

The centerpiece of Dr. Bell's final article for the *American Journal of Surgery* looks like a mail-order catalog for cheap Halloween suits: two rows of black-and-white ribcages, their X-rayed bones bowed as gracefully as the struts of a galleon. There are four shots: A routine checkup in October 1956, clear as a summer sky; March 1959, the right lobe blotted out by a white nimbus of cancer; by October, the bad weather is receding; and by April 1964, when he reported back to the hospital for a checkup, the X-ray sun shines through unobstructed. Animate the stills and it would look as if Joe had accidentally inhaled a cloud of tumor, then sneezed it all away in one magisterial *kerchooie*. In a final medical mug shot, Joe's eyes are blacked out for anonymity by a little bar, but the slightly sinister impression is erased by the shit-eating grin creasing his face and a tastefully muscled torso ripped straight from a Charles Atlas ad.

But perhaps we need to look at one more refraction of Joe's story, the one that appeared in the *Saturday Evening Post* after the popular glossy, tipped off by a local reporter, found him working as a security guard at the Naval Torpedo Station. The piece is patently an as-told-to. The Joe we met, a pragmatic "Apollonian" on the AOD scale, is a down-to-earth, plainspoken man, but the article has him speaking in oratorical flourishes. (He is said upon diagnosis to conjure the silent utterance, "My whole being strained for some ray of comfort, some hint of refutation," like some shipyard Thomas Aquinas.) Frills aside, Joe stands by the substance of the account.

For the most part, it is not very informative. The "magazine Joe" avers: "My questioners seem to hunger for particulars of the regimen I followed. They listen, as though expecting to unearth some as-yet-undiscovered truth, a detail which, while appearing ordinary, holds . . . the golden key that can open the door to re-gained good health. If I have the key, I don't know it." Joe is happy to reveal that he frequently ate his favorite "savory con-coctions of macaroni and cheese." The rest of his anticancer diet, he says, sparing no particulars, was canned tamales, frozen chicken pies, and raw onion sandwiches—this latter, he was told, being "germicidal in the intestinal tract."

A schematic of the stimuli to Joe Mayerle's healing system would seemingly include: the love of a father for an eagerly an-ticipated child; unexplained high fevers; social support (including the prayers of his mother's entire church); being outdoors (albeit jacking a Caterpillar tractor over mounds of detritus); and eating whatever he liked—all filtrated through the feisty personality of a "boogie-woogie bugle boy from Company B."

But Joe also recalls how he lay in bed after his exploratory surgery repeating over and over, "I'm going to die, I'm going to die," the cold shock washing over him, numbing him to the mar-row. At that point, the article reads (and Joe affirmed), "I became aware of a shift. Suddenly my mind no longer needed to dwell on death. Instead my thoughts veered to a new target: to make the best possible use of what remained of my existence." What followed is worth quoting verbatim:

> It was a time of discovery, of astonishment, as I observed myself carrying on the routine of everyday life. There was incredibly deep meaning in the simplest activity. In my state of heightened consciousness a simple act, such as scratching itchy stitches, left me stunned with the impact of awareness of the painful beauty of just *feeling,* being, living. The sound of water pouring, of paper rustling, of footsteps—all echoed in my innermost soul. . . . Sunshine and shadow, trees, grass, people, dogs—there was such indescribable beauty in the most mundane sights that tears would come to my eyes.

Joe, adjusting for the magazine's literary footwork, describes a world temporarily transfigured, an experience described by a number of our cases. Perhaps it was the shock of surgery, or painkilling drugs. But moments of dislocation, when suffering or annihilation seem inescapable are known to produce trancelike states. Dr. David Spiegel confirms that "hypnotic phenomena such as dissociation are intrinsic to the experience of trauma." He argues that to be properly recognized, trauma must be defined broadly: "Trauma can be understood as the experience of being made into an object, a thing; the victim of someone else's rage, of nature's indifference, of one's own physical or psychological limitations. . . . The kinds of events that mobilize dissociation as a defense also seem to be those in which the patient's volition is physically overridden. . . . The experience of involuntariness may be a link among hypnosis, dissociation, and trauma."

One study of a group of forty cancer patients who had received a recent diagnosis of recurrence revealed many of the signs of post-traumatic stress disorder (PTSD). "This finding is interesting," wrote one commentator on the study, "in that it provides support for conceptualizing events in the life of the cancer patients as analogous to physical traumas." The researchers Everson and Cole observed that some spontaneous remissions seemed to be triggered simply by "operative trauma," which was presumed to stimulate hormones that boosted the "host immune system." Perhaps the trauma of a fatal diagnosis can have a similar effect.

Says Dr. Charles Tart, author of the standard reference work, *Altered States of Consciousness,* "When your doctor says 'there's nothing we can do,' that's an *incredibly* potent psychological stimulus. It says every habit of thought you've had all your life, all your styles of thinking and feeling, don't mean a damn thing. It can certainly induce an altered state."

Many researchers believe one biological cause for such altered states may be the brain's endorphins—the so-called "natural opiates"—which can be released in quantity in a situation of shock. It is significant to our speculations about the innate synergy of the healing system that these chemicals, in addition to producing euphoria and reducing pain, may, according to some investigators, also enhance the immune system. It has led us to wonder if the unusual inner experiences sometimes described by our cases are more than the side effects of pathological processes, or secretions to numb pain, but an active part of the healing system itself.

Some researchers have suggested that the brain naturally secretes chemicals under stress that lead to an enhancement of symbolic and other "unitary" forms of perception. Neuro-ophthalmologist August Reader has noted that when the brain is significantly deprived of oxygen, it manufactures an excess supply of hormones which may produce the "life review" noted in reports of near-death experience, in which all people, places, and events of one's past are revealed as part of an interconnected pattern. This phenomenon, often experienced as deeply spiritual, Reader believes may also be a built-in survival response, a way for the brain to ransack its stored repertoire of experience in search of a life-saving strategy.

This curious notion—that not just biochemicals but *experiences* may be produced by the brain as part of a self-healing mechanism—has been speculated upon by other researchers. Raymond

Prince cites the famous African explorer David Livingstone's account of being mauled by a lion. Livingstone, in terms suggestive of both endorphin secretions and spontaneous hypnosis, recounted: "The shock . . . caused a sort of dreaminess, in which there was no sense of pain nor feeling of terror, though [I was] quite conscious of all that was happening. It was like what patients partially under the influence of chloroform describe, who see all the operation, but feel not the knife. . . ."

Prince notes that this same "analgesia-euphoria" is also a feature of shamanic healing ceremonies, which sometimes employ dramatic rituals of "psychological threat" which have "a potential for the defensive generation of endorphins." He surmises that such "artificial threat situations" may be created by the organism itself through "nightmares, deliriums, and psychoses."

It seems odd, he admits, that the mind-body would self-generate frightening images at a time when healing was most required. The key to this paradox, he believes, lies in the possible healing properties of endorphin secretions. Such vivid psychological experiences may be, he suggests, "a positive measure" used by the mind and body to produce "protective hormones." Though it sounds as convoluted as the healing system itself, it is intriguing in light of many remarkable recoveries who found themselves engulfed, as were Joe Mayerle and Peter Hettel, by a terror of imminent death just before a powerful survival instinct kicked in; or those who, like Garrett Porter and Wally Shore, had visualized dramatic inner battles with their disease. For that matter, Geertje Brakel's hallucination of fighting demons in her hospital room may have been not only a mirror of her body's internal battle with cancer cells, but a self-generated mechanism of the healing system to catalyze greater immune activity.

The catalytic effects of trauma have been creatively investigated by clinicians specializing in PTSD. Psychologist Eugene Peniston, for example, found that Vietnam veterans suffering from PTSD who were put in a state of relaxation through biofeedback often had spontaneous "abreactive" experiences in which they "relived" some of their most horrific combat experiences. Peniston found these sessions also altered their levels of endorphins. Coincidentally, he reports that as a result of such experiences, not a few of his patients seemed to go through a "complete personality change" that led to new feelings of wholeness. In a follow-up study two years later, he writes, "They said they had been restored to the way they used to be before they went to Vietnam." Another leading PTSD expert, Dr. Bessell van der Kolk, also found that the imaginary reliving of powerful emotional incidents causes the autonomic nervous system to activate and secrete neurohormones. He discovered that "if you show a Vietnam vet with PTSD the movie 'Platoon,' there is a massive secretion of endogenous opioids, equivalent to the ten-milligram morphine injection."

Certainly, emotional distress has been suggested by some researchers as a trigger for hormones that stimulate the *growth* of cancer. But emotional "abreactions" of traumatic experience have been associated by others with remarkable recovery, as in this famous case reported by psychologist Larry LeShan:

> A 32-year-old man had extensive metastases of a malignant melanoma. In his early adolescence he had undergone an unusually traumatic experience when he witnessed his father prepare to murder the only adult who had ever been warm and kind to him. The murder was committed and, for a long time, he had been overwhelmed by the fear that he would be called to court during one of his father's repeated trials. . . .
>
> During the course of psychotherapy, recurrent dreams and associations indicated that tension over his relationship to his father's guilt in the murder was mobilized. At the same time, he began to complain of pain in his throat and increasing difficulty in swallowing. Examination revealed a rapidly growing neoplasm in the right tonsillar and right glosso-epiglottic area. Preparations were made to remove it surgically so that he could continue to eat.
>
> In a psychotherapy session on the day before the opera-

tion was scheduled, he recalled the entire incident with all the emotion he had felt at the time. He recounted it in detail, weeping and trembling. Four hours later, he told the therapist that he had just finished the first meal he had been able to eat in a week without pain in his throat. Twenty-four hours later, the mass was markedly reduced; 48 hours later, it was even smaller; and within four days, it had disappeared. The surgical procedure was not carried out.

If vividly reliving a trauma can release a "massive secretion of endogenous opioids" in PTSD sufferers, could those same endorphins trip off a complex, perhaps irreproducible cascade of effects correlated with regression? Candace Pert, the co-discoverer of endorphins, believes the idea has some speculative merit. "There are many reports of emotional catharses sometimes accompanying healing," she told us. "Immune cells send out and receive the same chemicals that we conceive of as controlling mood in the brain. These findings mean we need to start thinking about how emotions are projected into various parts of the body. Perhaps a catharsis, which means literally a washing, could create a sudden healing shift in the pattern of the immune, endocrine, and nervous systems."

Perhaps, she adds, certain kinds of "emotional blockages" create "misinformation" preventing the immune system from functioning properly. The problem is to restore the missed signal, to cue the immune system to what it ignored."

One function of the healing system, we surmise, is to amplify these cues that produce health. It is known that certain cells biochemically signal various elements of the immune system to mobilize against an invading pathogen. These cells issue, in effect, a neuropeptide "call for help." It seems only logical such a "call for help" would echo through other levels of the healing system affected by neuropeptides, perhaps in the form of emotions, thoughts, and mental images.

Einstein once remarked that the fundamental question in science should be: Is the universe friendly? If it is not, then the peculiar inner states sometimes reported in remarkable recovery are either pathological or at best by-products of disease. But it can be stated beyond doubt that the universe of the healing system *is* friendly, for it is bent upon a single purpose—urgent recruitment of the mind-body-spirit in service of healing. When the body can no longer battle on its own, perhaps it sends out neuropeptide emergency signals that enlist the mind in the fray. If so, the debate over whether it constitutes false hope or wishful thinking for patients to deliberately try to stimulate their own mental, emotional, and spiritual resources is moot: This is what the healing system is already *striving* to do.

Dr. David Spiegel was striving, albeit with modest expectations, to do the same when he set out to study the effects of a "psychosocial intervention" on the mood and pain level of eighty-six metastatic breast cancer patients. Spiegel, a specialist in hypnosis and dissociative disorders at Stanford University, placed the women into two groups, one a "control" and the other an "intervention" group. The intervention group focused on enhancing mutual caring and support from their families. The women also trained in self-hypnosis for pain control.

"The whole point of the original study was that we could make them feel better," said Spiegel in a 1989 report in *Science*. "The challenge was to make the best use of whatever time remained for them."

The results were significant: The women's subjective "pain ratings," though not the incidence of pain itself, became less severe, and their coping abilities improved. Happy with this outcome, Spiegel and his colleagues published their paper and promptly forgot about it. Over the intervening years, however, he felt his ire swell over "media hype about patients being able to wish away their cancers." He remembered the woman who dropped out of his group, left off her conventional treatment in favor of visualization exercises, and died within a year; another woman who asked him plaintively if she would "have to become a Tibetan monk" to cope effectively with illness. "It seemed to me that the claims made about the powers of the mind to cure cancer were foolish and sometimes dangerous," he says.

Dr. Spiegel decided to reexamine the results of his initial study, certain "it would provide a perfect negative experiment revealing no effect on disease progression." His initial analysis confirmed his assumptions: As he had expected, given the grim progress of advanced metastatic disease, eighty-three of the original eighty-six women had died.

But further crunching the numbers, Dr. Spiegel was astounded to find that though *all* of the control group had died within four years, fully *one-third* of the intervention group was still alive after the same time interval. Spiegel waited years to publish these unexpected results, running the statistics through one exhaustive analysis after another. In the end, he was forced to admit that the group which had received his training had lived an average of 36.6 months, a doubling of the control group's 18.9 months' survival time.

Spiegel even found there was a "dose response"—the more therapy sessions the women had attended, the longer they had lived. But a dose of what? Dr. Spiegel himself believes it was social support. He also feels, noting that group discussion focused a great deal on fears of death and dying, that "honestly facing their own mortality and making rational choices about how to live their lives" had what he calls "an invigorating effect."

Other of Dr. Spiegel's observations, though he does not include them in his list of possible healing factors, are relevant to our schema. The women were allowed, for example, to vent sometimes intense emotions—their compassion for each other and themselves, their anger at being sick and at the way the world sometimes treats the ill, their love for family and children. They also encouraged each other to live more congruent lives. One woman had always wanted to be a poet and, egged on by the group, managed to publish two slim volumes before she died. When another patient told the group that her oncologist sat behind his typewriter while she was talking and dismissed her with a wave of his hand when she cried, the group insisted she confront him. Another woman decided to leave her husband and spend her time with her children.

In 1991, with two of the women in the original group still alive and two others only recently deceased, Spiegel interviewed one of the living survivors and the families of the other three on a grant from the Institute for Noetic Sciences. He told us that all four women possessed "quiet determination. They were not the feistiest ones we saw—not blindly optimistic, I'm-going-to-beat-this-thing types. They weren't rigidly set on pushing that stone uphill and having it roll back down on them. They were just determined to do the best they could."

All four had strong support from at least one very close person. They each felt they had a personal relationship with God, but were tolerant and disliked dogmatism. They came from large families, with unhappy childhoods and a family history of cancer. Though they felt they had good relationships with their doctors, Spiegel writes:

> Interestingly, they were quite non-compliant with medical care. Two of the four women refused to undergo a mastectomy in the early 1970s, when this was quite rare. Two refused chemotherapy, and a third interrupted her course of chemotherapy. Thus they had, on average, less intensive treatment than the short survivors.

David Spiegel is trying, he says, to chart a course between what he calls the "Scylla . . . [of] mindless materialism—viewing people as nothing more than the product of physical processes" and the "Charybdis . . . [of] disembodied spiritualism—the idea that if one fixes a problem in one's mind, it is fixed in the body." Still, Dr. Spiegel fails to suggest as a possible factor in his patients' longevity something we find potentially significant: He had taught his patients a combination of "self-hypnotic imagery and relaxation that helped them focus on a metaphor like floating or warmth or tingling numbness"—sensations that have cropped up throughout this book as possible correlates to healing system activity, and which are features of healing practices the world over.

We recently sat in on a demonstration of Chi Gong by a well-regarded Chinese practitioner. Frustrated by his own spotty command of English—how could he explain what he meant by "breathe into stomach"?—Master Ho finally unbuttoned his crimson silk polo shirt, Bruce Lee style, to reveal his torso. "Here is lung breath," he announced, and his chest rose while his stomach lay flat as paving stone. "Middle breath," and his belly swelled to a large, inverted coppery-golden bowl. "And here is *tan t'ien*," a spot three fingers below the navel that Oriental medicine says is the body's energetic center, a collection point for invisible *chi* energy thought to spill from universal sources and enter the body via the breath.

We noted that Master Ho—who, his assistant told us, had produced "documented increases in the immune system of HIV patients and people with some nonmetasized cancers"—began the session like a hypnotic induction. "Your palms are growing warm," he said, his voice soft and slow. "Imagine yourself between heaven and earth like a giant. You are collecting yin-yang energy, head in the heavens, feet on earth." Even the logic was that of a hypnotist aiming to create a state of absorption. The purpose of the visualization, he told us later, is "not superstition. When you imagine this, you don't think anything else, not family, not work problem."

Just as many hypnotists ask their subjects to imagine an arm growing light as a balloon, Master Ho instructed, "Use shoulder to pick up arm, arm may feel light," as his own arm floats slowly up from his side. Master Ho also suggested other sensations his audience might feel: "You may find your face or chest burning," he said soothingly. "Your hand feel numb, tingling, swollen. *T'an tien* may feel an electricity sensation. When you store energy, it first feel warm, then heavy, then burning, then . . . perfect." He beamed.

We have reported such sensations associated with some cases of remarkable recovery. Societies around the world, indeed throughout history, seem to use similar healing practices to stimulate what might be universal components of the healing response. Accounts of remarkable recovery are fraught with descriptions of symbolic processes, altered states, high emotion, special physical movements, and forms of social congregation that seem part and parcel of healing ceremonies everywhere.

Religions in particular seem to make use of such practices, leading us to wonder if this central human activity would take on a different coloration if looked at through the lens of the healing system. We spoke to an immunologist named Jeffrey Levin who as a young graduate student in the early 1980s set out to study the correlations between religion and health. Buffeted by professors who told him his search through the medical literature would yield no fruit, he was encouraged by one professor, an eminent social epidemiologist, whose kind words sent him on what he calls "my five-year wild goose chase." Dr. Levin eventually tracked down 250 studies in which some aspect of religion or spirituality had been studied in regard to health outcome.

Levin, who bears a slight resemblance to singer Paul Simon and composes country-western music in his spare time, came up with highly unexpected results. Although epidemiological studies usually show meaningful results only when comparing "matched populations" with similar characteristics, he found there was a "protective effect of religious involvement" which "emerged in persons regardless of gender, race or ethnicity, nationality, age, [or] social class." This effect cut across almost all diseases "including nearly every cancer site imaginable." In bad news to sectarians everywhere, it was also independent of religious affiliation, whether "Protestant, Catholic, Jewish, Hindu, Muslim, Zen Buddhist, Zulu, Parsi."

A portion of the correlations may be straightforward. Some churches forbid alcohol and tobacco or prescribe certain diets and regimens of hygiene. Many beliefs lead to what are called health-promoting behaviors. There are possible hard-data genetic variances—Ashkenazi Jews are at greater risk for Tay-Sachs Disease, Dutch Reformed Afrikaners for hypercholesterolemia, largely black congregations of the National Baptist Convention for sickle cell anemia. But the almost universal "efficacy" of religious practices seemed to us yet more evidence for the universality of the healing system itself. Religious affiliation, Levin suggests, produces "a sense of belonging and convivial fellowship" that seems to buffer stress and anger "perhaps via psychoneuroimmunologic pathways." Belief systems "may engender peacefulness, self-confidence, and a sense of purpose." (It is interesting to note that religious beliefs are often held passionately, fixedly, and emotionally, and are sometimes produced by cathartic conversion experiences.)

The "psychodynamics of religious rites," Levin continues, "may establish a 'sense of being loved' as well as 'actual physiological arousal' during worship and prayer . . . believed to be associated with health and well-being." He even leaves room in his analysis of the healing system for what he calls a "discarnate power" or "superempirical force" (as distinguished from a supernatural one) that goes by a variety of names (*prana, chi*, life force) which may be the active ingredient in such practices as yogic breathing or acupuncture."

Says hypnosis expert Dr. Herbert Spiegel, who professes himself to be fascinated by the commonalities among global healing ceremonies: "I think there are many roads to Rome, but once you're there it's the same city. The ability to turn inward and not allow static to interfere with the music is the shared goal."

Many researchers believe that music and art provide a way to bypass the "static" of purely rational thought and access deeper parts of the brain—the limbic system, for example—that may be key to the mind-body healing response. In our own study, we were interested to find that three-quarters of our cases reported artistic activities that were areas of proficiency and serious pursuit, nearly half of them citing playing a musical instrument or singing. (Nearly three-quarters of those who listed artistic activities also responded affirmatively to our question concerning "unusual experiences" that could not be rationally explained.)

In nearly all cultures, music and rhythm have been used as forces of healing. In ancient Greece, Apollo was both the god of music and of medicine. Modern science is just now playing catch-up. Avram Goldstein, a pharmacologist at Stanford University, asked 249 people what experiences gave them the most "thrills" or "chills" or "tingles." Most responded that it was listening to their favorite music, some even reporting that they found it more stimulating than sex. Dr. Goldstein has conducted physiological experiments that indicate such sensations are related to the release of the brain's natural opiates, the endorphins. Other research has shown that music influences heart rates, respiratory rate, stomach contractions, and the level of stress hormones in the blood.

Shamanic healing ceremonies almost invariably feature music and drumming. Researchers have found that a common rhythm noted in rituals around the world (four to seven beats per second) is correlated with frequencies of electrical activity in the brain associated with spontaneous imagery, ecstatic states, and creativity. In one innovative study, researcher Melissa Maxfield used biofeedback technology to monitor her volunteers' brainwaves while they listened to this typical drum rhythm. Half said they experienced marked temperature fluctuations in their bodies. All participants reported "visual and/or somatic imagery" in conjunction with the music, which most described as "vivid." If global healing practices are any indication, the healing system seems to respond well to combinations of stimuli. Several of our cases believed that music and vivid imagery combined to play an integral role in their remarkable recoveries.

In 1980, when he was twenty-nine years old, Tom Day, then a senior financial analyst at a Colorado computer company, started having blinding epileptic seizures. A biopsy revealed an astrocytoma, a brain tumor named for its radiating, tentaclelike pattern of growth.

Surprisingly, his oncologist suggested that along with radiation Tom might also consider "alternative therapies," handing him a copy of the Simontons' *Getting Well Again*. Tom, who opted for radiation treatment—"they put me in a God-blessed linear accelerator"—tried to imagine the radiation particles as bullets killing the tumor. But the image was flat, and despite the radiation, the tumor "took off like wildfire. They said I had at best six months to live." Further treatments were proposed—a "bulk reduction" that would have removed a substantial amount of brain tumor with uncertain results and possible disability, and chemotherapy or radium implants. Weighing the large risks and uncertain bene-fits, Tom declined.

His condition continued to worsen. Not knowing where to turn, he began to work with a local psychologist to help him with his attempts at imagery and healing. One afternoon, Tom recalls, he had a breakthrough: "I reached into my record collection and happened to pull out "The 1812 Overture." I cranked the music about as high as I could, lay on the bed, and *boom,* everything came together." What unfolded of its own accord before Tom's amazed inner eye was a nineteenth-century battle scene. "There were guard detachments with muskets, men in period military at-tire, caissons pulling cannons into position on a bluff overlooking a valley where the tumor sat."

"It started very pastorally," Tom remembers. "Then there was feverish preparation for battle, and finally at the climax of the music a cannonade blowing the living crap out of the thing." With his psychologist's guidance, Tom began to refine his images. "I replaced the musketry with light swords, like in 'Star Wars,' to hack the tumor to bits. I added huge garbage chutes, like at a con-struction site, to haul away the mess."

Whatever the reasons, to his doctors' surprise, CAT scans re-vealed the growth had halted. Encouraged, Tom began rushing home from his nearby job three times a day just to do his visual-ization. "I loved it, it was exciting, even fun. I'd never really been able to visualize before, and here this piece of music had made this . . . *movie* appear, like here comes the cavalry."

Barbara Crowe, past president of the National Association of Music Therapy, suggests music and rhythm create their healing effects by calming the "constant chatter" of the left brain. "A loud repetitive sound sends a constant signal to the cortex, masking input from other senses like vision, touch, smell," she explains. When sensory input is decreased, the normally noisy left brain with its internal conversations, analyses, and logical judgments subsides to a murmur, stimulating deeper parts of the brain that are throne rooms of symbols, visualization, and emotions. "This is the seat of ritual in tribal societies," she observes. "There is a clear, distinct parallel between traditional shamanism and the practices we do in music therapy today."

Music therapist and researcher Deforia Lane, for example, conducted a controlled experiment with a group of children hospitalized for a variety of diseases. She found that levels of salivary IgA—an immune factor that combats respiratory infections—increased significantly in children who received thirty-minute music therapy sessions. Deforia Lane sweeps into the room at Cleveland's Rainbow Babies and Children's Hospital with an almost visible contrail of irrepressible energy. Everything about the tall, strikingly beautiful black woman in the electric blue suit reads powerhouse. Her face radiates love; not the smarmy, sentimental kind one sometimes finds in hospital staffers worn down by the sorrow of insurmountable diseases, but the gravitational love that attracts the planets and binds them in mutual orbit.

Deforia grew up in a lower-middle-class family saturated with music. She remembers her father singing "Precious Lord, Take My Hand" in a magnificent, resonant baritone, "whirling and dancing" with her sister as her mother, a Wright-Patterson Air Force Base worker, played rippling classical piano. She had been struck by music's power to transform, how "Daddy was different when he sang, Mom was different when she played." Deforia who had taken piano lessons from the age of five and voice lessons from sixteen, had amazed herself by auditioning for the prestigious Curtis Institute of Music and being accepted. Her roommate was Kathleen Battle, today one of the world's great operatic sopranos.

But Deforia had washed out. "I was wonderful at emoting, but I didn't have the technique." She instead became a music therapist, working in a developmental center to enhance communication skills and self-esteem among people with IQ's of less than 50. Undaunted, she got the children "doing things they had never done before," eventually forming a choir, Sing and Sign, that

271

acted as "kind of ambassadors of the community, going to schools to teach children to treat 'different' kids more humanely."

Deforia is a devout Christian who says she always felt the sustaining "presence of the Lord." Her faith hadn't wavered when she'd had five surgeries in less than a decade for benign breast lumps. "I had quite a little road map, and had become quite cavalier about having them taken out and going about my business." When another lump appeared, she had waited until her son was born, and then waited some after that, before going to the doctor. "That was dumb. It had progressed to stage two cancer." As mastectomy was followed by recurrences, radiation, and Tamoxifen, she felt her faith wane.

Her husband buoyed her up with his own staunch belief. But Deforia, who in our testing fell at the "Dionysian" end of the AOD scale, finally found faith where she always had—in music. She recalls sitting down at the piano and opening a hymn book at random to a song that seemed to call out from her soul: "It was about going through the flood, going through the fire." She felt she had an answer then, a calm certainty that, as she puts it, "You're going to make it, kiddo!"

When another suspicious lump arose, she spent two weeks listening to the overture in "Carmen," and visualizing "God's fingers pointing at the lump and intense rays of sunlight coming from their tips and shrinking it." As with Tom Day, the music seemed to intensify the images. "I visualized lions clawing at it, and huge eagles swooping down getting pieces of it and flying away and never returning. In two weeks, the node was back to its normal size. Now I don't say that I imaged it away, but I think I helped my body out by at least getting back some sense of control, because I felt I was really losing it."

Her own experiences have helped her empathize with her patients. The success of music therapy, she believes, depends powerfully on the bond between patient and therapist. "I know there's a connectedness that transcends technique, procedure, or treatment plan. That's why it's so impossible to duplicate."

Deforia has witnessed what she calls "some remarkable responses." She describes a comatose patient with advanced colon cancer who had dulcimer music, which he dearly loved, played daily at his bedside. The doctors had recommended his life support be disconnected but the man had flabbergastingly roused from his coma, saying simply that he had heard music that he "had to get to." The man, Deforia recounts, "described it as not hearing the melody line, but these isolated drops of notes which he said were so alluring he had to shake himself out of it." He lived, she recounts, for a long time afterward, making and playing dulcimers and teaching others to do the same.

"I don't know whether the music was the catalyst," she says. "I would like to think so. The mystery is so intriguing I don't think we'll ever really understand it at all."

But it's not so hard to understand watching Deforia heft her Omnichord synthesizer and enchant a roomful of children suffering from terrible, ravaging diseases. The Omnichord, with its tinny-sounding tonalities and prefab rock rhythms, does not in itself produce celestial music. But in her hands, it becomes an instrument of mercy and power, through which every stimulus to the healing system pours forth as if from a cornucopia. "Don't give up," she sings to the hopeful circle of wounded children, to them a healing personage fully capable, as an ancient Greek text enjoined all physicians to be, of "loosening all bonds of sorrow."

Physicians, healers, patients—all instinctively find ways to stimulate the healing system, though the very concept, for the present, must remain a tangle of possibility and surmise. The healing system fairly begs for fresh coinage. It's also a broad-side-of-the-barn target for every neologist of science. One theorist suggests "cyberphysiology," which he categorizes as "the study of how neurally mediated autonomic responses, usually viewed as reactive reflexes, can be modified by a learning process that appears to be significantly dependent on image design or figures of thought."

No one terminology quite encompasses the healing system. Its seemingly hierarchical operations are structured like the better-charted systems, where higher levels direct lower ones to effect specific reactions, like the removal of unwanted substances or the cleansing of tissues. But other aspects are truly Lewis and Clark forays along tributaries unmapped, unnavigated, and unportaged. Here is a "meta-system" that can respond to signals, suggestions, and guidance emanating from the biological, mental, emotional, and spiritual life of every individual. Indeed, it may turn out to be an interface (with as many multicolored, permutational surfaces in as a Rubik's Cube) between the realms of mind and matter, operating by unique rules not identical to either.

As we have seen, to understand the healing system, we need to encounter it on all levels. In one sense, it is a system of information flow. On another, more immunological level, it is a system that distinguishes self from "non-self." (The immune system, in the way it learns, remembers, and recognizes patterns—in the way it "thinks"—has strikingly mindlike properties.) Further down the scale, it is perhaps our very selfhood, mediated by a corruscating sea of informational peptides. In what is now a well-known example, the same peptides found in the intestines have also been found to act in the brain and vice versa.

But there are other forms of information that seemingly interact with the physical ones—myth, symbol, and belief. The tantalizing unknown is: How are they linked together in the whole person?

The joke is told of the somewhat dim man who goes to his job every day with a lunch bucket containing a Thermos. One day, unable to contain his amazement, he motions a friend over. "It's amazing. On hot days I open my Thermos, and there's ice-cold lemonade in it. On cold days, it's filled with steaming cocoa."

"So what?" his co-worker asks indifferently.

"Well . . . *how does it know?*"

How, indeed? Such questions draw us inexorably back to Dr. Lewis Thomas' mental wart cure-inspired puzzlement as to the identity of the "skilled engineer and manager, chief executive officer, head of the whole place . . . landlord . . . who does supervise this kind of operation?" Dr. Walter Cannon, who in the 1930s pioneered the discovery that the central nervous system

(CNS) controlled many bodily functions, was at a loss to explain *how* it did so. Perhaps, he mused, the CNS in turn is subject to a regulatory mechanism "which in human beings we call the personality." More recently, Candace Pert has wondered, "Perhaps the mind is the information flowing among all of these bodily parts, holding the network together."

The more we gaze at it, the more dizzying it becomes, as if the healing system were an old-fashioned merry-go-round of painted giraffes, horses, bears, and dragons, some stationary, some bobbing up and down, all part of the same intricate gearworks, all somehow in thrall to the same orchestrating calliope.

Even if we were fortunate enough to study a person from disease onset to remarkable recovery, measuring every twist and turn of biology, we would find ourselves in a universe of simultaneous events, a Moebiuslike feedback loop rushing from mind to body and back again. "They tread in rings," wrote Hippocrates, before such circuitous notions were progressively banished from scientific medicine and recently reclaimed by dint of necessity. To find a language to talk about this suddenly unitary body-mind, it sometimes seems as if we must hopscotch back through millennia; back to the Greeks, for whom the living body implied not a singularity, but a plurality; not an insentient husk but a concretized awareness, containing "bodily parts or organs (heart, lungs, diaphragm, chest, guts); breaths, vapors, or liquid juices; feelings, drives, desires; and thoughts, concrete operations of the intellect such as comprehension, recognition, naming, and understanding."

Perhaps the healing system is not just mediated by our selfhood, but in the most fundamental sense, *is* our selfhood—the urge, stemming from our deepest nature, toward wholeness; our yearnings for self-congruence. The goal to discover and nourish this unknown system is worthwhile not only to scientific research, but to enable each of us to achieve his or her fullest capacity. If we are ever to practice a medicine that utilizes the near-celestial complexity of the healing system, it is here it must be firmly, immutably based—in the glorious complexity and infinite potential of each human being.

CHAPTER TEN

Toward a New Medicine

CASES OF REMARKABLE RECOVERY ARE INSPIRING HUMAN sagas, priceless raw material, sources of information and hope, and new clues to the healing process. But they are also an impetus and, in some way, a blueprint for the remarkable recovery of the medical system itself. There is today a grass-roots movement to bind the wounds between hard and soft sciences, between the ill and their caregivers; to forge a new medicine focused as much on the potential of the whole person as on the potency of treatment. It is no longer farfetched to envision a new science of spirit and values working hand in hand with biology and technology to create a new patient-centered medicine, one focused more on wellness than illness.

A long-held assumption in medical science has been that psychological, social, or spiritual factors are of little or no importance when stacked against cancer's relentless biology. Concerning his epiphanic encounter with the mystery that was Mr. DeAngelo (chapter two), Dr. Steven Rosenberg wrote wistfully, "If we could somehow understand the mechanisms, if we could somehow duplicate them in other patients . . . ," but never broadened his epic search for Tumor Necrosis Factor to include the X-factors of, for want of a better term, the human soul. He did not probe the dimensions of Mr. DeAngelo's experience; did not ask the man why *he* thought his metastasized stomach cancer had vanished into thin air.

To come to grips with the mystery—and the reality—of remarkable recovery calls for a new conceptual framework, new research techniques, and most certainly a fresh set of questions. If there are larger patterns—any patterns—associated with the disappearance or arrest of a tumor, they would suggest new, multipronged programs of prevention and treatment. In the course of our journey, our healing system "checklist" has swelled to dozens of synergistic factors. But it is unknown how many items would need to be checked off in a particular case—how many factors, in other words, are required to kick-start the healing system?

Some researchers would maintain the question is an oxymoron—that there *is* no healing system to kick-start; that remarkable recoveries are random statistical anomalies with no discernible cause; and that a handful of anomalies do not call for any change in the practice of medicine. Writes Yale radiologist Richard Peschel: "Scientific miracles are very rare and science does not—and does not have to—try to explain them. This may seem strange to a lay person, but it is enough for the scientist to know that extremely unlikely events do occur, that they *have* to occur, in fact, because they are statistically possible. Thus, scientific miracles do not need any explanation."

Peschel cites the case of eighty-three-year-old "Mr. G.," who had had metastasized lymphoma for three years. The man was too debilitated for chemotherapy, but hospital rules required he receive at least some treatment to qualify for a bed. His doctors kindly wished to keep him there for its excellent nursing care and for pain medication in his final days. They decided as a humanitarian gesture to pull off a ruse. Though Mr. G.'s cancer had spread to bone marrow, lymph nodes, and throughout his chest and abdomen, they began irradiating a single lymph node in his groin, knowing it could not possibly affect his disease but would be an acceptable charade for hospital authorities. Writes Peschel:

> At first it did look as if Mr. G. were going to expire. Gradually, though, he began to eat and get stronger. By the end of the first month, he was no longer in pain and had gained weight! Still, he continued to have obvious disease: an enlarged lymph node in his neck and a huge mass in his abdomen. Because he was so much better, however, he no longer needed hospital care and so his doctors let him return to his nursing home.
>
> On follow-up visits to the hospital, the masses in Mr. G.'s body were smaller. After several months it was clear that a scientific miracle had occurred. Most of Mr. G.'s disease had disappeared and his physical examination was almost normal. In fact, his physical condition was even better than before he got his lymphoma.
>
> Years passed. Mr. G. stayed alive in his nursing home. On physical examination he no longer had evidence of any cancer. And he kept telling his doctors he felt "better than ever."

Here was a case of well-documented remission, where the patient's terminal disease had been confirmed independently by two pathologists, yet he had inexplicably healed. Mr. G., of course, was told he was being treated with curative medical procedures. To Dr. Peschel, his remarkable recovery was just another "scientific miracle," which he defines simply as "an *extremely* unlikely event or an event that has an *extremely* low probability of occurring: a spontaneous remission, for example." The possibility of a placebo effect, of the power arising from Mr. G.'s belief in the useless treatment, is never raised. Nothing is hypothesized; nothing is learned. Mr. G.'s own testimony concerning his experience is never solicited.

So-called "patient attributions" are generally viewed with skepticism. Says Dr. Jimmie Holland, chief psychiatrist at Memorial Sloan-Kettering Cancer Center: "If you go to a hundred long-term survivors, it's fascinating why they *think* they survive. I would never take that away from somebody. But it oversimplifies the complexity of what might have happened. Why do some people progress and others don't? Why does one person respond to chemotherapy and another person gets zero response? We haven't the faintest idea."

Neither does Marilyn Koering. "Call me Ishmael," begins the epic *Moby Dick,* which ends with a line from Job: "For I only am escaped alone to tell thee." Sometimes, in her quiet moments, Marilyn feels as if she had crawled into the skin of the poignant, shipwrecked narrator. Hadn't she alone survived the furious thrashings of cancer's great white whale, clinging to life in a dark sea filled with blasted timber and broken bodies? Twenty patients who, like her, had incurable melanoma had embarked on the same experimental protocol; twenty hopeful, stricken people setting out toward unknown medical shores. All had perished horribly, leaving her to this day still clinging to a spar—a thin hypodermic of alpha-gamma interferon—that had failed to keep anyone else above water.

For I only am escaped alone to tell thee. She hadn't understood her isolation until she'd stumbled on a medical report years later, a write-up in *Cancer* spelling out a median survival of six months for twenty patients in a trial of recombinant interferon. The report mentioned in passing a "47-year-old previously untreated woman with biopsy-confirmed bone marrow involvement . . . [and] diffuse pelvic osseous metastases" who was the "one objective regression." With a chill, she recognized herself. It was eerie, to see oneself as an anonymous statistical exception. It made Marilyn, a respected professor of anatomy at George Washington University and, at one time, a researcher at the National Institutes of Health, want to shout from the domed roof of the nearby Capitol *I'm still alive, alive, alive!* But she would have to hear the echo of her own unanswered question: *Why? Why? Why?*

Melanoma had been a supreme irony. She had taught her medical students about it in her microscopic anatomy class. "I loved that disease because it had the fastest moving cells, and it gave them the clearest way to understand metastasis," she says. When, luxuriating after a set of tennis with the Sunday *Washington Post* spread out on the floor, she had spotted a blackened freckle on her ankle, she had thought irrationally, "Oh, my heavens, Marilyn, you loved that melanoma so much you brought it *home* with you." After several surgeries to remove the spreading growth, an MRI revealed the disease had spread into her bone marrow cavities, skull, ribs, vertebrae, and pelvis. "My hip bones were all chewed up," she says. "I knew it was a death notice."

Marilyn has written an essay, an oddly domestic episode about the dynamic machinery of death: She describes three cells named Jean, Jack, and Joe Melanocyte, who lived in a freckle. One day, Jean and Jack noticed that Joe was acting "a bit unusual. Instead of taking time to rest and enjoy himself, he was producing more melanin than was necessary." Jean and Jack, law-abiding sorts, became alarmed at his "hyperactivity" and "uncontrollable behavior." Joe soon "went astray," uprooting himself from his epidermal bungalow, traveling the "freeway system" of the body, dodging the "police force" of natural killer cells at lymph node truck stops, and instigating through his progeny an unchallenged reign of crime.

At least, till alpha-gamma interferon came along. Marilyn believes her daily shot, faithfully performed for eight years, "helped to stimulate my own police force. Now the disease is like a bunch of gangsters that stay undercover because the police are always around patrolling."

But what if the police weren't there? The question haunts her at nights, not only as a patient, but a scientist. For from all scientific appearances, alpha-gamma interferon doesn't *work* against malignant melanoma. The drug trial was basically a failure. The medical journal report had suggested the low dosage might have been "an important factor in our disappointing results," but Marilyn's maintenance dose is much less than even this ineffective experimental dose. She has surmised, with no evidence beyond her own survival, that "maybe a low dose is the answer, not overwhelming the system." But she's far from convinced, and eight years later it still gnaws at her.

"My concern now is that my remission may *not* be the result of the treatment, as no one else responded," she wrote in the 1990 letter that alerted us to her case. "It is believed by most investigators at the National Cancer Institute that interferon is of no benefit in the treatment of melanoma. Therefore, I really would like to know if this treatment has been effective, or if this was a spontaneous remission."

On the one hand, Marilyn's is a poignant existential question: *Why am I here?* But it is also a deeply pragmatic one: Should she, after nearly a decade of health, keep taking a drug that might have had nothing to do with her remarkable recovery? If she is actually now cured, is the interferon that worked on her and her alone mostly a placebo, or at best a minor immunologic stimulus acting in concert with her own healing system? Marilyn is more aware than most of the monumental scientific question hiding in the underbrush of her predicament. She even handed a colleague at the NCI's Biological Response Modifiers Program a vial of her own white cells. His results revealed nothing. "Like you," he wrote back, "I am very curious about what is going on."

But hers is an urgent curiosity. Here she is, an internationally recognized scientist at one of the country's most prestigious medical schools, a singular case of remarkable recovery, but research-wise, she can't get arrested. "In these studies," she objects, "people are treated en masse, not as individuals." Even as a patient, she says with a flash of acrimony, "my care in the last few years has been zero. They've literally dumped me." Maybe, the scientist in her wonders, she has stumbled on a new low-dose protocol that should then be used in new trials. If so, the medical research world should be beating a path to her door. Instead, she had to fight to keep the supply lines open for even her own daily self-administered shot. The drug company, having gotten no significant results, even suggested she begin purchasing the expensive drug herself, until she kicked up a ruckus "from the ethical standpoint of a guinea pig."

Gradually Marilyn has come to see herself, not like Ishmael, a hapless survivor, but rather more like Jonah, emerged miraculously from the belly of the whale, compelled to speak the truth to the citizens of Nineveh.

She shows us a crisply organized portfolio titled "Letters to the Editor: Published." One, in the *Wall Street Journal,* excoriates the press conference hoopla surrounding Interleukin-2, which she rails is driven by "increased publicity sought by firms more interested in the stock exchange than in human beings." Another, in *Time* magazine, twits the "political and medical-science establishment." She wrote the medical magazine *Hippocrates* as a researcher-turned-patient "appalled at the additional suffering that's caused by medicine's turmoil. . . . How can [cancer patients] know what to do if the medical community itself can't reach a consensus?" She met acclaimed NCI chief surgeon Dr. Steven Rosenberg at a Georgetown dinner party, who irked her by telling her it was "impossible" that interferon had cured her of disseminated melanoma.

To Marilyn, by nature a windmill-tilter, nothing is impossible. She will go to nearly any lengths, even in picayune matters, when convinced she's right. For years, she was accustomed to riding her bike to Constitution Gardens and settling on a bench with a good book and a small Coke. One day, she was told she could now only buy medium or large sodas. Marilyn punched out a letter to the National Park Service, then got the head of the service on the phone, then wrote *another* letter, and another. "I explained that I'm a citizen, these people have contracts with the U.S. government on my taxes, their signs say *small* Coke, which is all I want." Operation Restore Coke dragged on for months. The park service investigated, the concessionaires dug in their heels, the letters flew. Finally, she triumphed. "Now I sit there on the bench and just smile at how many people walk by me with small Cokes. It's quite a number."

Clearly, she wishes her recovery, whether due to her small-Coke doses of interferon or some mysterious biology of remission, could also be of benefit. "I've thought so much about this," she told us. "I've concluded, 'Marilyn, even if it was a fluke, you're supposed to use this to help others.' You'd think they'd want to look into this further, but they've closed the door." She is used to breaking down doors through sheer persistence. At fifty-seven, Marilyn is a veteran of a vanguard generation of women who stormed the barricades of professional power, infiltrating adamant male bastions and winning distinction, though often at a price. She often felt held to higher standards, scrutinized for signs of vulnerability or emotionalism (read femaleness) which would make her an unsuitable member of the club.

Cancer, she told us, catalyzed a rediscovery of her emotions; led her slowly, tentatively to a new life of the heart. In a set of privately circulated essays about her journey, she writes as if making a clinical discovery, her words still whalebone-stiff from years of wariness: "Crying is a normal human response that can be triggered by various emotions ranging from kindness to sadness. It is an action with which society is not comfortable as it is usually related solely to an expression of weakness."

Like Marilyn, her doctor Ed Creagan, the lead investigator in the interferon trial and the lead author of the *Cancer* report, is an overachiever, graduating second in his medical school class ("I'm probably the youngest professor in the Mayo Clinic Medical School"). He now teaches a pioneering course to med students on how to deal with the emotional side of illness.

Dr. Creagan has a lot of empathy for his perplexing, sometimes hectoring patient. "Her relationship with the medical world has been at times stormy and estranged," he says. "What has come through is her fiery determination." As we have noticed in a number of other cases, there is a congruity between caregiver and patient. They are, in fact, remarkably similar, both hard-driving, curious, outspoken, at times thorns in the side of their respective institutions.

Dr. Creagan professes a genuine curiosity about her case. "I certainly want to know why she's still here. Even though she's on amazingly low levels of alpha plus gamma interferon, I personally believe the treatment did something. But I tell her she's undoubtedly the only person in the world's medical literature who had this kind of medical reprieve.

"I do think," he adds, "there are traits which facilitate long-term survival, because these things can't just happen by luck. That's where I'm anguished, looking for the magical combination of characteristics. Certainly the civilians of the world want the formula of why she's done so well."

But he doesn't see where she fits any formula. "Dr. Koering is bright, intelligent, internationally renowned, a hard-driving, take-control patient," he says. "And yet some survivors have just blindly accepted their fate and have done well, while others like Dr. Koering have grabbed this thing by the horns and tried to wrestle it to the ground."

Marilyn is well aware of her crusty exterior but feels that, as a result, a lot of people don't really understand her. "I'm sensitive underneath. You probably know me better than most people do," she told us after we'd spoken only a few hours. We were often surprised at the level of emotion and intimacy our far-ranging set of interview questions elicited, highlighting the potential benefits for patient care if more physicians would take a similar tack. Even Dr. Creagan, it struck us, is still struggling to understand his patient. "You hear the idea that spirituality helps people get well," he told us, "but I don't get a sense of deep spirituality from her." Yet probing Marilyn's own account, we turned up striking, even overwhelming spiritual experiences.

She recalls, for example, a turning point as she lay alone on the gurney outside the operating room the day after Christmas. "Totally alone and with the fear of the unknown controlling my existence," she writes, "I made the most important decision of my life." Feeling pinned and helpless, her feet against the wall and her eyes on the ceiling, she suddenly was flooded with a vivid memory of attending a Stations of the Cross pageant in Catholic grade school, hearing Christ's final words, "Father, into your hands, I commend my spirit." Now, about to enter surgery, Marilyn had an experience reminiscent of Joe Mayerle's hospital-bed alteration in the previous chapter. She writes in an essay:

> . . . a peace came to me at that moment. When my cart was pulled back and pushed into the cold operating room, I felt like I may have already arrived in another life. All those welcoming me into this indirectly lighted chamber were decked out in gear that could have been from another place in space. For all I knew, they may not have had bodies as I saw only two eyes and possibly arms. . . . From that time on, I had a new freedom and peace.

Like Joe Mayerle, Marilyn falls at the "Apollonian" (low-hypnotizable) end of the AOD personality scale. But in the alchemy of the moment, she seems to have had a dissociative experience, an oft-described sense of sudden "differentness" and "existential shift" that began many journeys of remarkable recovery. The surgeon in his uniform, scarcely exotic to her under normal circumstances, was now an otherworldly Charon, ferrying her toward an unknown new life.

The threat of dying, she says, taught her "my spirit was an entity of its own." She was "forced," she says, to return to the philosophy texts of her college days as a disciplined way to approach "the realization that my being extends beyond the earthly environment to which my body responds." Indeed, tackling theology with the same zeal as she had science, she flew to Germany to seek out the great theologian Hans Küng at his home in Tübingen, feeling he had a "realistic understanding" of things mystical. She has now switched from teaching cell biology to the thorny issues of medical ethics.

Dr. Creagan, his fondness for Marilyn evident, seems to miss another possible stimulus to her healing system. "One common thread I've noticed in folks who do well is a feeling of connectedness with people. But she doesn't have that. Marlene Dietrich once said a friend is someone you can call at four in the morning. Dr. Koering's a Lone Ranger."

His view is curiously incomplete. Certainly, Marilyn's ambitious, "fast lane" scramble of a woman cracking a man's world gave her relationships a certain abrasive quality. A specialist in primate reproduction, Marilyn says she "professionally died" when her colleagues found out she had melanoma. A pathologist whose office was adjacent to her lab barged in "tornado style" one day to confess he'd been avoiding her because she had stirred up his own fears of mortality.

But she found new social cohesion in a support group of cancer patients more inured to such terrors. As many cases of remarkable recovery reported to us, she discovered new "kindness from people I had known all my life and people I had only met"; kindnesses that "often brought tears to my eyes, blurring my vision and wetting my cheeks. This was my reaction to their caring: It was not sadness, it was love." She spent three years going to weekly support group meetings where it was permissible to express feelings. (One of her essays is titled "OK to Cry.") When a woman who had lost a hard-won remission came to one meeting drained and frightened, some others counseled positive thinking. But Marilyn blurted out, "Bullshit!" Reality *hurts,* she assured the woman, who was then able to give free vent to her emotions.

The idea that there is any one "right" emotional attitude to healing disturbs her. When the article citing her survival in the interferon study was read to her group, they reacted with applause and cheers like "a pep rally." Discomfited, she described the gentleness of her "surrender" outside the operating room. "In unison they all nodded and said, 'Your way is a good way.' " She remembers feeling "elated" that there could really be "different ways for different people, but my way was right for me. When I was leaving," she writes, "each shook my hand and thanked me for being there . . . I now smile each time I think that they stated 'my way' was a 'good way' to address one's death."

Here, perhaps, is the most frequently cited healing force we encountered in our research—that of simply being treated as a unique individual, not a disease category or an errant statistic in a treatment protocol. In a single moment, a powerful axis of congruent perception was formed: *I am understood, cared for, accepted by another, seen for myself.* As a medical professional as well as a patient, Marilyn has had to learn, she says, "the uniqueness of each human being may dictate their course."

Marilyn has found her course. She feels different now as she jogs in her golden yellow running suit, the one with the heavily padded shoulders that make her look like "a Viking halfback in miniature," running across the Potomac, past the Pentagon, past the cherry trees lining the Tidal Basin, through Arlington Cemetery where the sign says "No Jogging" ("I run when I am alone with the thousands of deceased, who I figure won't tell on me"). She can't restrain a laugh—why should she?—every time she goes past a certain stop sign, the result of another blitzkrieg letter-writing campaign against "those Pentagon guys who speed right through the intersection."

She still seems like the control-freak she's had to be: quiet, well-organized, sedulous. But sometimes, a childlike rapture at being alive breaks through, overflooding the calculus of the hard scientist: "A glorious day! I pedaled past birds, ducks, and people. A slight breeze, warm sun, clear air, and color of fall leaves. I thought I was in heaven," she writes. "The old adage states, 'Without a storm, there is no rainbow.' "

She has found a way use her scientist's approach to satisfy her soul. She has taken to staining cytology slides in odd spectrums of color and then taking electron micrographs, the results so weirdly beautiful they've been hung in Washington galleries. Her melanoma, she says, "encourages a permanent feeling of 'living on the edge.' "

Dr. Creagan, too, skirts the edge when he speculates aloud there may be *some* unknown factors beyond interferon in Marilyn's remarkable recovery. But he finds little professional enthusiasm for his view. "My colleagues here think it's a lot of baloney. They say Marilyn Koering is just part of the natural expression of the bell-shaped curve."

The bell-shaped curve, the bell-shaped curve: The famously sinuous, snake-swallowing-an-elephant shape is one of science's great graphical icons. Technically, it is a "probabilistic distribution curve." Most tabulations of natural phenomena, psychological characteristics, sociological groupings, treatment outcomes, or life expectancies—damn near *any*thing when charted on a graph in sufficient numbers—reveals a curve shaped like a bell, a haystack, a hillock.

The great homogeneous bulge in the middle of the graph is the average, the mean, the usual, the many. The slope on either side steeply tapering to near zero represents the few rarities, cases virtually off the scale, referred to in statistics as "outliers." It is the outlier's doleful lot to be disregarded in calculations—less out of any cruelty of majority rule than as a necessary scientific precaution. If Marilyn Koering lives, as she seems well on her way to doing, for twenty-five or thirty years, and if her extended lifespan were then averaged with the tragically foreshortened ones of her original group, the whole group's median survival rate on paper would skew upwards, inaccurately representing the drug's efficacy and giving false hope in the worst sense. So Marilyn, as a statistical artifact, is unceremoniously given the boot.

But what happens to these outliers, these instances that don't fit the cluster pattern of predictable response, like the geek whose near-perfect test score ruins the class curve? On the positive end of the health spectrum, they are the superhealthy, the ones who never seem to get sick, or recover unusually quickly. In ordinary life, these might be what we call peak performers, athletes we watch with awe as they year after year trounce seemingly unbeatable records; a dancer who, like the young Baryshnikov, seems to have an occult ability to hover in midair. For them, there is no bell-shaped curve, only an ever upward-turning arc of performance. Their records are viewed even by amateurs as a challenge, an inspiration to go further.

Many patients have told us that hearing of a single remarkable recovery was similarly inspirational; the knowledge that even one person had survived their particular disease gave them the hope that life was still possible in the direst circumstance. But in some areas of science, an outlier may be experienced like a tone-deaf person singing loudly in G–flat when the rest of the group is in C: You'd just rather not listen. In calculations of treatment response, prognoses of survival, or predictions of mortality, the one or two or three dots on the graph that don't lie within the cloud of normalcy are irrelevant, perhaps dangerously misleading anomalies. But we would also suggest they are the "one white crow" who might be an exemplar of yet unknown healing mechanisms.

Dr. Karen Olness is a physician who has combined traditional medical practice and mind-body approaches in her quest to discover the mechanisms of the healing system. Today, she wipes the perspiration off her forehead with the back of her sleeve and grins. She's been pulling thistles, and she gulps the cold tap water, siphoned up from a deep well on her 260-acre farm, with greedy delight. She loves her swath of land, where she now grows commercial crops of peas and beans. She finds pulling weeds to be "therapeutic, like pulling weeds from your own mental processes. I started out majoring in botany, you know," she says, her eyes crinkling. "I was going to be a plant pathologist."

Instead, she became another nurturer of growing things, a pediatrician, renowned for teaching children strategies like self-hypnosis and imagery to reduce the frequency of migraines and chronic pain. The relationship between physiology and mental processes is her passionate specialty. In a case that became one of the most renowned gambits in mind-body medicine, Dr. Olness was able to condition the immune system of a little girl with lupus to respond to ordinary cod-liver oil as if it were a powerful drug, giving the child a degree of control over her symptoms. (At the end of two years, the amount of the drug the girl needed was reduced by half.)

Dr. Olness remains an enthusiastic pioneer, convinced that

though it may take well into the next century, the mind's role in healing will prove increasingly measurable. She hopes to convert an old farmhouse on her property into a retreat center to brainstorm new medical studies. "We even had a meeting of the Wart Consortium here a few years ago," she offers.

Her mischievous look suggests she's teasing. The *Wart* Consortium? But sure enough, at long last, Karen Olness has posthumously given Dr. Lewis Thomas his "National Institute of Warts and All." Dr. Olness has recently completed a study involving a consortium of eight institutions to see if warts could be coaxed to yield insights into how the mind affects the immune system. Discovering that there had been no previous immunological data on how warts grow or why they vanish, she enlisted the Edison Technology Center to design a custom-made "wart monitor," which "took longer than anybody could have *possibly* imagined. We are now," she says, raising her eyebrows in mock-horror, "the wart experts of planet Earth."

The eight Wart Consortium centers, from New York's Columbia University to the University of California at Berkeley, chose a total of ninety children around the country who had observable warts on their upper extremities. The children were told to choose a "sentinel wart" that they would pay particular attention to, then were taught relaxation and imagery exercises to "tell their warts to go away." One control group used only a traditional dermatology treatment. Preliminary results showed the children doing the imagery had better results than those using only medicine.

Virtually all children, Dr. Olness says, have prodigious self-hypnotic abilities, as does Olness herself. (She once underwent an operation on a torn ligament without anaesthetic, imagining a verdant scene from her childhood as her orthopedists painlessly sewed her flesh.) "A kid's heart rate will be pretty steady, and all of a sudden, you see a jump of forty points in the matter of ten seconds and ask him, 'What did you do?' And he'll say, 'Well, I was riding [my imaginary bicycle] too slow and I suddenly decided to ride real fast.' Normal school-age children showed the same level of autonomic response as athletes in special training programs. This absolutely has health repercussions."

But each kid does it differently. What Dr. Olness wants to know is how, and whether it affects their degree of wart-killing ability. Healing, she is convinced, is a highly individualized process, varying from person to person. "We have gathered data on whether a given child is better at visual or auditory or kinesthetic or some other kind of imagery." In a testing procedure reminiscent of Dr. Herbert Spiegel's AOD scale, Dr. Olness asks questions aimed at uncovering individual styles of cognition and perception: "I'll say, 'Tell me your favorite song. Now if you close your eyes can you imagine hearing that?' Some kids can and some can't. Or, 'Imagine a smell.' Some can, some can't."

But she admits, "We can't even conceive the kind of tools that we need to understand the mind–immune mechanisms. Thoughts seem to send a cascade of instruction using a cascade of neurotransmitters. But we need far more sophisticated ways of picking up the energy associated with thinking than brain wave measurements. I'm sure they'll laugh at us a hundred years from now."

Dr. Olness, when we asked her, remembered one case of remarkable recovery from her own practice, a boy named Charlie Roth. After some persistent detective work—she no longer had a number for the Roth family—we located Charlie, who at age twelve had been given a three-month prognosis. We found him the day after his thirtieth birthday.

Charlie's battle with cancer began around Christmas in 1976, when he had developed a racking cough and severe pains in his right leg. In spring 1977, his pediatrician ordered X rays and found a "fuzzy" area on his pelvis. Charlie was referred for biopsy to Minneapolis Children's Hospital, where he met Karen Olness and oncologist Larry Singher, the physicians who were to play irreplaceable roles in his fight for life.

Charlie's case, in fact, struck us as one blueprint for an emerging new medicine—a close, individualized collaboration between doctor and patient, between conventional medicine and other practices that stimulate the healing system, combining to save a boy from certain death. Dr. Olness introduced Charlie to relaxation and breathing exercises almost as soon as he arrived. "She told me to imagine I was walking down a path," Charlie describes, "and to try to smell the grass and see the trees. Then she said in this soft tone, 'Now you're walking down a hill and with each breath you will feel more and more relaxed.'

"When I came up the 'hill,' " he remembers, "I felt really good. It slowed my heart and breathing rate, which calmed me down when I went in for the operation." The surgeon found a grapefruit-sized tumor on Charlie's pelvic bone that couldn't be excised. X rays showed twenty more tumors in his lungs. The diagnosis was metastatic Ewing's sarcoma. "Just take him home and love him," the surgeon sadly told his parents; Charlie, he confided, had perhaps three months to live.

"Every time I saw that surgeon past those first three months," Charlie told us, "I'd walk by and say, 'Hi, Mac, I'm still here.' " Charlie hesitates. "He died of cancer, and I wish I had gone to his funeral. I would have liked to say once more, 'Hi, Mac. I'm still here.' "

Oncologist Larry Singher proved a perfect match for Charlie. From the first meeting, the straight-talking doctor included the unusually persistent child in every conversation, every consultation, every decision. Dr. Singher gave him access to all his records, test results, and treatment protocol, leveling unsparingly with the boy. "It was a good, open, honest relationship," says Charlie. "He told me plain and simple: Even with chemotherapy, the prognosis wasn't good, but with a lot of work, it might extend my life a little and make me a little more comfortable. But he also said, 'If you don't give it a try, you're never going to know. The ball's in your court.' "

"I was born with a survival instinct," Charlie told us. "And sometimes my survival instinct was to be adversarial, a real sarcastic little brat." Charlie's mother remembers Dr. Singher telling her he sometimes got up in the morning and said to himself, "That damn kid is coming in today." Charlie, who tested at the Apollonian end of the AOD scale, took on the fight for his life with a diligence leavened with childish élan. He and a boy with Hodgkin's disease, he says, used to have "races to see who could get their intravenous chemo in first. We used to do things like push the bottle up as far as we could and open it up as wide as possible, and lie on the floor. That drove the nurses nuts. But he didn't make it. Afterward, the only room that I would allow myself to be put in was the room he died in, because it seemed like there was some kind of energy there. Like he was there telling me, *You can do it, you can do it.*"

Charlie believed he could do it, and do it in his own way. He refused pain medication because "I didn't like the feel of it. I'm the kind of person who doesn't like to be out of control." Instead, Dr. Olness taught Charlie ways to control pain with biofeedback and self-hypnosis, which became his daily routines. Later, during chemotherapy and radiation treatment, Charlie used the same methods to help control his nausea. He approached his exercises in characteristic style. "She gave me a biofeedback monitor that measured finger temperature. I thought it was a challenge to make it go up and down. I got good enough that they brought me to a neuropsychiatric institute and hooked me up to a more sophisticated machine. I showed I could raise my finger temperature from 90 to 106 degrees." Remembers his mother, "Charlie had such intensity and dedication. He said he didn't want anything to interfere with his natural endorphins. They were really on speaking terms!" Dr. Olness also introduced Charlie to visualization techniques. Refusing any assistance, he quickly devised his own imagery, imagining his chemotherapy as "vicious beasts, like Tasmanian Devils on the Saturday morning cartoons."

Dr. Singher was no less aggressive. Charlie's mother remembers, "He let nothing stop him. I mean, if Charlie was due to come in for chemo on his birthday and complained, Singher would say, 'Do you want to have a birthday next year?' "

After six months of treatment, chest X rays revealed no tumors in Charlie's lungs. The tumor in his pelvis was shrinking. Almost a year after the original biopsy, his hip showed only the scarred remains of several lymph nodes. But Charlie says his imagery had already told him there was no cancer: "My white cells were actually coming to me at one point reporting they were cleaning up and that was it. I could see them like watching a movie." Singher elected to continue chemotherapy until, in the summer of 1980, after three years of grueling treatment, Charlie was declared in remission.

But his battle was not won yet. Less than a year after he was declared cancer-free, he bent over and felt a sharp pain in his back. He knew something was very wrong. A week later, he had surgery to remove a cancerous rib, and more chemotherapy. "I thought maybe it was time to check out," he said, "but something in me said, 'Hey dummy, quit it. You did it once, you can do it again.' " He insisted his rib be brought to him. "It was about a foot long, a thin thing with a little knot." Pointing to the little bump, he told his doctor, "Is *that* what we've been fighting all along? That's a piece of cake!" then yelled at the cancer, "I can beat you any day!' "

It's been eighteen years since Charlie was diagnosed. During that time, Dr. Singher died of stomach cancer. "I saw him a couple of times before he died," Charlie says, with sadness and respect in his voice. "He played a huge role, because without him, I wouldn't be here." In a newspaper article Marilyn Roth read to us, Dr. Singher attributed Charlie's remarkable recovery in part to Charlie's work with Karen Olness and the boy's "basically ornery disposition."

Charlie's description of himself is "Tough Nut," the name of his favorite brand of overalls. He works as a restaurant manager and reserve police officer who "pushes the envelope all day and night if there's a job to get done." When we asked Charlie, now married to a florist he met while buying flowers for a former girlfriend, what helped him survive, he said, "Every bit of it."

How can we account for Charlie's remarkable response to treatment? By his sense of fun and spirit of competition; excellent relationships with caring doctors; biofeedback and imagery; his childlike belief in his own invincibility; the loving support of his family; an unusual response to experimental chemotherapy that was only expected to buy him some time? Charlie is convinced it was all of the above, adding good humoredly, "But if it wasn't for *me,* I'd be dead!"

It has been suggested that each case of remarkable recovery is a unique "experiment of nature." But the study of the possible influence of moods and emotions, personality traits, social support, beliefs and attitudes lobs a quiet bombshell into the settled precincts of experimental medicine: Can we ever be certain whether "real" treatment does not owe an unknown portion of its curative power to these "nonmedical" factors? For that matter, how can we know the extent to which mind-body factors might account for the successes of even ostensibly well-proven treatments?

In 1994, at a meeting convened by the National Institutes of Health Office of Alternative Medicine, a paper was presented analyzing responses of various disease conditions to "nonspecific effects"—that is, placebos—using both alternative and standard medical therapies. It reported that for either approach "when both healers and patients believe that a treatment is likely to be effective, one can commonly expect improvements in up to seventy percent of patients treated, even when the treatment is entirely nonspecific." Said Dr. Alan Roberts, the paper's author, "Patients often improve after treatments that are not supposed to be effective. Depending upon our particular bias, we then say that improvement results from a placebo effect, a miracle, God's will, [or] spontaneous remission. . . ." Roberts reminds us, "Because a treatment is considered to be conventional and accepted does not necessarily imply that it is proven or specific. The thin line between applied scientific medicine and the power of the doctor-patient relationship is highly permeable. In clinical practice, they may become indistinguishable."

How accurately, then, can we assess the "real" efficacy of our medicines given the concept of the healing system? Science, after all, demands that all potential intervening variables be taken into consideration before a predictable effect can be ratified. But controlled, randomized drug studies typically select for, say, patients of a certain age, stage of disease, sex, and duration of illness, ignoring psychological, social, and spiritual factors. Until we know—and take into account—how varying states of mind, degrees of suggestibility, psychoneuroimmunological responsiveness, individual health practices, attitudes, social milieus, belief systems, and even religious experiences affect the progress or regress of disease, it is hard to have unbending faith in the results of experiments that never posed the questions.

In the model of the healing system we propose, individual differences become key. Some people, like the fully thirty percent of chemotherapy controls in one study who received only a placebo infusion of mild salt water and *still* lost all their hair as an unexpected "side effect," may be more susceptible to suggestions that can translate into profound physiological effects—effects perhaps more far-ranging than this startling exhibition of mind-over-follicles.

The extent to which individual differences are not taken into account in both the study and promotion of the healing response is not only a detriment to the healer's art, but a challenge to the scientific method itself. Could the "placebo responders" who lost their hair, for example, also be more adept at mobilizing their own "healing systems" to fight disease? What, then, if they had not been a control group, but had received the actual medicine and shown an inordinately strong response, positively skewing the apparent results of an experimental drug protocol? How can we even *begin* to know, when such "nonspecific effects" are viewed as insignificant or nonstudyable "complications" in data acquisition?

Jean Achterberg and Frank Lawlis, who have spent a combined total of forty-six years teaching research design and statistics to medical students, as well as serving as principal investigators on National Cancer Institute grants, pointed out in a 1992 article that randomized controlled trials were

designed chiefly for agricultural and horticultural studies. . . . Randomized control group designs have not and simply cannot yield satisfactory answers in complex behavioral or psychosocial studies with human beings. . . . To let a research methodology dictate the design and nature of the research question (instead of the other way around) is an aberration of the scientific method. The tail, quite plainly, is wagging the dog. . . .

It is not enough, they point out, to simply match diagnostic or demographic variables for equivalencies when "will to live, hope, trust, social support, personal beliefs, or imagery about the nature of health and disease or even nutritional status are equally or, in our opinion, more important determinants of outcome than the usually measured variables."

They call for setting aside "outdated, inappropriate methods" and paying more rigorous scientific attention to so-called anecdotal cases: "A single surviving patient in the [Dr. David] Spiegel group has a story which may be of far more interest and validity to our understanding of the experience than anything presented quantitatively to date." Finally, Achterberg and Lawlis suggest, "Depriving cancer patients of any treatment that meshes with their worldview or belief system and is probably helpful (at worst, benign) is unethical, inhumane, and unkind." To change the way we study illness and healing, they believe, "will create a vastly different science, a different psychology, and a different medicine."

The outlines of a "vastly different medicine" based on the unique qualities of the individual, the concept of a healing system, and the reality of remarkable recovery is already taking shape on both the edges and in the center of official medical practice, with support beginning to snowball among researchers and physicians. Dr. Steven Rosenberg, in his innovative treatment protocols, recognizes the cellular uniqueness of each patient when creating his individualized TNF "vaccine." Rosenberg's treatments, not unlike William Coley's in the nineteenth century, must be individually tailored. Unlike standard chemotherapy, each of Rosenberg's unique treatment batches is made up from cancer-fighting cells drawn from the patient's own body, treated in the laboratory, then reinfused. As Rosenberg told ABC News in April 1994:

> We can now, in about ten percent of patients with wide-spread kidney cancer, cause the complete disappearance of all malignancy—that's one in ten. And the overwhelming majority of those patients—over three-quarters of those—appear to be cured, that is, the cancer has not come back at times now lasting eight, almost nine years. And so in some small percentage of patients we can stimulate the immune system to completely eliminate the disease. It's a stepwise approach, but I think we're making progress to learn to harness the immune system to cause, in a deliberate way, what these spontaneous regressions appear to cause in a very mysterious way.

But still, what do we know about these ten percent long-term survivors and 7.5 percent remitters of kidney cancer, a disease known to, in a smaller percentage of cases, "naturally" remit? Who are they? What did they think, feel, do, imagine? Whom did they love, and who loved them? Which of them perceived the doctor, the treatment, and the hospital as supportive and congruent with their belief systems, and who found it frightening or alienating? If Rosenberg's treatment only works on a few, why *these* few?

The issue of just how much psychoemotional factors affect patient health has been rocking almost violently back and forth in what might be perceived as the birth pangs of a new medical paradigm. On one side are those who feel that "biology is destiny," and that to suggest that attitude can affect outcome encourages false hope. In a famous (and scathing) editorial in a 1985 issue of the *New England Journal of Medicine,* Marcia Angell called the idea that emotions can affect disease outcomes "folklore . . . a myth [that] serves as a form of mastery." She wrote:

> A view that attaches credit to patients for controlling their disease also implies blame for the progression of the

disease. . . . In addition to the anguish of personal failure, a further harm to such patients is that they may come to see medical care as largely irrelevant . . . and give themselves over completely to some method of thought control. . . . In our desire to pay tribute to gallantry and grace in the face of hardship, we sometimes credit these qualities with cures, not realizing that we may also be implying blame when there are reverses. . . . At a time when patients are already burdened by disease, they should not be further burdened by having to accept responsibility for the outcome.

Angell's article stirred up an unusually high volume of critical mail. Two past and one current president of the Society of Behavioral Medicine wrote to point out that Angell "fails to consider recent developments in the neurosciences that increase our understanding of the biologic basis of a variety of mental states." In another letter, researchers at the University of Rochester write, "A growing body of scientific literature indicates that biobehavioral factors influence a host of physiologic functions that lie at the foundation of homeostasis and resistance to disease . . . we simply do not know at present the extent to which, and the mechanisms by which, psychobiologic factors contribute to the induction and progression of, or recovery from, disease."

It is intriguing to consider that if there is such a thing as a "disease-prone" personality (a concept still being hotly debated), the therapies adopted by a new medicine to switch on the healing system, just like the strategies instinctively adopted by remarkable recoveries, might consist of reversing these pathological attitudes, beliefs, and behaviors. In study after study, repression of feeling, lack of expressiveness, depressed acceptance, a sense of helplessness, and hopelessness are cited. The research of Dr. Lawrence LeShan, for example, shows that many cancer patients have experienced severe emotional trauma, deeply repressed hostility, extreme feelings of psychological isolation, and despair. LeShan's therapy, not surprisingly, consists above all in restoring a sense of "enthusiasm."

But LeShan, a psychologist who reports a number of cases of remarkable recovery, admonishes, "You can't just look in a mirror and say, 'Every day in every way I'm getting more enthusiastic.' You've got to change your life."

The results of his approach are not always easy to accommodate within the medical contexts like hospitals, which often aim not so much at stimulating the healing system as creating an environment conducive to the efficient practice of technological medicine. "I know I'm doing my job," LeShan says, "when I come into the hospital for an appointment and the nurses snarl at me and hide the charts because my patient's been making trouble. It means the person is really fighting for their lives, is asking all the difficult questions, is making waves and making noises."

If the healing system is a "grand orchestration," can the orchestra in any way be conducted at will? One case of remarkable recovery told us, "No matter how much you dissect someone's experience, you might not be able to re-create it. It's like lightning." He had paused, looking for a better analogy. "Or like an amazingly delicious pot of soup, where there are all these ingredients plus something else, some art, that makes it *taste* so good." Said another: "You can't prescribe it, it can't be taught, and you *can* learn it."

Dr. Johannes Schilder of Rotterdam's Helen Dowling Institute has wrestled with the conundrum: Is there a way to reproduce the irreproducible, to catalyze a recovery? "I think it could be done," he says. "But if you took these cases as literal instructions, you would have to somehow create a dramatic replay of a pivotal event—or an entire set of circumstances in a person's life. It would certainly be a different type of psychotherapy than we're used to. And you can't just instruct a patient to 'become more autonomous.' It's a contradiction in terms." But he suggests that an "experiential diagnosis" might reveal specific patterns and situations where a patient could learn to break through "learned helplessness" and reassert his or her own power.

Tens of thousands of patients around the world are learning just that. The new medicine is emerging in large part through the grass-roots activities of the ill themselves, who are demonstrating a felt need for individualized treatment to stimulate the healing system.

Susan Silberstein, founder of the Center for Advancement in Cancer Education in Philadelphia, is a case in point. She was a professor of linguistics when her husband was diagnosed at age thirty with an extremely rare cancer of the spinal cord. Nothing could be done but palliative treatment. The doctors at Sloan-Kettering performed eight neurosurgeries in nine months, treating him with experimental chemotherapy and radiation along the way. Susan watched as a "six foot tall, two-hundred-pound young man turned into a shriveled great-grandfather who weighed sixty pounds on the day he died. But she feels that "he had been destroyed emotionally and mentally before he was physically."

While he'd been in the hospital, she'd virtually lived in medical libraries, looking for an alternative to the debilitating treatments her husband was stoically enduring at what seemed to her great cost and questionable benefit. "I knew so little about cancer, I'd never even heard the word 'chemotherapy,' " she says. "But I *was* a professional researcher." She tore through the stacks, piled up long-distance bills, found contacts in other countries and tantalizing leads, all too late to help her husband. After his death, she vowed she "wasn't going to bury with him everything I'd learned that might be of value to the next patient."

She set up her center in October of 1977, a few months after her husband had died, "not because I had any score to settle with the cancer establishment or with his doctors, who were all terribly sincere and totally broken up to have lost a young patient in such a vile way. It was because I was already intellectually persuaded there had to be other approaches."

She has now seen close to ten thousand patients, working with a staff of volunteers, never charging money. (Indeed, it is extraordinary how many of the centers we consider harbingers for the emerging new medicine are run at a shoestring, grass-roots level, turning few people away for lack of funds. There was a remarkable lack of profiteering, and indeed in some cases, lack of profit, harking back to an earlier model of medicine as first and foremost an act of *caritas,* or caring.)

Susan has had an opportunity to observe many of what she calls "not just spontaneous remissions, but 'hard-work miracles.' " She ticks off a list of common threads that are by now surprising only in the extraordinary degree of consensus with our and other findings: "They accept the diagnosis but reject the prognosis; they make decisions according to their own particular belief systems and understandings; there is at least one special healing relationship with a loved one, a health professional, a friend, a support group, or a therapist; they get in touch with unexpressed emotions; they rediscover joy, creativity, a purpose in life, a sense of worth, a reason to be on this planet, a feeling of fulfillment; they transform their lives, careers, cities, marriages. We're probably guilty," she says wryly, "of precipitating not a few divorces."

Her observations have led her to a form of intake interview and health care referral that is typical of the emerging new medicine: "Every referral we make is so incredibly individualized," she laughs ruefully, "that we drive ourselves nuts."

In a series of personal interviews, Susan looks carefully at each patient's physical, financial, and geographic limitations. She and her volunteers analyze physiological status and nutritional habits; beliefs; goals; and social support system. "We look at their mental or emotional readiness for a certain treatment approach. We never tell patients what they should or shouldn't do. We ask them what their doctors have told them, what the doctors are offering them, how they *feel* about what the doctors are offering them, how they feel about the *doctor,* what they feel comfortable doing in the conventional or unconventional medical world. Then we start offering them resources.

"You can't believe how intimately involved I can get with a patient at the end of one hour," she exclaims. "I know stuff about them that they swore they never told anybody. I don't think it's because I'm that brilliant a psychologist, I think it's because I've learned so much from what the other 9,999 patients have taught me."

If we have learned one thing from the extraordinary and inspiring people we met on our journey, it is that healing is as much wild as domesticated, as much raw as cooked. It requires a certain daring, a willingness to explore many dimensions of wholeness. Only a handful who got well did so without coloring outside the lines. A new medicine, too, must learn to color outside the lines: lines that sometimes artificially divide doctor from patient, fact from feeling, surgery from synergy, chemo from caring.

The more that remarkable recovery is recognized as a legitimate scientific occurrence, the more we may understand how to stimulate natural self-repair and create environments most conducive to self-healing. Clearly, the data of remarkable recovery could have important applications not only in our understanding of health and disease, but also in our search for new therapies. A combination of spirit, genetics, psychoneuroimmunology, and mind-body research are the puzzle pieces that could produce not only a new picture, but new techniques of integral healing.

A medical system sensitive to the genuine needs of patients would base health care as much on the individual's intangible values and beliefs as on tangible pharmaceuticals and operations. Therapeutic outcomes would also be measured in individuals' feelings about themselves, their connection to others, their sense of purpose, and their conviction that they have a unique place in the larger scheme of things. Only then can we hope to have a medicine that heals as well as cures.

Medieval mystic and healer Hildegard of Bingen, born in 1098 in what is now Bockelheim, Germany, in a curious way anticipated the emerging new philosophy and practice of medicine. Hildegard's theories stressed the interrelatedness of body, mind, emotions, and spirit. The cure for disease, she preached, could be found in the energy of life, which she called *viriditas,* "the greening power." Hildegard's use of this concept, according to one biographer, included "all living things, the energy of life which comes from God, the power of youth and of sexuality, the power in seeds, the reproduction of cells, the power of regeneration, freshness, and creativity."

Most of Hildegard's curative methods were at best folk medicine. But twenty-first-century medicine will have to be based firmly on her foundation of *viriditas* (and *caritas*) if it is to heal the lives of patients and, indeed, help restore and expand our notions of ourselves as human beings rather than mere biological mechanisms.

Medicine, once the crown jewel of reductionist scientism, has improbably opened up an unexpected vista of the human spirit. Guided in part by what we have witnessed in remarkable recovery, we believe we are on the cusp of a moment foreseen by Claude Bernard, the founder of modern physiology: "I have the conviction," he wrote, "that when Physiology will be far enough advanced, the poet, the philosopher, and the physiologist will all understand each other." Perhaps the common language will be that of the healing system. Then the study of remarkable recovery will have truly begun.

The
Remarkable Recovery
Registry

T HE STUDY OF THE ODD, THE UNEXPECTED, THE HARD-TO-
find and difficult-to-quantify has always been the challenge and glory of medicine. The study of autoimmune disorders,
for example, crucially advanced knowledge of immunology. But
there has been scant methodical study of remarkable recovery, not
in small part because of how infrequently these cases are reported
in the medical literature. The situation today is not that different
from the one noted by the early remissions researcher Dr. Joseph
DeCourcy in 1933, who explained the dearth of case reports:

> In view of the general conviction in the past that cancer is an
> incurable disease, there has been an inclination . . . to assume
> that the diagnosis was erroneous—a disconcerting reflection
> which has led the physician observing the case to keep silent
> about it, or to place a question mark against his report.

Even when there were reports, they contained little information
about the individuals who were their subjects. Attempting to lo-

cate the actual patients behind the sketchy details, we were surprised to discover that many doctors had lost track of their unusual patients entirely. How can the scattered data on the subject be retrieved from its orphaned status in medicine, and what steps can be taken to bring this knowledge to both the patients that need it and the medical profession that can use it? The publication of this book is intended as a first step in an ongoing effort to collect and learn from cases of remarkable recovery.

But we believe a much-expanded effort is needed. Our experiences pointed out what we feel is a vital, two-pronged task for the medical field: First, to improve the level of case reporting; and two, to track cases over a period of years through a Remarkable Recovery Registry modeled on (or perhaps even included within) the National Cancer Institute's Tumor Registry.

As we have pointed out, the rarity of extant reports stems in part from the lack of an appropriately broadened definition to include more complex healing events: unexpectedly long survival, recoveries that were treated conventionally yet "shouldn't have happened," unusual recoveries resulting from a combination of conventional and alternative treatment.

Indeed, when people have claimed that factors other than conventional medicine have been active in their cures, they have often been dismissed. Critics invoke Occam's razor, the cardinal scientific rule of thumb that prohibits attempting to explain one unknown with another unknown. But we must wonder which is a greater violation of this rule: to explain a remarkable recovery as merely "spontaneous remission" or to suggest that there may be unconventional "biological response modifiers" at work, whether alternative medicines or psychosocial factors.

Our principal source for this information, along with medical records and doctors' testimony, was our interviews with people who had remarkable recoveries. We found among some fellow researchers a pronounced skepticism about this approach. One prominent critic wondered aloud why we were bothering to gather this "subjective" data at all: "That information is notoriously unreliable," she expostulated. *"Nobody* believes it, and nobody pays much attention to it. No one will have any interest in it except the general public, who might be misled into thinking that they, too, can have a spontaneous remission. What people think about why they experienced a remission and what they believe about what was happening to their bodies is really not hard data."

But data, according to *Webster's,* consist of any information "from which conclusions can be inferred." Perhaps most significantly, it derives from the Latin *datum,* meaning "a gift, a present." Data are gifts, whether external observations or the internal ones from the world of thoughts and feelings.

Several decades ago these "inner" data were considered an acceptable scientific pursuit. We came across a 1957 article in which the author mentioned attending a "most interesting" conference at Houston's M. D. Anderson Hospital of "about forty psychologists and physicians from all over the United States, all of whom were actively engaged in cancer research from the psychological point of view." Until recently, the notion of such a meeting taking place on the premises of a federally funded cancer facility would be hard to imagine. With the emergence of the field of psycho-oncology, it is being increasingly recognized that psychological factors may play an important role. In 1984, an entire afternoon symposium at the Annual Meeting of the American Psychiatric Association entitled "Hope as a Factor in Remission from Illness" served to highlight the importance of this element in the patients' treatment environment. In fact, in a survey of specialists questioned about the importance of psychosocial factors in cancer care, ninety percent of the 649 oncologists who responded said that attitudes of hope and optimism, a strong will to live, confidence in the doctor, and emotional support from family and friends were of significant benefit to treatment.

Certainly, no one can solve the mystery of remarkable recovery using only anecdotal accounts. There are—and will be for the forseeable future—too many unknowns concerning why and how often the phenomenon occurs. But gathering and analyzing solid data on the incidence of remarkable recovery would give the concerned physician a means to provide "ethical hope" even to the most terminal-seeming patient.

In addition, a careful study of enough individual cases could lead us to a potential wealth of biological information. There is rising interest in studying the blood and tissues of patients who have had remarkable recoveries as a means of detecting clues about how to stimulate the phenomenon. With the advent of genetic screening techniques and other sophisticated tools for cloning rare biological substances, medical science may now be in a unique position to take advantage of instances of remarkable recovery to make groundbreaking discoveries.

In general, the field of psychoneuroimmunology has begun to allow us to analyze cases for possible mind-body factors in ways never before possible. By reexamining current therapeutic strategies in light of remarkable recovery, the testing of new medical protocols could be enhanced to the mutual benefit of patients, medical treatment, and medical education as a whole. By broadening case reports to include alternative as well as conventional medicine, a picture of the spectrum of self-repair could emerge that would improve. Introducing psychological, spiritual, and social assessments into intake procedures could lead to new individualized treatment models.

If remarkable recovery contains a social dimension, then providing social support to everyone who desires it will become an essential component of formal medical treatment. Given the frequent plea we have heard from cancer patients—"If I knew of just one person who had 'beat' this, then I would feel like I could fight it"—linking people struggling with disease with those who have unexpectedly recovered would provide a source of inspiration and hope to the sufferers. Peer counseling could reap great benefits both for the patients and the medical community as a whole.

With the publication of this book, we begin an initiative to create a Remarkable Recovery Registry, which we hope will spark greater international effort to collect and track cases in a systematic manner. Approached on a sufficient scale, such a registry might answer the following questions:

- Which types of cancer are most prone to RR?

- Are certain kinds of people more prone to RR?

- What is the frequency of RR?

- What is the distribution of RR in this country and world-wide?

- In which kinds of people, with which kinds of backgrounds, genetically, socially, psychologically and environmentally, does RR occur?

- Are there particular social, therapeutic, or other support settings that seem to contribute to RR?

- Are the factors involved genetic or psychobiological or both?

- Are there genetic or chromosomal patterns that predispose certain people toward RR? Is there a genetic combination that initiates self-repair mechanisms?

- With what kinds of behavioral changes, lifestyle, and habits does RR correlate?

- What are the attitudes and beliefs of people who experience RRs?

- What are the psychospiritual correlates of RR?

- What are the frequencies of RRs of primary tumors? Of metastases? Of the metastatic RRs, what are the relative frequencies in the various tissues (lung, liver, etc.)?

- What is the timing of RR? How long from the discovery of the primary tumor does it occur? Of the metastases? Over what period of time does the RR occur—one month, one week, overnight?

· Is there a relationship between incidence of RR and age? Between the longevity of the patient's parents and grandparents (suggestive of a genetic immune component)?

· What is the long-term health status—both physiological and psychological—of people who have experienced RR?

Without the answers to these most basic questions, the epidemiology of Remarkable Recovery will remain unknown. The creation of a registry could lead to greater understanding of disease and treatment; could increase the ability of physicians to advise patients regarding protective factors, practices, and lifestyle changes that might be adopted for prevention; and could provide new (and more dynamic) statistics on possible outcomes.

We would like to invite anyone who has had or has knowledge of someone who has had a remarkable recovery to join the Registry, including those who are long-term survivors of HIV/AIDS. On the pages that follow is a "Remarkable Recovery Registry" form based on the questionnaire we used in our research project. We would like to invite you to make a copy of the questionnaire, fill it out, and send it to:

THE REMARKABLE RECOVERY REGISTRY
CALL BOX 5009
BEN LOMOND, CA 95005-5009

THE REMARKABLE RECOVERY REGISTRY

Would you please take a few minutes to answer the following questions?

Name _____ Date of Birth _____

Place of Birth _____What is your sex? M _____ F_____

Address _____

_____

Phone _____ Fax _____

What is your marital status? Single __ Married __ Divorced __ Significant Other__

How long have you been/were you with your husband/wife/significant

other? _____

If you have been married or in a long-term relationship more than once, please

give the number of years of your longest relationship.

_____

Do you have children? Yes ____ No ____. If yes, how many and what are their

ages? _____

How old is your mother? _____ father? _____

(If deceased at what ages did they pass away? From what did they die?)

_____

How old is your maternal grandmother? _____ maternal grandfather? _____

(If deceased at what ages did they pass away? From what did they die?)

_____

How old is your paternal grandmother? _____ paternal grandfather? _____

(If deceased at what ages did they pass away? From what did they die?)

_____

What is the highest level of education completed?

elementary ____ high school ____ university ____ post graduate _____

If college graduate, in what subject(s) did you receive your degree? _____

_____

What is your profession? How long have you been working at that profession?

_____

Do you have/have you had an artistic or craft pursuit (drawing, painting, music, writing, singing, woodcrafts, etc.) in which you feel you have some talent? Yes ___ No ___ If yes, what art(s) or craft(s) have you pursued?

_____

_____

_____

What, if any, is your religious affiliation? your family's? (optional) _____

Have you had feelings or experiences (physical, psychological, spiritual) for which there seemed to be no logical/rational explanation? Yes ___ No ___. If yes, please describe your experience(s)

_____

_____

_____

Did any of the following practices contribute significantly to your survival/recovery? (please check all that apply)

meditation/relaxation techniques ___	hypnosis ___	self-hypnosis ___	yoga ___
	special diets/ nutrition ___	group support ___	group therapy ___
acupuncture ___	exercise ___	psychotherapy ___	dance/movement ___
music/singing ___	travel ___	storytelling ___	painting/drawing ___
guided imagery/ visualization ___	stress reduction techniques ___	visits to psychic or spiritual healers ___	unusual psychospiritual experiences ___
prayer ___	vivid dreams ___	therapeutic touch ___	gardening ___
research/information about illness ___	relationship with physicians ___	playing a musical instrument ___	alternative medicinal practices ___
social gatherings ___	volunteer work ___	rhythm/drumming ___	creative writing ___
reading/books ___	significant other ___	good luck ___	humor ___
homeopathy ___	herbal medicine ___	work/occupation ___	massage ___
art therapy ___	experiencing nature ___	walking/hiking ___	religious affiliation ___
medical treatment ___	play ___	spirituality ___	genetics ___

Other (please explain) _____

_____

Which, if any, of the following psychospiritual factors were important in your
survival/recovery? (please check all that apply)

religious/spiritual awakening or conversion ____	changes in beliefs or attitudes ____	social/family support ____	positive emotions /thinking/attitudes _____
faith ____	lifestyle changes ____	fighting spirit ____	denial of disease ____
previous experience with illness ____	environmental/social awareness ____	altruistic behavior/ helping others ____	altered sensory perception _____
self-nurturance ____	sense of control ____	commitment to life ____	expression of needs _____
seeing disease as a challenge ____	taking responsibility for disease ____	new sense of purpose ____	renewed desire and/ or will to live _____
belief in positive outcome ____	increased autonomy/ independence ____	changes in habits or other behaviors ____	changes in interpersonal relationships _____
future goals/orientation ____	acceptance of disease ____	laughter/humor ____	ability to say "no" _____

Other (please explain) _____

_____

Which of the following traits do you recognize in yourself? Please add other traits
in the blank spaces provided.

____ sensitive	____ strong	____ cowardly	____ mature
____ humorous	____ distant	____ self-confident	____ trusting
____ dependent	____ impulsive	____ happy	____ cooperative
____ proud	____ selfish	____ involved	____ tough
____ gentle	____ courageous	____ playful	____ serious
____ friendly	____ self-critical	____ rigid	____ independent
____ well-organized	____ discontented	____ rebellious	____ humble
____ unselfish	____ detached	____ lazy	____ logical
____ calm	____ shy	____ loving	____ consistent
____ messy	____ optimistic	____ hard-working	____ creative
____ emotional	____ bold	____ angry	____ unpredictable
____ neat	____ pessimistic	____ compassionate	____ forgiving
____ flexible	____ patient	____ cautious	____ aggressive
____ judgmental	____ philosophical	____ intuitive	____ assertive

___ dependable   ___ critical   ___ pragmatic   ___ tolerant

___ observant   ___ experimental   ___ unconventional   ___ enthusiastic

___ honest   ___ disciplined   ___ analytical   ___ practical

___ naive   ___ trustworthy   ___ passive   ___ curious

___ _____   ___ _____   ___ _____   ___ _____

___ _____   ___ _____   ___ _____   ___ _____

Primary Physician's

Name _____

Street

Address _____ City _____

State _____ Country _____ Phone _____ Fax _____

Do we have your permission to contact your physician? Yes ___ No _____

Are there other health care providers you would like us to contact? Yes ___ No ___

If so please provide names, addresses, and phone numbers in the space below.

_____

_____

_____

What is the Primary Site or Type of Cancer?

Breast ___ Ovarian ___ Uterine ___ Prostate ___ Testicular ___ Lung _____

Colon/Rectum ___ Stomach ___ Liver ___ Pancreas ___ Bone ___ Brain _____

Kidney ___ Peritoneal ___ Melanoma ___ Sarcomas ___ Lymphomas _____

Leukemias ___ Retinoblastoma ___ Neuroblastoma ___ Pituitary _____

Thyroid ___ Other (please explain) _____

_____

Date(s) of Diagnosis _____

If you have had metastatic or secondary sites, where did the metastases occur?

Lung ___ Colon/Rectum ___ Stomach ___ Liver ___ Bone ___ Brain _____

Peritoneum ___ Skin ___ Kidney ___ Lymph nodes ___ Other (please explain)

_____

Date(s) of Diagnosis _____

How was the cancer diagnosed? biopsy ___ X ray ___ surgery ___ blood tests ___

bone marrow aspiration _____

Other (please explain) _____

What kinds of standard therapies did you have? Please check all that apply. Please
provide, if possible, dates of treatment, duration of treatments, names of treating
physicians, where you were treated, and in the case of chemotherapy,
immunotherapy and experimental therapies, the kind of anticancer drugs used.

surgery _____

_____

radiation _____

_____

chemotherapy _____

_____

immunotherapy _____

_____

experimental therapies _____

_____

other _____

_____

Did you make use of any complementary cancer therapies or engage in any
personal practices that you think were beneficial? Yes ___ No ___ If yes, please list
the therapies you used and explain in what ways you found them beneficial.

_____

_____

_____

_____

To what do you attribute your remarkable recovery/survival? (Please use extra pages if necessary.)

_____

_____

_____

_____

_____

_____

_____

_____

(Optional) Please relate the history of your experience in your own words (How do you and/or your physician(s) view your remarkable recovery/survival?) Please use additional pages if needed.

_____

_____

_____

_____

APPENDIX TWO

The Remarkable Recovery Case Report

W E WOULD LIKE TO SOLICIT FORMAL CASE REPORTS TO help analyze the frequency and causes of remarkable recovery and the characteristics of those who experience it. Since, as we have pointed out, most reports in the literature in recent years contain very little information about the people who experience remarkable recovery, we are interested in establishing criteria for case reporting that include information about the person as well as the diagnostic and treatment history.

New methods of interviewing and reporting for medical case reports are needed to reveal the true dimensions of recovery and the real consequences of various methods of treatment. We have seen that each patient's unique characteristics are as vital as his or her biological measures. Often it is the support person, i.e., the family nurse practitioner, physician's assistant, nurse, or social worker who is more familiar with the patient than the doctor who might find this information extremely useful. The patient's account of his or her experience, often dismissed as subjective and "attributive," should be understood as a source of objective information in the context of the healing system. It is especially necessary to encourage physicians to publish their cases of remarkable recovery in refereed medical journals so that a true epidemiology of the phenomenon can finally emerge.

It is our belief that health and disease are a continuum in which many variables are pertinent. In order to develop an epidemiology of remarkable recovery, we need to understand the whole person, mind, body, and spirit. Therefore, some of the information we feel is important to gather from cases of remarkable recovery along with diagnosis and treatment would include:

- Life history, with as complete a biography of the person as possible, including information about his or her family of origin, marital status, religious background, social context, family members' medical history, education, schools attended, dates, psychologists or psychiatrists consulted, psychological tests taken, etc.

- Conventional *and* alternative treatments used, including surgery, radiation, chemotherapy, immunotherapies (partial or complete), vitamins, dietary changes, nutritional therapies, psychological and behavioral therapies, pharmacological or biological treatments, massage, biofeedback, homeopathy, acupuncture, herbal treatments.

- Behavioral factors, including lifestyle, diet, habits, exercise, social support, practices such as meditation, yoga, etc.

- Environmental factors, exposure to pathogens or carcinogens, and the nature of social, environment, religious, and family environments.

- Significant life events, including social, psychological, spiritual, physiological, environmental. Also a detailing of any particularly meaningful events prior to onset of disease and/or recovery.

· Subjective information, such as reasons for choice of treatment, books read, important dreams, insights, spiritual experiences, personal values.

APPENDIX THREE

Sample Patient Pie Charts

We would like to thank Jean Achterberg, PhD, and Warren Berland, PhD, for this research instrument.

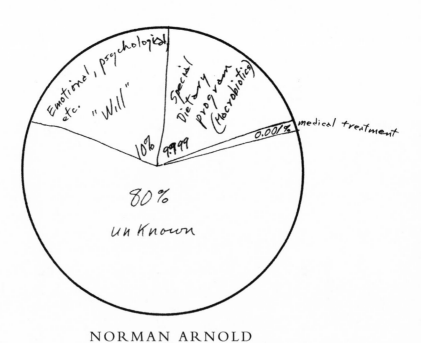

NORMAN ARNOLD

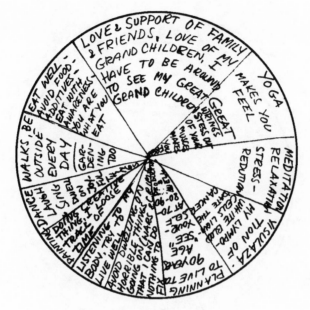

INGE SUNDSTROM

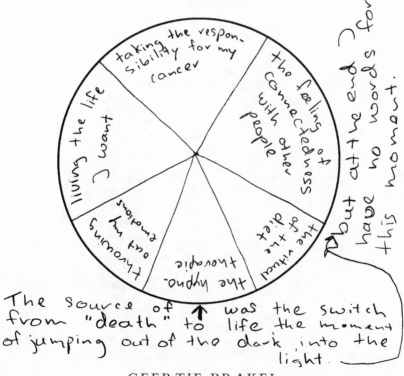

The source of ↑ was the switch from "death" to life the moment of jumping out of the dark into the light.

GEERTJE BRAKEL

ROB ANDERSON

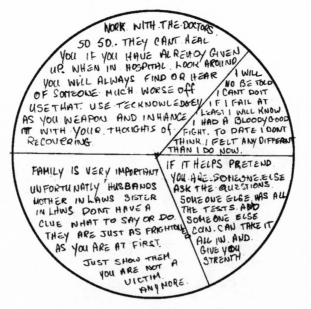

LESLEY BERMINGHAM

DR. WILLIAM CURTIS

APPENDIX FOUR

Psychosocial Characteristics of Remarkable Recovery: A Pilot Study

WHILE RESEARCHING THIS BOOK, WE BECAME CURIOUS IF there were ways to quantitatively measure what characteristics, if any, remarkable recoveries might hold in common. We wondered if there were similarities in emotional expression, coping style, beliefs, attitudes, hypnotic ability, or social support that might be correlated with exceptional healing.

Several studies published in the literature have linked psychosocial factors with the incidence, mortality, and survival of cancer. A "Type C" coping style—described as people who suppress anger (and other negative emotions) and put the needs of others before their own—has been postulated. It has been reported that personal qualities such as quiet determination, group affiliation, fighting spirit, denial, and expression of needs and emotions (both positive and negative) have been associated with survival. Also reported as possible positive factors in health maintenance are the "Three C's"—control, commitment, and challenge.

We requested advice from a number of psychosocial researchers recognized as expert in clinical and psychometric measurement tools. We asked Dr. Herbert Spiegel to conduct phone interviews using his ten-question clinical measurement profile, the AOD (for Apollonian, Odyssean, Dionysian) scale (see chapter six), a measure of what Dr. Spiegel has called "mind-styles." (The AOD is a clinical measurement which has been used with thousands of clients as part of patient assessment, though it is not a standardized measurement instrument.) The results of his ten-question phone interview (the AOD questionnaire) are presented in Figure I. They suggest that people with *all* types of mind/personality styles can recover from life-threatening disease. Furthermore, these results imply that a significant feature in recovery may be not so much what kind of individual a person is but whether his or her behavior, beliefs, attitudes, and approach to healing are congruent or resonant with his or her basic mind-style. Though the sample size is not large enough to generalize, there seems to be a sufficient spread to indicate that people of all different personality styles are in the remarkable recovery group. The data suggests that what we and Dr. Johannes Schilder refer to as "congruence" may be a powerful predictor of survival.

Because many of our cases remarked on the importance of prayer (68%) and faith (61%) as significant to their recovery, we sought a measure of religious/spiritual orientation. Dr. Jeffrey Levin, who has specialized in the study of religion and health, suggested the use of the Allport Intrinsic-Extrinsic Religiousity Scale. Findings from over 250 studies point to a generally positive correlation between health status and religious beliefs and affiliation. Writes Levin, "Recent epidemiological findings point to strong religious effects on outcomes such as cancer mortality rates, which persist despite adjusting for known demographic and environmental determinants of cancer." (Levin, Chatters, and Taylor, 1994 in press). Intrinsic religiosity is characterized by private, in-

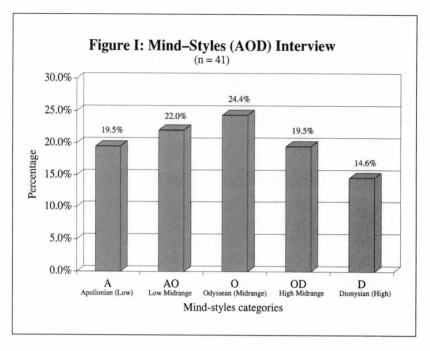

Figure I: Mind–Styles (AOD) Interview
(n = 41)

teriorly expressed religious beliefs. Individuals who are intrinsi-cally religious tend to be reflective and tolerant, with religiously informed moral views. Extrinsic religiosity is characterized by a more public and instrumental way of being religious—for exam-ple, church or synagogue attendance. Though the results of this measure were not statistically significant, there was a recognizable trend toward intrinsic in our cases.

We also contacted Ian Wickramasekera, Ph. D., whose High Risk Model of Threat Perception (HRMTP) postulates that a number of risk factors may be contributory to disease, among them, hypnotic ability, ability or lack of ability to express or rec-ognize negative emotions, coping styles, minor "hassles," major life changes, and support systems. Dr. Wickramasekera (Wickra-masekera, 1988) has further suggested that reversing these factors could conceivably stimulate recovery.

The HRMTP is a multidimensional model of the psychosocial factors that can 1) trigger, 2) amplify, and 3) attenuate biological disease. Dr. Wickramasekera uses several psychological testing in-struments to measure these risk factors. He suggested several to administer to our cases, each of which measures a component of behavior in his model: the Absorption scale, which measures the degree to which one can become absorbed in activities or thoughts or actions, a correlate of hypnotic ability; the Eysenck scale, which measures social extraversion and "neuroticism" (or negative affectivity); the Marlowe-Crowne scale, which is correlated with the degree to which someone represses his or her negative emotions; and the Coping Response Inventory, which measures whether one tends to deal with life's stresses through Approach (active) or Avoidance (passive) coping behaviors.

Dr. Wickramasekera analyzed the tests from over sixty people who kindly consented to participate in this study. Forty-five were those who had recovered from cancer, and we used this subgroup as the basis for our tabulations. It must be noted, however, that a wide range of cancer types and a variety of different treatments were represented in this sample. Some people had no medical treatment other than a biopsy or palliative treatments; others had a variety of traditional and alternative treatments. Given that our sample was both small and varied, the results must be viewed as very preliminary. But it is our hope that this pilot study will stimulate further research using many more people, some of whom may be generated by the Remarkable Recovery Registry.

Dr. Wickramasekera's HRMTP predicts a nonlinear relationship between stress-related disease and hypnotic ability; this means that, according to his model, people who measure *either* high *or* low in hypnotic ability are at greater risk for stress-related disease, although for different postulated reasons. Approximately fifty-five percent of the general population is found to be in this combined high-or-low risk group. Sixty-two percent of our Remarkable Recovery sample (people who have recovered from cancer, n=45) was found to be in the combined-risk (high and low hypnotic ability) group (see Figure II).

The Absorption scale was used as an indicator of hypnotic ability because it is positively but modestly correlated with other measures of hypnotic ability. Absorption represents "a disposition to enter under conducive circumstances psychological states that

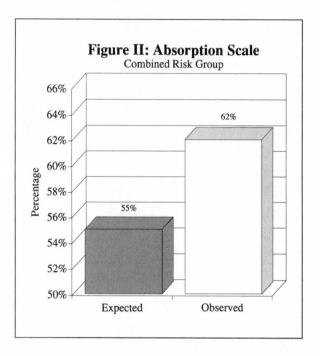

Figure II: Absorption Scale
Combined Risk Group

are characterized by marked restructuring of the phenomenal self and world. These more or less transient states may have a dissociated or an integrative and peak-experience-like quality. They may have an external 'sentient' focus, or may reflect an inner focus on reminiscences, images, and imaginings" (Auke Tellegen, 1992). Thirty-one percent of the sample was in the high range on the Absorption scale (vs. an expected norm of twenty-five percent), and thirty-one percent was low (vs. an expected norm of thirty percent). See Figure III.

It would appear that those at the high end of the scale, who are more prone to inner cues, may be able to mobilize their resources from within; whereas lows may tend to seek outside help, professional or personal, to aid in their recovery from life-threatening disease. Further research and evaluation are needed before conclusions can be drawn. However, this finding was not statistically significant, either because the sample size was too small or else too similar to the general population.

Negative affectivity (NA) describes the expression and/or recognition of negative emotions. It has been found in some stud-

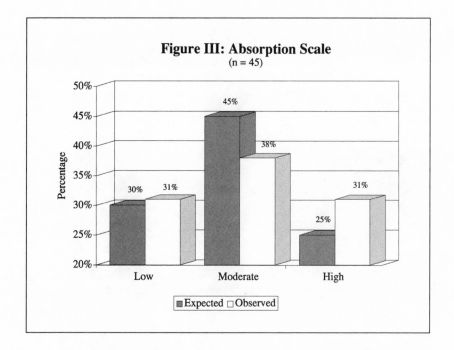

Figure III: Absorption Scale
(n = 45)

ies (Charles Spielberger, personal communication) that the absence of negative affect is correlated with disease (e.g., cancer and heart disease). In this study sample, sixty-nine percent of the cases are in the combined high and low group, suggesting either a consciously (high NA, 36%) or unconsciously (repression, 33%) high level of negative emotions (e.g., depression, fear, jealousy, anger, etc.). In other words, for the "repressors," these emotions may be "out of mind but not necessarily out of body" (Wickramasekera, 1988); whereas the high NA group is more fully conscious of their negative emotionality.

The HRMTP also predicts a nonlinear relationship between stress-related disease and negative affectivity (NA), so that people on the high end as well as a subset (repressors) on the low end of NA are at greater risk for such ailments (see Figure IV).

Norms predict that fifty-five percent of the general population would fall into this combined high and low group. It is worth noting that forty-four percent of the total sample in our study is low on NA. The percentage of these people who are "truly" low (i.e., not repressors) on NA is eleven percent. That means that

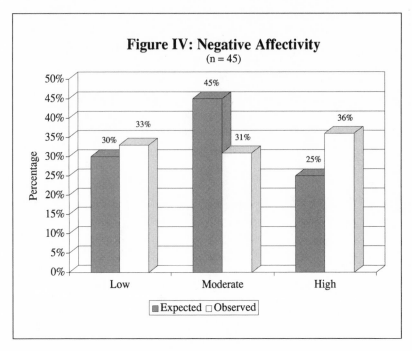

Figure IV: Negative Affectivity
(n = 45)

thirty-three percent of these people are either consciously or unconsciously inhibiting negative affect. This suppression of NA is known from several empirical studies to be associated with greater probability of cancer (Eysenck & Kissen, 1962). This hypothesis of conscious or unconscious suppression of NA is reinforced by the fact that 71 percent of the sample scored high on the Marlowe-Crowne scale. A high Marlowe-Crowne score appears to be related to the tendency toward "self-deception," particularly in terms of the failure to recognize negative emotions (see Figure V).

Dr. Wickramasekera speculates that if these high NA people are also high on absorption (hypnotic ability), there is the real possibility of distinct amplification of their baseline NA. A later analysis will explore the possibility of interaction between high hypnotic ability and high NA.

(Regarding the measurement of absorption/hypnotic ability, it is noteworthy that Dr. Spiegel's AOD scale shows, in our subjective analysis, a positive correlation with the Absorption Scale results. This suggests to us that if the AOD measure was statistically standardized and correlated positively with the Absorption scale,

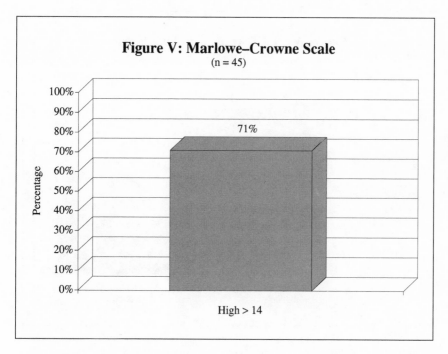

Figure V: Marlowe–Crowne Scale
(n = 45)

71%

High > 14

it could be used as an indicator of absorptive ability in situations where it is not possible to administer the Absorption scale itself.)

As measured on the Coping Response Inventory (CRI) devised by researcher Rudolf Moos, seventy-seven percent of the people in our forty-three-case sample tend to prefer, at least consciously, to confront their problems directly, rather than avoiding them (see Figure VI). The CRI measures eight different types of coping responses to stressful life circumstances: four that measure "approach" coping and four that measure "avoidance" coping. The norms for this test were not available, but Dr. Wickramasekera expects that this is a significantly greater approach style than that found in the general population. This preference for approach over avoidance coping is statistically significant. This may imply that once they recognize how psychosocial and other factors are contributing to their disease, the people in our sample would make a sustained effort, either alone or with coaching, to reverse the very psychosocial mechanisms that may have contributed to their physical disease process.

Eighty percent of the subjects tend to be high or moderate on

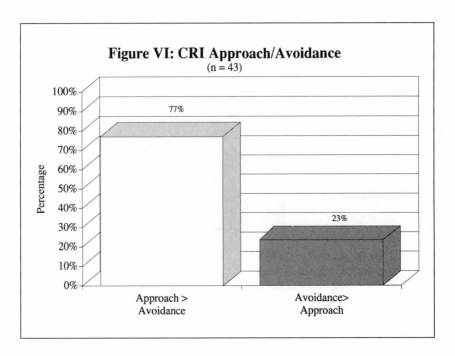

Figure VI: CRI Approach/Avoidance
(n = 43)

social extraversion (Eysenck "E" scale >31%) and, therefore, capable of positive mood states (see Figure VII). These positive mood states may have facilitated their ability to mobilize their cognitive and emotional resources to reverse the direction of activity of their psychosocial risk factors and to use social support (not measured in this study) to facilitate recovery from life-threatening disease. It is known that positive affect (PA) and negative affect (NA) are orthogonal (uncorrelated and independent dimensions) in verbal report data.

On our own personal information questionnaire, an expanded version of which is included as Appendix One, we asked people to check off activities that they believed contributed significantly to their recovery. Of the thirty items on that list, those checked with the greatest frequency ($\geq 50\%$) were as follows:

prayer	68%	walking	52%
meditation	64%	music/singing	50%
exercise	64%	stress reduction	50%
guided imagery	59%		

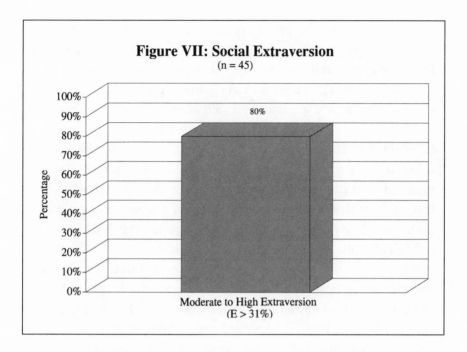

Figure VII: Social Extraversion
(n = 45)

We also asked people what psychospiritual factors they felt were important in their recovery. Of the twenty-six items on the list, those reported with the largest frequency (≥50%) are as follows:

belief in positive outcome	75%	positive emotions	64%
fighting spirit	71%	faith	61%
acceptance of disease	71%	new sense of purpose	61%
seeing disease as a challenge	71%	changes in habits/ behavior	61%
renewed desire/will to live/commitment to life	64%	sense of control	59%
taking responsibility for disease and outcome	68%	lifestyle changes	59%
		self-nurturance	57%
		social support	50%

Seventy-five percent of the people reported artistic pursuits at which they were somewhat proficient, and sixty percent reported having had feelings or experiences for which they had no logical/rational explanation.

The fact that all the present data were collected retrospectively is a limitation of this study. But it is well established that both hypnotic ability and neuroticism (NA) are very stable across situation and time (25 years) and are partly genetically based (Piccione, Hilgard, and Zimbardo, 1989; Morgan, 1973; Tellegen et al., 1988). Therefore, it is very likely that these personality features existed before the cancer developed, and this may have contributed to the biological disease process and might also, if reversed, contribute to the healing process. Another limitation of this study is that hypnotic ability was not measured directly but with a test (the Absorption scale) that correlates reliably but modestly (Tellegen, 1974; Tellegen and Atkinson, 1974) with hypnotic ability. The Absorption scale was used in place of scales that measure hypnotic ability directly (e.g., the Stanford Clinical Scale, the Harvard Group Scale of Hypnotic Susceptibility, or the Hypnotic Induction Profile). Another major limitation of this study was that social support systems were not measured by questionnaire (though verbal report data was collected). Social support is a major predictor variable of mortality (House, 1988) in the HRMTP.

Future research areas would include other measures of hypnotic ability (i.e., the Hypnotic Induction Profile or the Stanford or the Harvard scales) as well as other research instruments. The addition of a measure of life stresses and social support as well as measures of anger expression, anxiety, and lifestyle defense mechanisms should be included. Also, the verbal report data (from interviews) has not undergone formal qualitative analysis for this study; it could provide valuable additional information about how people viewed themselves before they were diagnosed with cancer and now. Perhaps with the information (from verbal reports) together with additional psychometric measures, clearer patterns of behavioral, belief, and lifestyle components associated with remarkable recovery will emerge.

NOTES

Chapter One

WHO, WHAT, WHERE, WHEN, WHY: IN QUEST OF A
MEDICAL MYSTERY

Page

2   Rosenberg's account briefly describes . . . S. A. Rosenberg, E. Fox, and
    W. H. Churchill, "Spontaneous regression of hepatic metastases from gas-
    tric carcinoma," *Cancer* 29, no. 2 (February 1972): 472–474.

3   ". . . *of spontaneous and complete remission of stomach cancer.*" Steven A. Rosen-
    berg and John M. Barry, The Transformed Cell: Unlocking the Mysteries
    of Cancer (New York: G. P. Putnam's Sons, 1992), 11–18.

3   *"No evidence of tumor or other masses could be found in the abdomen,"* Rosenberg,
    Fox, and Churchill, "Spontaneous regression," Rosenberg, 474

4   ". . . *and to discover what can be done to make her work easier.*" Joseph DeCourcy,
    "The spontaneous regression of cancer," *Journal of Medicine* 14 (May 1933):
    141–146.

4   ". . . *but many of these are based on inadequate evidence.*" H. J. G. Bloom, W. W.
    Richardson, and E. J. Harries, "Natural history of untreated breast cancer
    (1805–1933)," *British Medical Journal* 2 (July 1962): 213–221.

5   ". . . *the patient a something which can . . . effect a spontaneous cure?*" Charles
    MacKay, "A case that seems to suggest a clue to the possible solution of the
    cancer problem," *British Medical Journal* 2 (1907): 138–140.

5   *"The diseased parts that had not been treated with the X rays have undergone an ex-
    traordinary change."* Ibid., 140.

Page

6   ". . . *I think the sensation would have been but little less delightfully confound-ing.*" G. A. Boyd, "Arrested development of cancer," *Colorado Medicine* 11 (1914): 162–165.

8   ". . . *30 cigarettes per day for years but had quit 4 months before.*" Alexander D. Lowy, Jr., and E. Ralph Erickson, "Spontaneous 19-year regression of oat cell carcinoma with scalene node metastasis," *Cancer* 58, no. 4 (August 15, 1986): 978–990.

10   . . . "*no evidence of residual tumor identified grossly or by microscopic exam.*" Alexander D. Lowry, Jr., "Spontaneous 19-year regression of oat cell carcinoma with scalene node mestatasis," *Cancer* 72, no. 11 (December 1, 1993): 3366.

11   ". . . *since she appears 'cured,' we think there is no point in telling her.*" Charles Mayo, "Tumor clinic conference," *Cancer Bulletin* 15 (1963): 78–79.

13   ". . . *he/she felt was due to a psychological method.*" G. B. Challis and H. J. Stam, "The spontaneous regression of cancer: A review of cases from 1900 to 1987," *Acta Oncologica* 29, no. 5 (1990): 549.

13   (Of the three patients who had complete remission, one remained so for at least six years.) R. T. D. Oliver, "Surveillance as a possible option for management of metastatic renal cell carcinoma," *Seminars in Urology* 7, no. 3 (August 1989): 149–152.

14   "*The single most important element of good science is to ask an important question.*" Rosenberg and Barry, *The Transformed Cell*, 18.

14   . . . "*omitting two cases of alleged duration of 40–41 years.*" Bloom, Richardson, and Harries, "Natural history," 213–221.

Chapter Two

DEFINING THE IMPOSSIBLE

16   ". . . *a hypothetical straw to clutch in the search for cure,*" Lewis Thomas, *The Youngest Science: Notes of a Medicine Watcher* (New York: Viking, 1983), 205.

17   "*That, of course, is also absurd, for everything has a cause, apparent or inapparent.*" William Boyd, *The Spontaneous Regression of Cancer* (Springfield, IL: Charles C. Thomas, 1966), 6.

20   "*He had had no treatment except antiseptic gargles and sprays, and anodynes to relieve pain.*" Frank Godfrey, "Spontaneous cure of cancer," *British Medical Journal* 2, no. 2 (1910): 2027.

22   . . . "*aggressive histologic subtype*" in which regression is "*extremely rare.*" Jean L. Grem et al., "Spontaneous remission in diffuse large cell lymphoma," *Cancer* 57, no. 10 (May 15, 1986): 2042–2044.

23   ". . . *the physical exam was completely normal by late spring 1982.*" Ibid., 2044.

23   The median survival after diagnosis is one year. Ibid., 2044.

24   . . . through her own back records. Rose J. Papac, "Spontaneous regression of cancer," *Connecticut Medicine* 54, no. 4 (1990): 179–182.

26   ". . . *a case of genuine recurrence of the original tumour, and not of an independent new growth.*" Anthony A. Bowlby, "Long freedom from recurrence after operation for cancer of the breast," *British Medical Journal* 1 (January 31, 1925): 234.

26   *"When a tumor has been growing rapidly and then slows down or appears to halt . . ."* Boyd, *Spontaneous Regression*, p. 7.

31   *"no convincing evidence that chemotherapy offers any benefit whatsoever,"* Martin F. Shapiro, "Chemotherapy: Snake Oil Remedy?" *Los Angeles Times,* 9 January 1987, sec. II, 5.

31   *". . . response rates may not be much greater than the reported incidence of spontaneous regression!"* C. I. V. Franklin, "Spontaneous regression of cancer," in *Prolonged Arrest of Cancer,* ed. B. A. Stoll (London: John Wiley and Sons Ltd., 1982), 103.

31   *". . . the results produced by forces of the nature of which we are for the present entirely ignorant."* G. L. Rohdenburg, "Fluctuations in the growth energy of malignant tumors in man with especial reference to spontaneous recession," *Journal of Cancer Research* 3, no. 2 (1918): 193–225.

33   *". . . 20 consecutive patients with HCC. No detectable regression of tumor was observed in any patient."* K. C. Lam, J. C. I. Ho, and R. T. T. Yeung, "Spontaneous regression of hepatocellular carcinoma: A case study," *Cancer* 50, no. 2 (July 15, 1982): 332–336.

36   *"The holy man lived to the age of eighty and died in the order of sanctity."* S. L. Shapiro, "Spontaneous regression of cancer," *Eye, Ear, Nose, Throat Monthly* 46, no. 10 (October 1967): 1306–1310.

37   *"There was no evidence of carcinoma of the pancreas."* Ibid., 1306–1310.

38   *"She never even questioned for five seconds that this girl was going to get better."* Tamara Jones, "The Saint and Ann O'Neill," *The Washington Post,* Sunday, 3 April 1994, Style section, F1–F5

40   *". . . and concentrate a little on the angel's crown, which is immunity."* Boyd, *Spontaneous Regression*, 89.

40   *". . . medicine can learn to accomplish the same thing at will is surely within the reach of imagining."* Thomas, *The Youngest Science,* 205.

Chapter 3
POWERS OF THE BODY: IS THERE A BIOLOGICAL EXPLANATION?

41   *". . . to destroy the organisms at whose expense it survives."* Lucien Israel, *Conquering Cancer* (New York: Vintage Books, 1979) p. 22.

42   *". . . treatment only in the last quarter of the evolution of the disease, which is terribly late."* Lucien Israel, Ibid, 60.

42   *". . . a more satisfactory method of treating cancer than surgery or irradiation may be found."* Tilden Everson and Warren Cole, *Spontaneous Regression of Cancer* (Philadelphia: W. B. Saunders Co., 1966), pp. 519–520.

45   *". . . see them restored to life and health, was sufficient to keep up my enthusiasm."* William B. Coley, "The treatment of inoperable sarcoma by bacterial toxins (the mixed toxins of streptococcus of erysipelas and the bacillus prodigiosus)." *Practitioner* 83 (1909): 589–613.

45   . . . thirty-eight percent of patients suffering lymph node cancers (lymphomas) achieved five-year survival. Charlie O. Starnes, "Coley's toxins in perspective," *Nature* 357 (May 7, 1992): 12.

Page

45   In one analysis, only thirteen percent of those with inoperable disease survived
      five years.) Helen Coley Nauts, "Immunotherapy of cancer—The pioneer
      work of Coley," paper presented at the International Symposium on Endo-
      toxin: Structural Aspects and Immunobiology of Host Responses, Riva del
      Sole, Giovinazzo (Bari), Italy, May 29–June 1, 1986, 4.

48   *"He had a period of fever for four or five days which was really unexplained."* J. W.
      Bell, J. E. Jesseph, and R. S. Leighton, "Spontaneous regression of bron-
      chogenic carcinoma with five-year survival," *Journal of Thoracic and Cardio-
      vascular Surgery* 48, no. 6 (December 1964): 984–990

48   *". . . then all febrile diseases associated with . . . malignant tumors should show marked
      regression. Such we know is not the case."* William B. Coley, "Some thoughts
      on the problem of cancer control," *American Journal of Surgery* 14 (1931):
      605–619.

48   . . . (soft-tissue sarcomas comprise only 0.7 percent of all cancers). Vincent T.
      DeVita, Jr., Samuel Hellman, and Steven A. Rosenberg, *Cancer: Principles
      and Practice of Oncology* (Philadelphia: Lippincott, 1993), 1437.

49   . . . opened a new "issue" at the site of the abscess and allowed it to again sup-
      purate, the breast cancer once again disappeared. Helen Coley Nauts,
      "Bacteria and cancer-antagonisms and benefits," *Cancer Surveys* 8, no. 4
      (1989): 714.

50   *". . . gangrene, succeeded in doing so, and in a few days the ulcer became bright red and
      covered with healthy granulations."* Ibid, 714.

50   Dr. Coley, she writes, published 143 papers between 1896 and 1936 but failed
      to detail how, or how long, to administer the treatment. Helen Coley
      Nauts, "Coley Toxins—The First Century," read in Rome, May 1989 at
      the meeting of the International Clinical Hyperthermia Society.

51   . . . Coley's Toxins/chemotherapy combination responded more completely
      and had longer survival than those treated with chemotherapy alone. Vin-
      cent T. DeVita, Jr., Samuel Hellman, and Steven A. Rosenberg, *Biologic
      Therapy of Cancer* (Philadelphia: Lippincott, 1991), 97.

52   *"[But] he was in perfect health and the only trace of the growth was some smooth scar
      tissue."* Frank Godfrey, "Spontaneous cure of cancer," *British Medical Jour-
      nal* 2, no. 2 (1910): 2027.

53   *"In all cases the tumors have grown smaller; in some they have disappeared alto-
      gether."* Eugene Hodenpyl, "Treatment of carcinoma with the body fluids
      of a recovered case: A preliminary communication," *Medical Record* 77
      (1910): 359–360.

53   *". . . a method founded on imitating what appears to have taken place in this case may
      eventually be possible?"* Charles MacKay, "A case that seems to suggest a clue
      to the possible solution of the cancer problem," *British Medical Journal* 2
      (1907): 138–140.

54   *"I feel that nature has flaunted her cure under my eyes and they have been too blind to
      see."* G. A. Boyd, "Arrested development of cancer," *Colorado Medicine* 11
      (1914): 162–165.

54   *"We've got a hobbyhorse—let's thrash it for what it's worth!"* *Medical World News*
      (June 7, 1974): 13.

55   *"The order of Nature admits of no real anomalies, and is often best brought to light by*

the close study of apparent exceptions." W. S. Handley, "The Natural Cure of Cancer," *British Medical Journal* (1909): 582–589.

55 . . . "good" type of neuroblastoma—which affects some seven percent of babies with the disease . . . Gloria Hochman, "When Cancer Vanishes," *Science Digest* (Summer 1980): 95.

55 Only one in five children has recurrences in the "good" type, as opposed to ninety percent in the more aggressive "bad" kind. Stephen S. Hall, "Cheating Fate," *Health* (April 1992): 44.

55 *"We don't do anything further, and the disease doesn't come back."* Ibid, 44.

57 *"We can only assume that the patient with a lot of disease who is handling it himself is mounting some sort of rejection response."* Gloria Hochman, op. cit., 96.

58 In a series of stunning refinements, he detected almost 10,000 bands with an electron microscope. Kathleen McAuliffe, "The cell seer," *Omni* 8 (February 1986): 57.

60 *"found the tumor had nearly disappeared, there being apparently only a trifling thickening of the skin."* Ephraim Cutter, "Diet in cancer," *Albany Medical Annals* 8 (July 1887): 218–230.

60 *"The patient started a diet free of fruit, potatoes, sugar, animal proteins, and animal fats. Within a few months, his condition gradually improved."* B. Grillet, M. Demedts, J. Roelens, P. Goddeeris, and E. Fossion, "Spontaneous regression of lunge metastases of adenoid cystic carcinoma," *Chest* 85, no. 2 (February 1984): 289–291.

60 *"The vegetable compound tablets were analyzed and were found to contain asparagus, parsley, watercress, and broccoli."* Brian Blades and Robert G. McCorkle, Jr., "A case of spontaneous regression of an untreated bronchiogenic carcinoma," *Journal of Thoracic and Cardiovascular Surgery* 27 (1954): 415–419.

60 . . . to eating no meat; and, for a woman with malignant melanoma, eating "nothing but grapes." U. Niethe, "Spontaneous healing of a malignoma?" *Klinische Monatsblatter für Augenheilkunde und Augenarztliche Fortbildung* 166, no. 1 (January 1975): 137–138.

60 . . . substantial dietary changes, *"usually of a strict vegetarian nature . . . "* Harold Foster, "Lifestyle changes and the 'spontaneous' regression of cancer: An initial computer analysis," *International Journal of Biosocial Research* 10, no. 1 (1988): 17–33.

Chapter Four

TO WEAVE A TANGLED WEB: IS THERE A MIND–BODY MECHANISM?

70–71 Dr. West reports he had left his patient *"febrile"* on the fateful Friday he received his first shot. Bruno Klopfer, "Psychological variables in human cancer," *Journal of Projective Techniques* 21 (1957): 329–340.

71 *". . . and other devices of acting upon a patient's symptoms through his mind."* Quoted in Samuel S. Myers and Herbert Benson, "Psychological

factors in healing: A new perspective on an old debate," *Behavioral Medicine* 18, (Spring 1992): 7.

72 *"inspired magic, independent of higher degrees and laboratory gimmicks,"* Patrick Mallam, "Billy O," *Journal of the American Medical Association* 210, no. 12 (December 22, 1969): 2238.

73 *". . . machinery, as that the mind be disregarded or little thought of by the physician."* Myers and Benson, "Psychological Factors," 6.

73 *". . . summed up under the name 'placebo,' equated to some kind of noise in the system."* Norman Sartorius, quoted in Brendan O'Regan and Thomas J. Hurley, "Placebo—The hidden asset in healing," *Investigations* (Research Bulletin of the Institute of Noetic Sciences) 2, no. 1 (1985): 5.

74 . . . saltwater placebo in place of powerful chemicals—had experienced "alopecia." J. W. L. Fielding et al., "An interim report of a prospective randomized controlled study of adjuvant chemotherapy in operable gastric cancer: British Stomach Cancer Group," *World Journal of Surgery* 3, (1983): 390–399.

74 *". . . compresses to the area of his tumor. . . . He attributed his cure to prayer. . . ."* H. W. Baker, "Spontaneous regression of malignant melanoma," *American Surgeon* 30, no. 12 (December 1964): 825–829.

76 *". . . I give this as a remarkable case of self-induction, and the self-healing energies of the human organism."* M. A. Gravitz, "An 1846 report of tumor remission associated with hypnosis," *American Journal of Clinical Hypnosis* 28, no. 1 (July 1985): 16–19.

76 Only two of the boys developed a skin reaction to the plant. Yujiro Ikemi and Shunji Nakagawa, "A psychosomatic study of contagious dermatitis," *Kyushu Journal of Medical Science* 13 (1962): 335–350.

77 *". . . skin diseases, the production of skin inflammation and blisters, the inhibition of allergic responses. . . ."* Theodore X. Barber, "Changing 'unchangeable' processes by (hypnotic) suggestions: A new look at hypnosis, cognitions, imagining, and the mind-body problem," *Advances* 1, no. 2 (Spring 1984): 30–34.

78 *"hypnotic phenomena such as dissociation are intrinsic to the experience of trauma."* David Spiegel, "Hypnosis in the treatment of victims of sexual abuse," *Psychiatric Clinics of North America* 12, no. 2 (June 1989): 296–297.

82 . . . subjects could quickly raise or lower the temperature of specific areas of the skin by eight to fifteen degrees Fahrenheit. E. Taub, "Self-regulation of human tissue temperatures," in *Biofeedback: Theory and Research,* eds. G. E. Schwartz and J. Beatty (New York: Academic Press, 1977). Cited in Barber, "A new look," 27.

82 *". . . his perceptions will be imprinted and acted on in a manner similar to post-hypnotic suggestions."* Evelyn K. Stampley, "The healing power of suggestion," *Tourovues* (Summer 1989): 1.

82 *". . . teach the patient to control his pain, and then direct him through guided imagery."* Dabney M. Ewin, "The effect of hypnosis and mental set on major surgery and burns," *Psychiatric Annals* 16, no. (2): 115–118.

83 . . . while the other side produced a suppurating blister with subsequent scarring. Eugene Taylor, *William James on Exceptional Mental States: The 1896*

Lowell Lectures (Amherst: University of Massachusetts Press, 1984), 32, and Barber, "A new look," 23.

83 This second group experienced significantly less pain reduction than the first. Jon D. Levine, Newton C. Gordon, and Howard L. Fields, "The mechanism of placebo analgesia," *The Lancet* 2 (September 23, 1978): 654–657.

84 . . . prevent pain reduction in patients under hypnosis as it had for patients who took a placebo. E. Goldstein and E. Hilgard, "Failure of opiate antagonist naloxone to modify hypnotic analgesia," *Proceedings of the National Academy of Sciences* 95 (1975): 2041–2043, and D. Spiegel and L. H. Albert, "Naloxone fails to revers hypnotic alleviation of chronic pain," *Psychopharmacology* 81 (1983): 140–143.

84 And in yet another placebo study, pain reduction occurred even *with* the endorphin-blocker. R. H. Gracely et al., "Placebo and naloxone can alter post-surgical pain by separate mechanisms," *Nature* 306 (November 17, 1983): 264–265.

84 There are likely many mind-body routes, many mechanisms to create the same effects. In Leonard White, Bernard Tursky, and Gary Schwartz, eds., *Placebos: Theory, Research and Mechanisms* (New York: Guilford Press, 1985), 442, it is noted, "There is no single placebo effect having a single mechanism and efficacy, but rather a multiplicity of effects, with differential efficacy and mechanisms."

91 *". . . the quality of his life was beyond what we would have expected medically."* Stephanie Simonton, written communication, November 22, 1994.

92 *"When you visualize, you may also be creating a relaxation response, reducing stress and allowing the body to enhance lymphocyte proliferation."* Ibid.

92 *"Voluntary Modulation of Neutrophil Adhesiveness Using a Cyberphysiologic Strategy."* Howard R. Hall et al., "Voluntary modulation of neutrophil adhesiveness using a cyberphysiologic strategy," *International Journal of Neuroscience* 63 (1992): 287–297.

93 . . . then dry them in frigid weather using only a special *"psychic heat"* generated by their own bodies. Herbert Benson et al., "Body temperature changes during the practice of g Tum-mo yoga," *Nature* 295 (January 21, 1982): 234–236.

94 The warts on the other side flourished as brazenly as ever. A. H. C. Sinclair-Gieben and D. Chalmers, "Evaluation of treatment of warts by hypnosis," *The Lancet* 2 (October 3, 1959): 480–482. Cited in Lewis Thomas, *The Medusa and the Snail* (New York: Bantam Books, 1980), p. 62.

94 *"plausible notion that immunologic mechanisms are very likely implicated."* Thomas, *The Youngest Science*, 63.

95 *"It would be worth a War on Warts, a Conquest of Warts, a National Institute of Warts and All."* Ibid., 64–65.

95 the warts *"simply diminished and disappeared, shriveled up and left."* T. A. Clawson and R. H. Swade, "The hypnotic control of blood flow and pain: The cure of warts and the potential for the use of hypnosis in the treatment of cancer," *American Journal of Clinical Hypnosis* 17 (1975): 160–169.

95 *"the variations of their description point to the fact that the meditator or adept has to*

find them for himself." Terry Clifford, *Tibetan Buddhist Medicine and Psychiatry: The Diamond Healing* (York Beach, Maine: Samuel Weiser, 1984), 69.

98 . . . Stand by for releasing shells with those body white cells in them. Garrett Porter and Patricia A. Norris, *Why Me? Harnessing the Healing Power of the Human Spirit* (Walpole, NH: Stillpoint Publishing, 1985), 63–70.

98 *"Everyone can be a success at trying, and trying brings strength and energy of its own, which is a healing force."* Ibid., xiv–xv.

99 *". . . five-colored light beams emanating from numerous tiny triangular-shaped thunderbolts."* Garma Chang, *Teachings of Tibetan Yoga* (New York: Carol Publishing Group, 1993), 59.

99 . . . travel between mind and body—if such linear terms even apply—may be found in the fascinating instance of a neuropeptide called angiotensin. Candace Pert, personal communication, 7 July 1994.

100 *"All levels of organization are linked to one another in a hierarchical relationship, so that a change in one necessitates a change in others."* Yujiro Ikemi and Akira Ikemi, "An oriental point of view in psychosomatic medicine," *Advances* 3, no. 4 (Fall 1986): 150.

101 *". . . a skilled engineer and manager, a chief executive officer, the head of the whole place."* Thomas, *The Youngest Science*, 64.

101 *"The faith with which we work . . . has its limitations [but] such as we find it, faith is the most precious commodity without which we should be very badly off."* William Osler, "Medicine in the Nineteenth Century," in *Aequanimitas* (London: H. K. Lewis, 1914), 273–274.

Chapter Five
IN SEARCH OF THE MIRACULOUS

103 *". . . could have been worthy of a shrine or made the germ of a pilgrimage."* William Osler, "The faith that heals," *British Medical Journal* (June 18, 1910): 1471.

103 . . . who was said to heal the blind and the maimed. Richard E. Peschel and Enid Rhodes Peschel, "Medical miracles from a physician-scientist's point of view," *Perspectives in Biology and Medicine* 31, no. 3 (Spring 1988): 392.

103 . . . Nekumonta located a place of healing waters that miraculously cured his plague-ridden wife. Ibid., 394.

104 . . . millions of pilgrims—about one in six officially registered as sick St. John Dowling, "Lourdes cures and their medical assessment," *Journal of the Royal Society of Medicine* 77 (August 1984): 634–638.

104 *". . . cleverly conceived by astute ecclesiastics to lead erring followers back into the fold."* Ruth Cranston, *The Miracle of Lourdes* (New York: Image Books/Doubleday, 1988), p. 31.

104 . . . catching fire from car to car until *"the whole long train rang."* Ibid., 47.

105 *". . . people who have come from the four corners of the earth with but one purpose: prayer, and healing."* Ibid., 48.

105 . . . *"congruence of the belief system"* between pilgrim and place, sufferer and

healer. Jerome Frank, "The faith that heals," *Johns Hopkins Medical Journal* 137, no. 3 (September 1975): 130.

105   *"sentimental neurasthentics"* in the grip of *"hysteria"* and *"self-hypnosis,"* Cranston, *Lourdes,* 35.

106   *". . . what a splendid example of spiritual healing hers would have furnished!"* H. T. Butlin, "Remarks on spiritual healing," *British Medical Journal* (18 June, 1910): 1469.

106   *And if this can be induced by other states of the mind, why not by faith?' "* Ibid., 1468.

107   *". . . amazing efficiency to remove the toxic fluids and waste products of the fast-diminishing cancer."* Ernest Rossi, *Psychobiology of Mind-Body Healing: New Concepts of Therapeutic Hypnosis* (New York: W. W. Norton & Co., 1986), 8.

107   *". . . tissues such as skin are not restored but are filled by scar formation as in normal healing."* Jerome Frank, *Persuasion and Healing* (New York: Schocken Books, 1971), 71.

107   . . . sometimes undergo remission; they were *"potentially recoverable conditions."* Donald J. West, in Daniel J. Benor, *Healing Research: Holistic Energy Medicine and Spirituality,* vol. 1 (Oxfordshire, UK: Helix Editions, 1993), 258.

107   Twenty-seven of the sixty-five official Lourdes miracle cases—fully forty percent—were of tuberculosis. Steve Fishman, "What a lovely day to go hunting for a miracle!" *Health* 6 (February–March 1992): 56.

108   By contrast, during outgoing president Dr. Mangiapan's eighteen-year tenure, there were only three. Ibid., 56.

108   *". . . saying that we are facing a total penury of inexplicable cures,"* he told a journalist. Ibid., 56.

108   . . . if progress in genetics, immunology, and psychosomatic medicine would explain away the cures. Bertrand Vandeputte, "Le miracle entre science et foi," *La Croix* 23 October 1993, Hommes & Evénements section and Henri Tinco, "Lourdes: le miracle désenchanté," *Le Monde,* October 1993.

108   *"The miracles of Lourdes are, in the strict sense, a little old-fashioned."* Fishman, "What a lovely day," 59.

109   *". . . most notably to recent work by . . . researchers in this area."* Michelle Majorelle, "Clôture à Lourdes du congrés 'guérisons' et miracles," AFP; 25 October 1993 and Michelle Majorelle, "De la guérison unexpliques aû miracles," AFP, 20 October 1993.

109–110 The cure, which was written up in the *Journal of the Royal Society of Medicine* Dowling, "Lourdes cures," 634–638.

110   . . . (at most *"one to two weeks"*). Bernadette Wiemann and Charlie O. Starnes, "Coley's toxins, TNF and cancer research: A historical perspective," submitted manuscript, 1993), 24.

110   . . . *"upheavals" (bouleversements)* and psychological change *(réorganisatrice du psychisme).* Henri Tinco, op. cit.

110   *"He's our child, and you haven't got anything to do with this. We will find a way."* Johannes N. Schilder, "Long-term survival of cancer and its ultimate: Spontaneous regression of cancer: A study of psycho-social factors in-

volved," in *Healing: Beyond Suffering or Death,* ed. Luc Bessette (Quebec, Canada: MNH, 1994), 453.

111   *"Your boy's going to make it because of his blue eyes and blond hair."* Ibid., 453.

111   *". . . which is pulled along the roads by the family's dog."* Ibid., 453.

114   . . . *"so emaciated that, anatomically, they shouldn't have been strong enough to support him."* Paul C. Roud, *Making Miracles: An Exploration into the Dynamics of Self-Healing* (New York: Warner Books, 1990), 271.

114   . . . until it became visibly infected with *"this tremendous abscess."* Ibid., 174.

115   . . . dubbing De Orio a *"Vatican-Approved Wizard,"* James Randi, *The Faith Healers* (Buffalo: Prometheus Books, 1989), 225.

115   *". . . God is working throughout a person's life. It's not that important to prove it's extraordinary or divine intervention."* George Lange, quoted in Ibid., 222.

116   *". . . treated like a guest of honor; a path was cleared for him and he was ushered to the front."* Roud, *Making Miracles,* 194–195.

122   *". . . I am very happy and . . . just stress to them to maintain sobriety."* Medical report from Hdarmarville Rehabilitation Center, 23 June 1986, and "Rita Klaus: A Gift of Faith," video Grey Havens Films, 1993).

123   *"every evidence I could see would suggest that she is totally back to normal."* Deborah Deasy, "Medical mystery: Teacher's recovery is investigated as miracle," *The Pittsburgh Press,* 24 January 1988, A1, A11.

123   *She's had it for seventeen years. Tell me how this happened. I'll use it again."* Ibid., A1.

124   . . . reported a sensation of heat that moved through his body immediately upon entering the spring. Michael Talbot, *The Holographic Universe* (New York: Harper Perennial, 1992), 107.

124   *"a great warmth through all my body"* after being immersed in the bath. Cranston, *Lourdes,* 139.

124   . . . who described a sensation *"like the insertion of a red-hot iron under the skin."* Cranston, *Lourdes,* 266–267.

124   *"electricity going right through you right out of my body. Heat. A jolt of lightning, so to speak."* Roud, *Making Miracles,* 195.

125   . . . rolling to my fingertips and back up . . . I knew I had been healed. David J. Hufford, "Epistemologies in religious healing," *Journal of Medicine and Philosophy* 18 (1993): 186–187.

125   *"I can't explain it, but the x rays are perfectly normal.' "* Ibid., 186–187.

125   *". . . which is different from heat but which overlaps with it in some manner to stimulate the nerves."* Benor, 59.

126   *". . . which could throw a wholly new light on . . . the mysterious role of the nervous system."* Alex Carrel, *Voyage to Lourdes* (New York: Harper & Brothers, 1950)

126   *"something like an electric shock"* immediately before getting up from his wheelchair at Lourdes. Cranston, *Lourdes,* 287.

127   *". . . an Aeolian harp which discloses the motion of winds which we cannot see."* T. Claye Shaw, "Considerations on the occult," *British Medical Journal* (18 June 1910): 1473–1475.

127   *"injury current,"* a difference in electrical potential that arises between injured tissue (or a tumor) and the surrounding healthy flesh. Albert L. Huebner, "Healing cancer with electricity," *East West Journal* (May 1990): 48.

Page

128   . . . could be viewed, he writes, as an *"extrabiological guiding principle."* Björn
       E. W. Nordenstrom, *Biologically Closed Electric Circuits: Clinical, Experimental
       and Theoretical Evidence for an Additional Circulatory System* (Stockholm:
       Nordic Medical Publications, 1983), 1–10.

128   . . . *similar to a ball needing a slight push to get over a hump before it rolls down to a
       valley."* Frederic S. Young, "Theories and Mechanisms of Biomagnetic In-
       teractions: A Critical Review," review paper commissioned by the BioEn-
       ergy Medicine Program at the Institute of Noetic Sciences (1990), 25–30.

128   . . . once regarded as too low to be anything but benign—to affect dividing
       cells, immune system function, and neurohormones. Richard Leviton,
       "Current affairs: Exploring both the health risks and the medical benefits of
       electromagnetic fields," *East West Journal* (May 1990): 48.

128   . . . clearly capable of producing *"a cascade of changes"* in the body. Ibid., 48.

128   ". . . *the laws of physics guaranteed there could be no interaction between unseen fields
       and living things. It's not true."* Ibid., 49.

128   . . . clusters of cancer cases that show up in residential areas too close to trans-
       formers, power lines, and electrical substations. Ibid., 46–48.

129   *"control system that started, regulated and stopped . . . their healing was
       electrical."* Ibid., 102.

129   ". . . *regulating healing and growth through an intricate transfer of electromagnetic in-
       formation."* Personal communication, 1986.

129   *"Perhaps people who seem to be able to heal . . . frequency range that affects the body's
       own fields, and through them the cells of the body itself."* a videotape by Peter
       Walsh, "Bioenergy: A healing art," videotape (New World Media Alliance,
       1992).

129   . . . an effect almost identical to that obtained by immersing magnets in water
       for several hours. Benor, 97.

129   *Spiritual healing is one way of bringing the particles back into a harmonious relation-
       ship."* Benor, 65.

130   *"except it happened. Nobody knows what it means. But we saw the electrical side ef-
       fects."* Walsh, "Bioenergy: A healing art."

130   ". . . *upon another living system without using known physical means of interven-
       tion."* David Aldridge, "Is there evidence for spiritual healing?" *Advances* 9,
       (Fall 1993): 5.

133   ". . . *many minutes. Later, I realized it must have been quite a while."* Benor,
       14–15.

133   ". . . *make a "transition from materia medica to spiritual therapy."* Alan Cooper-
       stein, *The Myths of Healing: A Descriptive Analysis and Taxonomy of Transper-
       sonal Healing Experience* (Ph. D. diss., Saybrook Institute, 1990), 55–57.

133   *discursive and analytical thinking, resulting in a 'stilling of the mind.' "* Ibid., 112.

133   ". . . *forgotten experiences are remembered in elaborate detail."* Neher (1980) in
       Ibid., 63–64.

137   *"The only reason this case has not been written up is that I have been afraid
       to."* Tamara Jones, "The saint and Ann O'Neill," *The Washington Post,*
       Sunday, 3 April, 1994, Style section, F1–F5.

137   ". . . *treatment for the tumour, and regression therefore can be truly described as spon-
       taneous."* R. C. S. Ayres et al., "Spontaneous regression of hepatocellular
       carcinoma," *Gut,* 31, no. 6 (June 1990): 722–724.

Chapter Six

IS THERE A RECOVERY-PRONE PERSONALITY?

Page

Wickramasekera, "Observations, speculations and an experimentally testable hypothesis: On the presumed efficacy of the Peniston and Kulkosky procedure," *Biofeedback* vol. 21, no. 2 (June 1993): 19.

162   *"She is probably the best medically documented case of spontaneous regression I know of in the world."* Quoted in *The Heart of Healing* (Atlanta: Turner Broadcasting System, Inc., 1993).

162   *"If I really believed the pathologist in me, I wouldn't believe my eyes."* Ibid.

163   . . . experiences with imaginary playmates as well as *"bogeymen and monsters."* Theodore X. Barber, "Changing 'unchangeable' bodily processes by (hypnotic) suggestions: A new look at hypnosis, cognitions, imagining and the mind-body problem," *Advances* 1, no. 2 (Spring 1984): 31.

170   due to mortality, the same approximate 2:1 ratio of survival still obtained. K. W. Pettingale et al., "Mental attitudes to cancer: an additional prognostic factor," *The Lancet* (1985): 750.

170   *". . . denial is a creative stage, health professionals may come to respect its positive aspects. . . ."* Marco J. DeVries, "Healing and the process of healing: The synthesis of the mind and heart in medicine," *Humane Medicine* 1, no. 2 (October 1985): 55–56.

171   *"to have overcome cancer by accepting responsibility for resolving such a crisis for themselves,"* Yujiro Ikemi et al., "Psychosomatic consideration on cancer patients who have made a narrow escape from death," *Dynamic Psychiatry* 8, no. 2 (1975): 85.

172   . . . *your skin is now different, your left arm is now different, you are now different."* Cited in Howard Hall, "Hypnosis and the immune system: A review with implications for cancer and the psychology of healing," *American Journal of Clinical Hypnosis* 25, nos. 2–3 (October 1982–January 1983): 97.

173   . . . would switch into a *"boy alter"* personality who displayed no such symptoms. Dr. Gary Peterson, personal communication, 1993.

173   . . . muscle balance, pupil size, corneal curvature, keratomy, and intraocular pressure . . . Scott D. Miller and Patrick J. Triggiano, "The psychophysiological investigation of multiple personality disorder: Review and update," *American Journal of Clinical Hypnosis* 35, no. 1 (July 1992): 54, citing unpublished 1985 study by Shepard and Braun.

173   Levels of thyroid hormone (T4) in different personality states. Ibid., 55, citing unpublished 1986 study by Hunter.

174   (It has since been discovered that some areas of the brain contain more insulin than the pancreas itself.) Candace Pert, personal communication, July 1994.

175   *wounded part of personality that was so long unexpressed."* Johannes N. Schilder "(Lecture presented at Healing: Beyond Suffering and Death, First International Conference on Transcultural Psychiatry, Montreal, Quebec, Canada, June 1993).

175   Schilder performed an initial study of seven former cancer patients . . . Schilder and DeVries, "Psychological changes,"

176   making jokes with her doctor, a completely different person than she was the year before. Johannes N. Schilder, "(Lecture presented at Healing: Beyond

Suffering and Death, First International Conference on Transcultural Psychiatry, Montreal, Quebec, Canada, June 1993).

176 *"that 'I have very little time left, and I will have things the way I want them.' "* Johannes N. Schilder, "Het geheim van een lastige patiënt: Spontane regressie van kanker onderzocht," *MGZ* 19 (June 1991): 4–8 (translation).

176 *"body postures, gestures, feelings, behaviors, words, habits and beliefs."* Piero Ferrucci, *What We May Be: Techniques for Psychological and Spiritual Growth Through Psychosynthesis* (Los Angeles: J. P. Tarcher, 1982), 47.

177 *Spreading them out before the sun like stalks of flax to dry?* William Blake, from "The Four Zoas" in *Poetry and Prose of William Blake;* ed. Geoffrey Keynes (London: Nonesuch Library, 1961), 293.

178 apparently affected in some way we do not understand by associations reinforced over a lifetime. Bruce Bower, "Mind-survival link emerges from death data," *Science News,* 6 November 1993, 293.

178 *". . . which is not strange to it, but within which is the fulfillment of its potentialities. . . ."* 29. Paul Tillich, "The meaning of health," in *Religion and Medicine: Essays on Meaning, Values and Health,* ed. David Belgum (Ames, Iowa: Iowa State University Press, 1967), 9–10.

Chapter Seven
THE MIRACLE OF SURVIVAL

181 exercise control over their lives and jobs were by and large healthier, Suzanne C. Kobasa, Salvatore R. Maddi, and Stephen Kahn, "Hardiness and health: A prospective study," *Journal of Personality and Social Psychology* 42, no. 1 (1982): 168–177; and Clive Wood, "Buffer of hardiness: An interview with Suzanne C. Ouellette Kobasa," *Advances* 4, no. 1 (1987): 37–45.

181 selfish and unselfish, self-confident and self-critical. Al Siebert, *The Survivor Personality* (Portland, Oregon: Practical Psychology Press, 1993), 23–34.

186 *". . . that ultimate outcomes must be benign, that suffering can be endured."* Joel Dimsdale, "The coping behavior of Nazi concentration camp survivors," *American Journal of Psychiatry* 131, no. 7 (July 1974): 793.

191 *". . . may rise above himself, and by so doing change himself."* Viktor E. Frankel, *Man's Search for Meaning* (New York: Washington Square Press, 1984), 170.

191 Who knows? Ibid., 28.

192 *"Yes, a man can get used to anything, but do not ask us how."* Ibid., 35–36.

192 *"life was still expecting something from them."* Ibid., 100.

192 *"the uniqueness and singleness which distinguishes each individual."* Ibid., 101.

192 *"suddenly lowered his body's resistance against the latent typhus infection."* Ibid., 96–97.

193 *". . . to survive camp life better than did those of a robust nature".* Ibid., 55–56.

200 or as a biological effect of emotional states is not yet known.) Geoffrey M. Reed et al., "Realistic acceptance as a predictor of decreased survival time in gay men with AIDS," *Health Psychology,* in press.

202 with their physicians, rather seeing their doctors as partners. George F.

Solomon et al., "An intensive psychoimmunologic study of long-surviving persons with AIDS," *Annals of the New York Academy of Sciences* 496 (1987): 647–655.

202   men with T-cell counts of less than fifty. George F. Solomon et al., "Prolonged asymptomatic states in HIV-seropositive persons with fewer than 50 CD4+ T cells per MM³ [letter]," *Journal of Acquired Immune Deficiency Syndrome* 6, no. 10 (October 1993): 1172–1173.

Chapter Eight
THE SOCIAL CONNECTION

210   *"immune function . . . is one of the most robust findings in psychoneuroimmunology."* Janice K. Kiecolt-Glaser et al., "Negative behavior during marital conflict is associated with immunological down-regulation," *Psychosomatic Medicine* 55, no. 5 (19——): 395–409.

210   lymphocytes has been shown to depend in part on the quality of interpersonal bonds. Susan Kennedy, Janice K. Kiecolt-Glaser, and Ronald Glaser, "Immunological consequences of acute and chronic stressors: Mediating role of interpersonal relationships," *British Journal of Medical Psychology* 61 (1988): 77–85.

210–11 *". . . in comparison with single, separated, widowed or divorced persons."* James S. Goodwin et al., "The effect of marital status on stage, treatment and survival of cancer patients," *Journal of the American Medical Association* 258, no. 21 (December 4, 1987): 3125.

216   *". . . He wants to remain with those who love him."* Richard Katz, *Boiling Energy* (Cambridge, MA: Harvard University Press, 1982), 40–41.

216   . . . while only twenty percent of those who said they had little social support had survived. Daniel Goleman, "Doctors find comfort is a potent medicine," *The New York Times,* 16 February 1991, B5, B8.

217   *". . . feelings than it is to have a whole network of more superficial relationships."* Jane E. Brody, "Maintaining friendships for the sake of health," *The New York Times,* 5 February 1992, B8–B9.

217   *". . . where the psychodynamics were known before, during, and after the incident."* Margaretta K. Bowers and Charles Weinstock, "A case of healing in malignancy," *Journal of the American Academy of Psychoanalysis* 6, no. 3 (1978): 393–402.

221   . . . received intervention were three times less likely to suffer recurrence or death. Fawzy I. Fawzy et al., "A structured psychiatric intervention for cancer patients: I. Changes over time in methods of coping and affective disturbances; II. Changes over time in immunological measures," *Archives of General Psychiatry* 47 (August 1990): 720–725, 729–735; and Fawzy I. Fawzy et al., "Malignant melanoma: Effects of an early structured psychiatric intervention, coping, and affective state on recurrence and survival 6 years later," *Archives of General Psychiatry* 50, no. 9 (September 1993): 681–689.

Page
221   shown to take more formula and gain more weight. J. L. White and R. C. Labarba, "The effects of tactile and kinesthetic stimulation on neonatal development in the premature infant," *Developmental Psychobiology* 9 (1976): 569–577, quoted in Martin Reite, "Touch, attachment, and health: Is there a relationship?" in *Touch: The Foundation of Experience,* eds. Kathryn E. Barnard and T. Berry Brazelton, (Madison, CT: International Universities Press, Inc., 1990), p. 200.

226   "*. . . his profession he was already well aware of the pathology and prognosis of his condition.*" Ainslie Meares, "Regression of osteogenic sarcoma metastases associated with intensive meditation," *Medical Journal of Australia* 2 (October 21, 1978): 433.

227   "*activity of his immune system by reducing his level of cortisone.*" Ibid., 433.

228   "*could have been expected to offer given the advanced stage of their cancer.*" Goleman, "Doctors find comfort," B8.

229   "*His eyes no longer had their yellowish pall . . . I was stunned by the boy's recovery.*" Mark J. Plotkin, *Tales of a Shaman's Apprentice* (New York: Penguin, 1994), 79.

230   After protracted practice, she had a remarkable recovery. George J. Shen, "The study of mind-body effects and Qi Gong in China," *Advances* 3, no. 4 (Fall 1986): 139–140.

231   Wang, an engineer by profession, eventually became a Chi Gong tutor. Institute of Noetic Sciences, *The Heart of Healing* (Atlanta, GA: Turner Publishing, Inc., 1993), 131.

237   twice as likely to die as women treated with orthodox medicine. F. S. Bagenal et al., "Survival of patients with breast cancer attending Bristol Cancer Help Centre," *The Lancet* 336 (September 8, 1990): 606–610.

237   "*. . . visualization may have seriously damaged their health.*" T. A. B. Sheard, "Letters to the Editor," *The Lancet* 336 (November 10, 1990): 1186.

237   "*one of the most embarrassing episodes in British medical research history.*" Liz Hunt, "Cancer charities attacked for lack of fund control," *The Independent,* 7 January 1994, p. 15.

Chapter Nine

THE HEALING SYSTEM

242   . . . rat's immune system could be "conditioned" to respond to ordinary saccharine. Robert Ader and Nicholas Cohen, "Behaviorally conditioned immunosuppression," *Psychosomatic Medicine* 37, no. 4 (July–August 1975): 333–340.

243   "*nothing on the way the total organism is equipped to recover from abnormalities and illnesses.*" For a discussion of the healing system, see Norman Cousins, *Head First: The Biology of Hope and the Healing Power of the Human Spirit* (New York: Penguin, 1989) 122–124. See also Norman Cousins, *Human Options: An Autobiographical Notebook* (New York: W. W. Norton, 1981), 205.

Notes

245 *"But her much-hated husband suddenly died. Today a year and a half later she is entirely well."* Charles Weinstock, "Notes on 'spontaneous' regression of cancer," *American Society of Psychosomatic Dentistry and Medicine. Journal* 24, no.
4 (1977): 106–110.

246 *". . . there must always be added a free invention of the human mind that attacks the
heart of the matter."* Quoted in Georg Feuerstein, "Cultivating the Power of
Intuition," *The Quest* (Autumn 1994): 36.

248 *". . . look to fields lead us to consider it as an immunoblastic sarcoma that has likely
evolved from a plasmacytoma."* Letter, 5 November, 1986.

252 During the subsequent 2 to 3 months he slowly gained weight and developed
increasing strength and well-being. J. W. Bell, J. E. Jesseph, and R. S.
Leighton, "Spontaneous regression of bronchogenic carcinoma with five-
year survival," *Journal of Thoracic and Cardiovascular Surgery* 48, no. 6 (December 1964): 984–990.

252 (One data analysis of 224 cases of spontaneous regression found fevers or infections in 62 of them.) Hugh E. Stephenson, Jr., et al., "Host immunity
and spontaneous regression of cancer evaluated by computerized data reduction study," *Surgery, Gynecology and Obstetrics* 133 (October 1971):
649–655.

255 *"Frozen section was reported as a malignant neoplasm, probably poorly differentiated
squamous carcinoma."* J. W. Bell, "Possible immune factors in spontaneous
regression of bronchogenic carcinoma: Ten-year survival in a patient treated
with minimal (1,200 r) radiation alone," *American Journal of Surgery* 120 (December 1970): 804.

256 *". . . there has been ample opportunity for a new tumor to present; that a new lesion
has not developed suggests and acquired host immunity."* Ibid., 805.

256 *"immunity after induced or spontaneous regression is more effective than that after surgical removal"* Ibid., 805.

256 . . . Joe's immune potion reduced the cancer cells' colony formation by more
than half. Ibid.,

258 there was such indescribable beauty in the most mundane sights that tears
would come to my eyes. Joseph W. Mayerle as told to Ruth Bolotin,
"Cancer can be conquered," *The Saturday Evening Post,* May 1974, 24–29.

258 *". . . The experience of involuntariness may be a link among hypnosis, dissociation,
and trauma."* David Spiegel, "Dissociation and hypnotizability in post traumatic stress disorder," *American Journal of Psychiatry* 145, no. 3 (March 1988):
304.

258 *"conceptualizing events in the life of the cancer patients as analogous to physical traumas."* David Spiegel, "Psychosocial aspects of cancer," *Current Opinion in
Psychiatry* 4 (1991): 892.

259 *"operative trauma,"* which was presumed to stimulate hormones, William F.
Sindelar and Alfred S. Ketcham, "Regression of cancer following surgery,"
National Cancer Institute Monograph, no. 44 (November 1976): 82–83. Sindelar and Ketcham point out that "surgical procedures result in increases in
circulating steroids as well as catecholamines and various metabolites.
Steroids have been shown to cause tumor regressions in a variety of animal
systems, and certain human neoplasms are known to exhibit significant hormone responsiveness in terms of their growth patterns."

259   that boosted the *"host immune system."* Basil A. Stoll, "Restraint of growth and spontaneous regression of cancer," in *Mind and Cancer Prognosis* (New York: John Wiley and Sons, 1979), 23.

259   in addition to producing euphoria and reducing pain, may, according to some investigators, also enhance the immune system. Jeanne Achterberg, *Imagery in Healing: Shamanism and Modern Medicine* (Boston: Shambhala Publications, 1985), 175.

259   . . . a way for the brain to ransack its stored repertoire of experience in search of a life-saving strategy. Jeanne Achterberg, "Healing images and symbols in nonordinary states of consciousness," *ReVision* 16, no. 4 (Spring 1994): 150.

260   *". . . under the influence of chloroform describe, who see all the operation, but feel not the knife . . ."* Raymond Prince, "Shamans and endorphins: Hypotheses for a synthesis," *Ethos* 10, no. 4 (Winter 1982): 415.

260   may be created by the organism itself through *"nightmares, deliriums, and psychoses."* Ibid., 415.

260   *"a positive measure"* used by the mind and body to produce *"protective hormones."* Ibid., 416.

261   *"They said they had been restored to the way they used to be before they went to Vietnam."* Personal communication, 1993, and Eugene G. Peniston and Paul J. Kulkowsky, "Alpha-theta brainwave neuro-feedback for Vietnam veterans with combat-related post traumatic stress disorder," *Medical Psychotherapy* 4 (1991): 1–14.

261   *"there is a massive secretion of endogenous opioids, equivalent to the ten-milligram morphine injection."* From the videotape, "Trauma and Memory II: The Intrusive Past" (Cavalcade Productions, Inc., 1993).

261   as a trigger for hormones that stimulate the *growth* of cancer. Stoll, "Restraint of growth," 25.

262   *"within four days, it had disappeared. The surgical procedure was not carried out."* L. L. LeShan and M. L. Gassman, "Some observations on psychotherapy with patients with neoplastic disease," *American Journal of Psychotherapy* 12 (1958): 723–734.

263   *"psychosocial intervention"* on the mood and pain-level of 86 metastatic breast cancer patients. David Spiegel et al., "Effect of psychosocial treatment on survival of patients with metastatic breast cancer," *The Lancet,* 14 October 1989, 888–890.

263   *"The whole point of the original study was that we could make them feel better,"* said Spiegel in a 1989 report in *Science.* Marcia Barinaga, "Can psychotherapy delay cancer deaths?" *Science* 246, (27 October 1989): 448–449.

263   *"The challenge was to make the best use of whatever time remained for them."* Daniel Goleman, "Cancer patients benefit from therapy groups," *New York Times,* 23 November 1989, B7.

263   *"media hype about patients being able to wish away their cancers."* David Spiegel, "A psychosocial intervention and survival time of patients with metastatic breast cancer," *Advances* 7, no. 3 (Summer 1991): 15.

264   *". . . the powers of the mind to cure cancer were foolish and sometimes dangerous,"* Ibid., 15.

Page

264   *"it would provide a perfect negative experiment revealing no effect on disease progression."* Ibid., 15

264   *". . . honestly facing their own mortality and making rational choices about how to live their lives"* had what he calls *"an invigorating effect."* Ibid., 16–17.

265   *"Thus they had, on average, less intensive treatment than the short survivors."* David Spiegel, "The role of emotional expression on cancer survival" (Paper presented at the American Psychological Association annual meeting, San Francisco, 12 August, 1991), 11.

265   *"Charybdis . . . [of] disembodied spiritualism—the idea that if one fixes a problem in one's mind, it is fixed in the body."* Spiegel, "A psychosocial intervention," 10.

265   *". . . focus on a metaphor like floating or warmth or tingling numbness"* Spiegel, "A psychosocial intervention," 14.

267   *"Protestant, Catholic, Jewish, Hindu, Muslim, Zen Buddhist, Zulu, Parsi."* Jeffrey S. Levin, "Does religious involvement protect against morbidity and mortality?" *Bridges* (News magazine of ISSSEEM), in press.

268   *". . . which may be the active ingredient in such practices as yogic breathing or acupuncture."* Jeffrey S. Levin, "Religion and health: Is there an association, is it valid, and is it causal?" *Social Science and Medicine* 38, no. 11 (1994): 1478.

269   . . . what experiences gave them the most *"thrills"* or *"chills"* or *"tingles."* Avram Goldstein, "Thrills in response to music and other stimuli," *Physiological Psychology* 8, no. 1 (1980): 126–129.

269   . . . rituals around the world (four to seven beats per second). Melinda Maxfield, "The journey of the drum," *ReVision* 16, no. 4 (Spring 1994): 159, quoting a study by Wolfgang Jilek, 1974.

269   . . . brain associated with spontaneous imagery, ecstatic states, and creativity. Ibid., 159.

269   All participants reported *"visual and/or somatic imagery,"* Ibid., 160–161.

271   *"There is a clear, distinct parallel between traditional shamanism and the practices we do in music therapy today."* 42. Jeff Volk, "Of sound mind and body," videotape (Lumina Productions, 1992).

271   . . . increased significantly in children who received thirty-minute music therapy sessions. Deforia Lane, *"Music therapy: A gift beyond measure,"* Oncology Nursing Forum 19, no. 6 (1992): 863–867.

273   *". . . learning process that appears to be significantly dependent on image design or figures of thought."* Dennis Stillings, ed., "Cyberphysiology: The Science of Self-Regulation," no. 2 in *Time, Mind and Medicine,* (St. Paul, MN: Archaeus Project, 1988), 3.

274   *". . . head of the whole place . . . landlord . . . who does supervise this kind of operation?"* Lewis Thomas, *The Medusa and the Snail* (New York: Bantam Books, 1980), 81.

275   *". . . which in human beings we call the personality."* Walter Cannon, "Stresses and strains of homeostasis," *American Journal of the Medical Sciences* 189 (1935): 2. Cited by Steven Locke, *The Healer Within: The New Medicine of Mind and Body* (New York: E. P. Dutton, 1986), 13.

275   *"concrete operations of the intellect such as comprehension, recognition, naming and understanding."* Jonathan Crary, et al., eds., *Fragments for a History of the Human Body: Part One* (New York: Zone, 1989), 22.

Chapter Ten

TOWARD A NEW MEDICINE

Page

276–77   "*. . . if we could somehow duplicate them in other patients . . . ,*" Steven A. Rosenberg and John M. Barry, *The Transformed Cell: Unlocking the Mysteries of Cancer* (New York: G. P. Putnam's Sons, 1992), 18.

278   "*And he kept telling his doctors he felt 'better than ever.' *" Richard E. Peschel and
Enid Rhodes Peschel, "Medical Miracles from a physician-scientist's view-
point," *Perspectives in Biology and Medicine* 31, no. 3 (Spring 1988): 397–398.

278   "*. . . an event that has an* extremely *low probability of occurring: a spontaneous remission, for example.*" Ibid., 396.

279   "*Call me Ishmael,*" begins the epic *Moby Dick,* which ends with a line from the
Book of Job: "*For I only am escaped alone* to tell them." Herman Melville,
Moby-Dick or, The Whale (New York: Penguin Books, 1992), 625. Page 3:
"And I only am escaped alone to tell thee" (Job, 1:19).

279   "*. . .* [and] diffuse pelvic osseous metastases" who was the "*one objective regression.*" Edward T. Creagan et al., "A Phase I–II Trial of the Combination of
Recombinant Leukocyte A Interferon and Recombinant Human Interfer-
eon [gamma] in Patients with Metastatic Malignant Melanoma, *Cancer* 62,
no. 12 (December 15, 1988): 2473.

280   . . . cells at lymph node truck stops, and instigating through his progeny and
unchallenged reign of crime. Marilyn J. Koering, "When a cell goes astray
(melanocytes)," in privately circulated essays, *A New Beginning: Reflections of
a Cancer Survivor, A Collection of Inspirational Essays,* © copyright Marilyn J.
Koering (Washington, D. C., 1993).

282   "*increased publicity sought by firms more interested in the stock exchange than in human
beings.*" The *Wall Street Journal,* Letters to the Editor, 15 June 1988.

282   twits the "*political and medical-science establishment.*" *Time,* Letters, 12 March
1990.

282   How can [cancer patients] know what to do if the medical community itself can't reach
a consensus?" *Hippocrates,* Reflexes (May/June 1989), 8.

283   In a set of privately circulated essays Marilyn Koering, *A New Beginning: Reflections of a Cancer Survivor, A Collection of Inspirational Essays,* privately circulated essays, © copyright Marilyn J. Koering (Washington, D. C., 1993).

283   "*. . . society is not comfortable as it is usually related solely to an expression of weakness.*" Koering, "It is 'OK' to Cry," in Ibid.

285   "*. . . From that time on, I had a new freedom and peace.*" Koering, "Chasing the
Apricot Pit," in Ibid.

286   (One of her essays is titled, "*It is 'OK' to Cry.*") Koering, "It is 'OK' to Cry,"
in Ibid.

286   "*. . . I think that they stated 'my way' was a 'good way' to address one's death.*" Koering, "Which Way?" in Ibid.

287   ("*I run when I am alone with the thousands of deceased, who I figure won't tell on
me.*") Koering, "Today," in Ibid.

287   "*The old adage states, 'without a storm, there is no rainbow.' *" Koering, "Perfect
Moments," in Ibid.

Page

289   (At the end of two years, the amount of drug the girl needed was reduced by half.) Karen Olness and Robert Ader, "Conditioning as an adjunct in the pharmacotherapy of lupus erythematosus," *Journal of Developmental and Behavioral Pediatrics* 13, no. 2 (April, 1992): 125.

290   *"National Institute of Warts and All."* Lewis Thomas, *The Medusa and the Snail: Notes of a Biology Watcher* (New York: Viking Press, 1979), 80–81.

295   *". . . a placebo effect, a miracle, God's will, [or] spontaneous remission. . . ."* Alan H. Roberts, "The magnitude of nonspecific effects" (Paper presented at the Conference on Examining Research Assumptions in Alternative Medical Systems, NIH Office of Alternative Medicine, National Institutes of Health, Bethesda, MD, 11–13 July 1994), 2.

295   *In clinical practice, they may become indistinguishable."* Ibid., 18.

297   *The tail, quite plainly, is wagging the dog. . . ."* Jeanne Achterberg and G. Frank Lewis, "Letters: Human research and studying psychosocial interventions for cancer," *Advances* 8, no. 4 (Fall 1992): 2.

297   *our opinion, more important determinants of outcome than the usually measured variables."* Ibid., 3.

297   *. . . understanding of the experience than anything presented quantitatively to date."* Ibid., 3.

297   *"will create a vastly different science, a different psychology, and a different medicine."* Ibid., 4.

     . . . what there spontaneous regressions appear to cause in a very mysterious way. "The vanishing cancer," ABC News, "20/20," 1 April 1994.

299   . . . they should not be further burdened by having to accept responsibility for the outcome. Marcia Angell, "Disease as a reflection of the psyche," *New England Journal of Medicine* 312, no. 24 (13 June 1985): 1570–1572.

299   *". . . the mechanisms by which, psychobiologic factors contribute to the induction and progression of, or recovery from, disease."* Redford B. Williams, Jr., et al., "Disease as a reflection of the psyche: Letters to the editor," *New England Journal of Medicine* 313, no. 21 (21 November 1985): 1356–1359.

300   *". . . all these ingredients plus something else, some art, that makes it taste so good."* Mitchell May, private communication (July 1993).

300   . . . where a patient could learn to break through *"learned helplessness"* and reassert their own power. Johannes Schilder, MD, "Long-term surviving cancer patients and the ultimate: spontaneous regression of cancer, a study of psychosocial factors involved," in *Healing: Beyond Suffering or Death,* ed. Luc Bessette (Quebec, Canada: MNH, 1994), 449–454.

304   *". . . the power in seeds, the reproduction of cells, the power of regeneration, freshness, and creativity."* Wighard Strehlow and Gottfried Hertzka, *Hildegard of Bingen's Medicine,* trans. Karin Anderson Strehlow (Santa Fe, NM: Bear & Co., 1988), xxvi–xxvii.

304   *". . . the poet, the philosopher, and the physiologist will all understand each other."* Cited in Norman Cousins, *Head First: The Biology of Hope and the Healing Power of the Human Spirit* (New York: Penguin, 1989), 195.

INDEX